Western Gunslingers in Fact and on Film

ALSO BY BUCK RAINEY

The Cowboys: Six-Shooters, Songs, and Sex
(editor and contributor)

The Sage of Buck Jones

The Fabulous Holts

Shoot-Em-Ups

Saddle Aces of the Cinema

Heroes of the Range

The Shoot-Em-Ups Ride Again

Those Fabulous Serial Heroines

The Life and Films of Buck Jones: The Silent Era

The Life and Films of Buck Jones: The Sound Era

Sweethearts of the Sage

*The "Reel" Cowboy: Essays on the Myth
in Movies and Literature*

Western Gunslingers in Fact and on Film

HOLLYWOOD'S FAMOUS LAWMEN AND OUTLAWS

by

Buck Rainey

McFarland & Company, Inc., Publishers
Jefferson, North Carolina and London

British Library Cataloguing-in-Publication data are available

Library of Congress Cataloguing-in-Publication Data

Rainey, Buck.
    Western gunslingers in fact and on film : Hollywood's famous lawmen
and outlaws / by Buck Rainey.
      p.   cm.
    Includes bibliographical references and index.

    ISBN-13: 978-0-7864-0396-7
    (softcover : 50# alkaline paper) ∞

    1. Western films—History and criticism.   2. Outlaws—West
(U.S.)—Biography.   3. Sheriffs—West (U.S.)—Biography.   I. Title.
PN1995.9.W4R35   1998
791.43'6278—dc21   98-41807
                                                       CIP

Manufactured in the United States of America

McFarland & Company, Inc., Publishers
  Box 611, Jefferson, North Carolina 28640
    www.mcfarlandpub.com

Dedicated
to the memory of
Silver, Tarzan and Starlight,
the horses that thrilled me in my youth

Acknowledgments

I acknowledge my indebtedness to numerous historical, biographical and film books, pressbooks, magazines, journals and newspapers used in writing this book. *Yesterday's Saturdays, The TV Collector, Variety, The Hollywood Reporter* and *Film Daily* were especially helpful as was the National Film Information Service.

Special thanks go to the Department of Western Historical Collections of the University of Oklahoma for both its assistance and its waiver of the usual "use" fees which made possible the publication of a majority of the historical photos herein.

Thanks also to William (Bill) McDowell, film historian, who was called upon for assistance and who graciously shared with the author both his knowledge and film data.

Table of Contents

Acknowledgments   vi

Introduction   1

1 Billy the Kid   3

2 The James-Younger Gang   55

3 The Dalton-Doolin Gang   111

4 Myra Belle Shirley Starr   131

5 Wyatt Berry Stapp Earp   145

6 James Butler (Wild Bill) Hickok   177

7 William Barclay (Bat) Masterson   223

Bibliography   265

Index   305

Introduction

Throughout the history of motion pictures, scores of biographical films have been produced. A naive public often accepts these pastiches of fact and fiction as truthful representations of a person's life. The films are often advertised as "the true story of...," but all too often the only things one can depend on are the names of the main characters.

There are still many folks who honestly believe that Jesse James was a modern day Robin Hood, that Wyatt Earp was a staunch upholder of law and order and that Wild Bill Hickok was the greatest gunslinger the West produced. Generally speaking, they base these beliefs on what they have learned from film and novels.

"Dramatic license" has been the norm with most film productions, and nowhere has it been employed more than in western films supposedly based on the lives of America's most infamous outlaws or idolized lawmen.

This book allows the reader to compare film characters with their real life counterparts. In each chapter, a hero or outlaw's biography is followed by a catalog of the various films depicting that person. By comparing the film synopses with the biographies, the reader gets some idea of how accurate a film portrayal might be.

Selected bibliographies will aid readers who want to learn more about the subjects of this book.

1

Billy the Kid

For a punk kid, hardly dry behind the ears, William H. Bonney (Billy the Kid) has garnered much more literary space and film footage than a desperado of his ilk would usually receive. Today there are serial killers, rapists and other degenerates who are given only passing attention and then their deeds and names are forgotten. Not so with Billy. The news of his death electrified the sensation-loving world and the Territory of New Mexico in particular. One need only glance at the *partial* bibliography at the end of this book to get an idea of how much press he commanded. The films listed in this chapter show how popular he is as a screen personality. It has been estimated that upwards of a thousand writers have used Billy as a vessel into which to pour their passions, prejudices and opinions, though few of the portraits of him jibe. By the time he died, the public had already come to look on him as a larger-than-life desperado in a land full of desperadoes. True, he was a killer and an outlaw, but hardly on the scale represented by legend.

Supposedly the Kid was born, of all places, in New York City on November 23, 1859. His father died when Billy was about three; his mother moved the family to New Mexico because of her health, and there on March 1, 1873, married William H. Antrim. Billy's real name was Henry McCarty but he later took the name William H. Bonney ("William H." after his grandfather; the name Bonney was his own creation). At times he was referred to as Henry Antrim or Kid Antrim. Billy had a brother, Joe, who was five years older. Joe never took to outlawry and lived to the age of 76, dying in Denver in 1930.

Billy's mother died in 1874 and it was in that year that Billy's career as a "bad boy" began. He stole some clothes from a Chinese laundry, for which he was put in jail. He was only 15. He escaped to Arizona where he killed his first man, a rough-and-tough fellow by the name of F.P. Cahill. In Arizona he worked for various cattle outfits, gambled (which he loved to do) and rustled cattle on the side.

Billy had little conscience and his guns were soon for hire. Having worn out his welcome in Arizona, he moved first to Mesilla, New Mexico, but his stay was brief as he was accused (rightly) of being a horse thief. He fled to Lincoln County where for a brief time he rustled cattle with Jesse Evans and cronies. Later Billy worked for the Murphy–Dolan partnership, which was in the business of general merchandising to hide their more serious and lucrative business of stealing cattle (mostly from John Chisum). Along the way he met Englishman John H. Tunstall. Although they were from completely different backgrounds and had nothing in common, a mutual friendship developed. Billy went to work for Tunstall, who was associated with Alexander McSween, a local banker and merchant. Billy also rubbed elbows with Pat Garrett during this period. Allied against Tunstall and McSween was the Dolan–Murphy faction, which held a commercial hammerlock on the community. The enmity between these two factions exploded into the Lincoln County War when Tunstall was killed by a posse of Dolan's men. One of Billy's admirable traits was his loyalty. He swore to kill every man who had anything to do with Tunstall's death. He plunged into the Lincoln County War with a passion. An injustice to a friend was an injury to Billy; he held to the ancient law of an eye for an eye and a tooth for a tooth.

The nickname "The Kid" described Billy well. It was only in his final months of life that he began to be referred to as Billy the Kid. He had a boyish face, was of medium stature and slight build. The Kid's disposition was marked by good humor. He enjoyed a good time and he liked the girls.

In 1993 the *Albuquerque Journal* reported that a recently discovered tintype was of Billy the Kid. Until this time the world had only seen the one photo showing a slouched, slope-shouldered youth posing with a rifle. The owner of the tintype revealed that it was passed down from his great-grandmother, a medicine woman who treated the outlaw and became his friend.

A computer analysis of the images shows combined facial and physical characteristics that would exist in only one of 11 million people. The photo shows a clean-cut young man in a suit sitting with his hand on a book.

The purpose of this chapter is to discuss the films based on the life of the Kid, not to get too bogged down in discussing the Lincoln County War. Suffice it to say that when it was over, Billy and other participants were offered amnesty by Governor Lew Wallace (author of *Ben-Hur*). Billy refused and set about his life of crime.

Practically everyone is familiar with the story of Billy's death at the hands of his former friend, Pat Garrett. It occurred on Pete Maxwell's ranch, where the Kid had gone to see his girl. It was night and Garrett ambushed him as he stepped inside the door of Maxwell's room. The date was July 14, 1881.

Billy was the Southwest's most famous desperado and its last great outlaw. He died at the age of 21, claiming to have killed 21 men, "not counting Mexicans." However, historians place his killings at a more conservative figure, around 12 or 15. Of course, no one will ever know the exact number.

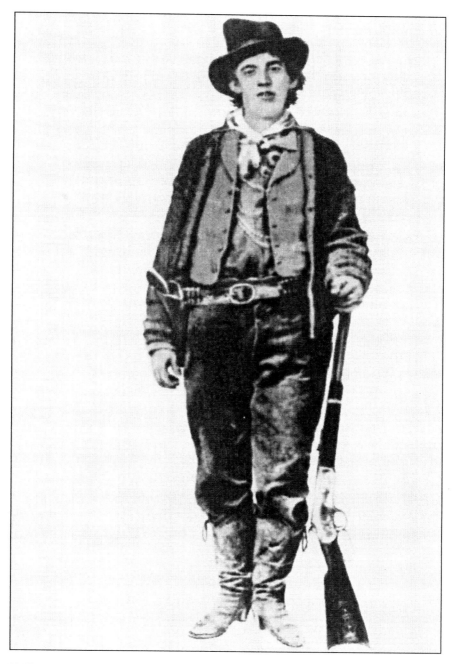

William H. Bonney, better known as Billy the Kid. (Courtesy Western History Collections, University of Oklahoma Library.)

Walter Noble Burns in his *The Saga of Billy the Kid* (Doubleday, 1926) states:

> Billy the Kid's legend in New Mexico seems destined to a mellow and genial immortality like that which gilds the misdeeds and exaggerates the virtues of such ancient rogues as Robin Hood, Claude Duval, Dick Turpin and Fra Diavolo. From the tales you hear of him everywhere, you might be tempted to fancy him the best-loved hero in the state's history. His crimes are forgotten or condoned, while his loyalty, his gay courage, his superman adventures are treasured in affectionate memory. Men speak of him with admiration; women extol his gallantry and lament his fate. A rude balladry in Spanish and English has grown up about him, and in every *placeta* in New Mexico, Mexican girls sing to their guitars songs of Billy the Kid. A halo has been clapped upon his scapegrace brow. The boy who never grew old has become sort of a symbol of frontier knight-errantry, a figure of eternal youth riding forever through a purple glamour of romance.

Two different versions of the Billy the Kid song are reproduced here.

BILLY THE KID
Version One

Billy was a bad man
And carried a big gun,
He was always after Greasers
And kept 'em on the run.

He shot one every morning,
For to make his morning meal,
And let a white man sass him,
He was sure to feel his steel.

He kept things boilin' over,
He stayed out in the brush,
And when he was full of dead eye,
T'other folkses better hush.

But one day he met a man
Who was a whole lot badder.
And now he's dead,
And we ain't none the sadder.

A second version goes like this:

I'll sing you a true song of Billy the Kid,
I'll sing of the desperate deeds that he did,
Way out in New Mexico long, long ago,
When a man's only chance was his own 44.

When Billy the Kid was a very young lad,
In the old Silver City he went to the bad;
Way out in the West with a gun in his hand
At the age of 12 years he first killed his man.

Fair Mexican maidens play guitars and sing
A song about Billy, their boy bandit king,
How ere his young manhood had reached its sad end
He'd a notch on his pistol for 21 men.

'Twas on the same night when poor Billy died
He said to his friends: "I am not satisfied;
There are 21 men I have put bullets through,
And Sheriff Pat Garrett must make 22."

Now this is how Billy the Kid met his fate:
The bright moon was shining, the hour was late,
Shot down by Pat Garrett, who once was his friend,
The young outlaw's life had now come to its end.

There's many a man with a face fine and fair
Who starts out in life with a chance to be square,
But just like poor Billy he wanders astray
And loses his life in the very same way.

Dorothy Johnson in *Western Badmen* (Dodd, Mead & Co., 1970) quotes Sallie Chisum, who knew the Kid well:

> He was brimming over with light-hearted gaiety and good humor.... He always looked as if he had just stepped out of a band box. In broad-brimmed white hat, dark coat and vest, gray trousers worn over his boots, a gray flannel shirt and black four in hand tie, and sometimes—would you believe it?—a flower in his lapel and quite the dandy.

This description supports the conclusion that the figure in the recently discovered tintype is actually of the Kid. It fits the description of his attire mentioned by Chisum, even though the well-known photo of Billy standing with his rifle is one in which his clothing sagged and bagged and he looked a slouchy man.

One of the better-known incidents in the life of Billy was the fight at the McSween home between Billy and his comrades and a sheriff's posse consisting of thirty to forty men. After considerable firing back and forth, the McSween home was set ablaze and eventually Billy and his friends had to make a run for it. Billy managed to get away but McSween was killed— and then some! (He had nine bullets in his body.)

The concluding event in Billy's life was his death at the hands of Pat Garrett. A number of people believed then and now that Billy and Pat concocted the story and that Billy fled the territory and started a new life.

Billy has proven a popular subject for motion pictures, having been portrayed in nearly 60 films and one television series. Never, however, have the portrayals been very authentic. The Kid fit perfectly the rebel role, fighting against various forms of social and legal injustice and made a dashing Robin Hood figure for a nation fascinated by outlaws.

The first film about Billy, *Billy the Kid*, was a one-reeler released by Vitagraph in 1911. It starred Teffi Johnson; however, there is no information available today as to the nature of the film. In 1916, *Billy the Bandit* was released by Victor Studios, but here again no information is available.

The first feature film about Billy was MGM's *Billy the Kid* (1930) starring John Mack Brown as Billy and Wallace Beery as Pat Garrett. Without bothering to stick with historical facts, the film allows Billy to ride off at the end. However, the European release version did adhere to the truth as we know it.

Roy Rogers played the Kid in a 1938 film, Bob Steele in six PRC oaters in 1940–41 and Buster Crabbe in 13 PRC programmers in 1941–43. These were "B" Westerns in which Billy was a whitewashed hero riding around the West with two pals, dispensing justice at every turn. There was no attempt in these Saturday matinee sagebrushers to portray Billy as the killer he was. Rather, Steele and Crabbe had halos that would do Saint Peter justice.

The second significant film was an MGM remake of *Billy the Kid (1941)*. Robert Taylor had the title role. It was a beautifully photographed picture but there was absolutely no resemblance between William Bonney (The Kid) and handsome Robert Taylor. In fact, Hollywood has never had a 20-ish actor play The Kid. It was evident to audiences that Taylor in his closeup riding sequences rode not a horse but a saddle mounted on a bouncing board. There is a strong element of self-sacrifice at the end of this version as Billy, facing his old friend Garrett, draws with his right hand instead of his left and thus meets his end. MGM made the assumption that Billy was left-handed. He was actually right-handed.

The Outlaw (1943) was entertaining and a pretty good Western, but was non-factual in its content. Jack Buetel played The Kid but it was Jane Russell's bosom that got the attention. Paul Newman in 1958 played Billy as a martyred illiterate striving for love and justice. Though Newman's *The Left Handed Gun* is one of the better "Kid" films, it was again a circumvention of the truth. Like previous actors, Newman was too old to be playing a 21 year-old.

Billy the Kid has continued to ride on in films of various quality. *Pat Garrett and Billy the Kid* (1973) is perhaps the best depiction of the Kid so far. The film covers the last months of the Kid's life, when he was a fugitive in New Mexico pursued by the relentless Garrett. There is some degree of historical accuracy here. However, director Sam Peckinpah takes many liberties with the truth as he contrasts the innocence of Billy with the corruption of Garrett. Kris Kristofferson plays Billy and James Coburn plays Garrett.

Dirty Little Billy (1972) with Michael J. Pollard in the title role is a definite attempt to debunk the "little punk," but it goes overboard in doing so.

Right: A rare photo of Billy the Kid, reportedly once owned by his great-grandmother. (Courtesy Western History Collections, University of Oklahoma Library.)

BILLY THE KID FILMOGRAPHY

Billy the Kid
(Vitagraph, July 1911) one reel.

Director: Larry Trimble. Screenplay: Edward J. Montagne, Teff Johnson, Edith Storey, Ralph Ince.

Billy the Bandit
(Special Victor, 1916) one reel.

Screenplay/Director: John Steppling. Producer: L.V. Waters.

Billy the Kid
(MGM, 1930) 99 min.

Director: King Vidor. Story from *The Sage of Billy the Kid* by Walter Noble Burns. Continuity: Wanda Tuchock. Dialogue: Lawrence Stallings, Charles MacArthur.

John Mack Brown (Billy the Kid), Wallace Berry (Pat Garrett), Kay Johnson (Claire Randall), Wyndham Standing (Tunston), Karl Dane

Johnny Mack Brown (right) played Billy the Kid (and Wallace Beery, left, was Pat Garrett) in the first feature about the outlaw, MGM's *Billy the Kid* (1930).

(Swenson), Russell Simpson (McSween), Blanche Frederici (Mrs. McSween), Roscoe Ates (Old Stuff), Warner Richmond (Ballinger), James Marcus (Donovan), Nelson McDowell (Hatfield), Jack Carlyle (Brewer), John Beck (Butterworth), Christopher Martin (Santiago), Marguerita Padula (Nicky Whoosiz), Aggie Herring (Mrs. Hatfield). *With* Soledad Jiminez, Don Coleman, Frank Hagney, Jack Rockwell, Blackjack Ward.

Cattlemen Tunston and McSween come into conflict with Hatfield, who wants to drive the newcomers out of the valley. Billy the Kid is caught stealing cattle from Tunston and is about to be hanged when Tunston decides that Billy's guns might be an asset in the pending war with Hatfield. Billy becomes Tunston's most devoted hand and when Tunston is killed by Ballinger, Hatfield's henchman, Billy decides to kill every man who took part in the fracas. He is particularly concerned for Claire, who was Tunston's intended wife. McSween, Billy and his friends are trapped in McSween's house by Sheriff Pat Garrett. When McSween tries to give up, he is killed and the house set afire. Only Billy escapes with his life. Billy is offered amnesty by General Wallace but refuses and retreats to a cave in the hills, where he is again trapped by Garrett. He is put in jail but escapes and is killed by Garrett when he returns to see Claire.

"The story is a disappointment for it does not follow 'the saga of Billy the Kid' all the way through.... True, it is far superior to the average program picture of its kind, but this due to the direction, dialog and acting and not to the story material."—*Hollywood Reporter,* September 8, 1930

"Mr. Brown gives an ingratiating performance. Mr. Beery also does his bit to make things interesting. Warner Richmond is capital as one of the scoundrels. James Marcus is excellent as the tyrannical sheriff. The rest of the cast do credible work, considering the nature of the tale."—*New York Times,* October 18, 1930

Billy the Kid Returns

(Republic, 1938) 58 min.

Director: Joseph Kane. Screenplay: Jack Natteford. Assoc. Producer: Charles E. Ford.

Roy Rogers (Roy Rogers, Billy the Kid), Smiley Burnette (Frog), Lynn Roberts (Ellen), Morgan Wallace (Morganson), Fred Kohler, Sr. (Matson), Wade Boteler (Pat Garrett), Edwin Stanley (Moore), Joseph Crehan (Conway), Robert Emmett Keane (Page). *With* Horace Murphy, Chris-Pin Martin, Al Taylor, George Letz [Montgomery], Jim Corey, Lloyd Ingraham, Bob McKenzie, Oscar Gahan, Jack Kirk, Art Dillard, Fred Burns, Betty Roadman, Rudy Sooter, Betty Jane Haney, Patsy Lee Parsons, Ray Nichols, Ralph Dunn, Dorothy Vaughn, Frank O'Connor, Bob Card.

The story begins with the shooting of Billy the Kid by Pat Garrett. The next day, Roy Rogers rides into the valley. He is an ex-deputy and a dead ringer for the dead Billy. He is arrested because of his resemblance to "The Kid," whose death has not been announced. Rogers is deputized to impersonate "Billy" in order to help the settlers fight the cattlemen. He and the sheriff hit upon the scheme of tricking the crooks into stealing army horses so that, if caught, they'll be brought before a federal court.

"This is the second of the Roy Rogers westerns. His first, *Under Western Stars*, received excellent notices and in them Rogers was heralded as the biggest western star discovery of the year. He is equally good in his second film. He complements a pleasing personality with one of the best singing voices in westerns."—*Motion Picture Herald,* September 24, 1938.

"Latest in Rogers series is equally as good if not better than the last, being an actioneer of the first order which, combined with Rogers-Burnette

Roy Rogers played a good guy who looked like Billy the Kid in *Billy the Kid Returns* (Republic, 1938). Lynne Roberts was his love interest.

name, Rogers' recording rep and a smart title should spell good b.o. where cactus rules. — *Variety,* September 21, 1938

Billy the Kid Outlawed
(PRC, 1940) 52 min.

Director: Peter Stewart (Sam Newfield). Story/Screenplay: Oliver Drake. Producer: Sigmund Neufeld.

Bob Steele (Billy the Kid), Al St. John (Fuzzy Q. Jones), Louise Currie (Molly Fitzgerald), Carleton Young (Jeff Travis), John Merton (Lije), Joe McGuinn (Morgan), Ted Adams (Sam Daly), Walter McGrail (Judge Fitzgerald), Hal Price (Sheriff Long), Kenne Duncan (Hendricks), Reed Howes (Whitey), George Chesebro (Tex), Steve Clark (Shorty), Budd Buster (Clem), Sherry Tansey (Outlaw). *With* Jack Ingram, Charles King, Carl Sepulveda, Jack Perrin, Carl Mathews.

Gun law rules Lincoln County, New Mexico, in 1872. Pete Morgan and Sam Daly, secretly bandit leaders, operate a general frontier store. Daly

PRC began its series of Billy the Kid films with *Billy the Kid Outlawed* (1940). In these films, Billy the Kid was a good guy. That's Bob Steele with his fist cocked, ready to dispense a little Billy-the-Kid-style justice to George Chesebro. Al St. John, who played Billy's pal Fuzzy Q. Jones, is at far right. John Merton is at left between the croupier and the woman; Reed Howes and Steve Clark are immediately to the right of George Chesebro.

expects to be elected sheriff. Once elected, he and Morgan intend to bring off a final coup and then disappear. The Bennett brothers, cattle ranchers, are murdered by the Morgan-Daly gang. Billy the Kid, with Jeff Travis and "Fuzzy" Jones, drives a herd through Lincoln County. Friends of the slain Bennetts, they seek revenge and engage in a gun skirmish with the killers, during which the stagecoach arrives with Judge Fitzgerald and his daughter Molly as passengers. The judge has been sent to take over the law enforcement in Lincoln County.

Later Fitzgerald is killed by the Morgan-Daly thugs. Sheriff Long deputizes Billy and his two friends to hunt down the murderers. But Daly is elected sheriff, and promptly outlaws Billy, Jeff and Fuzzy. Big rewards are offered for their capture. In a final battle, the gang members surrender after having killed their own bosses by mistaking them for Billy and friend.

Dave Hendricks, Molly's intended husband, tries to convince Billy that the governor has offered him a pardon, but the Kid had reached a stage in his career where he no longer trusts anyone. He refuses to accept the pardon and rides off with his companions to whatever Fate has in store for them.

"Following the windup of his 1939–40 series for Harry Webb's Metropolitan releases, Bob Steele signed for six 'Billy the Kid' films. This film was the beginning of Al St. John's seven-year PRC stay that would see him as 'Fuzzy Q. Jones' opposite Bob Steele, Buster Crabbe, George Houston, Bob Livingston and Lash LaRue. Any explanation as to why director Sam Newfield used the names of Peter Stewart during the latter part of 1939 and all of 1940, and Sherman Scott through 1941 and part of 1942, would be most appreciated."—Les Adams, *Yesterday's Saturdays*, Number 12, June 1977, page 45

Billy the Kid in Texas
(PRC, 1940) 58 min.

Director: Peter Stewart (Sam Newfield). Story/Screenplay: Joseph O'Donnell. Producer: Sigmund Neufeld.

Bob Steele (Billy the Kid), Al St. John (Fuzzy Q. Jones), Carleton Young (Gil Cooper), Terry Walker (Mary Morgan), Frank Larue (Jim Morgan), Charles King (Dave), John Merton (Flash), Charles (Slim) Whitaker (Windy). *With* Curley Dresden, Lew Meehan, Pasqual Perry, Chick Hannon, Denver Dixon, Sherry Tansey, Herman Hack, Ben Corbett, Art Dillard, Tex Palmer, Ray Henderson, Augie Gomez, George Morrell, Wally West, Oscar Gahan, Al Haskell.

On a trumped-up murder charge, Billy the Kid is held in a Mexico jail. He escapes and meets Fuzzy, his side-kick, in Corral City, which is taking a holiday to allow the cowpunchers of the Lazy A Ranch their periodic spree.

In the saloon, Billy is recognized by Dave and Flash, two of the Lazy A's bad men, as the lone rider who held them up after they robbed an express wagon a few hours earlier. They attempt to intimidate Billy, but are bested in a fight. Outside, however, Billy is ambushed and slightly wounded. Fuzzy and Jim, one of the town's leading citizens, take Billy to the express office where Mary Morgan, the local agent, agrees to tend the wounded man until the doctor arrives.

Jim brings in Billy's saddle bags containing the loot taken from Dave and Flash. Billy tells Jim he saw the robbery and that he robbed the robbers in order to return the money. Billy is appointed sheriff with Fuzzy as his deputy. The Lazy A gang brings in a noted gunfighter to deal with the trouble-making new sheriff, but the gunfighter, Gil Cooper, and Billy turn out to be old friends. Billy, Fuzzy and Gil eventually rout the outlaw gang, and Gil remains behind with Mary as Billy and Fuzzy ride off towards the setting sun.

"Bob Steele rides and shoots again as Billy the Kid in this new cactus opus. Picture is another in this series of adventures by the dashing 'Kid' character. Excepting this one is much duller than previous ones. Almost entirely quickie in acting and production, film likely will get most of the business from juvenile trade and lower-half double bills." — *Variety*, November 27, 1940

Billy the Kid's Gun Justice
(PRC, 1940) 59 min.

Director: Peter Stewart (Sam Newfield). Producer: Sigmund Neufeld. Screenplay: Joseph O'Donnell.

Bob Steele (Billy the Kid), Al St. John (Fuzzy Q. Jones), Louise Currie (Ann Roberts), Carleton Young (Jeff), Charles King (Ed Baker), Rex Lease (Buck Mason), Kenne Duncan (Bragg), Forrest Taylor (Roberts), Ted Adams (Sheriff), Al Ferguson (Cobb Allen), Karl Hackett (Lawler), Edward Peil, Sr. (Dave Barlow), Julian Rivero (Carlos), Blanca Vischer (Juanita). *With* Joe McGuinn, George Morrell, Curley Dresden.

Billy the Kid and his pals Fuzzy and Jeff are ambushed in a cabin. As they make their escape, Jeff is wounded. They decide to go to Little Bend Valley where Jeff's uncle has a ranch. On the way they have occasion to save Ann Roberts from thugs Baker and Mason. They learn from Ann that someone is trying to run them off their ranch.

Billy the Kid's Range War
(PRC, 1941) 60 min.

Director: Peter Stewart (Sam Newfield). Story/Screenplay: William Lively. Producer: Sigmund Neufeld.

Bob Steele (Billy the Kid), Al St. John (Fuzzy Jones), Joan Barclay (Ellen Gorham), Carleton Young (Jeff), Rex Lease (Buck), Buddy Roosevelt (Spike), Milton Kibbee (Leonard), Karl Hackett (Williams), Ted Adams (Sheriff), Julian Rivero (Romero), John Ince (Hastings), Alden (Guy) Chase (Dave Hendrix), Howard Masters (Ab Jenkins), Ralph Peteres (Jailer), Tex Palmer, George Chesebro, Sherry Tansey, Curley Dresden, Wally West (Outlaws).

Billy and his pals Jeff, Fuzzy and Romero learn of a plot by Williams to delay and stop work on a new stage line road. Williams has sent for Ab Jenkins to take the place of the construction foreman with instructions to demoralize the men. Billy captures Jenkins, whom Williams and the crooked sheriff have never met, and takes his place. Billy's true identity is soon uncovered, but he and his pals overcome the Williams gang and get the road open for the first stage.

"One of the less vigorous westerns. Meller is based on story material that impresses as too flimsy, though fist fights, a bit of gunplay and conventional horse-chase occasionally relieve tedious sequences.... Steele handles assignment capably."—*Variety*, March 12, 1941

Billy the Kid
(MGM, 1941) 94 min.

Director: David Miller. Suggested by Walter Noble Burns' book *The Saga of Billy the Kid.* Screenplay: Gene Fowler. Story: Howard Emmett Rogers and Bradbury Foote. Producer: Irving Asher.

Robert Taylor (Billy ["The Kid"] Bonney), Brian Donlevy (Jim Sherwood), Ian Hunter (Eric Keating), Mary Howard (Edith Keating), Gene Lockhart (Dan Hickey), Lon Chaney, Jr. ("Spike" Hudson), Henry O'Neill (Tim Ward), Guinn (Big Boy) Williams) (Ed Bronson), Cy Kendall (Cass McAndrews), Ted Adams ("Buz" Cobb), Frank Conlon (Judge Blake), Frank Puglia (Pedro Gonzales), Mitchell Lewis (Bart Hodges), Dick Curtis (Kirby Claxton), Grant Withers (Ed Shanahan), Joe Yule (Milton). *With* Earl Gunn, Eddie Dunn, Tom London, Slim Whitaker, George Chesebro, Arthur Houseman, Lew Harvey, Ray Teal, Buck Mack, Frank Hagney, Edwin J. Brady, Carl Pitti, Kermit Maynard, Ethel Griffies, Chill Wills, Olive Blakeney, Ray Henderson, George Sowards, Tom Smith, Wesley White, Priscilla Lawson.

The narrative carries the note of doom from the very first, when William Bonney is seen as a mercenary gunman for one of the lawless tycoons of the New Mexican frontier, and puts a deadly passion behind his shifting loyalties. Bonney and Jim Sherwood (the Pat Garrett counterpart) are friends at first but end up on opposite sides of the law. The marshal kills his boyhood pal to keep his legal oath.

This film doesn't seek to whitewash the outlaw. That would miss the whole point of the tragic story of a young outlaw's defiance and the inevitable retribution.

In spite of its elaborate coloring, beautiful scenery, competent supporting players and highly reputed star, *Billy the Kid* is just routine horse opera—another glorified fable about one of the West's more notorious outlaws—and not a very good one at that. As usual, the story here has it that the Kid pursued a roving career because of a grave injustice done to him in his youth. But even after he has gone through the regenerative phase, he is so dependent on the six-gun that he uses it to avenge the death of a friend. That, of course, means curtains for gallant but misguided Billy.

"David Miller, promoted from directing two-reelers on the Metro lot, was drafted to pilot *Billy the Kid*. His direction is crisp throughout, carrying the tale along at a consistently zippy pace, and generating the maximum amount of suspense possible from an oft-told tale."—*Variety*, May 21, 1941

Billy the Kid's Fighting Pals
(PRC, 1941) 57 min.

Director: Sherman Scott (Sam Newfield). Story/Screenplay: George Plympton. Producer: Sigmund Neufeld.

Bob Steele (Billy the Kid), Al St. John (Fuzzy Jones), Phyllis Adair (Ann Hardy), Carleton Young (Jeff), Charles King (Badger), Curley Dresden (Burke), Edward Peil, Sr. (Hardy), Hal Price (Borrows), George Chesebro (Sheriff), Forrest Taylor (Henson), Budd Buster (Marshal Mason), Julian Rivero (Lopez), Wally West, Sherry Tansey, Art Dillard (Outlaws).

Riding toward Paradise, Billy, Fuzzy and Jeff witness the murder of Marshal Mason. Fuzzy rides into town posing as the dead lawman and learns that it is being ruled by a mob, headed by Burke.

Burke and Badger, a henchman, force the editor of a crusading newspaper to auction off his plant. Billy outbids the others. Infuriated, Badger starts a fight and is whipped. The editor is murdered before Billy can talk to him. Ann Hardy, ward of the town banker, offers to help run the paper, and deliberately upsets some of the type scheduled for the next edition. Meanwhile, a sheriff rides into town, hunting for Billy the Kid.

While Billy is riding with Ann, attempts are made to ambush him, but he is saved through the help of Fuzzy and Jeff, who have been following. Badger, captured, informs Billy that Hardy is the real leader of the gang, which is working a smuggling racket by means of a tunnel, dug from Hardy's barn to a spot below the Mexican border. Ann arrives with news that Hardy plans to kill Badger, whom she loves, and the man is taken to Lopez's cafe for safety. The Kid manages to trick the gang members into assembling at the cafe, where they start accusing each other of double crossing. The sheriff overhears and arrests them all, thinking that Billy is one of them. In the confusion, Billy makes his getaway.

Nobody fares at all well in this early PRC mustanger because of an inferior screenplay and mediocre production values. It's a big letdown for Bob Steele fans, though he does his best while contending with a shoestring budget.

"Another in Sigmund Neufeld's seemingly interminable series. *Billy the Kid's Fighting Pals* is far below its predecessors in every department. Unbelievable situations, pathetic comedy and draggy dialog gang up on the players."—*Variety*, June 25, 1941

Billy the Kid in Santa Fe
(PRC, 1941) 56 min.

Director: Sherman Scott (Sam Newfield). Screenplay: Joseph O'Donnell. Producer: Sigmund Neufeld. TV title: *Battling Outlaws*.

Bob Steele (Billy the Kid), Al St. John (Fuzzy Jones), Rex Lease (Jeff), Marin Sais (Pat Walker), Dennis Moore (Silent Don Vincent), Dave O'Brien (Texas Joe Vincent), Charles King (Steve Barton), Karl Hackett (Davis), Steve Clark (Allen), Hal Price (Sheriff), Frank Ellis (Hank Baxter), Kenne Duncan (Scotty), Curley Dresden, Tex Palmer (Outlaws). *With* John Elliott, Reed Howes, Wally West, Art Dillard, Jack Evans, Chick Hannon, Milburn Morante, Foxy O'Callahan, George Morrell, Artie Ortego, Denver Dixon, Ray Henderson.

After framing Billy on a murder charge, Hank Baxter and Texas Joe head for Santa Fe to report to gang leader Steve Barton. The crooked sheriff frees Billy, planning to shoot him as he escapes, but is thwarted by Fuzzy and Jeff. The trio head for Santa Fe after Baxter and Texas Joe. They keep under cover at the home of an old friend, frontierswoman Pat Walker. Joe looks up his brother Silent Don Vincent, a reformed gunman. When Don tells Joe that Billy is in town, he heads for the hideout of the Barton gang and proceeds to get drunk.

As Baxter heads for the hideout, he is followed by Charlie, one of Pat's men, who suspects the gang of a recent holdup. Charlie walks into a trap and is killed. Baxter and Barton convince the drunken Joe that he is the real murderer, and induce him to remain in hiding. However, while riding back to town, Hank is captured by Fuzzy, who plans to keep him until he can find out why the man lied to convict Billy.

Texas Joe hides out in Don's house. When Billy calls on his old friend, Joe is found and submits to arrest. After one of his henchmen helps Joe escape, Barton blames the jailbreak on Baxter and arranges for a posse of gang members and dupe citizens to trail the escaped prisoner. Billy and Fuzzy confront Barton with the captive Baxter, and trick a confession out of the pair. When the posse returns, the men learn that they have hung an innocent man. Don swears revenge, and one by one the members of the death posse are tricked into gun fights. Their bodies are found with a playing card from Joe's deck on their chests.

Suspecting Don, Billy breaks into his house and finds a photograph of Texas Joe, inscribed "to my mother," and learns for the first time of the relationship between the men.

Knowing that Billy is coming after him, Don removes the cartridges from his gun, refusing to chance killing his friend. When the two men meet, Billy aims wide of the mark, and neither man is hurt. Billy decides that Don must stand trial, however, but before he can be taken to jail, Fuzzy gets the men together, forms a jury, has himself appointed honorary judge, and declares Don not guilty inasmuch as all the men he shot were outlaws.

Billy the Kid Wanted

(PRC, 1941) 64 min.

Director: Sherman Scott (Sam Newfield). Producer: Sigmund Neufeld. Screenplay: Fred Myton.

Buster Crabbe (Billy the Kid), Al St. John (Fuzzy Jones), Dave O'Brien (Jeff), Choti Sherwood (Jane), Glenn Strange (Matt Brawley), Charles King (Jack Saunders), Slim Whitaker (Sheriff), Howard Masters (Stan Harper), Joel Newfield (Little Boy), Budd Buster (Storekeeper), Frank Ellis (Bart), Pascale Perry, Reed Howes, Art Dillard (Deputies), Wally West, Augie Gomez, Frank Ellis, Kenne Duncan, Arch Hall (Outlaws). *With* Steve Clark, Chick Hannon, George Morrell, Ray Henderson.

Billy, Jeff and Fuzzy are hiding out with friendly farmers of the Paradise Land Development, a district mostly owned and totally controlled by unscrupulous Matt Bradley. When farmer Stan Harper attempts to protest Brawley's ruthless rule, all credit is withheld from the farmers. Accordingly, Billy robs the store and distributes the stolen food.

Jack Saunders, ex-partner of Brawley, arrives and cuts himself in on the new racket. Matt arranges to have Billy kill Saunders, hoping to rid himself of his ex-partner, and have Billy arrested for the murder. Jeff discovers the plan, and by charging Billy with double crossing him, picks a fight with his friend. The confusion prevents the gun battle with Saunders. Posing as Billy's enemy, Jeff is able to join Saunders' gang.

Billy leads Brawley's men into an ambush and, in a counter attack, Jeff manages to do the same with Saunders' outlaws. Each raid costs the rival gangmen. However, Jeff is caught signaling Fuzzy, and when Billy attempts to rescue him, he too is captured. The outlaw chiefs call a truce and, still thinking the captured Billy and Jeff are enemies, offer them the opportunity to fight a duel to the death, with freedom for the winner.

Jeff skillfully knocks Billy into Brawley. Billy grabs Brawley's guns, out shoots Saunders and, using Brawley as a shield, rounds up the rest of the gang. With the rival outlaw camps eliminated, the farmers elect their own sheriff, as Billy and his pals ride off to new adventures.

"*Billy the Kid Wanted*, latest in recent string of Billy the Kid westerns, is routine fare. It looks like it might be the start of a series from this producer, with Buster Crabbe in the title role. It has mild cowboy heroics and is lukewarm for lower half of dual setup."—*Variety*, November 26, 1941

Same shirt, different Billy: Buster Crabbe bursts onto the scene as Billy the Kid in *Billy the Kid's Round-up* (PRC, 1943). *Left to right:* Carleton Young, Al St. John, Buster Crabbe, player, John Elliott, Keene Duncan, Joan Barclay, player.

Billy the Kid's Round-Up
(PRC, 1941) 56 min.

Director: Sherman Scott (Sam Newfield). Producer: Sigmund Neufeld. Screenplay: Fred Myton.

Buster Crabbe (Billy the Kid), Al St. John (Fuzzy), Carleton Young (Jeff), Joan Barclay (Betty Webster), Glenn Strange (Vic Landreau), Charles King (Deputy Ed Slade), Slim Whitaker (Sheriff Jim Hanley), John Elliott (Dan Webster), Dennis Moore (Butch), Kenne Duncan (Joe), Curley Dresden (Curley), Richard Cramer (Bartender Harry), Wally West, Jack Hendricks, George Morrell (Outlaws), Tim Mason (Saloon Patron), Tex Palmer, Tex Cooper, Horace B. Carpenter (Townsmen). *With* Ray Henderson, Tex Phelps, Tom Smith, Augie Gomez, Art Dillard, Denver Dixon.

After writing Billy, Jeff and Fuzzy to come to his aid, honest sheriff Jim Hanley is murdered on the orders of saloon keeper Vic Landreau, among whose gang is deputy sheriff Ed Slade. Landreau sends Butch out to ambush the trio, but he fails and is captured. Billy drags him to Landreau's office and denounces him, hoping to force a showdown with the gang leader. Landreau keeps his head and a fight is averted.

When local newspaper editor Dan Webster attacks Landreau's gang in his paper, he is set upon by thugs, and only through the lucky intervention of Billy and his pals is the printing plant saved from being wrecked.

Billy decides to help Webster and his daughter Betty run the paper and to campaign for an honest government. The paper continues to oppose the crooked elements, and urges the defeat of Slade in the coming election.

Attempting to deliver a special pre-election issue to the voters of the outlying districts, Betty is kidnapped by members of Landreau's gang. Billy, Jeff and Fuzzy track the gang to its hideout and by a ruse rescue the girl.

Returning to town, they find the press wrecked, but manage to set up enough type for a single page denouncement of Landreau. Billy delivers the paper in person to the outlaw chief, and a fight ensues, with Butch attempting to shoot Billy while he is occupied with Landreau. Billy sees Butch's reflection in a mirror and beats him to the draw.

With Landreau beaten and in jail and the tough element of the town on the run, Billy, Jeff and Fuzzy ride into the sunset.

"Conventional western geared for nominal returns in situations using this type of product. ... Crabbe photographs well and gives a good account of himself in the top assignment as a quick-shooting, hard-riding sagebrush stalwart."—*Variety*, January 7, 1942

Billy the Kid Trapped
(PRC, 1942) 59 min.

Director: Sherman Scott (Sam Newfield). Producer: Sigmund Neufeld. Screenplay: Oliver Drake.

Buster Crabbe (Billy the Kid), Al St. John (Fuzzy Jones), Bud McTaggart (Jeff), Anne Jeffreys (Sally), Glenn Strange (Stanton), Walter McGrail (Judge McConnell), Ted Adams (Sheriff Masters), Jack Ingram (Red Barton), Milton Kibbee (Judge Clarke), Eddie Phillips (Dave), Budd Buster (Montana), Jack Kinney (Saloon Patron), Jimmy Aubrey, Wally West, Art Dillard, Jack Evans, Pascale Perry, Cactus Mack, Buck Bucko (Outlaws).

After Billy, Fuzzy and Jeff are rescued from a hanging by mysterious strangers, the countryside is terrorized by three men posing as Billy and his saddle partners.

When Sheriff Masters, ambushed by the masqueraders, is rescued by Billy and his pals, he puts them on the trail of the impostors. Clues lead them to Mesa City, an outlaw town run by Jim Stanton under whose orders three killers, Montana, Pete and Curly, have been robbing and murdering, disguised as Billy and his pals.

When Sheriff Evans begins to suspect Stanton, he is murdered. Billy brings in the killers, but they are released by crooked Judge Clarke. Stanton makes gang leader Red Barton the new sheriff, with orders to get Billy. Again assuming their disguises, Montana, Pete and Curly rob the stagecoach.

Sheriff Masters arrives in town and arrests Billy, Fuzzy and Jeff, thereby preventing an ambush, as Stanton killers have been posted at every exit. When they are clear of town, Masters releases them with the provision that they help him clean up the town.

After running crooked Judge Clarke out of town, the Sheriff leaves Mesa City to return later on the stage with honest Circuit Judge McConnell. Stanton and his gang ambush the stage, only to find Billy and his pals hidden within. A fight ensues, and the villains are rounded up.

"Acting is all good for a horse opera, with Buster Crabbe carrying off top honors with the fattest part. Al St. John lends his typical routine, and the balance of the support is properly villainous or defenseless, as the script requires. Photography is good and the horsemanship excellent. Direction is fast paced." — *Variety*, April 22, 1942

Billy the Kid's Smoking Guns
(PRC, 1942) 58 min.

Director: Sherman Scott (Sam Newfield). Producer: Sigmund Neufeld. Screenplay: George Milton.

Buster Crabbe (Billy the Kid), Al St. John (Fuzzy Jones), Dave O'Brien (Jeff), Joan Barclay (Mrs. Howard), John Merton (Morgan), Milton Kibbee (Dr. Hagan), Ted Adams (Sheriff Carson), Karl Hackett (Hart), Frank Ellis (Carter), Slim Whitaker (Roberts), Budd Buster (Rancher), Joel Newfield (Dickie Howard), Tim Mason (Outlaw). *With* James Mason, Curley Dresden, Art Dillard, George Morrell, Lou Fulton, Steve Clark.

Billy, Jeff and Fuzzy come upon a wrecked wagon with Dickie Howard grimly holding a gun over the figure of his wounded father. He tells them his father was shot by bandits.

They lift the wounded man from the wagon just as Sheriff Carson rides up and arrests them for the attack. They carry the wounded man to Dr. Hagan's office in town. Unknown to the three cowboys, the doctor and the sheriff are in with Morgan, whose gang is fighting the ranchers undercover. The doctor gives the wounded man a hypodermic and kills him so he cannot talk. The boys escape from jail and ride with little Dickie to his home to get information from his mother.

At the house they find three of Morgan's men threatening Mrs. Howard and drive them off. The sheriff arrives as the three buddies hide in the kitchen. They are amazed to hear him tell Mrs. Howard that her husband is dead, as he was not seriously injured. The sheriff tells her that Billy and his pals committed the crime.

Mrs. Howard tells the boys the story of the Cooperative Association that operates the only store in Stone City. Morgan operates it, offering ranchers credit for their supplies to be paid when their crops come in. Now Morgan is beginning to foreclose on their ranches ahead of time and refusing more supplies except for cash. When the ranchers try to haul in supplies from outside, they are shot like Howard was. Billy and Jeff now realize that the sheriff is in with Morgan, but they have no proof.

The ranchers try to bring in supplies and Jeff is wounded in a battle. The doctor tries to dispose of him the way he did Howard, but Billy arrives in time to save him. The gang is rounded up and after a quick trial the verdict is guilty.

"A routine, uninspired horseback opera headed for the second slot on twin bills. Cast and direction match the plot, with the audience hissing the villain and laughing at the suspense in real ten-twent'-thirt' fashion."— *Variety*, August 19, 1942

Law and Order
(PRC, 1942) 58 min.

Director: Sherman Scott (Sam Newfield). Screenplay: Sam Robbins. Producer: Sigmund Neufeld.

Buster Crabbe (Lt. Morrison, Billy the Kid), Al St. John (Fuzzy Jones), Dave O'Brien (Jeff), Sarah Padden (Aunt Mary), Wanda McKay (Linda Freemont), Charles King (Crawford), Hal Price (Simms), John Merton (Turtle), Kenne Duncan (Dugan), Ted Adams (Sheriff), Carl Mathews (Outlaw), Art Dillard (Soldier). *With* Jack Kirk, George Morrell, Bert Dillard, Tex Cooper, Jimmy Aubrey, Augie Gomez, Dan White, Steve Clark, Herman Hack.

Right after the Civil War, Billy, Jeff and Fuzzy are arrested by two U.S. Cavalrymen and brought to Fort Culver, a frontier post under the command of Lt. Morrison. Brought before him, Billy sees his double. Both he and the Lieutenant are amazed.

Learning of a plot to swindle the Lieutenant's rich blind Aunt Mary by marrying her off to an impostor named Simms instead of her sweetheart, Freemont, Billy and his pals escape and make their way to the ranch.

Crawford, head of the gang scheming to get hold of the blind woman's fortune, sends two men to waylay the stage bringing Freemont. The outlaws kill Freemont and also Lt. Morrison, who was on the way to the wedding.

Billy impersonates the dead officer, and Aunt Mary is fooled into believing he is her relative.

Linda, a niece of the murdered Freemont, arrives to see her uncle married to Aunt Mary. Billy meets her on the stagecoach and arranges to have her denounce Simms as an impostor just as the ceremony starts. This she does. A fight ensues with the gang rounded up.

Note: "Right after the Civil War," Billy the Kid would have been a lad of five or six, not a man of 30 or more years!

"Plot of this one is stretched a bit to fill out, causing some dragginess, but generally it is worthy western material, suitable for average demands... Story has been well mapped out, holding interest nicely, while along the route there is reasonable action." — *Variety*, October 21, 1942

Sheriff of Sage Valley

(PRC, 1942) 55 min.

Director: Sherman Scott (Sam Newfield). Producer: Sigmund Neufeld. Screenplay: George W. Sayre, Milton Raison.

Buster Crabbe (Billy the Kid, Kansas), Al St. John (Fuzzy Jones), Dave O'Brien (Jeff), Maxine Leslie (Janet Morley), Charles King (Sloane), John Merton (Nick Gaynor), Hal Price (Mayor Harrison), Kermit Maynard (Slim), Jack Kirk (Stage Driver), Jack Hendricks (Double), Curley Dresden, Lynton Brent, Art Dillard (Bandits). *With* Budd Buster, Roy Henderson, Al Taylor, Frank Ellis, Jack Evans, Bert Dillard, Carl Mathews, Dan White, Merrill McCormick.

A stagecoach holdup is interrupted by Billy, Jeff and Fuzzy after one passenger, the sheriff, has been killed. The other passengers are Nick Gaynor, faro dealer at the Casino at Sage Valley; the guard at the gambling place; and Janet Morley, sweetheart of Kansas, secret bandit leader of the gang. Kansas plotted the stage holdup to kill the sheriff and take over the town which is about to become the county seat.

The three stage bandits report to Kansas in his hideout and turn over a "Wanted" poster showing Kansas' photo. Kansas is later told by the faro dealer, the guard and Janet that the stranger Billy who interrupted the holdup is his twin. Sloane, who owns the property, has refused to renew the lease because ranchers have complained of being cheated by the crooked faro wheel. Kansas plans to dispose of Harrison, appoint his own sheriff and take over the town.

Carrying out the plot, Sloane picks a fight with Harrison in his office, but Billy arrives in time to prevent the murder of the banker/mayor. Billy gives Sloane a beating. Harrison offers the sheriff's job to Billy.

Billy and his pals go to the Casino as Sloane's gang are forcing the election of one of their men as sheriff. A fight starts, and the three best Sloane, the faro dealer and the would-be sheriff.

Later Billy is lured by Janet to the outlaw's hideout, where he is made a prisoner. Kansas, his double, takes the sheriff's badge and goes to town with his men to take over. Mayor Harrison and the ranchers are surprised to see the man they think is their new sheriff now siding with the outlaws.

With the help of Jeff and Fuzzy, Billy escapes. He meets Kansas alone, for he is now convinced that his double is his twin brother whom he has not seen since they were children. As Billy fights with the outlaw, Jeff breaks in and mortally wounds Kansas. The outlaw admits that he is Billy's brother. A grateful mayor and ranchers send the three pals on their way with their thanks for rounding up the gang.

There is no attempt in this film to adhere to historical fact. Not only was Billy the Kid *not* a hero made sheriff, but he had no twin brother.

"Again Buster Crabbe plays a dual role, this time two brothers who are outlaws, in an Indie-made western that ranks with the best in the field although palpably having cost less than most."—*Variety*, December 9, 1942

The Mysterious Rider
(PRC, 1942) 55 min.
(Reissued in 1947 in a 39-minute version titled *Panhandle Trail*)

Director: Sherman Scott (Sam Newfield). Producer: Sigmund Neufeld. Screenplay: Steve Braxton.

Buster Crabbe (Billy the Kid), Al St. John (Fuzzy Q. Jones), Caroline Burke (Martha Kincaid), John Merton (Dalton Sykes), Jack Ingram (Trigger Larson), Kermit Maynard (Joe), Charles (Slim) Whitaker (Rufe), Art Dillard, Augie Gomez (Outlaws), Edwin Brien (Johnny Kincaid). *With* Karl Hackett, Jimmy Aubrey.

Billy the Kid and Fuzzy, on the run from the U. S. marshal, ride into the apparently abandoned frontier town of Laramy. Here they find a reward poster for their capture. It is because of Billy's supposed outlawry that the townspeople have fled. Trigger Larson fires at Billy, and this gives the latter a hint as to why Laramy has become a ghost town.

Dalton Sykes, former sheriff of the town, searches for a vein of gold which was discovered by Frank Kincaid years before. (Sykes and his gang murdered Kincaid and have systematically cleaned out the town over a period of years in order to find the gold mine and keep others from stumbling on it.) Trigger notifies Sykes that there are two strangers in town.

Martha and Johnny Kincaid, children of the murdered miner, are chased by Sykes' men as they approach Laramy. Billy and Fuzzy rescue them. They all go to the deserted Kincaid ranch.

Fuzzy starts playing the dead man's violin. Sykes' men report in terror that Kincaid is haunting his old home. Investigating, Sykes discovers the strangers. In the gunfight that follows, the violin is broken and Billy discovers a map of the gold mine hidden inside. Billy tries to extract a confession from Trigger as to who murdered Kincaid, but is thwarted by the arrival of Sykes, acting in his old capacity of sheriff. Billy becomes suspicious and sends Johnny for the marshal.

Sykes tells Martha that Kincaid left them to his guardianship, and he had sent them East for schooling. Innocently believing Sykes a friend, she tells him about the mine map. In the meanwhile, Billy has made a false map in order to lay a trap for Sykes. The latter recognizes Billy as the notorious Kid and demands the map.

After being led on a false scent by the phony map, Sykes captures Billy and takes the genuine map. He is giving the signal to his men to shoot Billy when the marshal arrives. As Sykes makes a break, Billy pursues him. He overtakes him on the very spot where the gold mine lies.

Johnny and Martha are given legal possession of the property. The town of Laramy is restored to its former activity as the ranchers come back.

"This one, directed by Sherman Scott, will get by the budget market as has its predecessors. Al St. John provides the comedy expected of him as Billy's sidekick, and a capable leading woman is added in the person of Caroline Burke. ... Photography by Jack Greenhalgh is hampered by the blackness of his night effects."—*Hollywood Reporter*, January 5, 1943

The Outlaw

(United Artists, 1943) 128 min.

Director: Howard Hughes, Howard Hawks and Otho Lovering. Screenplay: Jules Furthman. Producer: Howard Hughes.

Jane Russell (Rio), Walter Huston (Doc Holliday), Thomas Mitchell (Sheriff Pat Garrett), Jack Beutel (Billy the Kid). *With* Martin Garralaga, Arthur Loft, Frank Darien, Ethan Laidlaw, Carl Stockdale, Julian Rivero, Dick Elliott, Dick Jones, Mime Aguglia, Joe Sawyer, Gene Rizzi, Nena Quartero, Pat West, Ed Brady, William Steele, Wallace Reid, Jr. Ed Peil, Sr., Lee (Lasses) White, Ted Mapes, William Newill, Lee Shumway, Emory Parnell, John Sheeham.

Doc Holliday befriends the notorious Billy the Kid and saves him from Sheriff Pat Garrett. Later, when Billy is shot, Doc leaves him in the hands of Rio, who crawls in bed with him to keep him warm. In the process she falls in love with Billy.

"...The public seems more than willing to forgive the faults of *The Outlaw*, if one is to draw conclusions from the attendance records. It would appear that I have never before quite realized to what lengths motion picture audiences will go, and what dross they will accept, just so long as it is an inspirational celluloid message that holds the screen."—Herb Sterns in *Rob Wagner's Script*, Vol. 32, No. 728, (April 27, 1946), p. 14

"Sitting in cans on a studio library shelf for a couple of years won't improve the product generally or the acting in particular. But then, neither will it hurt the appeal of the spectacular Jane Russell. Can't think of any other reason for catching this."—*Fortnight*, Vol. 8, No. 3 (February 3, 1950), p. 31

The Kid Rides Again
(PRC, 1943) 58 min.

Director: Sherman Scott (Sam Newfield). Producer: Sigmund Neufeld. Screenplay: Fred Myton.

Buster Crabbe (Billy the Kid), Al St. John (Fuzzy Jones), Iris Meredith (Joan), Glenn Strange (Tom), Charles King (Vic), I. Stanford Jolley (Mort), Edward Peil, Sr. (Ainsley), Karl Hackett (Texas Sheriff). *With* Ted Adams (Sheriff), Budd Buster, Ray Jones, George Morrell, Tex Cooper, Frank McCarroll.

Billy the Kid is arrested for an express robbery, but breaks away from the sheriff and joins his pal Fuzzy. He and Fuzzy set out to catch the real bandits but their job is difficult as the outlaw gang is protected by the sheriff. Consequently the ranchers have been suffering from cattle rustling without any protection.

John Ainsley, president of the local bank, addresses the townspeople and demands that the county be rid of the desperadoes. When Billy is seen in town, he is suspected of being the express robber. Joan, daughter of Ainsley, recognizes Billy and indignantly orders him out of town.

Mort Slade of the outlaw gang is trying to buy the mortgage on the Carter property after having rustled their cattle and leaving them penniless, but Ainsley refuses to sell. This infuriates Slade and he threatens Ainsley. Billy learns that Slade's brother Tom framed him on the express robbery and knows the Slades are the guilty ones, but no one can prove their guilt.

Billy and Fuzzy follow the Slades to their hideout and it is evident that they have been rustling cattle. Billy also overhears that they are after Ainsley because he will not sell the mortgage. He warns Ainsley but the banker ignores the warning.

Slade orders Billy out of town but Billy can't be discouraged, and he has it out with Slade in a gunfight. He is arrested by the phony sheriff for the shooting.

With Billy out of the way, Mort Slade robs the bank. His intention is to panic the people, forcing Ainsley to turn their money back to them and sell the ranch. But Fuzzy gets Billy out of jail in time to see the robbery and follow the outlaw gang. Meanwhile, Ainsley is holding off the people. They are demanding their money back as soon as the bank opens, but Joan now has faith in Billy and urges her father to hold out.

After a desperate gunfight, Billy and Fuzzy recover the money. They ride back to town in time to save the situation for Ainsley. The outlaws are arrested and Billy is made deputy.

"This is a true-to-formula addition to the 'Billy the Kid' series with Buster Crabbe. Action addicts will find all the ingredients present; rustling, gun fights, and chases. ... A deft comedy touch is injected by Al [Fuzzy] St. John, who is the only standout in the cast. Buster Crabbe makes a handsome but colorless title character." —*Variety*, March 24, 1943

Fugitive of the Plains
(PRC, 1943) 56 min.
(Reissued in 1947 as a 37-minute version titled *Raiders of Red Rock*)

Director: Sam Newfield. Producer: Sigmund Neufeld. Screenplay: George W. Sayre

Buster Crabbe (Billy the Kid), Al St. John (Fuzzy Jones), Maxine Leslie (Kate Shelly), Jack Ingram (Dillon), Kermit Maynard (Spence), Karl Hackett (Sheriff Packard), Hal Price (Sheriff Conley), George Chesebro (Baxter), Frank Ellis (Dirk), John Merton (Deputy), Artie Ortego, Curley Dresden (Outlaws), Budd Buster, Carl Sepulveda, Art Dillard, Jimmy Aubrey (Players).

The sheriff of Red Rock has issued orders for the arrest of Billy the Kid on robbery charges. Billy realizes that someone is impersonating him. He goes to Red Rock to find the guilty party and clear his name.

As Billy and his pal Fuzzy enter Red Rock they witness a holdup by a band of outlaws. Billy follows the outlaws to their ranch and is surprised to learn that the leader is a woman, Kate Shelly. Kate bargains with Billy and he agrees to join her gang. He does this to gain evidence enough to convict the outlaws.

Fuzzy is arrested but refuses to expose Billy. Meanwhile, Kate makes a deal with Billy to rob the stagecoach. Billy grimly accepts. Kate's partner Dillon tips off the sheriff that Billy is going to rob the stagecoach so that Billy will be caught red-handed. But Billy in the meantime has released Fuzzy from jail, captured two members of the gang and reported to Kate that the sheriff had been tipped off so that it was impossible to rob the stage.

Kate assigns Billy to help her on a bigger job which she will handle herself. They are to rob the Red Rock bank. Again the sheriff is tipped off, but this time by Billy. He captures more members of the gang so there are few members left. Billy tries to warn Kate not to go through with the robbery as he knows she will walk into the trap he has set. But Kate becomes suspicious of Billy and makes him her prisoner.

As Kate and her men enter the bank, they are met by the sheriff and his posse. A gunfight results, and Kate is seriously wounded. They make a getaway, with the sheriff in close pursuit. Kate is unable to keep up the pace. Meanwhile, Billy has escaped and arrives at the scene in time to save the wounded girl from toppling from her horse. He takes her to a hideout and is trying to get help when Dillon appears intent on killing him. With her last bit of strength, Kate kills Dillon to save Billy. She dies in his arms.

"In this one Buster Crabbe continues his adventures as 'Billy the Kid' in a vehicle good enough for the more rabid oats opera addicts. History's tail continues to be given a twist by this continuing characterization of 'Billy' as an upright citizen but that won't disturb the true-blue western film fan."—*Variety*, February 22, 1946

Western Cyclone
(PRC, 1943) 56 min.
(Re-released in 1947 in a 39-minute version titled *Frontier Fighters*)

Director: Sam Newfield. Producer: Sigmund Neufeld. Screenplay: Patricia Harper. (Re-released in 1947 in a 39-minute version titled *Frontier Fighters*)

Buster Crabbe (Billy the Kid), Al St. John (Fuzzy Jones), Marjorie Manners (Mary Arnold), Karl Hackett (Governor Arnold), Milton Kibbee (Senator Peabody), Kermit Maynard (Hank), Glenn Strange (Dirk Randall), Charles King (Ace Harmon), Hal Price (Sheriff), Frank Ellis, Frank McCarroll (Henchmen). *With* Artie Ortego, Herman Hack, Al Haskell, Jack Ingram, Lane Bradford, Cactus Mack, Steve Clark, Hank Bell, Jimmy Aubrey.

Billy and Fuzzy frame a holdup of the stagecoach which Fuzzy is driving in order to convince Senator Peabody that action should be taken by the state to curb a wave of lawlessness. Riding in the stage with the senator are Governor Arnold, his niece Mary and Dirk Randall, a local banker who is in cahoots with the criminal band.

Randall is scheming to get the governor impeached and arranges to kill one of his henchmen and frame Billy for the killing. Randall shoots his henchman in the back. Billy is arrested for the murder, tried and convicted.

Fuzzy gets Billy out of jail and the two start to track down the real murderer. The only clue they have is an empty shell which shows that the hammer of the gun which fired it was defective.

Randall realizes that Billy must be hanged on the specified date or his plan to have the governor impeached will fail. He has Mary kidnapped and gets word to Billy that if he doesn't give himself up, Mary will be harmed. Billy surrenders to the sheriff.

Billy arranges with the governor for 12 hours leave to find the murderer. The townspeople accuse the governor and sheriff of complicity with Billy.

Billy risks his life to take a shot in the shoulder from Randall's gun. He captures Randall and proves to the townspeople that the gun that killed Randall's henchman is the same one that fired the shell into his shoulder. The governor is cleared of all suspicion and Randall is exposed as the leader of the outlaw gang.

"This is one of the best of the 'Billy the Kid' series starring Buster Crabbe, not only because it has plenty of action and lively dialogue but also as a result of the laugh value. Al St. John has been provided with plenty of good comedy situations and, apparently with Crabbe's blessings, is given wide opportunity to show his stuff."—*Variety*, June 16, 1943

Cattle Stampede
(PRC, 1943) 58 min.

Director: Sam Newfield. Producer: Sigmund Neufeld. Screenplay: Joseph O'Donnell.

Buster Crabbe (Billy the Kid), Al St. John (Fuzzy Jones), Frances Gladwin (Mary Dawson), Charles King (Brandon), Edward Cassidy (Sam Dawson), Hansel Warner (Ed Dawson), Ray Bennett (Stone), Frank Ellis (Elkins), Steve Clark (Turner), Roy Brent (Slater), John Elliott (Doctor), Budd Buster (Jensen), Hank Bell (Stage Driver), George Morrell, Tex Cooper, Ted Adams, Hal Price (Townsmen), Rose Plummer (Townswoman), Frank McCarroll (Brawler), Ray Jones (Spectator). *With* Glenn Strange, Curley Dresden, Cactus Mack, Art Dillard, Roy Bucko, Carl Mathews.

In Arizona, Billy and Fuzzy are recognized by some men who figure to cash in on the reward offered for the pair. Billy is warned in time by Ed Dawson, but in the getaway Dawson is wounded. The boys learn from Ed that a range war is in progress across the border and that he is looking for men to make a cattle drive to the rail junction. Billy and Fuzzy decide to help Ed and his father. Bringing a doctor to attend to Ed, they leave.

They run across a Dawson man who has been killed from ambush. Mary, sister of Ed, thinks they did it, but they convince her of their innocence. At the ranch the news of the killing causes Brandon, the foreman, secretly working for the plotters, to try to get the rest of the Dawson men to quit. Billy and Fuzzy put a stop to this and agree to take the cattle through for the Dawsons. Brandon quits and rides to join the rest of the outlaw gang, headed by Coulter.

The cattle drive gets underway with Billy as trail boss. Brandon and Coulter have their henchmen stampede the cattle. Elkins, one of Coulter's men, meets Billy after the stampede and suggests that his boss will buy what cattle are left. Billy realizes that Coulter's gang is operating systematically to run off cattle. A trail patrol is organized, and Billy reports to Dawson of their loss.

Mary now recognizes Billy as Billy the Kid, but he convinces her father that he is going to help them. Mary is not convinced and visits the town where Coulter is located to do some investigating. Later Billy is recognized by Coulter and agrees to work for him for a cut of the money received for the stolen Dawson cattle.

Billy and Fuzzy plan to rob the stage, bringing Coulter money for the cattle he has illegally sold. Billy intends to give the money from the robbery to Dawson. Mary happens to be on the stage and recognizes Billy and Fuzzy.

Later Mary is kidnapped by members of Coulter's gang and taken to Coulter. Coulter plans to use her to force her dad to give him a quit-claim to the Dawson ranch. Both Coulter and Mary find out that Billy is not working for Coulter. Later Billy reports to Coulter's office where a wild fight ensues. Billy learns that Mary has been taken away to Coulter's ranch. He rides there and rescues her. Coulter and his henchmen are captured, and the cattlemen are able to send their herds through the pass without being molested.

"...a routine dual western. Buster Crabbe and Al St. John are featured, with the latter's comedy providing the highlight."—*Variety*, December 29, 1943

The Renegade
(PRC, 1943) 58 min.
(Re-released in 1947 as *Code of the Plains*)

Director: Sam Newfield. Producer: Sigmund Neufeld Story: George Milton. Screenplay: Joseph O'Donnell.

Buster Crabbe (Billy the Kid), Al St. John (Fuzzy Jones), Lois Ranson (Julie), Karl Hackett (Dan Martin), Ray Bennett (Mayor Hill), Frank Hagney (Saunders), Jack Rockwell (Sheriff), Tom London (Pete), George Chesebro (Bart). *With* Wally West, Dan White, Jimmy Aubrey, Carl Sepulveda, Silver Harr.

When Dan Martin's bank is robbed of $50,000, he calls on Billy and Fuzzy to capture the robbers. Billy figures that sooner or later some of the stolen bills will be put into circulation, and through the serial numbers the outlaws can be identified.

Billy suspects that Mayor Hill is the man who controls the outlaws. Billy and Fuzzy break into his office and find the stolen money. The mayor catches them in the act of breaking open his safe. He threatens to kill them and blame the robbery on them. But the sheriff hears him boasting of his vicious plans and with Billy's help captures the mayor and his gang.

Blazing Frontier
(PRC, 1943) 59 min.

Director: Sam Newfield. Producer: Sigmund Neufeld. Screenplay: Patricia Harper.

Buster Crabbe (Billy the Kid), Al St. John (Fuzzy Jones), Marjorie Manners (Helen), Milton Kibbee (Clem Barstow), I. Stanford Jolley (Luther Sharp), Kermit Maynard (Pete), Frank Hagney (Sheriff Ward Tragg), George Chesebro (Deputy Slade), Frank Ellis (Deputy Biff), Hank Bell (Bartender), Jimmy Aubrey (Man in Bar), Charles King, Curley Dresden, Cactus Mack, Frank McCarroll (Outlaws).

When a feud develops between settlers and railroad detectives in Red Rock Valley, Clem Barstow, lawyer for the settlers, sends for that ubiquitous pair, Billy the Kid and Fuzzy Jones.

Billy and Fuzzy hire out as detectives in order to get evidence against Ward Tragg, chief of the railroad detectives. Billy suspects that Tragg and Luther Sharp, land agent for the Western Railroad Company, are defrauding the settlers without the knowledge or sanction of their employer.

Billy and the settlers rustle cattle which had been confiscated by Tragg and his men in order to raise money for Barstow to bid on a ranch which Sharp is auctioning off.

When Barstow receives his deed from the railroad company, it is apparently in order, but Billy discovers that the purchase price recorded on the deed has been altered. Barstow writes to the railroad company and they send out a representative to investigate.

When Tragg learns about this, he plans to kidnap the railroad official to prevent him from meeting with Barstow, but Billy rescues the official. The railroad company makes an amicable settlement and the settlers are allowed to return to their homes from which they had been evicted.

(Following this film, Billy's last name was changed from "the Kid" to "Carson." Crabbe obtained a palomino called "Falcon" and became known as "The King of the Wild West.")

Alias Billy the Kid
(Republic, 1946) 56 min.

Director: Thomas Carr. Story: Norman Sheldon. Screenplay: Betty Burbridge, Earle Snell. Assoc. Producer: Bennett Cohen.

Sunset Carson (Sunset Carson), Peggy Stewart (Ann Marshall), Tom London (Dakota), Roy Barcroft (Matt Conroy), Russ Whiteman (Pewee), Tom Chatterton (Ed Pearson), Tex Terry (Buckskin), Pierce Lyden (Sam), James R. Linn (Jack). *With* Jack Rockwell, Jack Kirk, Stanley Price, Steve Clark, Edward Cassidy.

A ranger lets a convicted murderer escape from jail so he can trail him to his gang, but the man gets away and the ranger becomes involved with a female outlaw leader.

Return of the Bad Men
(RKO, 1948) 89 min.

Director: Ray Enright. Screenplay: Charles O'Neal, Jack Natteford and Luci Ward. Story: Jack Natteford and Luci Ward. Producer: Nat Holt.

Randolph Scott (Vance), Robert Ryan (Sundance), Anne Jeffreys (Cheyenne), George "Gabby" Hayes (John Pettit), Jacqueline White (Madge Allen), Steve Brodie (Cole Younger), Richard Powers [Tom Keene] (Jim Younger), Robert Bray (John Younger), Lex Barker (Emmett Dalton), Walter Reed (Bob Dalton), Michael Harvey (Grat Dalton), Dean White (Billy the Kid), Robert Armstrong (Bill Doolin), Tom Tyler (Wild Bill Yeager), Lew Harvey (Arkansas Kid), Gary Gray (Johnny), Walter Baldwin (Muley Wilson), Minna Gombell (Emily), Warren Jackson (George Mason), Robert Clarke (Dave), Jason Robards, Sr. (Judge Harper). *With* Ernie Adams, Bud Osborne, Forrest Taylor, Lane Chandler, Charles Stevens, Kenneth MacDonald, Earle Hodgins, Harry Shannon, Larry McGrath, Billy Vincent, Brandon Beach, Ida Moore, John Hamilton, Charles McAvoy.

The plot mainly concerns conflict between Marshal Vance and Sundance; the former, retired, takes up his guns again when Sundance and assorted outlaws launch a series of train and stage holdups in the territory.

"Nat Holt ... has packed *Badmen* with all the ingredients that pay off in the action market. Enright's direction insures swift action despite the abundance of story material and makes it add up to neat filmfare. Much use is made of outdoor movement by J. Roy Hunt's lensing, and action is backed with good music score by Paul Sawtell."—*Variety*, May 26, 1948

Son of Billy the Kid

(Western Adventure/Screen Guild, 1949) 65 min.

Director: Ray Taylor. Producer: Ron Ormond. Screenplay: Ron Ormond and Ira Webb.

Lash LaRue (Jack Garrett), Al St. John (Fuzzy Q. Jones), Marion Colby (Norma), June Carr (Betty Raines), George Baxter (Jim Thorn), Terry Frost (Cy Schaeffer), John James (Colt), House Peters, Jr., Clarke Stevens (Outlaws), Bob Duncan (Yantis), Cliff Taylor (Jake), William Perrott (Billy the Kid), Felipe Turich (Jose Gonzales), Rosa Turich (Rosa Gonzales), Jerry Riggio (Sanchos), Eileen Dixon (Dance Hall Girl), Frazer McMinn (Joe), I. Stanford Jolley (Fergus), Bud Osborne (Guard).

Baldwin City, a sleepy frontier town, will soon be welcoming the railroad, but in the meantime, the stagecoach driven by Fuzzy (who is also the sheriff, postmaster and express agent), brings in travelers, mail and money shipments. On the latest trip the passengers include town banker Jim Thorn, who is carrying a shipment of money, and Betty Raines, a dance hall girl always on the hunt for a man to marry her.

The stage is attacked by a gang of outlaws, one of whose leaders is a handsome young man named Colt. The stage's "shotgun" knocks off a couple of the bandits and then he is hit. It looks like curtains for the stagecoach until a dashing young rider in black appears on the scene. He is Jack Garrett, a special U. S. Marshal heading for Baldwin City. He joins the fracas and turns the tide. The remaining bandits flee.

It turns out that Garrett is in Baldwin City to see Jim Thorn and make arrangements for his bank to handle the railroad's cash. Meanwhile, Cy Schaeffer, a supposedly respectful real estate man, is conniving with the bandits. He wants to block money shipments so he can squeeze mortgages and then hold the railroad up for high prices.

The bandits, after attempting to trap Jack Garrett, finally try a raid on the town bank, but the main bunch is double-crossed by young Colt, who gets away with the money. Jack Garrett concocts a plan which he reveals only to Thorn and his adopted niece Norma, who is also his secretary. The big shipment of money has arrived by covered wagon and its safety was insured by a trick Garrett rigged up. Now he is sending the money out again, but when the bandits stage their raid, the wagon is full of well-armed deputies and the gang is rounded up. Meanwhile, Thorn is putting away the money in his vault when his niece pulls a gun on him and reveals herself as the one who tipped Schaeffer off to Thorn's moves. But before she can shoot or get the money, young Colt quietly disarms her. Finally, Thorn admits the truth—he *was* Billy the Kid, and Colt is his son who joined the outlaws to protect his father.

Thorn is ready to give himself up, but Jack Garrett refuses to believe the law could be stern with a man who has completely rehabilitated himself.

"The yarn makes a good entry in the Lash LaRue series and affords plenty of opportunity for shooting, fighting, and the usual western action. Ron Ormond and his associate, Ira Webb ... utilize the slim budget to the best advantage. Ray Taylor's direction has the kind of pace sagebrush devotees prefer. The item will do well when LaRue is a favorite."—*Hollywood Reporter*, August 12, 1949

I Shot Billy the Kid
(Lippert, 1950) 58 min.

Director/Producer: William Berke. Screenplay: Orville Hampton.

Donald Barry (Billy the Kid), Robert Lowery (Sheriff Pat Garrett), Wendy Lee (Billy's Girlfriend), Wally Vernon (Father of Billy's Girlfriend), Tom Neal (Outlaw). *With* Claude Stroud, John Merton, Henry Marco, Bill Kennedy, Archie Twitchell, Jack Perrin, Richard Farmer, Felice Richmond, Jack Geddes, Tommy Monroe, Barbara Woodell, Dick Lane, Sid Nelson.

This standard story, deals with the tracking-down and killing of Billy. The story has a large vein of sympathy for Billy but ends up showing that he has a homicidal urge which would make his rehabilitation impossible. Billy is shown battling in range wars and then, when other gunmen are given amnesty, refusing to make a deal that would require him to give up his guns and go straight. He continues his outlawry and in the end is shot dead by Pat Garrett in the home of his Mexican girlfriend.

"William Berke's production and direction chores are performed with skill, although the action of the story lags somewhat in places. Photography, particularly of horsemen riding, is well done by Ernest Miller. Orville Hampton's screenplay finds hard going at times to take audience sympathy away from Barry."—*Variety*, July 1950

"A routine story of Billy the Kid, this latest saga of the famous gunman is produced and directed with sufficient skill to give it a good entertainment rating in the secondary field."—*Independent Film Journal*, August 12, 1950

The Kid from Texas
(Universal-International, 1950) 78 min.

Director: Kurt Neumann. Screenplay: Robert Hardy Andrews, and Karl Lamb. Story: Robert Hardy Andrews. Producer: Paul Short.

Audie Murphy (Billy the Kid), Gale Storm (Irene Kain), Albert Dekker (Alexander Kain), Shepperd Strudwick (Jameson), Will Geer (O'Fallon), William Talman (Minister), Martin Garralaga (Morales), Robert H. Barrett (Governor Wallace), Walter Sande (Crave), Frank Wilcox (Pat Garrett), Dennis Hoey (Major Harper), Ray Teal (Sheriff Rand), Don Haggerty (Morgan), Paul Ford (Copeland), Rosa Turich (Marita), Pilar Del Rey (Margarita). *With* John Phillips, Harold Goodwin, Zon Murray, Tom Trout, Dorita Pallias, Jack Ingram, Edmund Cobb, Pierce Lyden, William Fawcett, Terry Frost, Rory Mallinson, Johnny Carpenter.

The story of Billy the Kid is subject to many variations, and quite a number of them have already been tried. *The Kid from Texas*, though, is the first effort at presenting the story of the Kid as psychological melodrama. The film just doesn't swing into action until the very last reel.

"Producer Paul Short missed on both story supervision and in choice of director. While Kurt Neumann's megging is solid as concerns characters, his pacing of action fell far short."—*Variety*, February 22, 1950

Captive of Billy the Kid
(Republic, 1952) 54 min.

Director: Fred C. Brannon. Screenplay: M. Coates Webster, Richard Wormser.

Allan Lane, Penny Edwards, Grant Withers, Clem Bevans, Roy Barcroft, Mauritz Hugo, Gary Goodwin, Frank McCarroll, Clayton Moore, Richard Emory, Steve Clark.

Deputy marshal Rocky Lane is on the trail of murderers who tried to steal a piece of a map from their victim. He arranges for all five owners of pieces of the map to make a trip together to locate the buried treasure hidden by Billy the Kid. One of the five owners, however, is the ringleader of the gang trying to secure the complete map. During the trip he kills one of the party. The rest, unaware of the killer, decide to put their maps together. Rocky pretends to turn crook and steals the map. This ruse works and he flushes out the ringleader, disposing of him in hand-to-hand fighting on a cliff.

"Lane maintains his usual aplomb in fighting off hordes of villains and adds several notches to his handle in the deputy marshal character. Penny Edwards is competently attractive and unobtrusive, with Clem Bevans providing the light touches in his character role. Excellent heavy work by Grant Withers and Roy Barcroft prop the action. Fred C. Brannon's direction accents action, with good photography by John MacBurnie and music by Stanley Wilson."—*Hollywood Reporter*, January 1952

"This is a pretty stereotyped ragged entry in the Rocky Lane series, which usually can be depended upon to provide strong, fast-paced western entertainment. Lane tries hard, but uncertain direction of a complicated story line tells against picture as a whole and only at infrequent intervals does the action hold spectator."—*Variety*, January 16, 1952

The Law vs. Billy the Kid
(Columbia, 1954) 72 min.

Director: William Castle. Screenplay/Story: John T. Williams [Bernard Gordon]. Producer: Sam Katzman.

Scott Brady (Billy the Kid), Betta St. John (Nita Maxwell), James Griffith (Pat Garrett), Alan Hale, Jr. (Bob Olinger), Paul Cavanagh (John M. Tunstall), William (Bill) Phillips (Charlie Bowrie), Benny Rubin (Arnold Dodge), Steve Darrell (Tom Watkins), George Berkeley (Tom O'Folliard), William Tannen (Dave Rudabaugh), Richard Cutting (Pete Maxwell), John Cliff (Carl Trumble), Otis Garth (Governor Wallace), Martin Garralaga (Miguel Bolanos), Frank Sully (Jack Poe), William Fawcett (Parsons), Robert Griffin (L. G. Murphy). *With* Gregg Barton, Bud Osborne, John Cason, Rory Mallison.

This is a sympathetic look at the life of Billy the Kid, with his killings depicted as acts of self-defense and revenge for the deaths of others. The story telescopes the more favorable events that caused young Billy Bonney to turn outlaw and become one of the most enduring legends of the American West. We see how the truculent hero, who is ever ready to use his gun to keep from being pushed around, forms a friendship with the more even-tempered Pat Garrett and how he is befriended by an Englishman, rancher John Tunstall. When Tunstall is murdered by a sheriff's posse, the Kid becomes a reckless killer seeking revenge. After circumstances force him to refuse an amnesty by the military governor, Garrett is appointed sheriff to bring him in. He succeeds, but the Kid makes a sensational jail break. Seeing that he will never become a law-abiding citizen, Garrett reluctantly shoots him after catching him in a rendezvous with Nita Maxwell.

"Scott Brady, in the title role, reads his lines intelligently, but he looks more like a college boxing champion than a kid."—*Hollywood Reporter*, July 1954

The Boy from Oklahoma
(Warner Bros., 1954) 83 min.

Director: Michael Curtiz. Screenplay: Frank Davis and Winston Miller. Story: Michael Fessier. Producer: David Weisbart.

Will Rogers, Jr. (Tom Brewster), Nancy Olson (Katie Branisan), Lon Chaney, Jr. (Crazie Charley), Anthony Caruso (Barney Turlock),

Wallace Ford (Wally Higgins), Clem Bevans (Pop Pruty), Merv Griffin (Steve), Louis Jean Heydt (Paul Evans), Tyler MacDuff (Billy the Kid), Sheb Wooley (Pete Martin), Slim Pickens (Shorty), Skippy Torgerson (Johnny Neil), James Griffith (Joe Downey), Charles Watts (Harry). *With* George Chesebro, Forrest Taylor, Guy Wilkerson, Harry Lauter, John Cason, Denver Pyle.

Rogers drifts through a small western town and dallies long enough to become sheriff, solve a murder, bust up a bad gang and find a girl. Plot gimmick is that he is a peaceable man who doesn't bother to carry a gun and has to perform his heroics with only a lariat and a prayer. Both put him in good stead, as does a native shrewdness that helps him beat the baddies even when the odds are mighty uneven.

"Rogers, Jr.'s homespun playing carbons his late father's to some extent, although not so broadly, and his physical likeness to the parent should jog the memories of the oldsters. Miss Olson dons the range wear required attractively and counts in helping Rogers show to advantage. Lon Chaney has only one scene, that of the town drunk gone berserk, and he makes it register strongly."—*Variety*, January 14, 1954

"It's a good cast with Anthony Caruso a particularly forceful villain, and Tyler MacDuff doing an outstanding short assignment as his brother, Billy the Kid. It has the great benefit of being directed by Michael Curtiz who makes the good old western subject come alive with notes of novelty."—*Los Angeles Times*, February 15, 1954

Last of the Desperados

(Associated Film Releasing Corp., 1955) 75 min.

Director: Sam Newfield. Screenplay/Story: Orville Hampton. Producer: Sigmund Neufeld.

James Craig (Pat Garrett), Jim Davis (Deputy Sheriff), Bob Steele, Barton MacLane (Gang Members). *With* Margia Dean, John Hart, Brad Johnson, Herbert Viagran, Donna Martell, Myrna Dell, Stanley Clements, Mike Ragan, Frank Sully, Thomas Browne Henry, Jack Perry.

Pat Garrett kills Billy the Kid, ending his outlaw career. However, it appears that Billy was a hero to half the people in his area, not to mention four members of his gang who plan to kill Garrett. After several innocent people are killed by the gang, Garrett, with no backing from the townspeople, resigns and moves to another town under an alias, believing this will save lives. It doesn't work, so on goes his sheriff's badge and the four baddies are soon sprawled in the dust.

"There will, of course, be many desperados in many pix to come, but

Last of the Desperados wipes out five of them, including Billy the Kid—again. Overall pic shapes as a good programmer, with story line sustaining interest and James Craig coming through with a good performance in the lead role. ... As produced by Sigmund Neufeld, pic shows its modest budget physically, but other departments shape up adequately. Sam Newfield's direction is good, highlighting the action values without sacrificing plot."—*Variety*, January 19, 1956

Strange Lady in Town
(Warner Bros., 1955) 112 min.

Producer/Director: Mervyn LeRoy. Story/Screenplay: Frank Butler.

Greer Garson (Julia), Dana Andrews (O'Brien), Cameron Mitchell (Davis), Lois Smith (Spurs), Walter Hampden (Father Gabriel), Gonzales Gonzales (Martinez Martinez), Joan Camden (Norah), Anthony Numkena (Tomasito), Jose Tovay (Bartolo), Adele Jergens (Bella Brown), Bob Wilke (Karg), Frank De Kova (Hatlo), Russell Johnson (Haddock), Gregory Walcott (Scanlon), Douglas Kennedy (Wickstrom), Ralph Moody (General Lew Wallace), Nick Adams (Billy the Kid), Jack Williams (Rebstock), The Trianas (Dance Specialty).

Rejected by Boston society, Julia turns her back on the town and heads for Santa Fe to practice medicine. However, her ne'er-do-well brother's reputation tarnishes her own. Local Mexicans, Indians and a competitive male doctor, however, want her to stay.

"Critics may call it pure 'corn' and carp at its occasional inconsistencies, but I'm betting the cash-paying public will relax and thoroughly enjoy every moment of *Strange Lady in Town*. Why? Because it's uncomplicated, unsophisticated and often completely unreal drama, excitement and fun by turns."—*Los Angeles Examiner*, April 28, 1955

"Shot in CinemaScope in mellow tones of WarnerColor, this expensive outdoor picture highlights the beauty, charm and graciousness of Greer Garson against the drowsy, sun-baked glamour of the old Southwest."—*Hollywood Reporter*, April 12, 1955

Parson and the Outlaw
(Columbia, 1957) 71 min.

Director: Oliver Drake. Screenplay: Oliver Drake and John Mantley. Producer: Charles (Buddy) Rogers.

Anthony Dexter (Billy the Kid), Sonny Tufts (Jack Slade), Marie Windsor (Tonya), Buddy Rogers (Reverend Jericho Jones), Jean Parker (Mrs. Jones), Robert Lowery (Colonel Morgan), Madalyn Trahey (Etta

McCloud). *With* Bob Steele, Joe Sodja, Bob Duncan, Bob Gilbert, Jack Lowell, John Davis, Paul Spahn, Herman Pulver, Richard Reeves.

Billy the Kid, supposedly killed but actually spared by a friendly law officer, swears he will never use his guns again. He tries to forget the past when he was forced to permanently puncture 21 hombres. This was a difficult period in Billy's life; he found it difficult to live with himself knowing that he had ended the lives of so many men.

But even in the present he can't avoid violence. Billy's old friend, Rev. Jones, gets himself plugged while taking on the town's heavies. Billy steps in and mows them down, but he too gets a Colt .45 clobbering.

"*The Parson and the Outlaw* is an old-fashioned melodrama with neither novelty nor charm to rescue it from being an almost total loss ... ineptly directed from start to finish. Despite some good cast names, *Parson and the Outlaw* can be used only as double-bill material and fortunately it is comparatively short."—*Hollywood Reporter*, August 30, 1957

"This one might have been taken from the files of a Junior Lone Ranger. An old-fashioned oater, the Charles (Buddy) Rogers production might rate a nod in undemanding sagebrush situations but otherwise rates only the brush."—*Variety*, September 4, 1957

Tales of Wells Fargo
(NBC/Overland Productions, 1957) 30 min.
(segment entitled *Billy the Kid*)

Dale Robertson

The Left Handed Gun
(Warner Bros., 1958) 105 min.

Director: Arthur Penn. Screenplay: Leslie Stevens. Producer: Fred Coe.

Paul Newman (Billy the Kid), Lita Milan (Celsa), John Dehner (Pat Garrett), Hurd Hatfield (Moultrie), James Congdon (Charley Boudre), James Best (Tom Folliard). *With* Colin Keith-Johnston, John Dierkes, Bob Anderson, Wally Brown, Anne Barton, Jo Summers, Ainslie Pryor, Martin Garralaga, Denver Pyle, Paul Smith, Nestor Paiva, Robert Foulk.

Billy the Kid and three other fugitives are given sanctuary by a gunsmith in a New Mexico town. One by one Billy's companions are killed. The fugitive becomes intimate with the gunsmith's wife and more violence ensues.

"...smart and exciting western paced by Paul Newman's intense

Paul Newman won praise for his portrayal of Billy the Kid in *The Left Handed Gun* (Warner Bros., 1958).

portrayal of the young killer. There is plenty of action for western buffs and the added value of a psychological story for general appeal…. Leslie Stevens' screenplay is based on a teleplay by Gore Vidal that was called *The Death of Billy the Kid.*"—*Variety*, April 23, 1958

"The scenes are worked out so carefully the tension builds without creating sympathy for the central character, played effectively by Paul Newman.

"A strong cast which obviously had been carefully rehearsed keeps the action moving. The feminine interest, Lita Milan … presents an emotional portrayal. Hurd Hatfield, a finished performer who was last seen in *Anastasia,* is convincing as the heavy."—*Motion Picture Herald*, April 26, 1958

"…Doesn't try to justify the infamous killer known as Billy the Kid, but to explain him. The screenplay … is full of psychology and symbolism; and Fred Coe's production, directed by Arthur Penn and beautifully photographed in 1880 sets and the great outdoors, is determinedly arty. While the picture tries to handle everything on a high-class, intellectual plane, it also includes too much shock, violence and rough-and-tumble."—Phillip T. Hartung, *The Commonwealth*, May 23, 1958, p. 207

The Tall Man

(NBC-TV, September 10, 1960-September 1, 1962) 30 min. episodes.
Syndicated—75 episodes.

Clu Gulager (Billy the Kid), Barry Sullivan (Pat Garrett).

The cast changed from episode to episode. Here again, Billy was portrayed as a good guy, similar to the Bob Steele–Buster Crabbe series of feature films. Garrett is portrayed as his friend.

OTHER TELEVISION APPEARANCES OF BILLY THE KID

Ray Stricklyn—*Cheyenne*
Joel Grey—*Maverick*
Robert Conrad—*Colt 45*
Robert Vaughn–*Tales of Wells Fargo*
Dennis Hopper—*Sugarfoot*
Stephen Joyce—*Bronco*
Richard Bakalyan—*The Deputy*
Andrew Prine—*The Great Adventure*
Glenn Whitrow—*Bret Maverick*
Gore Vidal—*Billy the Kid*.

Billy the Kid

(Carthago [Spain], 1962)

Director: Leon Klimovsky. Screenplay: Bob Sirens and Angel Del Castillo. Camera: Manuel Hernandez Sanjuan. Music: Daniel White.

George Martin (Billy the Kid). *With* Jack Taylor, Juny Brunell, Tomas-Blanco, Alberto Dalbes, Luis Induni, Esther Grant.

Apparently poor distribution and promotion sent this Billy the Kid feature to the cinematic boneyard.

Bullet for Billy the Kid

(Associated Distributors, 1963) 61 min.

Director: Rafael Baledon. Screenplay: Raymond Obon. Producer: Alfred Ripstein and Jerry Warren.

Gaston Sands, Steve Brodie, Lloyd Nelson, Marla Blaine, Richard McIntyre, Gilbert Cramer, Rita Mace, Peter Guillon.

Having decided to start a new life, Billy the Kid starts his 1,000-mile journey to his sister's ranch. Plagued and trailed by both lawmen and gunslingers, he writes his sister to have friends on guard at the ranch. No sooner does he arrive than the killers, who have intercepted the letter, surround the ranch. Escaping into the night after a blazing battle, he realizes that Billy the Kid can never find peace.

The Outlaws Is Coming
(Columbia, 1965) 89 min.

Producer/Director: Norman Maurer. Screenplay: Elwood Ullman.

The Three Stooges, Adam West, Nancy Kovack, Mort Mills, Don Lamond, Rex Holman, Emil Sitka, Henry Gibson, Murray Alper, Tiny Brauer, Joe Bolton, Bill Camfield, Hal Frayer, Johnny Ginger, Wayne Mack, Ed T. McDonnell, Bruce Sedley, Paul Shannon, Sally Starr.

Larry, Moe and Curley Joe, printers, go west with a magazine editor to conduct a campaign against the slaughter of the plains buffalo. They discover that the killings constitute part of the plot of a gang of desperadoes who plan to set the Indians against the whites, then against the U. S. Cavalry in order to take over the entire West for themselves.

Par for the Stooges' course, the usual anachronisms abound. For instance, the film has "Bob Dalton," "Wyatt Earp," "Johnny Ringo," "Billy the Kid," "Cole Younger," "Wild Bill Hickok," "Bat Masterson," "Jesse James" and "Belle Starr" in the crime dynasty, organized like TV's *The Untouchables*.

"Columbia is releasing another feature-length comedy starring The Three Stooges, this one with the ungrammatical title of *The Outlaws Is Coming*, apparently a take-off on the ad campaign for Alfred Hitchcock's *The Birds*. Let it be added, hastily, that that is the only resemblance, if such may be called, and the new effusion from the zany trio will undoubtedly find great response with audiences composed of extremely unsophisticated 12-year-olds and under. If anything, the picture is quite above the usual cut of Stooges' antics, an attempt having been made to give the trio more of a story line to follow, which they do to the accompaniment of their usual sight gags."—*Hollywood Reporter*, January 8, 1965

Billy the Kid Versus Dracula
(Embassy, 1966) 72 min.

Director: William Beaudine. Story/Screenplay: Carl K. Hittleman. Producer: Carroll Case.

Chuck Courtney (Billy the Kid), John Carradine (Count Dracula), Melinda Plowman (Betty Bentley), Virginia Christine (Eve Oster),

The meeting of two legends: Vampire (John Carradine) greets reformed outlaw (Chuck Courtney) in *Billy the Kid vs. Dracula* (Embassy, 1966). Frontier beauty Melinda Plowman looks on.

Walter Janovitz (Franz Oster), Bing Russell (Red Thorpe), Lennie Geer (Yancy), Roy Barcroft (Marshal Griffin), Olive Carey (Dr. Henrietta Hull), Hannie Landman (Lila Oster), Marjorie Bennett (Ann Bentley), William Forrest (James Underhill), George Cisar (Joe Flake), Charlita (Nana), Harry Carey, Jr. (Ben). *With* Richard Reeves, Max Kleven, Jack Williams, William Challee.

Arriving by stagecoach at Wickenburg, a small Southwestern town, Count Dracula poses as the uncle of Betty Bentley, who owns the Bar-B Ranch. Almost immediately he arouses the suspicions of the ranch foreman, the reformed outlaw Billy the Kid. As Billy sets out to prove the uncle is an impostor, he is unaware that Dracula already has Betty in his power. The local doctor eventually comes to Billy's aid by holding a mirror up to Dracula's face and exposing him as a vampire when no reflection appears in the glass. Although Dracula escapes, Billy, the doctor and the marshal trace him to a silver mine. Bullets proving to be of no help, Billy fights off Dracula's attack with a scalpel and drives it into the vampire's heart. As his body dissolves, Betty recovers from the mesmerized state in which Dracula had placed her.

"...a 1966 zinger returning Carradine as a top-hatted Dracula with eyebrows that look like they were painted on with shoe polish... Working out of a deserted mine and so desperate he is draining the blood of sheep, he has his luminous eyes on a lovely young woman whose foreman is (gulp) Billy the Kid. While awaiting the inevitable confrontation, you keep wondering when Dracula will get on a horse."—*Los Angeles Times*, August 3, 1979

The Man Who Killed Billy the Kid
...E Divenne il Più Spietato Bandito del Sud

(Kinesia/Altor, 1967) 86 min.
Alternate Title: **A Few Bullets More**
Opened in Madrid in May 1967 as
El Hombre Que Mató a Billy el Niño (100 min.)
Distributed in the U.S. by RAF Industries

Director: Julio Buchs. Story/Screenplay: Julio Buchs, Rederico De Urrutia, Carlo Veo. Producer: Silvio Battistini. Camera: Miguel Mila. Music: Gianni Ferrior. Filmed in France and Italy.

Peter Lee Lawrence (Billy the Kid/William Bonney), Fausto Tozzi (Pat Garrett), Dianik Zurakowska [Diane Zura] (Helen Tunstall), Gloria Milland (Billy's Mother), Luis Prendes (Mark Liston), Carlos Casaravilla, Barta Bani, Antonio Pica, Paco Sanz, Tomas Blanco, Luis Induni, Enrique Avila, Orlando Baralla, Luis Riveria, Alfonso Rojas, Jose Canalejas.

Billy Bonney kills the man who assaulted his mother and is shielded by prospector Pat Garrett, an old friend of the family. In spite of Garrett's protection, however, Billy shoots those pursuing him and flees to Mexico, where he becomes widely known as "Billy the Kid."

He attempts to reform when Englishman Henry Tunstall and his daughter Helen befriend him. Billy goes to work on the ranch and falls in love with Helen. When Tunstill is murdered, Billy turns killer again. Governor Lew Wallace offers amnesty to criminals on the run.

Helen persuades Billy to go back. Back home he finds that his poor mother has died through shame at her son's activities. Billy's love for his mother may seem a little excessive because he kills another man who taunts him about her death. This time he has gone too far and the law decides that enough is enough. Mother or no mother, it's time Billy cashed in his chips.

By this time his friend Garrett has become a lawman, but when Billy is cornered, Pat refuses to shoot his former friend. Pat tries to convince the youth to mend his ways, but Billy kills again. Once again Billy becomes a fugitive and flees to Helen's home, where the two plan to build a new life together in another territory. Billy convinces the pursuing Garrett of his sincerity, but he is ambushed by one of his old enemies.

Helen accuses Garrett of the killing, which he denies, but the blame nevertheless follows him for many years.

"Billy the Kid is flaunted as a golden-haired martyr who only kills people in self defense. The film does touch on Billy's rumored unhealthy 'love' for his mother. Other than this rather tawdry segment, the action is humdrum and grossly inaccurate."—*Spaghetti Westerns—The Good, The Bad and The Violent*, 1961–1977

Chisum

(Batjac/Warner Bros., 1970) 111 min.

Director: Andrew V. McLaglen. Producer/Screenplay: Andrew J. Fenady. Exec. Producer: Michael Wayne.

John Wayne (John Chisum), Forrest Tucker (Lawrence Murphy), Christopher George (Dan Nodeen), Ben Johnson (James Pepper), Glenn Corbett (Pat Garrett), Bruce Cabot (Sheriff Brady), Andrew Prine (Alex McSween), Patric Knowles (John Tunstall), Richard Jaeckel (Jess Evans), Geoffrey Deuel (Billy the Kid), Pamela McMyler (Sally Chisum), Lynda Day (Sue McSween), John Agar (Patton), Lloyd Battista (Neemo), Robert Donner (Morton), Ray Teal (Justice Wilson), Edward Faulkner (Dolan), Ron Soble (Bowdre), John Mitchum (Baker), Glenn Langan (Dudley), Alan Baxter (Governor Axtell), Alberto Morin (Delgado), William Bryant (Jeff), Pedro Armendariz, Jr. (Ben), Christopher Mitchum (O'Folliard), Abraham Sofaer (White Buffalo), Gregg Palmer (Riker), Trinidad Villa (Blacksmith). *With* Josh McLaglen, Mari McLaglen, Ralph Volkie, Hank Worden, Chuck Roberson, Pedro Gonzales Gonzales, John Pickard.

In 1878 John Chisum, the owner of a huge New Mexico cattle ranch, discovers that Lawrence Murphy, a corrupt businessman, is trying to gain control of the surrounding land by illegally foreclosing mortgages.

When Chisum comes upon some of Murphy's men rustling cattle, he enlists the aid of John Tunstall, his English neighbor, and the notorious Billy the Kid Bonney to gun the cowboys down. Stranger Pat Garrett arrives and informs Chisum of Murphy's growing power and particularly his influence on Sheriff Brady, who was appointed by Murphy. When the ranchers attempt to set up a general store of their own and Murphy's men interfere, Tunstall rides to report his actions to the governor. On his way, he is killed by Sheriff Brady.

Billy Bonney, enraged by the killing of his friend, shoots Brady and his deputies in revenge. Chisum's niece Sally, who had been attracted to Billy, realizes the extent of his violent nature and turns her affection to Pat Garrett.

Murphy then uses the killings to persuade the governor to send bounty hunter Dan Nodeen to apprehend Billy and his gang.

Murphy joins Nodeen in the fierce gunfight against Billy. Chisum stampedes his cattle through town and in the resulting confusion, Billy chases Nodeen out of town and Chisum kills Murphy. The town is left in ruins, but Garrett is appointed sheriff and Chisum is once again in control of his cattle empire.

Freedom to Love

(Reginald Puhl Filmproduktion/Grove Press, 1970) 96 min.

Director/Story: Phyllis Kronhausen. Producer: Reginald Puhl.

Kess Vanderwusten (Chuck), Franulka Vanderwusten (Lucy), Per Massini (Robert), Irene De Graaf (Anne), Sacha Kraamwinkel (Brigitte), Monique Kraamwinkel (Christine), Billy Dixon (Jean Harlow), Richard Wright (Billy the Kid), Kenneth Carr (Little Bill), Dan Halaleck (Hank), Paula Shaw (Sandy), Marie Antoinette (Deborah), John Fraser (The Poet), Brian Phelan (Alfred Hodge), Anne Fairbanks (Secretary). *With* Margit Mecklenburg, Gaby Esche, Annemarie Graf, Simon Spies.

Psychotherapists Phyllis and Eberhard Kronhausen advance the view that sexual freedom benefits society and that suppression of sexuality contributes to crime, juvenile delinquency, family breakdowns and divorce. They draw from their own case histories and interview celebrities such as Hugh Hefner who support their view. Included in the film are three short plays, one of which is "The Beard" by Michael McClure. In this segment we see Billy the Kid and Jean Harlow demonstrate their sexual bravado in Heaven.

This one is pretty far-out!

Gas-s-s-s

(American International, 1970) 79 min.

Producer/Director: Roger Corman. Screenplay: George Armitage

Robert Corff (Coel), Elaine Giftos (Cilla), Pat Patterson (Demeter), George Armitage (Billy the Kid), Alex Wilson (Jason), Alan Braunstein (Dr. Drake), Ben Vereen (Carlos), Cindy Williams (Marissa), Bud Cort (Hooper), Talia Coppola (Coralle), Country Joe and the Fish (F. M. Radio), Lou Procopio (Marshall McLuhan), Jackie Farley (Ginny), Phil Borneo (Quant).

This film is ostensibly about the actions of the under-25s of the world, as displayed by a sample group in Texas. When an experimental gas kills off all of those over that age, a group of six young people travel to a New Mexico commune where they have heard "a brave new world" awaits them.

Obstacles appear in the form of automobile rustlers, headed by a character who calls himself Billy the Kid. After a night of rest, recuperation and rocking at a drive-in theater, they encounter a gang of football players who try to force them to join the team, but they escape.

(Note: This Billy the Kid is obviously not the historical Billy the Kid. The film is included lest I be accused of having overlooked a Billy the Kid film by someone who has not seen this film.)

"Producer-director Roger Corman, who has a good batting average in the low-to-medium budget, has struck out with this one. An assortment of unproven talent, with the possible exception of the rock group, Country Joe and the Fish, *Gas-s-s-s* doesn't even have the usual fine Corman color photography and art direction to make it palatable."—*Variety*, August 24, 1970

A Girl Is a Gun (U. S. Title)
Une Aventure de Billy le Kid

(Moullet Production, 1971) 80 min.

Producer/Story/Screenplay: Luc Moullet. Music: Patrice Moullet. Camera: Jean Gonnet and Jean Jacques Flori.

Jean-Pierre Leaud (Billy the Kid), Rachel Kesterber (Ann), Jean Valmont (Hunter), Bruno Kresoja (Indian), Michael Minaud (Sheriff Holiday), Bernard Pimon (Soldier), Kathy Maloney (Squaw).

A wacky, offbeat rendering of the Billy the Kid legend. Here Billy is a hapless fellow who falls into one calamitous disaster after another. But he is also a vicious gunfighter. After pulling a holdup, Billy tracks down and kills a witness. On his way back, he stumbles upon Ann, a girl who has buried herself in the sand in an attempt to commit suicide. It's her way of dealing with the death of her boyfriend (the witness that Billy killed).

Love blooms as Billy is tracked down by a posse. Billy and Ann flee into the wilderness on Billy's reluctant donkey. On their trail is a posse headed by Sheriff Holiday and a tribe of war-hungry Indians.

It all ends happily as the two lovers (wounded, mangled and nearly scalped) limp off together into the sunset.

"Mixture of attitudes in development limit playoff for buff or special situations. Jean-Pierre Leaud's performance seems like frenzied ineptness. A sentimental sendup, a sort of impish homage, a mixture of Italo western salting, it is not completely clear."—*Variety*, March 17, 1971

Dirty Little Billy
(Columbia, 1972) 93 min.

Director: Stan Dragoti. Producer: Jack L. Warner. Screenplay/Story: Charles Moss and Stan Dragoti.

Michael J. Pollard (Billy the Kid), Lee Purcell (Berle), Richard Evans (Goldie), Charles Aidman (Ben), Fran Hamilton (Catherine), Willard Sage (Henry), Josip Elic (Jawbone), Mills Watson (Ed), Alex Wilson, Ronnie Graham, Dick Van Patten.

Seventeen-year-old Billy, his mother and his stepfather arrive in Coffeyville, Kansas, a mean little mudhole whose mayor sells them a run-down farm. The mayor is in the business of enticing settlers to Coffeyville where he owns most of the real estate. Of course, it is to his advantage to get the filthy, depressing little place filled up with people. He even finds time to gloat when the next town is virtually devastated by an epidemic and the survivors are forced to move to Coffeyville.

Billy finds the town a bit of a bore and farm life downright tedious. Following a family squabble, he is advised by his stepfather to run away. He runs straight for the local saloon which is presided over by likable gambler Goldie and his whoring girlfriend Berle, the one with a heart of etc.

Billy is introduced to sex by Berle, to the use of guns by Goldie and to friendship, as he is readily accepted by the saloon crowd. He is also introduced to frontier morals and politics when it is revealed to him that the civic-minded mayor also owns the saloon. The interplay between the three lonely outcasts holed up in the tacky backstreet saloon approaches a level of folk art.

"...an unusual film of Americana that could find its audience at home and abroad with good handling. Extremely well textured lensing also helps as well as editing, and director Stan Dragoti ... throws the usual gimmicks overboard for a fluid, clear and fresher look into the Old West."—*Variety*, October 25, 1972

"*Dirty Little Billy* aspired to be a great film and missed its target by just enough to inspire pangs of ingratitude for its failures.... Granted that *Billy* is not all that it should have been, it is nevertheless a highly enjoyable film."—*Hollywood Reporter*, October 31, 1972

Pat Garrett and Billy the Kid
(MGM, 1973) 106 min.

Director: Sam Peckinpah. Producer: Gordon Carroll. Screenplay: Rudolph Wurlitzer.

James Coburn (Pat Garrett), Kris Kristofferson (Billy the Kid), Bob Dylan (Allas), Richard Jaeckel (Sheriff Kip McKinney), Katy Jurado

Michael J. Pollard (right) played William Bonney in *Dirty Little Billy* (Columbia, 1972), a film that returned Billy to his rough and tumble roots.

(Mrs. Baker), Chill Wills (Lemuel), Jason Robards (Governor Wallace), R. G. Armstrong (Ollinger), Luke Askew (Eno), John Beck (Poe), Richard Bright (Holly), Matt Clark (J. W. Bell), Rita Coolidge (Maria), Jack Dodson (Howland), Jack Elam (Alamosa Bill), Emilio Fernandez (Paco), Paul Fix (Maxwell), L. Q. Jones (Black Harris), Slim Pickens (Sheriff Baker). *With* Jorge Russek, Charlie Martin Smith, Harry Dean Stanton, Claudia Bryar, John Chandler, Mike Mikler, Aurora Clavel, Rutayna Alda, Walter Kelly, Elisha Cook, Jr., Barry Sullivan, Gene Evans, Donnie Fritts, Dub Taylor, Don Levy.

Bob Dylan provided the music for this acclaimed film. It is the story of Pat Garrett's sworn mission to arrest or kill Billy the Kid, and of how his life collapses as he hunts down his man. The movie's scenes are filled with sadness as the insane battle between men leads to inevitable chaos, destruction and death.

...[has] all the elements for an extraordinary movie—a mixture of conservative macho energy and counter-culture humor and mysticism... The performances are uniformly excellent. Coburn is subtle and controlled, the perfect counterpoint to Kristofferson's extraordinary mixture of savagery, innocence and freedom. Bob Dylan, a non-actor used extremely well, plays a mischievous imp who follows Billy, suggesting mystical wisdom."—*Hollywood Reporter*, May 22, 1973

"Technically the film is above average. John Coquillion's Metrocolor photography is a pleasing merger of realism and stylization.... Ted Haworth's art direction is unostentatiously believable. "The editing, faulted in recent interviews by the director, conceals the reported post-production tinkering but also reduces such players as Jason Robards and Richard Jaeckel and Katy Jurado to walk-on status."—*Variety*, May 30, 1973

Young Guns
(20th Century-Fox, 1988) 107 min.

Director: Christopher Cain. Screenplay: John Fusco. Producer: Joe Roth and Christopher Cain. Co-Producer: Irby Smith and Paul Schiff. Exec. Producer: John Fusco and James G. Robinson.

Emilio Estevez (William H. Bonney [Billy the Kid]), Kiefer Sutherland (Doc Scurlock), Lou Diamond Phillips (Chavez Y Chavez), Charlie Sheen (Dick Brewer), Dermot Mulroney (Dirty Stephens), Casey Siemaszko (Charlie Bowdre), Terry O'Quinn (Alex McSween), Terence Stamp (John Tunstall), Jack Palance (L. G. Murphy), Sharon Thomas (Susan McSween), Geoffrey Blake (J. McCloskey), Alice Carter (Yen Sun), Brian Keith (Buckshot Roberts), Tom Calloway (Texas Joe Grant), Patrick Wayne (Pat Garrett), Jenny Wright (Jane).

Young William Bonney finds employment with Englishman John Tunstall. Although they have nothing in common, Bonney develops an admiration for the kindly Tunstall. Trouble has been brewing in Johnston County for some time, and when Tunstall is ambushed and killed, the fireworks really begin. Bonney swears vengeance on those responsible for Tunstall's death. He becomes the leader of a band of young cowboys called the Regulators and soon becomes known as Billy the Kid.

Surprisingly the film adheres closely to historical fact, but is done in a light-hearted way. Emilio Estevez is good as the fun-loving Billy. It's a film that will appeal to fans of the film's young cast but does nothing to advance the popularity of the Western genre. However, it did well enough at the box office to justify a sequel.

"*Young Guns* is a lame attempt at a brat pack *Wild Bunch*. Executed without style or feel for the genre and, for the most part, colorlessly populated by some of the more fashionable new actors of the moment, pic will do nothing to help restore the reputability or popularity of the Western. A short ride at the b.o. seems in store."—*Variety*, August 17, 1988

"The Western *Young Guns* is less like a real movie that an extended photo opportunity for its trendy young stars.... However, *Young Guns* doesn't make the mistake of taking itself too seriously. It's a good-humored exercise, if also a transparent one, and it sustains its spirit of fun right up to the point of a final shootout, in which the young heroes are badly outnumbered. Even so, the film manages to end on a cheery note."—*The New York Times*, August 12, 1988

Bill and Ted's Excellent Adventure
(Orion, 1989) 90 min.

Director: Stephen Herek. Screenplay: Chris Matheson, Ed Solomon. Producer: Scott Kroopf, Michael S. Murphey and Joel Soisson.

Keanu Reeves (Ted Logan), Alex Winter (Bill S. Preston), George Carlin (Rufus), Terry Camillerj (Napoleon), Dan Shot (Billy the Kid), Ted Steadman (Socrates), Rod Loomis (Freud), Al Leong (Genghis Khan), Jame Wiedlin (Joan of Arc), Robert V. Barron (Abraham Lincoln), Clifford David (Beethoven), Hal Landon, Jr. (Captain Logan), Bernie Casey (Mr. Ryan), Amy Stock-Poynton (Missy), J. Patrick McNamara (Mr. Preston).

Bill and Ted discover a magic phone booth that transports them back in history where they hob-nob with such people as Napoleon, Billy the Kid and Joan of Arc.

Billy the Kid
(Turner Network, 1989)

Director: William A. Graham. Story: Gore Vidal. Producer: Phillips Wylwy, Sr., and Gregory Prange.

Val Kilmer (Billy the Kid), Duncan Regehr (Pat Garrett), Wilfred Brimley (Governor Lew Wallace), Julie Carmen (Billy's Girlfriend), Rene Auberjonois (Town Drunk). *With* Michael Parks, Red West, Tom Everett, Albert Salmi, Clark Ray, Tiny Wells, Patrick Massett, Jack Dunlap, Will Hannah, Ned Vaughn, Sam Smiley, Nate Esformes, Richard Glover, Andrew Bicknell, Ed Adams, Billy Joe Patton, Roberto Guajardo, Rick Wheeler, Kirk Nelson.

A number of significant events in the life of the Kid are left out of the film, and some fictitious events are included. The story begins with the end of the Lincoln County War and Billy's revenge for the killing of rancher John Tunstall. After killing Sheriff Brady he is offered amnesty by Governor Wallace if he will appear before a Grand Jury and testify against crooked businessman Dolan. Things go awry, however, and Billy is held for trial for murder against the wishes of the governor.

Billy is able to escape jail and starts cattle rustling. His friend Pat Garrett is appointed sheriff and at first tries to persuade Billy to leave the territory. Failing in this, he vows to capture or kill Billy, which he does at Pete Maxwell's ranch house one night when Billy is not aware of his presence.

Billy is not given a "whitewash" job but is presented as the killer he was. Kilmer makes a good Billy, being close to Billy's youthful age. All in all, the film is good entertainment.

Young Guns II
(20th Century-Fox, 1990) 105 min.

Director: Geoff Murphy. Screenplay: John Fusco. Producer: Irby Smith and Paul Schiff.

Emilio Estevez (Billy the Kid [William Bonney]), Kiefer Sutherland (Doc Scurlock), Lou Diamond Phillips (Chavez Y Chavez), Christian Slater (Arkansas Dave Rudabaugh), William Peterson (Pat Garrett), Alan Ruck (Henry William French), R. D. Call (D. A. Ryerson), Jenny Wright (Jane Greenhouse), Scott Wilson (Governor Lew Wallace), James Coburn (John Chisum), Balthazer Getty (Outlaw), Leon Rippey (Bob Orlinger), Tony Frank (Judge Bristol), Tom Kurlander (J. W. Bell). *With* Robert Knepper, Jack Kehoe, Brad Whiteford, Richard Shiff, Iris Pappas, Nicholas Sean Gomez, Tom Byrd, Carlotta Garcia, Joey Joe Hamlin, Dale Gibson, Ed Adams, Joy Bolton, Dan Simpson, Robert Harvey, Boots Sutherland, Holt Parker.

Young Guns II takes up where *Young Guns* left off. The story follows Billy the Kid's descent to death, although the film leaves the door slightly ajar for his survival.

Billy enters into an agreement with Governor Lew Wallace to testify against the Dolan gang in exchange for a pardon. Prosecutors will not honor the governor's promise to Billy, and Billy remains an outlaw on the run. He has a falling out with Pat Garrett and then John Chisum, who refuses to pay Billy money that Billy believes he is owed. Garrett becomes a sheriff and vows to kill Billy.

In a final shootout (set in a burning house), the young Regulators are badly outnumbered. However, Billy escapes and continues killing and laughing as the film ends. Little attention is paid to historical facts.

"...*Young Guns II*, which tells of the split between Billy and Pat Garrett (William Peterson) that eventually led to the whole gang's apparent annihilation, concentrates principally on the drawing power of the post-adolescent heartthrobs in its cast. This approach has its appeal in limited doses, but it makes for a western that's smaller than life."—Janet Maslin, "Emilio Estevez in Reprise of Billy the Kid Role," *The New York Times*, August 1, 1990

The Untold West
(TBS, December 13, 1993) 60 min.

Narrator: Lou Diamond Phillips

This documentary on the outlaw gang presents the Old West and its inhabitants as they really were, without pulling any punches or whitewashing anyone in the telling.

2

The James-Younger Gang

"When the legend becomes fact, print the legend." This seems to have been the rule by which a vast majority of all biographical films have adhered. This is especially true of the Western badmen, foremost of whom was Jesse James, labeled by pulp writers as "the Robin Hood of the Old West." With his brother Frank, Jesse headed the most celebrated gang of bank and train robbers in American history.

More has been written about Jesse than any other outlaw, with the possible exception of Billy the Kid, and he has been portrayed in 40 or more films. Dramatic license has always been the norm in these films, as well as in much of the literature. The truth about Jesse and Frank James became more and more distorted as the years passed, with countless legends and pure fiction written and filmed about the pair. Typical of the stories about Jesse is the tale of the poor widow whose mortgage was about to be foreclosed. Jesse gave her the money to pay off the banker holding the mortgage and then lay in wait until she had done so. As the banker returned to town, he was held up by Jesse, who took his money back. This fictitious incident was depicted in the film *The True Story of Jesse James* (1957) and in several written accounts.

Legend had the James brothers robbing the rich to give to the poor who had suffered unjustly at the hands of the railroad. Their sins were washed away in countless dime novels, with known details of their lives being consistently presented incorrectly. Just as writers washed away many of the James brothers' sins, so did the movies.

Robert and Zerelda James migrated from Kentucky to Kearney, Missouri, in 1842. Kearney was located in Clay County, touching on the Kansas border. It was here that James bought a small farm and worked it to supplement his income from the ministry.

Alexander Franklin James was born January 10, 1843; Jesse Woodson James on September 5, 1847. They had a sister, Susan, born in 1849.

Robert left his family in 1850 to join the California gold rush, hoping to strike it rich and thus be able to provide his family a better living. Unfortunately he died before he could achieve his goal.

Frank (seated) and Jesse James. (Courtesy Amon Carter museum, Fort Worth, Texas.)

The boys' mother then married a man named Benjamin Simms, but they separated after about six months and he died shortly thereafter. In 1855 she married Dr. Reuben Samuel. This marriage lasted until her death. He loved the children and they loved him. He was a good husband, a good provider and a good stepfather to Jesse, Frank and Susan.

When the James boys were growing up, life along the border of the free state of Kansas and the slave state of Missouri became a living hell as the plunder and murder of Missourians became commonplace. Soon a deadly group of young Missouri guerrillas formed to fight fire with fire. They were led by the infamous William Clarke Quantrill. When the Civil War erupted there was a whole generation of teenage toughs living in the tier of Missouri counties bordering on Kansas, all of them handy with guns, all of them staunch supporters of Missouri as a slave state, all of them itching to start a rumble.

Among these hellions were Frank James, 18; his brother Jesse, 14; Cole Younger, 17; Jim Younger, 13; Jim Reed, 16; Ed Shirley, about 18; and his sister Myra Belle (Belle Starr), 13. Two of the Younger brothers, Bob and John, were still just children.

With the outbreak of the war, Frank joined the Missouri State Guard, a Confederate force. After a fierce battle near Springfield, Frank returned home only to be arrested and jailed by Union soldiers. His mother obtained his parole, which he soon broke, and joined the guerrilla band led by Quantrill.

A slightly different story of what happened to Frank James after the Battle of Eilson's Creek says that he came down with measles shortly after the battle and was left at a hotel in Springfield, where he was found by Union forces. He was allowed to return home on his promise not to take up arms again against Union forces. Frank gave his word, returned to Clay County, and was soon back on the firing line as a member of Quantrill's newly formed guerrillas. Cole Younger, Frank's cousin, was soon to join also. Cole's brother Jim also rode with Quantrill.

Cole (just 17) had fought with Confederate forces under General Sterling Price in 1861, the same year he joined Quantrill's band of guerrillas.

Thomas Coleman Younger, commonly known as Cole, was born January 15, 1844, to Henry Washington Younger and Bursheba Fristoe. The elder Younger was a respected civic leader and a prosperous businessman. There were a total of 14 children (nine girls and five boys) in the Younger family, Cole being the seventh child. James (Jim) was born in 1848, John Harrison in 1851, and Robert (Bob) in 1853. The birth year of the eldest son, Dick, is uncertain, but his death date is August 17, 1860. The Younger family was southern in sympathy. Colonel Younger owned slaves, and the Younger siblings were reared in ease and indulged with what luxury the border could afford at that time. However, being Southern sympathizers, it was inevitable that conflict with Yankees would occur.

Henry was murdered on July 20, 1862, while en route home from a business trip. He was ambushed by a group of Missouri militia. The Younger brothers' career of crime began not only in retaliation for grievous wrongs enacted against the parents, but because of their Southern sympathies. It is not surprising that some of them would gravitate to the guerrilla bands roaming the Missouri-Kansas territory, making quick surprise attacks on those supporting the union cause. Union forces and Jayhawkers tried their best to stamp out the guerrilla raids without much success. There were too many people with Southern sympathies to tip off the guerrillas that union forces were about.

Both Cole Younger and Frank James were with Quantrill, in August 1863 when the town of Lawrence, Kansas, was sacked and 183 of its citizens killed. When he was old enough, Jim Younger also joined Quantrill's guerrillas and was captured with him and served time as a prisoner of war at the Federal military prison at Alton, Illinois.

In June 1863, 16-year-old Jesse James was still at home with his mother and stepfather when Union soldiers attempted to hang Dr. Samuels. His life was saved by Mrs. Samuels, who managed to cut him down. At about the same time, the soldiers found Jesse working in the field and gave him a severe beating. Soon thereafter Jesse was old enough to join Quantrill's guerrilla forces, serving under Quantrill's lieutenant, Bloody Bill Anderson. He was with this band at the Centralia massacre in September 1864 when Anderson's guerrillas held up a train on which there were twenty-three Union soldiers. They were made to remove their clothing and then were shot. A band of Union soldiers out to kill or capture the guerrillas was ambushed shortly after the Centralia massacre and about 125 soldiers were killed. Jesse is credited with killing the commander, Major H. J. Johnson.

Not long afterwards, Anderson was instructed to ride into northern Missouri and destroy railroad track on the line that ran from Hannibal to St. Joseph. However, Anderson and his guerrillas were ambushed in southern Ray County. It was Bloody Bill Anderson's last fight. He was killed along with most of his men, but Jesse and a few others managed to escape and rode south into Texas.

Shortly after the end of the war, Quantrill and his men were ambushed. Quantrill was seriously wounded and died about a month later. The federal government announced that it would not punish any guerrillas if they gave up and returned to their homes to become law-abiding citizens. Jesse and a small group of guerrilla companions rode toward a schoolhouse designated a surrender point. Before reaching the schoolhouse, they were attacked by Union soldiers. Jesse was badly wounded but managed to get away and make his way to Nebraska where his parents lived after being run out of Kearney. For months it was touch-and-go for Jesse, as he had been shot several times. Expressing a desire to return to Missouri, he was taken by his mother to the home of relatives in Kansas City. Here his cousin Zee took over the job of nursing him back to health. During this time Jesse and Zee fell in love and made plans to be married later.

Cole Younger and Frank James refused to surrender and were considered outlaws by Missouri and the federal government. While Jesse was still recovering, Cole and Frank, along with several other men, robbed the Clay County Bank in Liberty, Missouri, on February 13, 1866, killing a young man in the getaway. This escapade is generally considered the birth of the James-Younger gang. Recovered from his injuries, Jesse was with the gang, when it hit the bank at Gallatin, Missouri, on December 7, 1869. Jesse shot the cashier because he looked like the man who had killed Bloody Bill Anderson. He wasn't.

In January 1866, John Younger and brother Bob were in Independence stocking up on supplies for their mother when a former Union soldier taunted them and knocked John down. In the fracas that followed, John killed the bully right in front of the sheriff's office. Several people witnessed the struggle and a coroner's inquest concluded that John had acted in self-defense.

By the fall of 1868, Bursheba thought it might be in the family's best interest to join her daughter Ann Jones in Dallas County, Texas. Once there, Cole and Jim, along with a reluctant Bob, were soon involved in a fairly successful cattle business. John took a clerking job in Dallas where he could sow his wild oats in night life, women and gambling. Being young, his main interest was having a good time, not nurse-maiding a bunch of cows. Bursheba's health began to deteriorate. John, Bob and sister Retta returned with her to St. Clair, Missouri, in 1870.

There a posse appeared at the Younger farm looking for Jim and Cole. Bob was held down while others dragged John to the barn, where they put a rope around his neck, threw the end of the rope over a beam and hoisted John into the air until he lost consciousness. Bursheba, her heart broken by such incidents, died at the age of 45. John survived his hanging.

John, Bob and Jim spent several months in Texas before once again returning to St. Clair. Restless, however, John quickly returned to Texas, a clerking job and riotous living. There wasn't anything mean about John, he just was young and wanted a good time.

On the night of January 15, 1871, John was drinking with friends in Soyene, Texas. Being a little drunk, he began to harass a slow-witted fellow by the name of Russell. John got a few laughs out of his friends by trying to shoot a pipe out of Russell's mouth. Soon tiring of the sport, he quit.

Encouraged by John's "friends," Russell, somewhat shaken and scared, got the sheriff, a friend of John's, to issue a warrant for his arrest. Deputy Charles Nicholas, another friend, was assigned to bring John in. At most he would be fined for disturbing the peace.

Nicholas and a friend found John eating breakfast with his friend Tom McDaniels. John said he would report to the sheriff's office as soon as he finished eating. This was okay with Nicholas and his colleague McMahan, and they agreed to meet John and McDaniels in front of the dry goods store. On the way over, John noticed that a guard had been placed over his horse in the livery stable. It incensed him that his word would be questioned. When John and McDaniels reached the dry goods store, heated words were exchanged and suddenly gunfire erupted. McMahan drew his pistol first and fired a split second ahead of John. His bullet missed the mark; John's didn't. McMahan was fatally wounded. Nicholas drew his gun and shot John while McDaniels was shooting Nicholas, who died of his wound. John, though wounded, was able to beat it out of town on a "borrowed" horse, along with McDaniels. The two were indicted for murder, though never arrested. John was riding fast on a beeline northeast toward Missouri.

John later spent some time in California and wrote Jim to come rescue him, as he was being pressured to marry a girl (though she was not pregnant by him). On their way back to St. Clair, John and Jim spent some time in the Black Hills. Once back in St. Clair, Cole invited them to participate in a bank holdup along with Frank and Jesse James. Jim declined but John gladly accepted and with Cole, Frank and Jesse James robbed the St. Genevieve Savings Bank of about $4,000.

Bob had been living in Louisiana. When he returned to Missouri he was enticed to join the outlaw gang. Although his heart was set on farming, he lacked the capital to get started. Thus, he accepted the invitation.

The July 21, 1873, robbery of the Chicago, Rock Island and Pacific Railroad near Adair, Iowa, was probably the only time that all four Youngers took part in a robbery together. On January 31, 1874, Jesse, Frank, Bob, Cole and John pulled off the Iron Mountain railroad stick-up at Gad's Hill. Jim had declined to go along. Realizing that such stick-ups were likely to continue, the railroad hired the Pinkerton Detective Agency to hunt down the gang.

While Cole and Bob were relaxing in Hot Springs, John was enjoying the night life in LaCygne, Kansas, with its five saloons and plenty of whores. In fact, when he was feeling especially good, he would buy the services of two or three girls the same evening. Jim did not approve of the robberies and refused to help his brothers spend the money. However, John finally talked him into attending a dance at the Monagaw Hotel in St. Clair County on March 16, 1874. The following day there was a clash between two Pinkerton detectives and the Youngers. John was killed by detective Louis Lull while Jim was busy killing detective Ed Daniels. Wisely, Jim made a hasty exit from Kansas. Friends buried Frank in a grave marked only by a rusted steel stake.

In early February 1866, the Clay County Bank of Liberty, Missouri, was robbed in broad daylight. The gang, composed of several men, rode off with over $60,000 after killing one bystander. Jesse, still recovering from wounds, was not involved in this holdup, but Cole Younger and Frank James are believed to have spearheaded it. Banks in Savannah, Missouri, Richmond, Missouri, and Russelville, Kentucky, were hit prior to the Gallatin, Missouri, holdup previously mentioned. However, it was not Jesse who gunned down the cashier who offered no resistance. On his deathbed, Cole Younger stated that it was Frank who did the shooting.

There was so much bad feeling about the Gallatin killing that the gang laid low for nearly a year. Jesse and Frank used many aliases, but they were relatively safe as long as they remained inactive, as authorities had no photographs from which to identify them.

On June 3, 1871, the gang robbed the bank at Corydon, Iowa, of $6,000 and in the spring of 1872 a bank in Columbia, Kentucky was their target. In the fall of 1872 they held up the cashier of the Kansas City fairgrounds in the presence of a number of onlookers. At this point John Newman Edwards wrote a glowing article in which he praised Frank and Jesse as former guerrillas. A strong Southern sympathizer and former Confederate soldier, Edwards defended the James brothers in articles written over a period of years. His descriptions were fictitious; he never met either brother. The following descriptions by Edwards are quoted verbatim as found in Robert L. Dyer's *Jesse James and the Civil War in Missouri* (University of Missouri Press, 1994):

> Jesse James, the youngest, has a face as smooth and innocent as the face of a school girl. The blue eyes, very clear and penetrating, are never at rest. His form is tall, graceful and capable of great endurance and great efforts. There is always a smile on his lips, and a graceful word or a compliment for all with whom he comes in contact. Looking at his small white hands, with their long tapering fingers, one would not imagine that with a revolver they were among the quickest and deadliest hands in all the West.
>
> Frank is older and taller. Jesse's face is a perfect oval—Frank's is long, wide about the forehead, square and massive about the jaws and chin, and set always in a look of fixed repose. Jesse is light-hearted, reckless, devil-may-care. ... Neither will be taken alive.

The gang turned to train and stagecoach holdups in 1873, continuing through July 1876. Between holdups the gang members scattered here and there. (Jim Younger whiled away the time by serving as deputy sheriff in

Dallas, Texas!) Jesse was baptized and joined the Kearney Baptist Church (under an assumed name) and became an active member, though it did not stop his criminal pursuits. He married his cousin Zerelda Mimms on April 24, 1874. That same year Frank married Annie Ralston. By this time there was a $10,000 reward for either brother, dead or alive.

In 1873–74 the gang pulled two train holdups—one near Council Bluff, Iowa, and one at Gads Hill, Missouri. In the first the engineer was killed when the engine was thrown off the track.

The Younger brothers were trapped by Pinkerton detectives at Osceola, Missouri, but fought their way out of the trap, taking the lives of several lawmen in the escape. The James-Younger gang was by now known to too many people, and in several states any group of horsemen was under suspicion. The bandits had to range farther away from home, to places where nobody worried about the Jameses or the Youngers. The gang committed crimes in at least seven states—Missouri, Texas, Arkansas, Iowa, West Virginia, Kentucky and Minnesota. However, a reversal of the gang's luck was inevitable. Disaster met them at Northfield, Minnesota, on September 7, 1876.

Eight outlaws planned to rob the First National Bank. The group consisted of Jesse and Frank James, Cole, Bob and Jim Younger, Charlie Pitts, Clell Miller and Bill Chadwell. Once in town they were recognized and the citizens quickly mounted a defense. In the gun battle that followed, Bill Chadwell and Clell Miller were killed. Jim Younger's jaw was shot away and Bob's elbow smashed. Jesse led the six remaining bandits out of town and into a swamp called "The Big Woods." Jesse wanted to shoot Jim, who was holding up their flight, but Bob stood ready to kill Jesse should he try such a thing. Even Frank was against it. Jesse's character was hardly enhanced by this cowardly, selfish proposition. Jesse and Frank, in an "every man for himself" move, took leave of the others and made a clean getaway.

Several days later, a posse found the Youngers and Charlie Pitts in the swamp and once again a violent gunfight ensued. Jim Younger received five wounds, the most serious being the bullet that lodged beneath his brain. Cole Younger received 11 wounds. Bob Younger, already shot in the right elbow, was shot through the right lung. Charlie Pitts was killed.

The Youngers were no longer a thorn in the side of the law.

Under Minnesota law a felon could escape the death penalty by pleading guilty. This the three Youngers did, and each received a sentence of life imprisonment in the state penitentiary at Stillwater. Bob came down with consumption and died in prison in 1889 after serving 13 years of his sentence. He had been a model prisoner and had won the friendship of the warden, guards and prisoners alike.

Cole and Jim were pardoned in July 1901 after serving 25 years of their

Clockwise from top: Henrietta, Cole, Jim, and Bob Younger. Photo made in 1889 while the brothers were serving time in the Stillwater penitentiary in Minnesota. (Courtesy Western History Collections, University of Oklahoma Library.)

Robert Ford, who killed Jesse James. Photographer: Lozo, St. Joseph, Missouri. (Courtesy Western History Collections, University of Oklahoma Library.)

life terms. On October 19, 1902, Jim committed suicide, his health and spirit broken.

Cole took a temporary job selling tombstones and then organized a touring wild west show in partnership with Frank James, but that is getting ahead of Frank's story. Cole lived to be 72, still carrying a dozen or more bullets in his body. He died in 1916.

After eluding pursuers in Minnesota, Jesse and Frank headed into the Dakotas where they forced a doctor to dress Frank's leg wound. Afterwards they are believed to have traveled down to Kentucky where they holed up awhile before proceeding on to Missouri. Later they took up residence in Tennessee along with their wives. Jesse and Zee were known as Mr. and Mrs. Howard, and Frank and Annie became Mr. and Mrs. B. J. Woodson.

Jesse's son, Jesse Edwards James, was later called Jesse James, Jr., when he wrote a book and appeared in two movies portraying his father. He was born August 31, 1875, at Nashville, a year before the Northfield fiasco. Frank and Annie had a boy, Robert Franklin James, shortly after the Northfield disaster. The two families lived quietly, went to church, and made no trouble for anyone. Soon Jesse decided to become a rancher and went west to pursue this dream. However, he couldn't put together enough money to purchase a spread. He returned home to find that a daughter, Mary, had been born in his absence.

Disgusted with his failure to acquire a ranch, he put together a small gang and on October 8, 1879, robbed a train at Glendale, Missouri. After several more holdups, Frank joined him and the two families moved around a bit. In November 1881, Jesse and his wife were living in St. Joseph, Missouri, as Mr. and Mrs. Howard. On April 3, 1882, two of his gang members, Bob and Charlie Ford, were visiting him with ulterior motives. Unbeknownst to Jesse, Bob and Charlie Ford had been to see Governor T. T. Crittenden, who offered $10,000 for Frank or Jesse, dead or alive. While visiting with the brothers on a Sunday morning, Jesse took off his coat and laid it across the bed where his guns also lay. Getting up on a chair to straighten a picture, his back was to Bob and Charlie. Bob seized the opportunity, took out his own gun and shot Jesse in the back of the head. He and Charlie were captured, tried and sentenced to hang, but were pardoned by the governor.

The body of Jesse James was given to his widow for interment and, in accordance with the wishes of his mother, it was arranged for the outlaw to be buried at the old homestead at Kearney. Frank James arrived in St. Joe on Tuesday morning following the shooting and registered at the World's Hotel. On Wednesday morning Frank left St. Joe and went to the homestead at Kearney. He remained there during the last rites. If anyone knew of his presence there, nothing was ever said.

Bob and Charlie took to the boards as actors, reliving their real life roles. The play was appropriately titled "How I Killed Jesse James." This dramatization of their "heroism" was popular in the East but met with disapproval in most other areas of the country. It was a cowardly, disloyal act that most Americans could not quite stomach. Perhaps it was only justice that Bob was killed in his own makeshift saloon in Jim Town, near Creede, Colorado, and that Charlie Ford committed suicide.

Jesse James in death. Photographer: Uhlman. (Courtesy Western History Collections, University of Oklahoma Library.)

Jesse James rode roughshod over the country for 16 years and the law never laid a hand on him. Frank James was never taken; he turned himself in after traitor Bob Ford, "the dirty little coward" of song and ballad, cut Jesse down. Frank was tried on several charges over a three-year period but public sympathy was such that prosecutors could never get a conviction. So of all the outlaws making up the James-Younger gang, Frank was the one who came away with the least scratches.

The canonization of Jesse and Frank began early with the articles by John Newman Edwards and gained momentum with the first book about the two. Other books followed. Almost all the literature about the brothers portray them as authentic heroes. By the time of Jesse's death, the brothers were already well on their way to becoming legendary characters. The early biographers were inclined to create myth rather than report facts and later writers picked up and perpetuated much of these fictitious stories. Jesse was the subject of the bulk of the writing.

Jesse's "deification" proceeded along the lines laid down by the *Police Gazette*—his prankish charm, his courteous behavior to women involved in his stick-ups, his protection of widows from villainous bankers, his fighting the railroads and all the rest. But in his case a unique attribute was added, one guaranteed to inflame the partisan passion bred of the Civil War. Jesse symbolized the gallant rebel, ground down beneath the boot of the victorious Yankee oppressor, and such was the potency of this bogus magic that his death kept the sovereign state of Missouri in an uproar for a decade.

Plays about the Jesse James gang were popular in small town opera houses through the Midwest. *The James Boys in Missouri* toured the country playing to packed houses.

Soon after Jesse's death, someone composed a many-versed ballad of mawkish sentimentality about him that has persisted to this day. Credit for the composition has been given to Billy Gashade, though no one seems to know anything about him.

> Jesse James was a lad that killed a-many a man;
> He robbed the Danville train.
> But that dirty little coward that shot Mr. Howard
> Has laid poor Jesse in his grave.
>
> CHORUS:
>
> Poor Jesse had a wife to mourn for his life,
> Three children, they were brave;
> But that dirty little coward that shot Mr. Howard
> Has laid poor Jesse in his grave.
>
> It was Robert Ford, that dirty little coward,
> I wonder how he does feel,
> For he ate of Jesse's bread and he slept in Jesse's bed,
> Then laid poor Jesse in his grave.
>
> Jesse was a man, a friend to the poor,
> He never would see a man suffer pain;

And with his brother Frank he robbed the Chicago bank,
And stopped the Glendale train.

It was his brother Frank that robbed the Gallatin bank,
And carried the money from the town;
It was in this very place that they had a little race,
For they shot Captain Sheets to the ground.

They rallied out West for to live upon the best,
The Fletchers asked their names;
They laughed and smiled as they made their reply,
"We are Frank and Jesse James."

It was on Wednesday night, the moon was shining bright,
They robbed the Glendale train;
The people they did say, for many miles away,
It was robbed by Frank and Jesse James.

It was on Saturday night, Jesse was at home
Talking to his family brave,
Robert Ford came along like a thief in the night
And laid poor Jesse in his grave.

The people held their breath when they heard of Jesse's death,
And wondered how he ever came to die.
It was one of the gang called little Robert Ford,
He shot poor Jesse on the sly.

Jesse went to his rest with his hand on his breast;
The devil will be upon his knee.
He was born one day in the County of Clay
And came from a solitary race.

Jesse went down to the old man town,
Thinking he would do as he'd please;
But he will dwell in the City of Hell
And he'll go to the devil on his knees.

This song was made by Billy Gashade,
As soon as the news did arrive;
He said there was no man with the law in his hand
Who could take Jesse James when alive.

Not to be outdone by the authors of the ballads about Billy the Kid and
Jesse James, someone composed the following ballad about Cole Younger
before the turn of the century. It proved far less popular than the ones to

James or Billy the Kid and in a few short years was forgotten by most folk singers.

> I am one of a band of highwaymen, Cole Younger is my name;
> My crimes and depredations have brought my friends to shame;
> The robbing of the Northfield, the same I can't deny,
> For now I am a prisoner, in the Stillwater jail I lie.
> 'Tis of a bold, high robbery, a story to you I'll tell,
> Of a California miner who unto us befell;
> We robbed him of his money and bid him go his way,
> For which I will be sorry until my dying day.
> And then we started homeward, when brother Bob did say;
> "Now, Cole, we will buy fast horses and on them ride away.
> We will ride to avenge our father's death and try to win the prize;
> We will fight those anti-guerrillas until the day we die."
> And then we rode towards Texas, that good old Lone Star State,
> but on Nebraska's prairies the James boys we did meet;
> With knives, guns and revolvers we all sat down to play,
> A-drinking of good whiskey to pass the time away.
> A Union Pacific railway train was the next thing we did surprise,
> And the crimes done by our bloody hands bring tears into my eyes.
> The engineerman and fireman killed, the conductor escaped alive,
> And now their bones lie molding beneath Nebraska's skies.
> Then we saddled horses, northwestward we did go,
> To the God-forsaken country called Min-ne-so-te-o;
> I had my eyes on the Northfield bank when brother Bob did say,
> "Now, Cole, if you undertake the job, you will surely curse the day."
> But I stationed out my pickets and up to the bank did go,
> And there upon the counter I struck my fatal blow.
> "Just hand us over your money and make no further delay.
> We are the famous Younger brothers, we spare no time to pray."

Over the years numerous Jesse James impersonators have claimed that a member of his gang was shot by Ford in a plot to allow Jesse James to begin a new life. In 1948 J. Frank Dalton of Lawton, Oklahoma, at the age of 100, "revealed" himself as Jesse James. For three years he was interviewed by newspapermen from all over the world. He knew many of the details of Jesse's life. Was he really Jesse James? In 1971, St. Louis historian Carl W. Breihan wrote an expose, noting that Dalton couldn't correctly recite the James family tree and didn't even know Frank James' full name. However, there continues to be some doubt as to whether the real Jesse James lies in his grave.

Jesse James' grave at Kearney, Missouri, was opened in 1995 and a team of scientists led by forensic scientist James E. Starrs examined the remains.

(Starrs became intrigued with the project after being contacted by longtime Jesse James researcher Emmett C. Hoctor, who proposed that the body in James' grave be exhumed and DNA tests be made. Starrs had the cooperation of James' heirs.) Starrs told the *Kearney Courier*, "There is no question in my mind that this is Jesse James." DNA tests later confirmed it.

In a related development, descendants of J. Frank Dalton—the man who insisted he was Jesse James up to his death in August, 1951—were pushing for Dalton's remains be exhumed and tested so that they could prove the true Jesse James died at the age of 103. So far as this author knows, it was never done.

JAMES-YOUNGER GANG FILMOGRAPHY

Of all the outlaws who have ridden across the screen, the most memorable was Jesse James. Portrayed on the screen roughly 40 times, he was nearly always given a whitewash job in the major films. The "reel" Jesse first appeared in 1911 in a one- or two-reeler. No information is available on this film. It is possible that he was portrayed in other short films prior to 1921.

Jesse James Under the Black Flag
(Mesco Pictures, 1921)

Director/Story: Franklin B. Coates.

Jesse James, Jr. (Himself, Jesse James, Sr.), Harry Hoffman (Cole Younger), Marguerite Hungerford (Zee Mimms), Diana Reed (Lucille James), Franklin B. Coates (Himself), James Neil (Robert Standing), Harry Hall (Charles William Quantrill), Sunshine Baker (Mrs. Sam Clifton), Mrs. Jesse James, Jr. (Herself), J. P. McCabe (Bill Anderson), Dan Peterson (Murdock), Hortense Espey (Mrs. Bowman), Ralph Johnson (Judge Bowman), Jack Wall (Captain Andy Clements), Chief Red Fox (Himself), Stonewall (Himself [a horse]).

Franklin Coates has written a book about Jesse James. As he discusses it with Jesse James, Jr., the latter's daughter Lucille has an encounter with Robert Standing, who has landed his airplane in a nearby field to get his bearings. He falls in love with Lucille and several months later visits Mr. James to get permission to marry her. James gives him a copy of the book about his dad and asks him to read it first. Robert learns the story of Jesse James, Sr., beginning in 1863 when Jesse was a boy on the family farm near Kearney, Missouri.

Desiring revenge on the soldiers who mistreated his family, Jesse joins Quantrill's Missouri guerrillas and swears allegiance to their Black Flag. Cole Younger, Jesse's cousin, is also a guerrilla and plays a prominent part in Jesse's survival.

Because of a serious wound, Jesse is mustered out of Quantrill's guerrillas and thus is not with them when they surrender after the war. However, he receives the kind hospitality of Judge Bowman and his daughter Zee, who falls in love with him.

Robert now understands why Lucille is reluctant to marry him.

Jesse James as the Outlaw
(Mesco Pictures, 1921)

Director/Story: Franklin B. Coates.

Jesse James, Jr. (Himself, Jesse James, Sr.), Diana Reed (Lucille James), Marguerite Hungerford (Zee Mimms James), James Neil (Robert Standing).

(This is a sequel to *Jesse James Under the Black Flag*, although it does not begin where the other leaves off.)

Jesse returns home after the war determined to live a peaceful life. It is not long, however, before the Missouri Home Guards (Union sympathizers) accuse him of a bank robbery. He is forced to run.

Branded an outlaw, he lives like one, constantly on the run from the law. He becomes an outlaw when his half-brother is killed and his mother's arm blown off by agents of the railroad who pitch a bomb into the James' home.

Many of Jesse's exploits, both for good and evil, are detailed. He manages to marry Zee Mimms and lives quietly under a different name until one of his old gang, Bob Ford, shows up and shoots him in the back of the head for the reward money offered.

Standing's devotion to Lucille is only intensified from reading about her grandfather, and Jesse James, Jr., gives his permission for them to wed.

Jesse James
(Paramount, 1927) 8 Reels.

Director: Lloyd Inghaham. Story/Screenplay: Frank M. Clifton. Technical Advisor: Jesse James, Jr. Supervisor: Alfred L. Werker. Presented by Adolph Zukor and Jesse Lasky.

Fred Thomson (Jesse James), Nora Lane (Zerelda Mimms), Montagu Love (Frederick Mimms), Mary Carr (Mrs. Zerelda Samuels), James Pierce (Frank James), Harry Woods (Bob Ford), William Courtwright (Parson Bill), Silver King (Himself).

Opening scenes show Jesse as a member of Quantrill's Partisan Rangers. The horse Silver King gets a chance to do his stuff in these early scenes by limping and showing signs of extreme weariness when Quantrill casts a covetous eye on the magnificent mount.

As the dusty horsemen approach a river, they are given permission to go swimming. Jesse comes up under a willow tree and startles Zerelda Mimms and Martha Sumner. Zerelda is interested in the debonair soldier in spite of his haughty dignity.

That night, General Grant and his men camp at the Sumner plantation and are received with cold courtesy by the Southerners. A Union sergeant is yanked into a bush and Jesse appears before Grant in the sergeant's clothes. Zerelda threatens to expose him. He saves her the trouble, disappearing into a fireplace. He beats pursuing bloodhounds to the river and gets away on Silver King, who has followed him into the water in response to a whistle.

There are some exciting battle scenes in which Jesse and Frank James keep the Confederate colors flying and save the life of Bob Ford. At the end of the war, Jesse is warned by his old friend Parson Bill to be ready for bad news. He finds that his mother's arm has been blown off by fanatic Union sympathizers in his home town, and that she has been threatened with expulsion from the town by a citizens' committee headed by Frederick Mimms.

Jesse is about to wreak vengeance on Mimms when his daughter Zerelda enters, and he discovers she is the girl who had interested him at the Sumner plantation. Her screams bring help and Jesse is forced to flee again in a spectacular manner. He is now a peace-time outlaw.

During three succeeding days the stagecoach is robbed at a pass in the hills. Jesse's home is burned. Zerelda helps his mother to escape.

Citizens attempt to trap Jesse into a surrender with the aid of Bob Ford, who has turned against Jesse as a result of having developed a secret fondness for Zerelda. Jesse appears at a dinner in the home of Frederick Mimms. They tell him he will have to betray his friend. He backs to the door, shielded by Zerelda, leaps into the darkness onto Silver King and grabs a tree branch. As a pursuer rides beneath, Jesse drags him into the tree, changes clothes with him and reappears among the pursuers as a Union soldier. In the meantime, Silver King, riderless, is leading the soldiers on a merry chase into the open country.

Zerelda and Jesse are reunited and drive away as it begins raining. They seek shelter near some rocks. As the stagecoach comes by, Jesse holds it up only to discover Parson Bill aboard. He marries them as Jesse guides the coach at top speed with Zerelda beside him. A lurch throws Parson Bill off as he concludes the strange service, but Silver King finds him. Together they pursue the disappearing coach.

Jesse James grossed $1.2 million at 1927 prices. The picture made Thomson the biggest western star of the day and (to many western fans) elevated him over Tom Mix in popularity.

Jesse James
(20th Century–Fox, 1939) 105 min.

Director: Henry King. Producer: Darryl F. Zanuck. Screenplay/Assoc. Producer: Nunnally Johnson.

Tyrone Power (Jesse James), Henry Fonda (Frank James), Nancy Kelly (Zerelda (Zee), Randolph Scott (Will Wright), Henry Hull (Major Rufus Cobb), Slim Summerville (Jailer), J. Edward Bromberg (Mr. Runyan), Brian Donlevy (Barshee), John Carradine (Bob Ford), Donald Meek (McCoy), John Russell (Jesse James, Jr.), Jane Darwell (Mrs. Samuels), Charles Tannen (Charles Ford), Claire Du Brey (Mrs. Bob Ford), Willard Robertson (Clarke), Harold Goodwin (Bill), Ernest Whitman (Pinkie), Eddy Waller (Deputy), Paul Burns (Hank), Spencer Charters (Minister), Arthur Aylesworth (Tom Colson), Charles Middleton (Doctor), Charles Halton (Heywood), George Chandler (Roy), Harry Tyler (Farmer), Virginia Brissac (Boy's Mother), Ed Le Saint (Judge Rankin), John Elliott (Judge Mathews), Erville Alderson (Old Marshal), George Breakston (Farmer Boy), Lon Chaney, Jr. (One of James Gang), Harry Holman (Engineer), James Flavin (Cavalry Captain), George O'Hara (Teller), John Beck (Turnkey), Victor Kilian (Preacher).

This is a superb Western which presents a highly romanticized view of the legendary outlaws Jesse and Frank James, from the time of their idealistic revolt against the railroads to their disastrous raid on a Minnesota bank.

By 1867 the St. Louis Midland Railroad moved toward Sedelia, Missouri, hiring land-grabbers to secure right-of-way privileges in any way they saw fit. A gang of these bullies headed by Barshee finds a difficult obstacle in Mrs. Samuels, a farm woman. When the gang threatens her, her two sons Jesse and Frank James step in and drive them away. Warned to go into hiding for their own safety, the James brothers leave the area. Later, however, Jesse's sweetheart Zee informs them that Barshee has killed their mother. Upon hearing this, Jesse rides into Sedalia and kills Barshee, vowing that he will make the railroad pay for his mother's death.

When the railroad starts the initial train to Sedalia, Jesse pulls off the first train holdup in history. Thus begins the fabulous careers of Jesse and

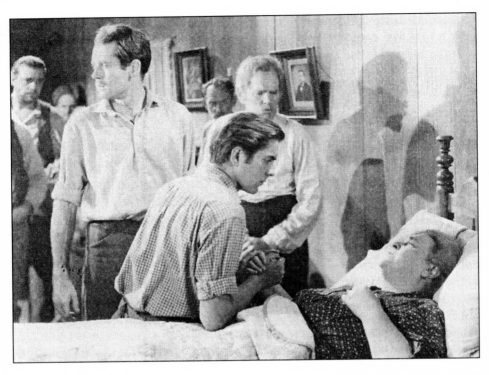

Highly romanticized but lots of fun to watch, *Jesse James* (20th Century–Fox, 1939) featured Tyrone Power as the infamous outlaw. Here, Jesse attends the deathbed of his mother (Jane Darwell); Frank (Henry Fonda) stands just behind and Major Cobb (Henry Hull) is to his left.

Frank James. Hunted continually by U. S. Marshal Will Wright, the brothers carry out one daring bank and train holdup after another until they are the most wanted men in Missouri.

The film traces their daring exploits until the moment when Bob Ford shoots Jesse in the back to collect a reward.

"About the only connection the film has with fact," said Jo Frances James, a descendant of the outlaw, "was that there was once a man named James and he did ride a horse." Nevertheless, upon release on January 13, 1939, *Jesse James* was a box office sensation. The *New York Times* praised the film: "Handsomely produced by Messrs. Darryl Zanuck and Hunnally Johnson, stirringly directed by Henry King, beautifully acted by its cast ... an authentic American panorama."

Both Power and Fonda gained new legions of fans as a result of *Jesse James*, with Power rising to second place in the box office polls in 1939. Fonda went on to score big in *The Return of Frank James*.

For all its glamorizing and distortion, this film remains the definitive saga of Jesse James—melodramatic enough to build up sympathy for his adventures, and honest enough to hammer home the crime-does-not-pay theme that makes the film a true tragedy.

"Vigorous and intensely dramatic in its unfolding, *Jesse James* is box-office smacko that will wind up in the top list of biggest grossers for the first half of 1939. It's a cinch extended run attraction with plenty of exploitation angles to attract."—*Variety*, January 11, 1939

Days of Jesse James
(Republic, 1939), 63 min.

Director: Joseph Kane. Assoc. Producer: Joseph Kane. Screenplay: Earle Snell. Story: Jack Natteford.

Roy Rogers (Roy Rogers), George F. Hayes (Gabby Whittaker), Pauline Moore (Mary Whittaker), Donald Barry (Jesse James), Harry Woods (Captain Worthington), Arthur Loft (Sam Wyatt), Wade Boteler (Dr. Samuels), Ethel Wales (Mrs. Samuels), Scotty Beckett (Buster Samuels), Michael Worth (Frank James), Glenn Strange (Cole Younger), Olin Howard (Undersheriff), Monte Blue (Fields), Jack Rockwell (McDaniels), Fred Burns (Sheriff), Bud Osborne (Deputy), Jack Ingram (Deputy), Fred Toones (Bank Janitor), Carl Sepulveda (Jim Younger), Forrester Dillon (Bob Younger). *With* Hansel Warner, Lynton Brent, Pasquel Perry, Eddie Acuff.

When the Midwest is plagued by the various bank and train robberies of the James-Younger gang, Roy Rogers is brought in by the Bankers' Association to track down the James boys. The railroads also join in the manhunt, engaging Captain Worthington, head of one of the nation's largest detective agencies, and offering $50,000 reward.

Roy and Worthington clash from the start. Worthington suspects that Roy has inside knowledge of Jesse James' whereabouts.

Rogers is particularly indignant over the Muncie bank robbery in which old Gabby Whittaker, grandfather of Mary, the girl in whom Roy is interested, loses his life's savings. He suspects that this is an inside job, although it is attributed to the James gang. He and Gabby join the James mob in order to obtain first-hand information.

Worthington and his men storm the home of Dr. Samuels, Jesse James' stepfather. They throw a naphtha torch into the interior of the home; it explodes and Jesse's step-brother is killed.

Jesse James thinks that Rogers is responsible for this attack and vows to have his revenge, not knowing that Rogers is a member of his own gang, using the name of "Leavenworth."

The James boys, with the Younger brothers, plan a spectacular bank robbery. Roy is unsuccessful in his attempt to prevent it. He and Gabby are named as accomplices by Worthington.

In the getaway, Jesse James is wounded, and Roy exhibits pronounced surgical skill in binding his wounds and in treating Jesse's sick wife and baby. Grateful, Jesse offers Roy the entire booty of the James gang to use as a stake in the study of medicine. Roy declines the offer but is touched by this kindly gesture, and all but admits his identity.

Returning to Muncie to find that the bank president has reported a far greater amount of money taken than the meager booty displayed by Jesse James, Roy deftly lets it be known to the Wyatt brothers, executives in the bank, that they are suspected of robbing their own bank and blaming the James gang. The Wyatt boys leave town with the bank's stolen money but are captured by Roy. The money is returned to the depositors, Roy explains to the authorities his ruse in joining the James gang, and Jesse and his outlaws remain free to roam the countryside.

"The film is swift paced and has more than enough action to hold audience attention for the full 63 minutes running time."—*Motion Picture Herald*, December 23, 1939

"...interesting enough, though the story and direction leave many loose ends still unraveled at the finale. However, faults aren't so glaring that action fans won't derive satisfaction. It's replete with the usual gun-throwing, battles and chases, etc."—*Variety*, December 27, 1942

The Return of Frank James
(20th Century–Fox, 1940) 92 min.

Director: Fritz Lang. Screenplay: Sam Hellman. Producer: Darryl F. Zanuck. Assoc. Producer: Kenneth Macgowan.

Henry Fonda (Frank James), Gene Tierney (Eleanor Stone), Jackie Cooper (Clem), Henry Hull (Major Rufus Todd), John Carradine (Bob Ford), J. Edward Bromberg (George Runyan), Donald Meek (McCoy), Eddie Collins (Station Agent), George Barbier (Judge), Ernest Whitman (Pinky), Charles Tannen (Charlie Ford), Lloyd Corrigan (Randolph Stone), Russell Hicks (Prosecutor), Victor Kilian (Preacher), Edward McWade (Colonel Jackson), George Chandler (Roy), Irving Bacon (Bystander), Barbara Pepper (Nellie Blane), Louis Mason (Watchman), Stymie Beard (Mose), Davidson Clark (Officer), William Pawley, Frank Sully (Actors). *With* Milt Kibbee, Lee Phelps, Adrian Morris.

The story begins with a reprise of the shooting of Jesse by Bob and Charlie Ford. Frank, who is minding his own business on a little farm, sets out to even things. In the search, young Clem joins Frank. Frank begins by robbing an express office to get funds for the manhunt; in the ensuing struggle, the station agent is killed by his own friend's guns. In Denver, Frank meets up with Eleanor Stone and also the Fords. The Fords ride out of town with Frank and Clem on their trail. Charlie Ford slips and falls to his death from a cliff. Frank learns that his Negro servant Pinky is about to be hung for the station agent's killing. Eleanor convinces Frank to turn himself in, which he does. In the resultant trial Frank and Pinky are freed, just in time to see Clem and Bob Ford kill each other.

"Fritz Lang managed to evoke the spirit but not the truth of the real west by instilling the film with a revenge motif of European subtlety and shuttling to the background conventional Western characters."—*Shoot-Em-Ups* (1978), p. 171

"From standpoint of production and cast, Darryl Zanuck has spared nary a horse. And it's on this angle that the picture may be expected to do moderately good biz. ... Film suffers from too much rationalization of the necessity for Frank's wiping-out job and not enough of the old one-two with the six shooter. Makin' bad men good is okay, pardner, but keep the hosses movin' and guns a-blazin'."—*Variety*, August 14, 1940

Jesse James at Bay
(Republic, 1941), 56 min.

Producer/Director: Joseph Kane. Screenplay: James R. Webb. Story: Harrison Jacobs.

Roy Rogers (Jesse James, Clint Burns), George F. Hayes (Sheriff Gabby Whittaker), Gale Storm (Jane Fillmore), Sally Payne (Polly Morgan), Hal Taliaferro (Paul Sloan), Pierre Watkin (Phineas Krager), Roy Barcroft (Vern Stone), Jack Kirk (Rufe Balter), Billy Benedict (Davis), Jack O'Shea (Burt), Rex Lease (Gregg), Ed Peil (The Marshal), Kit Guard (Bartender), Jack Rockwell, Hank Bell, Curley Dresden, Bill Wolfe (Townsmen), George Kesterson (Art Mix). *With* Chester Conklin, Charles Moore, Ken Card, Ted Lorch, Pascale Perry, Al Taylor, Luke Cosgrove, Rick Anderson, Bob Reeves, Paul Sells.

Clint Burns, a gambling double, is hired to blacken the name of Jesse James. The scheme is successful with all but Jesse's friends, Sheriff Whittaker and young Polly Morgan, who can distinguish the two men intuitively. To bring justice to the farmers who are being cheated by the railroad, Jesse himself takes advantage of the resemblance. He plays Robin Hood, robbing the land grabbers so the farmers can pay off the exorbitant claims. A number of pitched gun battles and chases keep things moving at the proper gait to a satisfactory conclusion.

"Joseph Kane, director-producer, has paced his yarn with the skill usually found in better programmers, and James R. Webb's scripting is above par."—*Variety*, October 22, 1941

Bad Men of Missouri
(Warner Bros., 1941) 75 min.

Director: Ray Enright. Screenplay: Charles Grayson. Story: Robert E. Kent.

Dennis Morgan (Cole Younger), Jane Wyman (Mary Hathaway), Wayne Morris (Bob Younger), Arthur Kennedy (Jim Younger), Victor Jory (William Merrick), Alan Baxter (Jesse James), Walter Catlett (Mr. Pettibone), Howard da Silva (Greg Bilson), Faye Emerson (Martha Adams), Russell Simpson (Hank Younger), Virginia Brissac (Mrs. Hathaway), Erville Anderson (Mr. Adams), Hugh Sothern (Fred Robinson), Sam McDaniel (Wash), Dorothy Vaughan (Mrs. Dalton), William Gould (Sheriff Brennan), Robert Winkler (Willie Younger), Ann Todd (Amy Younger), Roscoe Ates (Lafe). *With* Duncan Renaldo, Tom Tyler, Charles Middleton, Spencer Charters, Jack Mower, Leah Beard, Bud Osborne, Frank Mayo, Milton Kibbee, Ben Corbett, Vera Lewis.

The Younger Brothers return home after the Civil War to find that carpetbaggers have taken charge of everything. Hank Younger, the brothers' father, is killed and other old settlers run off their land. As a result, Hank's sons turn to robbery and murder. Eventually the brothers join forces with Jesse James' gang for wholesale pillaging of banks and trains until they are wounded and captured during the Northfield, Minnesota, bank holdup. The film does its bit to whitewash and glorify the exploits of the Youngers.

"Picture makes little pretext of providing anything more than plenty of riding, holdups and chases. Script and story both fail to establish credulity, and use technique of a quarter century ago." — *Variety*, August 6, 1941

The Remarkable Andrew
(Paramount, 1942) 80 min.

Director: Stuart Heisler. Story/Screenplay: Dalton Trumbo. Assoc. Producer: Richard Blumenthal.

William Holden (Andrew Long), Ellen Drew (Peggy Tobin), Brian Donlevy (General Andrew Jackson), Rod Cameron (Jesse James), Richard Webb (Randall Stevens), Porter Hall (Art Slocumb), Frances Gifford (Halsey), Nydia Westman (Miss Van Buren), Montagu Love (George Washington), George Watts (Ben Franklin), Brandon Hurst (Justice Marshall), Gilbert Emery (Thomas Jefferson), Jimmy Conlin (Henry Smith), Spencer Charters (Dr. Upjohn), Wallis Clark (R. R. McCall), Tom Fadden (Jake Pearl), Minor Watson (Orville Beamish), Milton Parsons (Sam Savage), Thomas W. Ross (Judge Krebs).

The tale, although utilizing fantasy, is human and real. A young lad, named after Andrew Jackson, is a bookkeeper in City Hall. He unearths a discrepancy in the balancing of the figures which involves the grafting politicians in City Hall from the mayor down. Instead of covering up, he attempts to expose it and is in turn arrested by the politicians.

His hero Andrew Jackson appears in full regalia to help him. Only the lad can see him. Jackson is continually at his side giving him advice, and people began to think the lad is crazy and talking to himself. Jackson calls upon the ghosts of Jesse James, George Washington, Thomas Jefferson, Ben Franklin, Justice Marshall and an unsung private from the Revolutionary War for counsel. The ghosts unearth the evidence the boy needs and as a result all of the politicians resign.

"Every so often, but not often enough, a picture emerges from the lesser budget brackets with true, dramatic distinction. *The Remarkable Andrew* attains such rating because of the sincere and eloquent manner in which it combines entertainment and a reaffirmation of the fundamental truths of our democracy. It is the kind of picture which will build through word of mouth and is worthy of astute showmanship."—*Film Daily*, January 19, 1942

"*The Remarkable Andrew* has been well-produced and is consistently engaging and timely in recalling memorable words that have long since been placed in American archives. But it all adds up as confusing."—*Variety*, January 21, 1942

Jesse James, Jr.

(Republic, 1942), 56 min.

Director/Assoc. Producer: George Sherman. Story: Richard Murphy. Screenplay: Richard Murphy, Taylor Caven and Doris Schroeder.

Don Barry (Johnny Barrett), Lynn Merrick (Joan Perry), Al St. John (Pop Sawyer), Douglas Walton (Archie McDonald), Bob Kortman (Blackie Deane), Karl Hackett (Amos Martin), Lee Shumway (Tom Perry), Stanley Blystone (Sam Carson), Jack Kirk (Sheriff), George Chesebro (Bull), Frank Brownlee (Councilman), Forbes Murray (Mr. Forbes), Jim Corey (Deputy Sheriff), Kermit Maynard (Wilson). *With* Ken Cooper, Tommy Coates.

The frontier town of Sundown seeks to become the western terminus of the National Telegraph Company, but it is suddenly shattered by a series of robberies and raids by an organized band of hoodlums. Amos Martin, a member of the town council, is the secret leader of the gang; he will profit if the neighboring Fargo is made the terminus.

Johnny Barrett, son of a former Sundown sheriff, is called in by the town council. To their disappointment, Johnny turns out to be a pacifist. Johnny and Archie McDonald, an Englishman who heads National Telegraph's investigating committee, become friends. When McDonald is robbed and seriously wounded by Martin's henchman Blackie Deane, Johnny casts aside his pacifist notions and goes after Blackie. The gunman accidently shoots himself during a fight with Johnny, and the latter is charged with murder and becomes a fugitive.

Working secretly, Johnny soon establishes his own innocence while uncovering Martin as the gang leader.

There is no one in the cast named Jesse James, Jr., nor is Jesse James mentioned. Republic misled its audience.

"Unspectacular western which falls a trifle below par."—*Variety*, April 8, 1942

Badman's Territory

(RKO, 1946) 97 min.

Director: Tim Whelan. Story/Screenplay: Jack Natteford and Luci Ward. Producer: Nat Holt.

Randolph Scott (Mark Rowley), Ann Richards (Henryette Alcott), George "Gabby" Hayes (Coyote), Ray Collins (Colonel Farewell), James Warren (John Towley), Morgan Conway (Bill Hampton), Virginia Sale (Meg), John Halloran (Hank McGee), Andrew Tomes (Doc Grant), Richard Hale (Ben Wade), Harry Holman (Hodge), Chief Thundercloud (Chief Tahlequah), Lawrence Tierney (Jesse James), Tom Tyler (Frank James), Steve Brodie (Bob Dalton), William Ross (Grat Dalton), Nestor Paiva (Sam Bass), Isabel Jewell (Belle Starr). *With* Emory Parnell, Ethan Laidlaw, Kermit Maynard, Bud Osborne, Chuck Hamilton, Ben Johnson, George Chesebro.

Mark Rowley, a Texas sheriff, flees his home state with a price on his head because of a clash with ruthless Texas State Policeman Bill Hampton. He enters the Oklahoma Territory to take the post of sheriff of the town of Quinto. He has not escaped Hampton, however, for the manhunter instigates a new feud by wounding Rowley's younger brother while attempting to arrest Coyote, one of the boy's pals.

Quinto newspaper editor Henryetta Alcott and her spinster telegraph operator friend Meg try to dissuade Rowley from carrying out his duties as sheriff, but the peacemaker is forced to ferret out the James brothers in order to find his brother. He finds the boy and brings him back to town after a terrific fight.

A short time later Rowley moves in on the Dalton boys and subdues them to a degree. However, his real nemesis is tracking down Hampton, and before the last reel he too is vanquished. Rowley is acquitted by a jury which brings in a verdict of justifiable homicide.

"An intriguing saga of the West, capably directed, remarkably cast, and well produced."—*Film Daily*, April 22, 1946

"RKO has a vigorous encompassing saga in *Badman's Territory*, which covers in one film portions of the careers of most of the early West's badmen and runs the gamut of outdoor action, from hard riding to massacre."— *L. A. Examiner*

Jesse James Rides Again

(Republic, 1947) 13 chapters.

Director: Fred C. Brannon, Thomas Carr. Screenplay: Franklin Adreon, Basil Dickey, Jesse Duffy and Sol Shor. Assoc. Producer: Mike Frankovich. Photography: John MacBurnie. Music: Mort Glickman. Special Effects: Howard and Theodore Lydecker.

Clayton Moore (Jesse James, John C. Howard), Linda Stirling (Ann Bolton), Roy Barcroft (Frank Lawton), John Compton (Steve Lang, Steve Long), Tristram Coffin (James Clark), Tom London (Sam Bolton), Holly Bane (Tim), Edmund Cobb (Wilkie), Gene Stutenroth [Roth] (Duffie), Fred Graham (Amos Hawks), Leroy Mason (Finlay), Edward Cassidy (Grant), Dave Anderson (Sam), Eddie Parker (Flint), Tom Steele (Goff), Dale Van Sickel (Brock, Boyd, Gow, Raider), Robert Blair (Bartender), Ted Mapes (Bass), Tex Terry (Blair), Gil Perkins (Cody), Tex Palmer (Doty), Casey MacGregor (Jim Doyle), Emmett Lynn (Drunk), Duke Taylor (Gil), Monte Montague (Green), Lee Shumway (Hammond), Carey Loftin (Harlan), Loren Riebe (Haynes), Charles Morton, Walter Downs (Farmers), Frank Marlowe (Joe), Herman Hack (Kaw), Chuck Roberson (Lafe), Carl Sepulveda (Mort), Ken Terrell (Price), Bert LeBaron, Pascale Perry (Raiders), Nellie Walker (Rose), Chester Conklin (Roy), Tommy Coates (Saloon Patron), George Chesebro (Gus Simmons), Charles King (Trent), Bud Wolfe (Stock), Tom Chatterton (Mark Tobin), Robert Riordan (Waldon), Howard Mitchell (Ward), Richard Alexander (Clem Williams), Keith Richards (Wynn). *With* Victor Cox, Helen Griffith, and Don Summers.

CHAPTER TITLES

1. The Black Raiders
2. Signal for Action
3. The Stacked Deck
4. Concealed Evidence
5. The Corpse of Jesse James
6. The Traitor
7. Talk or Die
8. Boomerang
9. The Captured Raider
10. The Revealing Torch
11. The Spy
12. Black Gold
13. Deadline at Midnight

Jesse James, trying to go straight, flees into Missouri where he helps the Bolton family fight off an attack by hooded raiders. Jesse and his friend Steve discover oil under Peaceful Valley and they stay around to rout the outlaws and expose the leaders.

Clayton Moore (left) and Steve Darrell played the James brothers in Republic's 13-chapter serial *Adventures of Frank and Jesse James* (1948).

Republic simply used the name "Jesse James" to attract an audience. The film has nothing to do with the historical Jesse James.

Adventures of Frank and Jesse James
(Republic, 1948) 13 chapters.

Director: Fred Brannon and Yakima Canutt. Screenplay: Franklin Adreon, Basil Dickey and Sol Shor. Assoc. Producer: Franklin Adreon. Photography: John MacBurnie. Music: Morton Scott. Special Effects: Howard and Theodore Lydecker.

Clayton Moore (Jesse James, John Howard), Steve Darrell (Frank James, Bob Carroll), Noel Neill (Judy Powell), George J. Lewis (Rafe Henley), Stanley Andrews (Jim Powell), John Crawford (Amos Ramsey), Sam Flint (Paul Thatcher), House Peters, Jr. (Sheriff Towey), Dale Van Sickel (Thomas Dale, Art Carter, Jones), Tom Steele (Mike Steele, Gus), James Dale (J. B. Nichols), I. Stanford Jolley (Ward), Gene Stutenroth (Marshal), Lane Bradford (Bill), George Chesebro

(Jim), Jack Kirk (Casey), Steve Clark (Sheriff Barton), Duke Taylor (Bull), Carey Loftin (Carlson, Pete), Duke Green (Carver), Frank Ellis (Citizen), Roy Bucko (Citizen), Art Dillard (Citizen), Ralph Bucko (David), Augie Gomez (Hall), Joe Yrigoyen (Grady), Fred Graham (Dirk 1), Guy Teague (Dirk 2), Victor Cox (Dick), Joe Phillips (Zeb), Ken Terrell (Tim), Eddie Parker (Jergens, Joe), Bud Osborne (Bat Kelsey), Bob Reeves (Tim), Bud Wolfe (Moody), Rose Turich (Rosita), David Sharpe (Seth).

CHAPTER TITLES

1. Agent of Treachery
2. The Hidden Witness
3. The Lost Tunnel
4. Blades of Death
5. Roaring Wheels
6. Passage to Danger
7. The Secret Code
8. Doomed Cargo
9. The Eyes of the Law
10. The Stolen Body
11. Suspicion
12. Talk or Die
13. Unmasked

Frank and Jesse plan to make amends for their past crimes. Miner Jim Powell and his daughter Judy are friends of the James brothers and help them to devise a plan to repay the victims their gang has robbed. Jim owns several mines and believes that one of them, with a little more work, will pay off handsomely. Jesse borrows money from Thatcher to buy the necessary equipment and work begins. Gold is found but Amos Ramsey, mine foreman, kills Powell and conceals the discovery.

Ramsey hires Rafe Henley's gang to prevent any attempts to work the mine, but Frank and Jesse fight off Henley's outlaws. Ramsey is not suspected until the Jameses catch him and Rafe Henley extracting gold from the mine. In the shoot-out that follows, both villains are killed.

Return of the Bad Men
(RKO, 1948)

For full writeup see page 33.

The Younger Brothers
(Warner Bros., 1949) 76 min.

Director: Edwin L. Marin. Screenplay: Edna Anhalt. Story: Morton Grant. Producer: Saul Elkins.

Wayne Morris, Janis Paige, Bruce Bennett, Geraldine Brooks, Robert Horton, Alan Hale, Fred Clark, James Brown, Monte Blue, Tom Tyler, William Forrest, Ian Wolfe.

While the brothers (Wayne Morris, Bruce Bennett and James Brown) are camping near Cedar City, their young brother Robert Horton and Geraldine Brooks, Bennett's fiancée, arrive in town. As the unarmed Youngers ride into town, they are turned back by armed citizens, aroused by Fred Clark, an ex-detective with a grudge against the brothers.

Janis Paige, outlaw leader of her dead brother's gang, asks Morris and the others to join her in a bank robbery in the next town. They refuse. Horton gets into a saloon brawl, instigated by Clark, and kills a man in self-defense. His brothers help him out of town and across the state line.

Morris and Horton are captured by Paige's men and taken along as prisoners when they go to rob the bank, so that they will be blamed for the crime. Bennett and Brown follow, armed with stolen guns. Paige is killed during the holdup, and Wayne takes her gun. The four brothers dispose of the escaping robbers and throw the money sacks back into the bank. The brothers are finally pardoned and set out for Missouri to live as farmers.

The picture whitewashes the Youngers, but to oater fans it makes "no never mind." Edwin L. Marin's direction is exactly what Edna Anhalt's actionful script called for. Producer Saul Elkins spared neither the horses nor the ammunition in this superior Western.

I Shot Jesse James
(Screen Guild, 1949) 80 min.

Screenplay/Director: Samuel Fuller. Producer: Robert L. Lippert, Carl Hittleman. Suggested by the *American Weekly* article by Homer Croy.

Preston Foster (John Kelley), Barbara Britton (Cynthia Waters), John Ireland (Bob Ford), Reed Hadley (Jesse James), J. Edward Bromberg (Kane), Victor Kilian (Soapy), Barbara Woodell (Mrs. Zee James), Tom Tyler (Frank James), Tom Noonan (Charles Ford), Byron Foulger (Room Clerk), Eddie Dunn (Bartender), Jeni Le Gon (Maid), Robin Short (Troubadour), Margia Dean, Gene Collins, Chuck Roberson, Stanley Price.

The story opens with a bank holdup by the James Brothers, whose gang includes the Ford brothers. Bob Ford loves roadshow actress Cynthia Waters, and decides to shoot Jesse James in order to gain amnesty and live his life openly. But Cynthia's love for Ford is ended by his crime.

John Kelley is a prospector, also in love with the actress, whose path crosses Ford's before and after the killing, and finally in Creede, Colorado, where Ford has struck it rich and Kelley has become sheriff. Kelley shoots Ford to death after the latter, refusing to listen to reason, has fired at and wounded him.

"John Ireland is typed perfectly for the Bob Ford role, and does an excellent acting job. Reed Hadley, looking a bit like Abraham Lincoln with his whiskers, his skinny frame and mournful eyes, also draws sympathy. Preston Foster, of course, is entirely adequate in the role of the man whom the girl finally falls in love with. Barbara Britton is dainty and skillfully convincing as the girl."—*Los Angeles Times*, January 29, 1949

"As an exploitation picture, *I Shot Jesse James* should ring up heavy returns for Screen Guild. Most ambitious ever made under this distribution banner, film carries strong appeal and touches a topic known to greater majority of theater-goers, which gives added impetus to interest picture is sure to generate."—*Variety*, January 27, 1949

Fighting Man of the Plains
(20th Century–Fox, 1949) 93 min.

Director: Edwin L. Marin. Story/Screenplay: Frank Gruber. Producer: Nat Holt.

Randolph Scott (Jim Dancer), Bill Williams (Johnny Tancred), Victor Jory (Dave Otham), Jane Nigh (Florence Peel), Douglas Kennedy (Ken Vedder), Joan Taylor (Evelyn Slocum), Barry Kroeger (Cliff Bailey), Rhys Williams (Chandler Leech), Barry Kelley (Slocum), James Todd (Hobson), Paul Fix (Yancey), James Millican (Cummings), Burk Symon (Meeker), Dale Robertson (Jesse James), Herbert Rawlinson (Lawyer), J. Farrell MacDonald (Partridge), Harry Cheshire (Lanyard), James Griffith (Quantrill), Tony Hughes (Kerrigan), John Hamilton (Currier), Cliff Clark (Travers), John Halloran (Harmer), Anthony Jochim (Holz), James Harrison (Slattery), Matt Willis (Ferryman), Kermit Maynard.

Jim Dancer, one of Quantrill's Raiders, becomes a fugitive for killing the man he thought had slain his brother. He picked the wrong target. Justice catches up with him but he escapes from detectives and comes into a town overrun by lawlessness. His quick trigger hand and ability to defend himself get him the post of sheriff. Dancer drives the lawless element out with the assistance of Jesse James and Dave Otham, operator of the local gambling emporium. There is a romantic triangle to complicate Jim's life, and inevitably his true identity is revealed. But he has performed his duty well and has at least some good deeds to his credit.

"… despite a lush Cinecolor dressing along with competent acting, this latest entry in the big-budget sagebrush sweepstakes will be held to average business in most situations. … Long string of super westerns which have preceded it will tend to dull the edge of *Plains*. While the tale generates simple action the plot is hackneyed."—*Variety*, October 12, 1949

The Great Missouri Raid
(Paramount, 1950) 84 min.

Director: Gordon Douglas. Story/Screenplay: Frank Gruber. Producer: Nat Holt.

Wendell Corey (Frank James), Macdonald Carey (Jesse James), Ward Bond (Major Trowbridge), Ellen Drew (Bee Moore), Bruce Bennett (Cole Younger), Bill Williams (Jim Younger), Anne Revere (Mrs. Samuels), Edgar Buchanan (Dr. Samuels), Lois Chartrand (Mary Bauer), Louis Jean Heydt (Charles Ford), Barry Kelley (Mr. Bauer), James Millican (Sgt. Trowbridge), Paul Lees (Bob Younger), Guy Wilkerson (Clell Miller), Ethan Laidlaw (Jim Cunnings), Tom Tyler (Allen Parmer), Steve Pendleton (Arch Clements), Bob Bray (Charley Pitts), Paul Fix (Sgt. Brill), James Griffith (Jack Ladd), Bob Osterloh (August), Alan Wells (Liddil), Whit Bissell (Bob Ford).

A Union soldier is killed while brutally questioning the James parents as to the whereabouts of Frank, a Quantrill Raider. The soldier's brother Major Trowbridge swears that he will bring Frank and Jesse to justice if it takes him a lifetime. This vow sets off a chain of circumstances that sees the brothers, the Youngers and others taking to a life of crime after being hounded away from a respectable existence. Major Trowbridge particularly wants to catch Jesse, who marries Bee Moore between holdup operations. Frank, who is hiding out under an assumed name, joins up for a railroad holdup which proves disastrous. This fiasco returns the brothers to their homestead, presided over by their mother, who lost an arm when Trowbridge's men attacked the farmhouse. Trowbridge plots the killing of Jesse with Bob Ford, and Jesse is killed as he is about to leave for the East.

"More Jesse James history. Accent is on spectacular action, a plentitude of gunplay, the romantic angles, and the relentless, vindictive hunting of the brothers by an ex-army officer who turns detective to avenge the death of his brother during the Civil War when the Jameses were with Quantrill."— *Film Daily*, December 1, 1950

"Gordon Douglas' direction swings the footage through many exciting moments. The bank holdups that follow the personally-inspired raids against the Jameses, the train robberies, the flights through rugged terrain, the more intimate family and romance incidents are all told most acceptably."— *Variety*, December 6, 1950

The Return of Jesse James
(Lippert, 1950) 73 min.

Director: Arthur Hilton. Screenplay: Jack Natteford. Story/Producer: Carl K. Hittleman.

John Ireland (Johnny), Ann Dvorak (Sue Younger), Henry Hull (Hank Younger), Hugh O'Brian (Lem), Reed Hadley (Frank James), Victor Kilian (Rigby), Byron Foulger (Bakin), Tom Noonan (Charley Ford), Clifton Young (Bob Ford). *With* Carleton Young, Barbara Woodell, Margia Dean, Sid Melton, Sam Flint, Robin Short, Paul Maxey, Earle Hodgins, I. Stanford Jolley, Hank Patterson.

Johnny, a small-time desperado, gets into the big time by teaming up with the former James gang headed by Hank Younger. Due to Johnny's strong resemblance to James, and the fact that the same James tactics are being used once again, the populace get the idea that James was never killed. This brings Frank James, now a respected citizen under a different name, into the picture to persuade Younger to discontinue the supposed James robberies. By this time, however, Johnny has other ideas on the subject, and these eventually lead to his death during a holdup.

"Slightly off the beaten track for a Lippert oater, *The Return of Jesse James* proves a successful experiment for the company. Original yarn by Carl K. Hittleman injects the needed action and includes some finely developed characters and a slight psychological overtone which holds interest."—*Variety*, September 9, 1950

Kansas Raiders
(Universal-International, 1950) 80 min.

Director: Ray Enright. Story/Screenplay: Robert L. Richards. Producer: Ted Richmond.

Audie Murphy (Jesse James), Brian Donlevy (Quantrill), Marguerite Chapman (Kate Clark), Scott Brady (Bill Anderson), Tony Curtis (Kit Dalton), Richard Arlen (Union Captain), Richard Long (Frank James), James Best (Cole Younger), John Kellogg (Red Leg Leader), Dewey Martin (James Younger), George Chandler (Willie). *With* Charles Delaney, Richard Egan, Dave Wolfe, Buddy Roosevelt, Jack Perrin, Ed Peil, Sr., Mira McKinney, Sam Flint, Larry McGrath.

In July 1865, five youths led by the very young Jesse James ride into Lawrence, Kansas, on their way to join Quantrill's guerrilla band. A captain in command of the Union forces holding the town saves the lads from being hanged by the citizens. At the Southerners' guerrilla camp, Quantrill accepts the recruits and, impressed by Jesse's bravery in a duel-to-the-death with one of the men, makes him a lieutenant. But on their first raid Jesse is shocked by the brutal killings and wanton destruction. Quantrill's housekeeper Kate advises him to leave the band and offers to go with him. On the next raid, Quantrill saves Jesse's life, and Jesse's loyalty for the leader keeps him with the raiders. Lawrence is taken, looted and burned. Union cavalry are searching for Quantrill and the band breaks up. Only Kate, Jesse and the lads stay with their leader, who has been blinded by gunfire. Eventually Quantrill throws away his life to force Jesse to escape with the others.

"The competent direction by Ray Enright sustains all the excitement in the raids and killings, brings out the human interest in the yarn, and gives his players every opportunity to display their acting abilities."—*Hollywood Reporter*, November 8, 1950

"Story and screenplay by Robert L. Richards are floundering affairs that would have had a lot more interest if developed along a straight line without attempting to explain Jesse James and Quantrill, its two principal characters. Both characters get a whitewash that doesn't make much sense as screened."—*Variety*, November 8, 1950

The James Brothers of Missouri
(Republic, January 1950) 12 chapters.

Director: Fred C. Brannon. Screenplay: Royal Cole, William Lively and Sol Shor. Assoc. Producer: Franklin Adreon. Photography: Ellis W. Carter. Music: Stanley Wilson. Special Effects: Howard and Theodore Lydecker.

Keith Richards (Jesse James, John Howard), Robert Bice (Frank James, Bob Carroll), Noel Neill (Peg Royer), Roy Barcroft (Ace Marlin), Patricia Knox (Belle Calhoun), Lane Bradford (Monk Tucker), Gene Stutenroth [Roth] (Rand), John Hamilton (Lon Royer), Edmund Cobb (Sheriff), Hank Patterson (Duffy), Dale Van Sickel (Harry Sharkey), Tom Steele (Slim, Drake), Nolan Leary (Pop Keever), Marshall Reed (Dutch), Lee Roberts (Brandy Jones), Frank O'Connor (Citizen), Wade Ray (Deputy), Duke Green Brad, Cowl), Ken Terrell (Stark, Trent), Tommy Coats, Robert Wilke, Ray Morgan (Townsmen), Post Parks (Wagoner), Hank Patterson (Waller), Cactus Mack, Al Ferguson, Ralph Bucko, Roy Bucko, Herman Hack (Heavies), Duke Taylor (Flint, Pete), Ray Morgan (Driver), Jim Rinehart (Davis), John Crawford (Carson), Art Dillard (Blears, Townsman), Dave Sharpe (Bailey), Joe Phillips (Jackson), Bert LeBaron (Price), Ted Hubert (Ed Thorne). *With* Forest Burns, Helen Griffith, Rocky Shahan, Frosty Royce, Chuck Roberson, Bud Wolfe, Chick Hannon.

Jesse and Frank James help Peggy Royer run a freight line after her brother, who was their friend, is killed by thugs employed by a rival freight line. After they finally bring about the downfall of the outlaws, a grateful marshal allows them to remain free.

CHAPTER TITLES

1. Frontier Renegades
2. Racing Peril
3. Danger Road
4. Murder at Midnight

5. Road to Oblivion
6. Missouri Manhunt
7. Hangman's Noose
8. Coffin on Wheels

9. Dead Man's Return
10. Galloping Gunslingers
11. The Haunting Past
12. Fugitive Code

Gunfire

(Lippert, 1950) 59 min.

Producer/Director: William Berke. Screenplay: Victor West and William Berke.

Don Barry (Frank James, Fenton), Robert Lowery (Marshal Kelly), Wally Vernon (Clem), Pamela Blake (Cynthy), Claude Stroud (Mundy), Leonard Penn (Simons), Gaylord [Steve] Pendleton (Charlie Ford), Tommy Farrell (Lerner), Dean Reisner (Cashier), Paul Jordon (James' son), Steve Conti (Riley), Roger Anderson (Bob Ford), Gill Fallman (Bank President), Kathleen Magginetti (James' daughter), Bill Bailey (Officer), Barbara Woodell (Mrs. James), Jane Adrian (Flo). *With* Charles King, Carol Henry, Lee Roberts, Dale Van Sickel.

Some time after the death of Jesse James, members of his band ask his brother Frank to lead a reorganized gang. When he refuses, Fenton, who is almost his double in appearance, takes over the job. The new James gang makes some rich hauls and everyone believes their leader is Frank James. Marshal Kelly, out to break up the gang, sees Frank and is convinced of his innocence. Frank rides out alone to kill the man who is impersonating him. One of the outlaws tries to mislead Clem, Kelly's deputy, about their hideout, while they rob the bank. But Kelly and a posse corner the gang in a shack where they are holding Cynthy as hostage. Kelly captures or kills the outlaws, while Frank James kills his double.

"The yarn is very contrived and some of the situations are entirely unconvincing, but there is enough excitement, ridin' and shootin' to help put it over with juveniles and action fans. William Berke as producer-director gives the film adequate sagebrush production values, and Ernest Miller's fine photography provides some pictorially beautiful footage. But Mr. Berke's direction is about on a par with the screenplay, and he resorts far too often to establishing the doings of the outlaws in newspaper headlines."—*Hollywood Reporter*, July 17, 1950

"*Gunfire* is more outdoor melodrama than oater and crowds a lot of characters into a short 59 minutes. Yarn brings back outlaw Frank James and features actionful lensing of the outdoor locales. It measures up as acceptable supporting fare for secondary situations."—*Variety*, July 19, 1950

Best of the Badmen
(RKO, 1951) 83 min.

Director: William D. Russell. Screenplay: Robert Hardy Andrews and John Twist. Story: John Twist. Producer: Samuel Bischoff.

Robert Ryan (Jeff Clanton), Claire Trevor (Lily Fowler), Jack Buetel (Bob Younger), Robert Preston (Matthew Fowler), Walter Brennan ("Doc" Butcher), Bruce Cabot (Cole Younger), John Archer (Curley Ringo), Lawrence Tierney (Jesse James), Tom Tyler (Frank James), Barton MacLane (Joad), Bob Wilke (Bob Younger), John Cliff (John Younger), Lee MacGregory (Lieutenant), Emmett Lynn (Oscar), Carleton Young (Wilson). *With* Byron Foulger, Harry Woods, Robert Kortman.

At the end of the Civil War, Jeff Clanton, Union officer, brings in a band of Confederate guerrillas with a promise of freedom if they take the oath of allegiance. Trouble starts when Matthew Fowler, a protection agency operator, attempts to take the prisoners for the reward money and frames a murder charge against Clanton.

Clanton is driven into outlawry. He joins up with the James brothers, the Younger brothers and Curley Ringo to launch a series of raids on banks under Fowler's protection. Lily Fowler, estranged wife of Matthew, joins with the outlaws to try to ruin Fowler. Along the way she falls in love with Clanton.

Windup of film sees Clanton ready to give up to the law so he can begin life anew with Lily, by now the widow of Fowler.

"This is indeed a robust number, cut from a standard pattern and bedecked with a sturdy cast. Moreover, all of the action, centering around an episode in the exploits of the James boys and the Younger brothers, is resplendently dressed in Technicolor, reputedly an important consideration in any calculation of a Western's box office possibilities."—*Motion Picture Daily*, May 3, 1951

"Credit for the quality of the flicker—aside from the fact that it has a terrifically competent cast—probably should go to director William D. Russell, who has never directed a western before. And maybe that's a good idea. A new boy might conceivably bring fresh, new ideas."—*L. A. Daily News*, June 15, 1951

"...follows the rather routine groove of outdoor settings and action, dressed in Technicolor, backing a plot that offers little unusual or dramatically worthy. Its chances are no better than average in the houses where such features rate their best playing time."—*Variety*, May 2, 1951

The Great Jesse James Raid
(Lippert, 1953) 73 min.

Director: Reginald LeBorg. Screenplay: Richard Landau. Producer: Robert L. Lippert, Jr.

Willard Parker (Jesse James), Barbara Payton (Kate), Tom Neal (Arch Clements), Wallace Ford (Elias Hobbs), James Anderson (Jorrette), Jim Bannon (Bob Ford), Richard Cutting (Sam Wells), Barbara Woodell (Zee), Mary Treen (Mrs. Angus), Earl Hodgins (Soapy Smith), Tom Walker (Jesse James as a Youth), Joann Arnold (Brunette), Helene Hayden (Redhead), Steve Pendleton (Todd), Bob Griffin (Morgan), Robin Morse (Anderson), Ed Russell (Sheriff), Rory Mallinson (Cavalry Officer). *With* Frank Ellis, Ray Jones, Ted Mapes, Fred Graham.

Bob Ford, a former partner of Jesse James, tries to enlist Jesse's help in a $300,000 gold dust robbery from a mine in Colorado. Jesse is living in Missouri under an assumed name when Ford comes to him with the proposition. Jesse supplies a gunman, a powder expert, and a getaway driver who accompany him to the scene of the proposed raid. Ford is planning a double-cross, tipping off the local townsmen to Jesse's identity. The whole gang is wiped out with the exception of Jesse and Ford, who get back to Missouri where they separate. Ford is obviously working on a plan to collect the reward money for Jesse.

"A 'retired' Jesse James agrees to join Bob Ford in stealing gold hidden in a closed mine tunnel. Tawdry melodrama made to get box office mileage out of the romance between plump Barbara Payton and Tom Neal, although neither has much to do in the proceedings."—*Western Movies*, 1986, p. 150

The Woman They Almost Lynched
(Republic, 1953) 90 min.

Director: Allan Dwan. Screenplay: Steve Fisher. Story: From the *Saturday Evening Post* story by Michael Fessler.

John Lund (Lance Horton), Brian Donlevy (Quantrill), Audrey Totter (Kate Quantrill), Joan Leslie (Sally Maris), Ben Cooper (Jesse James), James Brown (Frank James), Nina Varela (Delilah Courtney), Ellen Corby (First Woman), Fern Hall (Second Woman), Minerva Urecal (Mrs. Stuart), Jim Davis (Cole Younger), Reed Hadley (Bitterroot Bill), Ann Savage (Glenda), Virginia Christine (Jenny), Marilyn Lindsey (Rose), Nacho Galindo (John Pablo), Richard Simmons (Captain), Gordon Jones (Sergeant), Frank Ferguson (Bartender), Post Park (Driver), Tom McDonough (Quantrill's Henchman), Ted Ryan (Soldier), Richard Crane (Lieutenant), Carl Petti (Hangman), Joe Yrigoyen (Guard), Jimmie Hawkins (Boy), James Kirkwood (Old Man), Paul Livermore (Bill Anderson).

This Civil War yarn is set in Border City and deals with a feud between ladylike but accurate-shooting Sally Maris and Kate Quantrill, as mean and sadistic a wench as has reached the screen. They mix in a free-swinging brawl, with Sally beating the daylights out of Kate. This is followed by a rather ludicrous gun duel between the two which is more likely to arouse laughter than suspense. Then Sally saves her enemy from Union troops and Kate pulls a complete reversal, going soft and tearfully renouncing her villainy. Overshadowed by this is a good story of Confederate espionage.

"For its first 45 minutes it is ... a fine western filled with rousing action and well-motivated characters. But then the story goes to pieces, submerged by incredible character reversals. Allan Dwan's production is good and his direction is excellent, particularly in his staging of the action scenes which have a realistic quality that is genuinely exciting."—*Hollywood Reporter*, March 30, 1953

Jesse James vs. the Daltons
(Columbia, 1954) 65 min.

Director: William Castle. Screenplay: Robert E. Kent. Story: Edwin Eestrate. Producer: Sam Katzman.

Brett King, Barbara Lawrence, James Griffith, Bill Phipps, John Cliff, Rory Mallinson, William Tannen, Richard Garland, Nelson Leigh, Raymond Largay, Bud Osborne, Syd Saylor, Wally West, Norman Frederic.

Brett King suffers at the hands of society because he is believed to be the son of Jesse James. He rides into Coffeyville in time to rescue Barbara Lawrence from being lynched by a mob because she killed the son of the community's most respected citizen. Learning from King about his doubts about being the son of James, Barbara promises to help him. King believes James to still be alive and hopes to contact him through the Dalton brothers. The Daltons, however, prove to be inaccessible, and so King hits upon a new scheme to meet them. He holds up a train, quietly returning the robbed money to the president of the railroad, and gets himself declared a "wanted" man.

This device soon puts him in touch with the Daltons with whom he agrees to share his loot on the understanding that they should inform Jesse James that King was out to unearth $100,000 hidden by James. Accepting the deal, the Daltons try hard to lay their hands on the hidden money while one of them tries to lay his hands on Barbara in spite of King having declared her his wife. This leads to a fight in which King beats up the Dalton. After some frantic double-crossing, the Daltons force a friend of the James family, Rory Mallinson, to reveal to them the hidden money. The money turns out to be useless Confederate money. The Daltons feel cheated and tie up King and Mallinson and set out to rob Coffeyville's banks, with Barbara as their prisoner.

Mallinson informs King that he is not a son of Jesse James but is an orphan. The two men manage to free themselves and rush to Coffeyville to alert the citizens. Forewarned, the sheriff collects his men and they wipe out the Dalton gang. King prepares to marry Barbara.

"This is a typical disgusting blood-and-bullets-filled "Western" which deserves to be avoided by all. Violence and lawlessness being its only recognizable features, the picture should be given no room in India."—*Filmindia*, April 1954

"William Castle's megging is vigorous, the action scenes being forcefully handled. Lester H. White's effective lensing makes good use of the 3-D process."—*Variety*, January 22, 1954

"The combination of lively action and the kind of sharp shooting that oater fans like goes a long way toward covering a vague story with hazy motivations that consistently leave the viewer wondering what is going on. While the title of this Sam Katzman 3-D Technicolor opus leads one to suspect that, tired of shooting up the forces of law and order, the boys are now fighting among themselves, it is a misnomer, Jesse James failing to appear in the story."—*Hollywood Reporter*, January 22, 1954

Jesse James' Women
(United Artists, 1954) 83 min.

Director: Donald Barry. Screenplay: D. D. Beauchamp. Producer: Lloyd Royal and T. V. Garraway.

Don Barry (Jesse James), Jack Buetel (Frank James), Peggie Castle (Waco), Lita Baron (Delta), Joyce Rhed (Caprice Clark), Betty Brueck (Cattle Kate Kennedy), Laura Lee (Angel Botts), Sam Keller (Cole Younger)

Jesse and Frank James, along with cohorts, are on the lam in a small Mississippi town. In rapid succession Jesse is enamored of saloonkeeper Waco, songstress Delta, banker's daughter Caprice and cattle owner Kate. Taunted by his followers, he asserts he's merely using the femmes as a means of stealing enough coin to make the trek back west.

"Jesse James, Hollywood's favorite outlaw, has been depicted as a man of many faces and moods. Through the years he has been portrayed as a latter-day Robin Hood, a cold-blooded killer and a misunderstood farm boy who fell into bad company.

"In *Jesse James' Women* changeable old Jesse becomes an irresistible ladies' man. It is quite a lump to swallow after following him from Quantrill's

Don Barry played Jesse James, the ladies' man, in *Jesse James' Women* (United Artists, 1954). Here, he cuddles up to Lita Baron while Peggie Castle expresses disapproval.

Raiders to the modest living room where he was shot in the back. James, as played by Donald Barry, is such a lad with the lassies that the spectacle of a woman not falling into his arms at first glance is almost beyond belief." — *Los Angeles Times*, November 26, 1954

The True Story of Jesse James
(20th Century–Fox, 1957) 93 min.

Director: Nicholas Ray. Screenplay: Walter Newman (from a screenplay by Nunnally Johnson). Producer: Herbert B. Swope, Jr.

Robert Wagner (Jesse James), Jeffrey Hunter (Frank James), Hope Lange (Zee), Agnes Moorehead (Mrs. Samuels), Alan Hale (Cole Younger), Alan Baxter (Remington), John Carradine (Rev. Jethro Bailey), Rachel Stephens (Anne), Barney Phillips (Doctor Samuels), Biff Elliott (Jim Younger), Frank Overton (Major Cobb), Barry Atwater (Attorney Walker), Marian Seldes (Rowena Cobb), Chubby Johnson (Askew), Frank Gorshin (Charley), Carl Thayer (Robby), John Doucette (Hillstrom), Robert Adler (Sheriff Trump), Clancy Cooper

(Sheriff Voe), Sumner Williams (Bill Stiles), Tom Greenway (Deputy Leo), Mike Steen (Deputy Ed), Jason Wingreen (Peter), Aaron Saxon (Wiley), Anthony Ray (Bob Younger), Clegg Hoyt (Tucker), Tom Pittman (Hushie), Louis Zito (Clell Miller), Mark Hickman (Sam Wells), Adam Marshal (Dick Liddell), Joseph Di Reda (Bill Ryan), J. Frederik Albeck (Jorgenson).

The True Story of Jesse James explains why Jesse James became an outlaw in the post–Civil War years. Through many flashbacks, his story is told by both his friends and enemies.

The film's premise is that the James boys were forced outside the law by the antagonism of their neighbors in Missouri. The James family had been Confederates during the Civil War, a fact that caused their northern-sympathizing neighbors to persecute them after the conflict ended. Jesse planned just one robbery to get enough money so he and his fellow Confederates could face their farming futures with some confidence. The gist of the "true" account is that Jesse robbed at first because he felt he had to. Like many others, he came to like the means and forgot the end so he wound up robbing and wantonly killing because it satisfied some twisted urge within him. The picture ends as Robert Ford shoots Jesse as he is preparing to go straight.

"*The True Story of Jesse James* is a first-rate adventure story that gains freshness and novelty by a modern psychological approach to a historical problem. The picture has an excellent cast, and one that will appeal to younger fans, and Nicholas Ray's direction is analytical and well-paced, probing, and exciting."—*Hollywood Reporter*, February 15, 1957

"[T]he real star is a fellow named Nicholas Ray, the director. Profiting by his experience with *Johnny Guitar*, a prairie fiasco, he has admirably utilized his sprawling cast, the CinemaScope expense, and the very color itself. His keen-eyed staging imbues an obvious tale with a handsome, dynamic spaciousness and sweep that are often thrilling to watch."—*New York Times Index*, March 23, 1957

Tales of Wells Fargo
(NBC/Overland Productions, 1957) 30 min.
Segment entitled *Jesse James*

Dale Robertson

Hell's Crossroads
(Republic, 1957) 73 min.

Director: Franklin Adreon. Screenplay: John K. Butler, Barry Shipman. Story: John K. Butler. Producer: Rudy Ralston.

Stephen McNally (Vic Rodell), Peggie Castle (Paula Collins), Robert Vaughn (Bob Ford), Barton MacLane (Clyde O'Connell), Harry Shannon (Clay Ford), Henry Brandon (Jesse James), Douglas Kennedy (Frank James), Grant Withers (Sheriff Steve Oliver), Myron Healey (Cole Younger), Frank Wilcox (Governor Crittenden), Jean Howell (Mrs. Jesse James), Morris Ankrum (Wheeler).

Vic Rodell is a long-time friend of Jesse James and a member of his gang. However, he decides to give up his life of crime so that he can marry Paula Collins. Another member of the gang wanting to give it all up is Bob Ford. Paula is instrumental in getting the governor to promise to grant them a pardon if either of them brings in Jesse James—dead or alive. Ford shoots Jesse in the back, the pardons are granted and Vic is able to settle down with Paula.

"The James boys, Bob Ford and the Younger brothers are among the outlaws romping through *Hell's Crossroads*. The basic storyline holds little interest, however, so it all shapes up as a below-par programmer. ... Acting runs along acceptable lines, newcomer Robert Vaughn making the best impression. Showing up well, too, as Jesse James, is Henry Brandon."— *Variety*, May 16, 1957

Cole Younger, Gunfighter
(Allied Artists, 1958) 78 min.

Director: R. G. Springsteen. Story: Clifton Adams. Screenplay: Daniel Mainwarning. Producer: Ben Schwalb.

Frank Lovejoy (Cole Younger), James Best (Kit Caswell), Abby Dalton (Lucy), Jan Merlin (Frank), Ainslee Pryor (Follyard), Myron Healey (Phil Bennett), George Keymas (Price). *With* Douglas Spencer, Frank Ferguson, Dan Sheridan, John Mitchum.

Texas in 1873 is under the oppressive rule of Governor E. J. Davis and his state police, the "Bluebellies." Kit Caswell and his friend Frank are thrown in jail for taking part in a demonstration. They manage to escape and meet up with Cole Younger. Frank returns to town to turn Younger in but Kit stays with Younger.

Kit and Younger meet Phil Bennett, who tells Kit that his father has been killed by the Bluebellies. Kit returns to seek revenge. He is stopped from killing Follyard and Price by the sudden appearance of Younger. They disarm the pair and ride off. Frank, who has been hiding under the table, shoots Follyard and Price in cold blood.

This crime is blamed on Kit. He writes Lucy to meet him in Abilene, but the letter is intercepted by Frank, who tips off the state police as to Kit's whereabouts. Kit is brought back to face trial for the killings, and Frank

Frank Lovejoy (left) is *Cole Younger, Gunfighter* (Allied Artists, 1958); James Best is Kit Caswell.

testifies against him. Again Younger comes to Kit's rescue and forces Frank to tell the truth. Kit and Lucy are reunited, while Younger rides off alone.

"The story moves along well enough to satisfy grownup action fans, and won't give the youngsters any nightmares."—*Film Daily*, April 2, 1958

Alias Jesse James
(United Artists, 1959) 92 min.

Director: Norman McLeod. Screenplay: D. D. Beauchamp and William Bowers. Story: Robert St. Aubrey and Bert Lawrence. Producer: Jack Hope.

Bob Hope (Milford Farnsworth), Rhonda Fleming (Cora Lee Collins), Wendell Corey (Jesse James), Jim Davis (Frank James), Gloria Talbott (Indian Maiden), Will Wright (Titus Queasley), Mary Young ("Ma" James). *With* Glenn Strange, Dick Alexander, Roy Rogers, Gail Davis, Gary Cooper, Bing Crosby, Michael Whalen, George E. Stone, Hugh O'Brian, James Arness, Mike Mazurki, Mickey Finn, Bob Gunderson, Fred Kohler, Jr., Ethan Laidlaw, Sid Melton, I. Stanford Jolley, Ward Bond, Jay Silverheels, Fess Parker, James Garner.

Milford Farnsworth is a cowardly, greenhorn insurance salesman who has made the mistake of selling Jesse James an insurance policy, with Jesse's girl Cora Lee Collins as beneficiary. Jesse gets the idea of substituting Milford for himself. Milford will then be killed, and Jesse will collect the insurance money along with Cora Lee. Milford fights back and with the help of every TV lawman in the West wipes out the whole James gang.

"This is a fair enough premise for the kind of gags and situations that Hope can play off his left hand. Unfortunately not enough script has been given him for even one finger of the left hand, and the result is an extremely mild comedy that will find fans only among the staunchest Hope adherents." — *Variety*, March 18, 1959

Bronco
(Warner Bros. TV) 52 min.
A segment entitled *The Shadow of Jesse James*
First Air Date: 1/12/60

Ty Hardin (Bronco), James Coburn (Jesse James), Jeanne Cooper (Belle Starr), Richard Coogan (Cole Younger).

Young Jesse James
(20th Century–Fox, 1960) 73 min.

Director: William Claxton, Screenplay: Orville H. Hampton and Jerry Sackheim. Producer: Jack Leewood.

Ray Stricklyn (Jesse James), Willard Parker (Cole Younger), Merry Anders (Belle Starr), Robert Dix (Frank James), Emile Meyer (Quantrill), Jacklyn O'Donnell (Zerelda), Rayford Barnes (Pitts), Rex Holman (Zack), Bob Palmer (Bob Younger), Sheila Bromley (Mrs. Samuels), Johnny O'Neill (Jim Younger), Leslie Bradley (Major Turnbull), Norman Leavitt (Folsom), Lee Kendall (Jennison).

The formative years of the outlaw Jesse James are examined in this film from a psychological perspective.

Having witnessed the hanging of his stepfather by Union soldiers, young Jesse James leaves his sweetheart, Zerelda Mimms, and his mother, and rides off to join Quantrill. Jesse's brother Frank is already a member of the group. Although dubious of the youth's ability, Quantrill lets Jesse join his band. Frank's cousin Cole Younger is also a member and is extremely wary of Jesse's hotheaded disposition.

An attack on a Union ammunition dump is planned by Quantrill to cover a raid on Union supply wagons. Frank captures the wagons and some prisoners, among whom is the Union soldier who hung Jesse's stepfather. In a hate-filled moment, Jesse guns the unarmed soldier down, to Frank and Cole's disgust. Later, during a raid on a jail to release Zack, Jesse kills the sheriff without cause. Cole sees Jesse becoming more and more like Quantrill every day.

During a raid, Jesse is thrown from his horse and breaks an ankle. Cole takes him to the home of one of his old flames, Belle Starr. Jesse proves to be an ungrateful patient while Cole finds the old romance rekindled. In talking to Belle about the war situation, Cole decides to leave Quantrill.

Back in camp, Jesse finds that Zee has been captured and is being attacked by Zack. Jesse kills him, has a run-in with Quantrill and returns home with Zee. There he finds his mother hurt. His old bitterness returns. After being shot by a trigger-happy soldier, Jesse marries Zee from his bedside while he is recuperating from his wounds.

Frustrated that they can't get the old farm going again, Frank and Jesse join Cole for a series of bank robberies. On their way to the holdup, Jesse doesn't know that the United States has granted him a full pardon for his wartime activities. The holdup has barely begun when Jesse kills the bank manager. The gang flees town, leaving Jim Younger and two other outlaws dead. Outside of town, Cole makes it plain he doesn't want the kill-crazy Jesse in the gang anymore. As Jesse rides off, Frank realizes that blood is thicker than water and rides after him.

"...western fans and aficionados of JJ's cantankerous career will find little to grow enthused over in Jack Leewood's production. Mrs. James' son, Jesse, has, through overexposure, become a caricature of himself. It is an easy matter now for an educated audience to anticipate his reactions—an element of familiarity that ought to curb future filmland inclinations to tackle the hackneyed story."—*Variety*, August 10, 1960

The Outlaws Is Coming
(Columbia, 1965)

The Three Stooges, printers in the Old West, contend with a number of real-life lawmen and outlaws. See full writeup on page 43.

The Legend of Jesse James
(ABC Television, 1965-1966) 30 min.
26 Episodes.

Chris Jones (Jesse James), Allen Case (Frank James), Robert J. Wilke (Sheriff Sam Corbett), Ann Doran (Mrs. James [first episode]).

Avenging their mother's death, Frank and Jesse James strike and rob the Great Western Railroad and attempt to return rightful property to the survivors of innocent victims.

Jesse James Meets Frankenstein's Daughter
(Embassy, 1966) 82 min.

Director: William Beaudine. Story/Screenplay: Carl K. Hittleman. Producer: Carroll Case.

John Lupton (Jesse James), Cal Bolder (Hank Tracy, Igor), Narda Onyx (Maria Frankenstein), Steven Geray (Rudolph Frankenstein), Felipe Turich (Nina), Estelita Rodriguez (Juanita), Jim Davis (Marshal McFee), Rayford Barnes (Lonny), William Fawcett (Jensen). *With* Page Slattery, Nestor Paiva, Dan White, Roger Creed, Fred Stromsoe, Mark Norton.

In escaping from a posse, Jesse James and Hank Tracy, a wounded member of his gang, obtain aid from Juanita, a young Mexican señorita who leads them to an ancient mission inhabited by the grandchildren of the original Doctor Frankenstein. In Jesse's absence, Maria performs a brain operation on Hank and transforms him into Igor, a monster somewhat like the one her grandfather created many years before. When Jesse returns, Igor no longer recognizes him as his friend and knocks him out. Maria prepares to perform a similar operation on Jesse. However, Juanita arrives with Marshal McFee and both Igor and Maria are killed. Jesse is taken in by the marshal, but Juanita promises to wait for him.

Hondo
(MGM TV/Batjac Prod.) 52 min.
A segment entitled *Hondo and the Judas*
First Airdate: 11/3/67

Asso. Producer/Story: Andrew J. Fenady. Director: Lee H. Katzin. Teleplay: Frank Chase.

Ralph Taeger (Hondo), Rick Nelson (Jesse James), John Agar (Frank James), Forrest Tucker (William Cantrell), Roger Perry (Johnny Ringo), Roy Jenson (Bob Ford), Fritz Ford (Charlie Ford), Kip Whitman (Jim Younger), Richard Bakalyan (Cole Younger), John Carradine, John Crawford, Ken Mayer, Charles Maxwell.

The Intruders
(Universal, November 10, 1970) 120 min.

Director: William A. Graham. Teleplay: Dean Riesner. Story: William Lansford.

Don Murray (Sam Garrison), Anne Francis (Leora Garrison), Edmond O'Brien (Colonel William Bodeen), John Saxon (Billy Pye), Gene Evans (Cole Younger), Edward Andrews (Elton Dykstra), Shelly Novack (Theron Pardo), Dean Stanton (Whit Dykstra), Stuart Margolin (Jesse James), Zalman King (Bob Younger). *With* Phillip Alford, John Hoyt, Harrison Ford, Marlene Tracy, Ken Swofford, Robert Donner, Edward Faulkner, James Gammon, Gavin MacLeod, Len Wayland, Mickey Sholdar, Kay E. Kuter, Ted Gehring, Robert P. Lieb, William Phipps.

A Western town is in crisis as the James-Younger gang rides in, and the local marshal, having lost both his nerve and his skill with a pistol, is put to the test. Originally this was to have been titled *Death Dance at Madelia*.

A Time for Dying

(Fipco, 1969) 67 min.
Not released until 1982 and then only briefly.

Producer: Audie Murphy. Director/Story/Screenplay: Budd Boetticher. Photographer: Lucien Ballard. Music: Harry Betts. Editor: Harry Knapp.

Richard Lapp (Cass Bunning), Anne Randall (Nellie Winters), Bob Random (Billy Pimple), Beatrice Kay (Mamie), Victor Jory (Judge Roy Bean), Audie Murphy (Jesse James), Willard Willingham (Frank James), J. N. Roberts (Bob Ford), Ron Masak (Bartender), Walter Reed (Mayor), Walt LaRue (Shotgun), Burt Mustin (Ed), Peter Brocco (Seth), Louis Ojena (Blacksmith), Maria Desti, Betty Rowland, Tina Stuart, Joannie Shields, Miki McDonald, Darla Paris, Arlette Thomas, Nancy Lewis, Athena, Jo Linn, Suzette DeCarlo (Mamie's Girls), Annette Gorman (Mamie's New Girl), Charles Wagenheim (Milton), Ira Angustain (Pepe), Terry Murphy (Sonny), Skip Murphy (Curly), Randy Shields (Cauliflower), Bob Herron (Rankin), William Bassett (The Southerner), Casey Tibbs (Sidekick to Jesse), Dick Spangler, Robert Grever (Sidekicks to Billy).

Audie Murphy's role as Jesse James is a cameo one, major roles being filled by Richard Lapp as a would-be gunfighter, Victor Jory as the nasty, self-appointed judge of the "one-dog" town of Vinegaroon, Anne Randall as a prostitute and Bob Randon as a young punk hoping to make a name for himself as a fast gun.

Director Budd Boetticher built a reputation as a western director with the Randolph Scott vehicles *Seven Men from Now* (1956), *The Tall T* (1957), *Decision at Sundown* (1957), *Buchanan Rides Alone* (1958), *Ride Lonesome* (1959), *Westbound* (1959), and *Comanche Station* (1960); as a group they are the best westerns of the 1950s.

Author Jim Kitses (*Horizons West*, Cinema One Series, 1969) writes that Boetticher had his hand in every detail from original script to final cut of the film and that it is more studied in its play of formal and dramatic elements than many of his earlier works. Thus, the film describes a perfect circle for all of its principals: the aspiring gunfighter Cass dying outside the brothel from which he saves Nellie at the outset; Nellie herself returned again alone, to the setting she had fled; Billy Pimple with his reputation intact rides out of town. Victor Jory as a bitterly farcical Judge Roy Bean pretty well steals the film.

"Pic is a terse, compact western that takes a solid look at violence of post–Civil War days as seen through the early death of a young farm boy out to become a bounty hunter. No heroics, but a paredown, succinct handling of story, mood and atmosphere…. It is an offbeat oater that should get critical attention."—*Variety*, October 6, 1971

"Both Murphy and Boetticher had long backgrounds in movie-making, but, almost incredibly, they wound up with a feature picture that was too short in running time. Around $800,000 was invested in the 'negative costs' without a guaranteed release by a major studio."—*Films and Career of Audie Murphy*, 1996, p. 163

"Boetticher's great quality has always been his narrative power, in particular his realization of strong characters, a firm foundation on which he could play creatively. *A Time for Dying* departs sharply from Boetticher's traditional terrain in concentrating on a love story. And the film fails finally because his quirky hero and the surprisingly hard Nellie at the center of the action never truly marry. The looseness flows less from its cameoed villains than from the failure of its heart to come alive."—*Horizons West*, pp. 129–30

The Great Northfield, Minnesota Raid
(Universal, 1972) 91 min.

Director/Screenplay: Philip Kaufman. Producer: Jennings Lang.

Cliff Robertson (Cole Younger), Robert Duvall (Jesse James), Luke Askew (Jim Younger), R. G. Armstrong (Clell Miller), Dana Elcar (Allen), Donald Moffat (Manning), John Pearce (Frank James), Matt Clark (Bob Younger), Wayne Sutherlin (Charley Pitts), Robert H. Harris (Wilcox), Jack Manning (Heywood), Elisha Cook Jr. (Banker), Royal Dano (Gustavson), Mary Robin Redd (Kate), Bill Calloway (Calliopist), Arthur Peterson (Jefferson Jones), Craig Curtis (Chadwell), Barry Brown (Henry Wheeler), Nellie Burt (Doll Woman), Liam Dunn (Drummer), Madeleine Taylor Holmes (Granny Woman), Herbert Nelson (Chief Detective), Jack Manning (Landlord), Erik Holland (Sheriff), Anna Barton (Clell's Wife), Marjorie Durant (Maybelle), Inger Stratton (Singing Whore), Velda J. Hansen (Nude Girl), William Challee (Old Timer), Robert Gravage (Farmer).

Cliff Robertson (left) as Cole Younger and Robert Duvall as Jesse James in *The Great Northfield Minnesota Raid* (Universal, 1972).

The Great Northfield, Minnesota Raid is a Western which attempts to humanize famous outlaws Cole Younger and Jesse James. The film follows them and their gang as they plan and execute an ill-fated bank robbery in Minnesota.

"...utter lack of sustained narrative, confused and inept writing, overabundance of characters difficult for ready identification, often apparent indecision whether to make this drama or comedy, and a mishmash of irrelevant sequences which combine to give chief protagonists the impossible task of trying to make sense out of their roles."—*Variety*, April 12, 1972

The Long Riders

(United Artists, 1980) 100 min.

Director: Walter Hill. Screenplay: Bill Bryden, Steven Smith, Stacy Keach and James Keach. Producer: Tim Zinnemann. Music: Ry Cooder.

David Carradine (Cole Younger), Keith Carradine (Jim Younger), Robert Carradine (Bob Younger), James Keach (Jesse James), Stacey Keach (Frank James), Dennis Quaid (Ed Miller), Randy Quaid (Clell Miller), Kevin Brophy (John Younger) Harry Carey, Jr. (George

Preparing to rob the bank in Northfield, the James gang looks nervously down toward the town in *The Long Riders* (United Artists, 1980). Left to right: David Carradine, Randy Quaid, Stacy Keach, James Keach, and Keith Carradine. This film used brother actors to portray real-life brothers.

Arthur), Christopher Guest (Charlie Ford), Nicholas Guest (Bob Ford), Shelby Leverington (Anne Ralston), Felice Orlandi (Mr. Reddick), Pamela Reed (Belle Starr), James Remer (Sam Starr), Fran Ryan (Mrs. Samuel), Savannah Smith (Zee), Amy Stryker (Beth), James Whitmore, Jr. (Mr. Rixley), John Bottoms (Mortician), West Buchanan (McCorkindale).

The Long Riders comes close to being the most accurate chronicle of the James-Younger Gang filmed thus far. The film starts at the height of the Gang's activities. Most of the populace of Missouri and surrounding states have some respect for the gang's continued fight against the North. Their main opposition comes from the Pinkerton Detective Agency. The film is partly a study in different styles of gallantry.

The Long Riders gives Western fans a fast, rough ride for their money, telling its story with the elemental directness and vigor of a Colt .45 at ten paces. The old gambling, boozing, boasting, shooting, fighting type of Western that more or less went out of style with the production of such adult Westerns as *High Noon* (1952) and *Shane* (1953) is back in full cry in this boisterous film. Deep characterization and accurate history are discarded as director Hill and his writers buck the tendency of current Westerns to be concerned withi psychological and sociological motivations.

The Long Riders scores with its ability to sustain interest and suspense, as well as its abundant action. It is worth noting that the film lacks the proverbial clinch or happy ending.

It's a big-time Western, a bit fuzzy in the story department but otherwise rigorous, convincing adventure fare. The script is inclined to go overboard somewhat, attempting to weave too many threads into one, making for more compl;ications and longer running time than are really necessary. The failed bank robbery at Northfield and the killing of Jesse by Bob Ford will keep audiences excitedly gulping their popcorn, even though they know what the outcome will be.

Hill's ace craftsmen are responsible for high-grade technical attainments.

"There are ... great moments scattered like buckshot throughout even the last part of the film. In the spectacular final gunfight, the bodies reel in slow motion at each bullet's impact. This is the most visceral depiction yet of what it meant to be hit by a bullet at a time when you could sustain five or six shots—and live. Cole Younger himself survived 11 bullets in the Northfield raid. The sound of the bullets, too, goes into slo-mo, their whiz becoming an other-worldly, buzzing death knell."—Michael Bragow, "A Wild Bunch of Good Ol' Boys," *Los Angeles Herald Examiner*, May 16, 1980

"...striking in several ways, not the least of which being the casting of actor brothers as historical kin, but narrative is episodic in the extreme and disparate artistic qualities fail to completely jell into satfisfactory whole. ... What is ultimately missing is hardly style, but a definable point of view which would tie together the myriad events on display.... Only character which noticeably changes over pic's duration is Jesse James, who becomes something of an authoritarian dandy with his increased celebrity."—*Variety*, May 7, 1980

"Yet another retelling of the sordid exploits of the Younger-James gang is detailed in this visually gripping Western. Director Walter Hill brought this property to the screen with great care for period authenticity, although its historical merits are a bit dubious."—Parish and Pitts, *The Great Western Pictures II*

Belle Starr
(Hanna-Barbera/CBS-TV, April 20, 1980) 100 min.

Director: John A. Alonza. Teleplay: James Lee Barrett. Producer: Doug Chapin.

Elizabeth Montgomvery played *Belle Starr* in the 1980 Hanna-Barbera/CBS-TV production, which featured Cliff Potts as Cole Younger and Michael Cavanaugh as Jesse James.

Elizabeth Montgomery (Belle Starr), Cliff Potts (Cole Younger), Michael Cavanaugh (Jesse James), Fred Ward (Ned Christie), Jesse Vint (Bob Dalton), Alan Vint (Grat Dalton), Gary Combs (Frank James), Geoffrey Lewis (Reverend Weeks), Sandy McPeak (Pratt), David Knell (Ed Reed), Geno Silva (Blue Duck), Michelle Stacy (Pearl Younger), Peter Hobbs (Jenkins), Morgan Paull (Latham), Sarah Cunningham (Mrs. Chandler), Stony Bower (Summerville), Burt Edwards (Bank Manager), James Burke (Fuller), Dee Cooper (Morris), Gilbert Combs (Baggage Clerk), Kate Williams (Woman), John Edwards (Stockyard Clerk).

"Belle Starr (real name: Myra Belle Shirley, 1848–1889), one of the legends of the Old West, dipped into cattle rustling and was the girl friend of Cole Younger. Hardly an attractive woman, Belle Starr has been glamorized on screen and has shown up in a number of features…"—James Robert Parish and Michael R. Pitts, *The Great Western Pictures II*, pp. 31–32

The Last Days of Frank and Jesse James
(NBC-TV, 1986) 100 min.

Director: William Graham. Teleplay: William Stratton. Producer: Phillip Cates.

Johnny Cash (Frank James), Kris Kristofferson (Jesse James), Ed Bruce (Major Edwards), Gail Youngs (Anna Young), David Allen Coe (Whiskeyhead Ryan), Andy Stahl (Dick Liddil), June Carter Cash (Mother James), Willie Nelson (General Jo Shelby), Marcia Cross (Sarah Hite), Darrell Wilks (Bob Ford), Margaret Gibson (Zee James), James Sinclair (Charlie Ford), Charie Elledge Grapes (Martha Bolton), Peter Bradshaw (Peter Hite), Earl Pooderall (Squire Farnum), Jack Barlow (Uncle George Hite), Mac Bennett (Clarence Hite), John Brown (Gentleman), Dan Butler (New York Reporter), Glen Clark (Angry Man), David Cobb (Dr. Samuel), Bruce Darnham (Sedalia Reporter), Ed Evans (Governor Tom Crittenden), Marshal Falwell (Jim Ward), Buck Ford (William Pinkerton), Donnie Fritts (Jury Foreman), Lucille Harris (Bartender), Mary Jane Herrill (Actress), Dan Hoffman (Conductor Westfall), John Jay Hecker, Jr. (John Phillip), Slick Lawson (Ed Kelly), William Newman (Sheriff Timberlake), John Jackson Routh (Jesse at age 3), Jimmy Tittle (Jim McDaniels), Denis Tucker (Bud McDaniels), Charlie Williams (Judge).

The story opens with the shooting of Jesse James by gang member Bob Ford. Then, in flashbacks, the story turns back to 1877 when Frank and Jesse James decide to retire and lead normal lives. Frank assumes the name Bob Woodson and becomes a farmer while Jesse calls himself John Davis Howard and attempts domesticity, which is harder for him than it is for Frank. The brothers cannot shake the outlaw life and soon organize their gang and continue their outlaw life until Jesse is killed.

"The adventures of Jesse and Frank James have been recounted on film numerous times and yet another airing of the good and bad times of the famous outlaws seemed a bit superfluous. Overall, though, this TV film sustains interest. With the catchlines 'The Most Wanted Men in the West. By the law ... and by the ladies,' this production pegs its appeal to country music stars in the lead assignments."—James Robert Parish and Michael R. Pitts, *The Great Western Pictures II*

The Untold West
(TBS, December 13, 1993) 60 min.
Narrator: Lou Diamond Phillips

Bonanza: Under Attack
(NBC, 1995)

Director: Mark Tinker. Story: Dennie Bart. Producer: Kent McCroy.

Ben Johnson (Bronc), Leonard Nimoy (Frank James), Jack Elam (Buckshot). *With* Michael Landon, Jr., Dennis Farina, Dirk Blocker, Emily Warfield, Richard Roundtree, James Karen.

Frank James, wounded and chased by Pinkerton detectives, takes refuge on the Ponderosa, having fought in the Civil War with Bronc and Buckshot.

Pinkertons capture Josh and two of the Cartwrights. Captain Sirango demands that James be turned over to the Pinkertons or they will kill Josh; however, Bronc is able to outsmart them and Josh is freed. In the end, Frank rides away free of pursuit.

Frank and Jesse
(HBO, Trimark Pictures, 1995)

Director/Teleplay: Robert Boris. Producer: Rob Lowe, Andrew Hersh, Cassian Elwes and Elliott Kastner. Exec. Producer: Mark Amin.

Rob Lowe (Jesse James), Bill Paxton (Frank James), Randy Travis (Cole Younger), William Atherton (Alan Pinkerton). *With* Dana Wheeler-Nicholson, Maria Pitillo, Luke Askew, Alexis Arquette, Sean Patrick Flanery, Todd Field, John Pyper-Ferguson, Nick Sadler, Tom Chick, Mary Neff, Richard Maynnard, Jim Floeers, Mari Askew, William Michael Evans, Lyle Armstrong, Cole McKey, Dennis Lettis, John Stiritz, Micah Dyer, Jackie Stewart, Chad Linley, Rhed Khilling, Jerry Saunders, D. C. (Dash) Goff, Robert Moniot, Norman Hawley, Jeffrey Paul Johnson, Bryce Anthony Thomason, John Paxton, Elizabeth Hatcher-Travis, Sudie Henson, Cole McKay.

The film offers a provocative angle on the story of the James brothers, placing responsibility for the outlaws' behavior directly on the North's treatment of the South following the Civil War

"Boris' approach undercuts much of the delight audiences derive from Western heroes (or antiheroes) raidin', ridin' and takin'. Fair enough. Deconstructing the Western is all the rage. Yet telling it from the James' p.o.v. is one thing—turning Jesse into a martyred Christ figure is going a bit too far."—John McCarthy, *Daily Variety*, April 26, 1995

Dr. Quinn, Medicine Woman
[An untitled episode]
(CBS-TV, February 25, 1995) 60 min.

Director: Jerome London, Producer: Timothy Johnson, Created by Beth Sullivan.

Jane Seymour (Dr. Quinn), Joe Lando (Sully), Melissa Clayton (Belle Starr), Oscar Bean (Loren Bray), Chad Allen (Matthew), Jonelle Allen (Dorothy), Shawn Toovey (Brian), Jessica Bowman (Colleen). *With* Barbara Babcock, William Shockley.

Belle Starr, age 14, is shot from her horse when she and two male companions, Jim and Cole Younger, attempt to rob the town bank. The Younger brothers escape, and Dr. Quinn assumes responsibility for Belle, against the wishes of most of the townsfolk.

Dr. Quinn and her adopted daughter Colleen come close to rehabilitating the young bandit but because of the actions of the town's troublemakers, the saloon keeper and the barber, Belle is compelled to ride away with Jim and Cole in the end to pursue her life of crime.

Although this is an entertaining segment in the "Dr. Quinn" teleseries, there is nothing factual about the story.

3

The Dalton-Doolin Gang

The Dalton brothers of Oklahoma achieved immortal fame in the world of Western outlawry when they attempted to rob two Coffeyville, Kansas, banks simultaneously in 1892. Cousins of the more famous Younger brothers, their saga has intrigued both Western history buffs and cinema fans.

Adeline Younger Dalton, a devout Christian lady and wife of Louis Dalton, a saloonkeeper-farmer, gave birth to 15 children. All were born in Missouri. The family ultimately moved to the Indian Territory and for a time lived near the border of Kansas, a few miles from Coffeyville. Little is known about the brothers' youth. It can be assumed that they led the lives of typical farm boys. Mrs. Dalton did her best to see that her children received religious instruction. Perhaps she did a pretty good job, considering the fact that only four of her brood went bad.

The first of the Dalton boys to die with his boots on was Frank, a deputy marshal working under the famed hanging judge, Isaac Parker. Frank had an excellent reputation as an honest lawman and normally was very careful to protect himself. However, his luck ran out when he was killed in a gun battle with several gents he attempted to arrest for whiskey running.

Grat, Bob and Emmett also became lawmen, even though Bob and Emmett were still in their teens. They served briefly as law enforcers in the Osage Nation and surrounding areas. They became dissatisfied when their pay was not forthcoming for months at a time. Grat was dismissed for action unbecoming a lawman when he forced a scared Negro boy to stand while he shot an apple off his head. Grat thought it was funny; his superiors didn't. He trekked off to California where his brothers Bill and Littleton lived. Bob and Emmett were fired when they stepped outside the law to rustle cattle. There was talk of their holding up a faro game in New Mexico when they thought they had been cheated. Bob soon followed Grat to California. There he, Grat, Bill and a fourth (unknown) bandit held up a train. The date was February 6, 1891. Things went sour and Grat and Bill were arrested while Bob escaped. In court, Bill was cleared but Grat was convicted and sentenced to 20 years in prison. However, he served very little of that sentence.

Bob Dalton and Eugenia Moore, 1889. Studio portrait by Fowler of Vinita, Indian Territory. (Courtesy Western History Collections, University of Oklahoma Library.)

Escaping, he made a bee-line for Oklahoma. Bob had already joined Emmett, who had prepared a crude dugout hideaway for the boys to use whenever necessary.

Although Grat was the oldest, it was Bob who had the necessary leadership qualities. Emmett was the youngest, not yet 21. The old adage about blood being thicker than water was exemplified by the brothers, who were extremely loyal to each other. Their gang was composed of Bill Doolin (perhaps the smartest of the lot), Bill Powers, Dick Broadwell, George Newcomb, Charles Bryant, Bill McElhanie and Charley Pierce. The gang was aided by Bob's girlfriend Eugenia Moore, who posed as a newspaper writer and squeezed information out of railroad officials, and by Julia Johnson, Emmett's girl.

Frank Dalton, deputy U.S. marshal, age 28. (Courtesy Western History Collections, University of Oklahoma Library.)

The gang was quite elusive and managed to outsmart lawmen or to extricate themselves from ticklish situations. After a number of successful train holdups, the gang was eager to try a bank holdup—not just one but two simultaneously! It seemed a good idea at the time. After all, the banks were only the width of a street apart. In their minds it was to be the last holdup by the Dalton brothers before disbanding the gang. Bob, Grat and Emmett wanted to give up their life of crime; the others could do what they wished. The foray would eclipse anything ever attempted by the James or Younger brothers. Even after the haul was split, there would be enough for each of the gang members to put aside outlawry and start their lives anew. Emmett had a desire to marry Julia Johnson and settle down somewhere to farm. Bob and Grat thought they would like to go to South America for a while. Bill Doolin was harboring the idea of starting his own gang. Powers and Broadwell kept their future plans to themselves.

On the morning of October 5, 1892, the gang proceeded to Coffeyville,

Left to right: The bodies of Bill Powers ("Tom Evans"), Bob Dalton, Grat Dalton and Dick Brodwell ("Texas Jack") after the Coffeyville shootout. (Courtesy Archives & Manuscripts Division, Oklahoma Historical Society.)

where the robbery turned into a major disaster. Part of the gang was to hold up one bank while the rest of the gang held up the bank across the street. Things quickly went awry, as the outlaws were recognized before they could exit the banks. The street gunfight that followed proved to be far more exciting than the Wyatt Earp shoot-out at the O.K. Corral in Tombstone. Killed were Bob and Grat Dalton, Bill Powers, and Dick Broadwell. Four Coffeyville citizens were killed and three others wounded. Emmett had a chance of escaping with a bag containing $21,000 even though he was badly wounded himself. However, brotherly love would not let him ride away if there was a chance of saving Bob or Grat. He hesitated to pick up the dying Bob, was hit in the back with buckshot and went down. He lingered near death for weeks. Once recovered, he was sentenced to life imprisonment and entered the Kansas State Penitentiary in 1893 at the age of 21. Fourteen years later, at the age of 35, he was pardoned. Julia Johnson faithfully waited for him and they were married. Emmett became a model citizen. At the time of his death on July 13, 1937, he was 73 years of age and living in Los Angeles.

The saga of the Daltons was not yet complete. Bill Dalton, who had been in on the California train robbery with Bob and Grat, organized his own gang shortly after the Coffeyville massacre. (He had been pressured to give up his seat in the California legislature because of the bad publicity generated by his brothers.) He quickly engraved the Dalton name deep into the annals of the Old West, soon becoming the most prominent of the Dalton brothers.

Though most historians have assumed Bill returned to Indian Territory to begin his reign of lawlessness after the death of his brothers, historian Harrell McCullough (*Selden Lindsey*, Paragon Publishers, 1994) thinks otherwise. A leading authority on Bill Dalton, his thoughts are not to be taken lightly. He says that Dalton returned to Indian Territory about a year before the Coffeyville holdup and that prior to that time he was secretly a member of his brothers' gang while posing as a law-abiding citizen, a pose that he continued for a period after Coffeyville.

Bill Doolin, who backed out of the Coffeyville caper at the last minute, joined forces with Dalton upon his return to

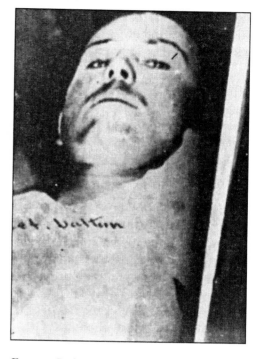

Emmett Dalton after being wounded 21 times in the Coffeyville fight; he lived another 43 years. (Courtesy Western History Collections, University of Oklahoma Library.)

Indian Territory. Others in the newly-formed gang included "Arkansas Tom," "Dynamite Dick," Bran Miller, "Bitter Creek" Newcomb, Jim Wallace, "Big Asa" and Jim Nite.

The gang was on their good behavior with the citizens of the small town of Ingalls, where they often went for rest and relaxation. When Federal lawmen learned of this, they kept a close watch over the hamlet. When the Dalton gang again hit town, the lawmen slipped in hidden in a covered wagon. They outnumbered the gang 13 to five and had the element of surprise. However, in the gunfight that ensued three deputy marshals and one bystander were killed, others wounded. "Arkansas Tom" was captured but the rest of the Dalton gang shot their way out of the ambush with only Bill Doolin and "Bitter Creek" slightly wounded.

Three days later the gang held up a train at Mound Valley, Kansas. The Pawnee, Indian Territory Farmers and Citizens Bank was next on the agenda. Shortly thereafter Dalton and Doolin stole $6,500 from the train depot in Woodward, O.T. Mill Creek, I.T., Clarkson, I.T., Cushing, I.T., Stillwater, I.T. and other banks, trains, or towns were hit, with Dalton and associates always winning fights with lawmen.

Dalton was a personable, intelligent man who quickly became a folk hero. Historian Harrell McCullough (*Selden Lindsey*, p. 78) wrote:

> The newspaper accounts of the time clearly show that Bill Dalton commanded the respect of his fellow Westerners and that he fired the romantic instinct of the rest of the nation as no other Western outlaw ever did. It has been forgotten that back in the waning days of the Old West Bill Dalton was the most widely known, and considered the most daring, fearless and awesome of all the Old West outlaws.
>
> Bill Dalton became a legend during his lifetime, but his legend died in the later gross distortions of Western history, so that today even serious scholars of Western history do not realize his significance in the Old West tradition.

One of Dalton's most infamous crimes took place in Longview, Texas on May 23, 1894. Dalton and fellow outlaw Jim Wallace had been hiding out on the farm of Jim's brother about 25 miles from Ardmore, Oklahoma Territory. Their plans mapped out, they rode south to Longview, Texas, where they were joined by Big Asa Nite and his brother Jim Nite, two of Longview's less desirable citizens.

Dalton and Jim Nite entered the First National Bank while Big Asa and Jim Wallace took the four horses to an alley in back of the bank. Once inside the bank, Dalton leveled his pistol at the tellers while Nite scooped up money. One of the tellers managed to grab Dalton's gun and as they grappled over it two bank customers had an opportunity to run out the door and shout an alarm.

Then all hell broke loose. Wallace was able to kill George Buckington, who had run carelessly into the alley with a pistol. Then, shooting at anyone he saw, Wallace killed citizen Charles Learn and seriously wounded Marshal Matt Muckleroy and a man named J. W. McQueen. Big Asa was busy holding the horses until Dalton and Jim Nite got there with the loot. Another man was wounded by a shot from one of the bandits as they left town, using as shields two brothers they had grabbed. Jim Wallace lay dead in the alley.

Releasing their hostages a short way out of town, Dalton and the two Nite brothers made their way back to the farm of Houston Wallace with over $2,000. The Nite brothers took their share of the money and went their way. Dalton remained and his wife Jennie and their two children joined him there. Houston Wallace got his dead brother's share of the stolen money.

U.S. Deputy Marshal Selden Lindsey of Ardmore was contacted by Texas officials who believed the bandits might be headed to the Arbuckle Mountain area of Indian Territory. The lawman formed a posse and set about finding the infamous gunmen.

Newspapers as far away as London wrote of the bank robbery and escape. The nation had long been interested in the exploits of Bill Dalton who, believe it or not, would often send word to a pursuing posse which road he would take for an escape. Such unadulterated gall was a thorn in the saddles of embarrassed law enforcement officers. On Dalton's part it did not make good sense to flirt with capture or death in that manner.

Citizens clamored for news about the infamous gunman whose boldness led him into Ingalls, Indian Territory, where he, Bill Doolin and their gang were surrounded. Outnumbered more than two to one, they simply shot their way out leaving three dead lawmen.

Three days later the gang robbed another bank. On yet another occasion, and to the horror of some good church ladies, Dalton and his gang dropped in on their oyster supper and after stacking their guns outside the door, behaved like well-bred gentlemen while enjoying the tasty meal.

On June 7, 1894, Lindsey spotted and detained Jennie Dalton, another woman and Houston Wallace on the charge of possession of illegal whiskey in Indian Territory. Discovering Jennie's identity, and knowing that Houston's brother was in on the Longview holdup, Marshal Selden decided to investigate the Wallace farm. A posse surrounded the farmhouse on June 8. Sighting the lawmen, Dalton attempted to escape through the back door of the house and into a ravine a short distance away. He was able to get off only one shot at the officers before either Marshal Lindsey or Marshal Loss Hart shot him in the stomach. He died almost instantly.

Dalton's body was taken to Ardmore where it was embalmed and put on public display for several days. News that Bill Dalton was finally dead electrified the western world. Trains brought people from other cities and roads to Ardmore were lined with those who came to view the body of the fallen outlaw. Reporters from across the country journeyed there to get the story for their newspapers.

In his book, *Selden Lindsey*, author Harrell McCullough writes, "Word that the king of the western outlaws had finally reached the end of his trail flashed to every state and every city in the nation and to nations across the sea, for Europe had long been fascinated by the American West. The shot that had echoed through the little vale so far away now echoed through the newspaper headlines from coast to coast and the public realized instinctively that the echo spelled the death knell of the Old West. It was thrilling but sad."

Dalton's body was sent to California for burial, and Jennie and the two children also returned to California.

No one will ever know what it was that triggered Bill Dalton to become an outlaw. He was well aware of what had happened to his brothers. Why did he make such a decision? Was it simply the lure of "easy" money? Whatever the reason, the Dalton crime spree had ended. Mrs. Dalton's other children managed to live law-abiding lives.

Bill Doolin was a member of the Dalton gang when the Coffeyville caper was planned. However, on the ride to town he dropped out, for whatever reason. Some say his horse went lame. Probably the smartest of the gang, he may have sensed disaster and wished to avoid it. Learning of the fate of his comrades, he saddled up and returned to Oklahoma where he formed his own gang and became one of the most noted outlaws on the frontier. Besides Bill Doolin, his gang was composed of "Bitter Creek" Newcomb, George Waightman, "Dynamite Dick," "Little Bill" Raidler, Jack Blake, Charley Pierce and "Arkansas Tom." Under the leadership of Doolin, the gang successfully pulled off a number of holdups. Luck seemed to ride with them. When almost cornered in the hamlet of Ingalls, they killed three marshals and escaped. It was not easy to capture or kill the Doolins because they had many friends among the ranchers. Doolin himself once hid out on the ranch of famed Western writer Eugene Manlove Rhodes.

Aiding the gang in minor ways were Jennie Stevens (Cattle Annie) and Annie McDougal (Little Britches), two teenage girls who imagined themselves lady bandits. They did not commit any really serious crimes. Captured by marshals Tilghman and Burke, they each received a two-year sentence, which they served at the penitentiary in Boston. Upon release they became model citizens, Jennie returning to Oklahoma and Annie remaining in Boston.

Doolin was married in 1894 to the daughter of a minister. Devoted to his wife, he tried to go straight but to no avail. He couldn't resist the temptations of the outlaw trail. His gang was always a few

Bill Doolin in death. (Courtesy Western History Collections, University of Oklahoma Library.)

miles ahead of the posses. For a little while the gang rode fearlessly across the territory.

Famed marshal Bill Tilghman, along with marshals Heck Thomas and Chris Madsen, was assigned to run down the gang. The first casualty was Bill Dalton. "Tulsa Jack," "Bitter Creek" Newcomb and Charley Pierce followed in that order. "Little Bill" Raidler was almost killed by a shotgun blast from Bill Tilghman but lived to stand trial. Shortly after imprisonment he was pardoned for health reasons.

Doolin was taken at Eureka Springs, Arkansas. While awaiting trial at the Guthrie, Oklahoma, federal jail, Bill managed to escape and to free others prisoners as well. Hiding out in New Mexico he was relatively safe, but missing his wife and child he returned to Oklahoma only to be gunned down by Marshal Heck Thomas on a lonely country road one night as he traveled by wagon with his wife and baby.

The Doolin gang was now history.

DALTON-DOOLIN GANG FILMOGRAPHY

Passing of the Oklahoma Outlaw
(Eagle Film Company, 1915) 6 Reels.

D: William Tilghman (?). Scenario: William Tilghman, Colonel Lute Stover. Photography: J. B. Kent.

William Tilghman, E. D. Nix, Chris Madsen, Bud Ledbetter, Arkansas Tom (Themselves).

The outlaw gangs of Al Jennings, Bill Doolin, Emmett Dalton and Henry Starr were passing from the scene in Oklahoma. Arkansas Tom, the last of the Doolin gang, is captured by federal authorities, as are the female outlaws Cattle Annie and Little Britches.

All of the cast names listed here were well-known historical personages of the time. Arkansas Tom was the only real-life outlaw in the film. Tilghman, Nix, Madsen and Ledbetter were former U.S. marshals. Tilghman owned the film company. Some sequences closely reflected the actual events as they took place.

The Last Stand of the Dalton Boys
(Circa 1918) 3 Reels.

D: Jack Kenyon.

Cast: Emmett Dalton.

No other information can be found on this film. It was probably made by Emmett Dalton's Southern Feature Film Corporation and surely must have centered on the Coffeyville, Kansas, bank robbery, which was the last stand of the Daltons.

The film was probably made in 1918. It was never copyrighted.

Beyond the Law
(Southern Feature Film Corp., 1918) 6 Reels.

Director: Theodore Marston. Scenario: William Addison Lathrop. Based on the novel *Beyond the Law* by Emmett Dalton. Producer: Emmett Dalton. Photography: Robert A. Olsson.

Emmett Dalton (Himself, Bob Dalton, Frank Dalton), Harris Gordon (Young Emmett Dalton), Ida Pardee (Mother Dalton), William Dunn (Grat Dalton), Mabel Bordine (Eugenia Moore), Jack O'Loughlin (William McElhanie), Dick Clark (Charles Bryant), Virginia Lee (Ruth Lane).

Frank Dalton, a U.S. deputy marshal, is killed in Indian Territory while trying to make an arrest. His brothers Bob and Grat Dalton also become U.S. marshals for a short time. Bob is cheated in a card game and uses his gun to retrieve his money. He is tagged as a crook and loses his marshal job. Grat is sentenced to prison for a train robbery he did not commit. He escapes from prison and joins Bob. They plan to get even with the railroad by actually robbing the train.

Bob's sweetheart Eugenia Moore is killed while attempting to warn the brothers of an approaching sheriff and deputies. His heart hardened by the death of Eugenia, Bob plans to rob two banks simultaneously. Things go awry and both Grat and Bob are killed. Emmett survives a number of gunshot wounds and spends the next 15 years in prison. Upon his release, he marries the girl who has faithfully waited for him.

When the Daltons Rode
(Universal, 1940) 80 min.

Director: George Marshall. Screenplay: Screen credits list Harold Shumate, but non-screen sources give credit to Stuart Anthony and Lester

Bob Dalton (Broderick Crawford, left) keeps an eye on the prostrate Tod Jackson (Randolph Scott), while Bob's fiancée (Kay Francis) mourns the sad result of this romantic triangle in *When the Daltons Rode* (Universal, 1940).

Cole. Story: Emmett Dalton, Jack Jungmeyer, Sr. Consultant: Mrs. Emmett Dalton.

Randolph Scott (Tod Jackson), Broderick Crawford (Bob Dalton), Brian Donlevy (Grat Dalton), Kay Francis (Julie King), George Bancroft (Caleb Winters), Andy Devine (Ozark), Stuart Erwin (Ben Dalton), Frank Albertson (Emmett Dalton), Mary Gordon (Ma Dalton), Harry Stevens (Rigsby), Edgar Dearing (Sheriff), Quen Ramsey (Wilson), Bob McKenzie (Photographer), Dorothy Granger (Nancy), Fay McKenzie (Hannah), Walter Soderling (Judge Swain), June Wilkins (Suzy), Mary Ainslee (Minnie), Erville Alderson (District Attorney), Sally Payne (Annabella), June Wilkins (Suzy), Edgar Buchanan (Wheelwright), Harry Cording, Bob Kortman, Ethan Laidlaw (Henchmen), Charles Murphy (Tim), Ian MacLaren (Second Cronie), Joe King (Sheriff), Henry Roquemore (Juror Norris), James Flavin, Dan Rowan (Annabella's Brothers), James Morton (Juror Osborne), John Beck (Native), Cyril Thornton (First Cronie), Stanley Blystone, Jack Clifford, Walter Long, George Guhl, Ed Brady (Deputies), Tom Chatterton (Landlord), Robert Dudley (Court Clerk), Eddie Parker

(Mason), Lloyd Ingraham, Russ Powell (Engineers), Lafe McKee (Doctor), Kernan Cripps (Freight Agent), James Pierce, Charles McMurphy (Deputy Sheriffs), Alan Bridge (Billy Eagle). *With* Jack Baxley, Tom London, Mary Cassidy, Pat West, Dorothy Moore.

Tod Jackson, a young lawyer motivated by friendship for the Dalton family, defends Ben Dalton who is on trial on murder charges trumped up by Rigby, head of the Kansas Land and Development Company. At the trial events occur which force the Dalton Brothers to fight their way out, and from that time they remain hunted men whose crimes pile up in legendary fashion throughout the southwest.

Ben is shot in the back by vigilantes as the Dalton home is burned. Tod falls in love with Bob's fiancée Julie King, creating a romantic triangle of an explosive nature. Tod finally uncovers evidence proving that the development company is a front for Caleb Winters. Tod confronts him and walks out the door. Caleb sees the Daltons on the street and gets word to the sheriff. With the exception of Emmett, who is shot a number of times, the Daltons meet their death on the streets of Coffeyville.

"Wherever and whenever this pulsating production plays, audiences will spend most of their time on the edge of theater chairs. It's that sort of picture—packed to virtual capacity with action, whirlwind situations and horses, if indeed the almost superhuman exploits of the quartet of outlaw Dalton brothers can be strictly classified in conserving eyes as 'heroic.'"— *Film Daily*, July 29, 1940

"George Marshall hits a speedy pace of direction at the start, catching attention immediately, and maintains it without a letdown in the final fade-out. Despite the rough-and-tumble formula of the piece, Marshall injects plenty of human interest and sympathy for the Dalton boys in the unreeling."— *Variety*, July 31, 1940

The Daltons Ride Again
(Universal, 1945) 70 min.

Director: Ray Taylor. Screenplay: Roy Chanslor and Paul Gangelin. Producer: Howard Welsch.

Alan Curtis (Emmett Dalton), Kent Taylor (Bob Dalton), Lon Chaney, Jr. (Grat Dalton), Noah Beery, Jr. (Ben Dalton), Martha O'Driscoll (Mary), Jess Barker (Jeff), Thomas Gomez (McKenna), Milburn Stone (Graham), John Litel (Botannon), Walter Sande (Wilkins), Douglas Dumbrille (Sheriff), Virginia Brissac (Mrs. Walters). *With* Stanley Andrews, Fern Emmett, Cyril Delevanti, Wheaton Chambers, Davidson Clark, Jack Rockwell, Robert Wilke, Dick Dickinson, George Chesebro, Ethan Laidlaw, Edward Cassidy, Paul Birch, Henry Hall.

Alan Curtis as Emmett Dalton and Martha O'Driscoll as Mary in *The Daltons Ride Again* (Universal, 1945).

The Daltons are unjustly accused of a series of robberies and murders. In order to square themselves they raid a vigilance meeting and expose the real criminal, a land-grabbing company out to control the railroad right of way. Three of the Daltons then ride off toward the Argentine and on the way hold up the Coffeyville banks, where they are killed in ambush. The fourth Dalton, Emmett, rushes in to warn them and is wounded. He gets a stiff sentence for his pains.

"Action-packed outdoor melodrama has plenty to offer fans who like film entertainment rough and raw with a western flavor. Pic has enough production values and robust elements to give it a good rating for any but the deluxe situations, and should play well all down the line. Action emphasis and neat results make up for lack of box office weight among the cast names, although all are familiar."—*Variety*, November 21, 1945

Badman's Territory
(RKO, 1946)

See full writeup on page 80.

Return of the Bad Men
(RKO, 1948)

See full writeup on page 33.

The Dalton Gang
(Lippert, 1949) 62 min.

Director/Screenplay: Ford Beebe. Producer: Ron Ormond.

Donald Barry (Larry West), Robert Lowery (Blackie Mullet), James Millican (Sheriff Jeb Marvin), Betty [Julie] Adams (Polly), Byron Foulger (Amos Boling), J. Farrell MacDonald (Judge Price), Greg McClure (Missouri Gany), George J. Lewis (Chief Irahu), Marshall Reed (Joe), Ray Bennett (Gorman), Lee Roberts (Mac), Cliff Taylor (Doctor), Cactus Mack (Stage Driver). *With* Dick Curtis, Stanley Price.

Larry West is a deputy marshal assigned to track down the Dalton Gang. While riding in Dalton territory he witnesses the shooting of Joe by a band of white men dressed as Indians. He takes Joe into town where he recovers from his wound. Larry talks Joe into posing as the marshal, while he (West) works undercover. West finds the Dalton gang in control of the cattle country and promoting war between Indians and settlers. West rides to the Indian reservation and listens to their side of the story and is convinced the Indians are telling the truth.

When the Daltons learn that West is the marshal, they frame him in the same way they did the Indians. Polly, believing in West, rides to the reservation and persuades the Indians to spring West from jail. Now free, West finds Blackie Mullet, a Dalton, and forces a confession. Mullet escapes from West and is not recaptured until the Indians move in and put an end to the entire Dalton clan.

"*The Dalton Gang* chalks up strong performance credits straight down the line. Film rolls off as tailor made lower rung material which should keep theatre goers happy. Picture, however, doesn't generate anywhere near the action its title would suggest.... Robbery and murder scenes are covered with newspaper headlines and reward posters in a montage effect at film's outset."—*Variety*, November 2, 1949

The Doolins of Oklahoma
(Columbia, 1949) 90 min.

Director: Gordon Douglas. Screenplay: Kenneth Gamet. Producer: Harry Joe Brown. 2nd Unit Director: Yakima Canutt.

Randolph Scott (Bill Doolin), George Macready (Sam Hughes), Louise Albritton (Rose of Cimarron), Noah Beery, Jr. (Little Bill), Virginia Huston (Elaine Burton), John Ireland (Bitter Creek), Charles Kemper (Arkansas Tom Jones), Dona Drake (Cattle Annie), Robert H. Barrat (Heck Thomas), Lee Patrick (Melissa Price), Griff Barnett (Deacon Burton), Frank Fenton (Red Buck), Jock O'Mahoney (Tulsa Jack), James Kirkwood (Rev. Mears), Robert Osterloh (Wichita), Virginia Brissac (Mrs. Burton), John Sheehan (Dunn).

The story follows Doolin from the time he becomes an outlaw, after having seen his friends the Dalton brothers killed. Thereafter, Doolin organizes his own gang, stages countless bank holdups, gets married to a young woman who doesn't know about his background and is finally is killed by a U.S. marshal who has been tracking him for years.

"Standard story is boosted into first-rate category through clever treatment, which gives audience maximum of chases, gunplay, and other action calculated to hold spectator throughout film's 90 minutes. Grosses will reflect draw of Scott and show neatly."—*Variety*

The Daltons' Women
(Western Adventures, 1950) 77 min.

Director/Screenplay: Ron Ormond. Producer: Joy Houck and J. Francis White.

Lash LaRue, Tom Neal, Pamela Blake, Jacqueline Fontaine, Jack Holt, Al St. John, Raymond Hatton, Lyle Talbot, June Benbow, Archie Twitchell, Duke Johnson, J. Farrell MacDonald, Terry Frost, Bud Osborne, Stanley Price, Lee Bennett.

Lash LaRue is assigned to track down the Dalton gang. He is mistaken for one of the gang and is hired as a gambler in the local saloon. The saloon owner is in cahoots with the Daltons. In fact, the sheriff, the mayor, a local rancher and sundry other characters are all crooks. Jack Holt is the chief heavy. He and the other crooks are eventually exposed and captured by LaRue and St. John.

"...carelessly assembled oater that moves erratically from a thin story line to irrelevant little subplots and gives the general impression that the film was slapped together from bits of disconnected pieces. ... the women involved have no relationship to the Dalton brothers, who themselves are only slightly concerned in the proceedings...."—*Hollywood Reporter*

The Cimarron Kid

(Universal, 1951) 84 min.

Director: Budd Boetticher. Screenplay: Lewis Stevens. Producer: Ted Richmond.

Audie Murphy (Bill Doolin), Beverly Tyler (Carrie Holly), Hugh O'Brian (Red), Leif Erickson (Marshal Johnson), Noah Beery, Jr. (Bob Dalton), Yvette Dugay (Rose), James Best (Bitter Creek Newcomb), Roy Roberts (Pat), John Hubbard (George Webber), Tris Coffin (Cafe Patron), Harry Harvey (Store Clerk). *With* John Hudson, William Reynolds, Frank Silvera, Rand Brooks, Rory Mallinson, Richard Garland, David Wolfe, Jack Ingram, Eugene Baxter, John Bromfield, Ted Richmond, Dave Sharpe, Lee Roberts, Lee Morgan, Ann Robinson.

This film is a loose remake of *The Doolins of Oklahoma* (1949). There is no attempt at historical accuracy. In this version of the Bill Doolin story, he is with the Dalton gang at the ill-fated Coffeyville fiasco. He later organizes his own band of outlaws, but in the end love wins out over greed.

Montana Belle

(RKO, 1952) 81 min.

Director: Allan Dwan. Screenplay: Horace McCoy and Norman S. Hall. Story: M. Coates Webster and Howard Welsch.

Jane Russell, George Brent, Scott Brady, Forrest Tucker, Andy Devine, Jack Lambert, John Litel, Ray Teal, Rory Mallinson, Roy Barcroft. *With* Holly Bane, Ned Davenport, Dick Elliott, Eugene Roth, Stanley Andrews, Rex Lease, Dennis Moore, Frank Ellis, Iron Eyes Cody, Glenn Strange, Hank Bell, Franklyn Farnum, George Chesebro, Pierce Lyden, Gregg Barton, Kenneth MacDonald, Rodney Bell, Charles Soldani.

Story concerns an alliance between Belle Starr and the Daltons, a rift in the union and then the grandiose plans to rob a bank. Things go wrong and the Daltons are captured and Belle is sent to prison.

Overall the film is a disappointment, even though it has big names, Trucolor and good production quality. The plot is weak and none of the actors fare very well.

Jane Russell, of course, plays Belle Starr, but not even her pretty face and other major assets keep this film from being just a little above mediocre. George Brent does his best.

"Filmed originally at Republic Studio two or three years ago, it was taken over lock, stock and gun barrel by Howard Hughes for eventual RKO release. Apparently the time has now been deemed right. As a matter of fact it is overripe. I like to think the Western has progressed a little, at least in its best manifestations, since *Montana Belle* was made. But let's not use the word 'best' around *Montana Belle*."—*Los Angeles Times*, date unknown

Jesse James vs. the Daltons
(Columbia, 1954)

See full writeup on page 92.

The Dalton Girls
(United Artists, 1957) 71 min.

Director: Reginald LeBorg. Screenplay: Maurice Tombragel. Story: Herbert Perdum.

Merry Anders, Lisa Davis, Penny Edwards, Sue George, John Russell, Ed Hinton, Glenn Dixon, Johnny Western, Malcolm Atterbury, Douglas Henderson, Kevin Enright, Al Wyatt, H. E. Willmering, Red Morgan, K. C. MacGregor, David Swapp.

Merry Anders, Lisa Davis, Penny Edwards and Sue George are sisters of the Dalton brothers. They turn to crime themselves when their brothers are wiped out and Anders kills a man in self-defense. John Russell, a traveling gambler held up by the quartet, begins to put chinks into the group's solidarity when Edwards falls in love with him. Anders and Davis are the two hard members of the sisters, while Edwards and George carry the sympathy in wanting to live decent lives. The career of the girls eventually ends in a hail of bullets as they attempt to pull their biggest job and fail.

"*The Dalton Girls* proves pretty conclusively that the female of the species can be as deadly a gunslinger as the male. Far-fetched switcheroo, in which femmes play the baddies and men the good guys, is sufficiently novel as carried out in an okay story line and action to rate good acceptance in the western market."—*Variety*

Tales of Wells Fargo
(NBC/Overland Productions, 1959) 30 min.
Segment entitled *The Daltons*.

Dale Robertson.

The Dalton That Got Away
(Dalton Film Co., 1960) 69 min.

Director: Jimmy Salvador. Story/Screenplay: E. L. Erwin. Producer: Henry A. Lube.

Michael Connors, Elsie Cardenas, Carlos Rivas, Felix Moreno, Zachary Milton, Stilman Segar, George Russell, Reed Howes, Francisco Reynolds, Quinton Bulnes, Sam Murphy, Arlene King.

The Last Ride of the Dalton Gang
(Dan Curtis Productions/NBC, November 20, 1979) 150 min.
(Working Title: *The Raid on Coffeyville*)

Producer/Director: Dan Curtis. Teleplay: Earl W. Wallace.

Jack Palance (Will Smith), Dale Robertson (Judge Isaac Parker), Cliff Potts (Bob Dalton), Larry Wilcox (Emmett Dalton), Randy Quaid (Grat Dalton), Sharon Farrell (Flo Quick), Matt Clark (Bitter Creek), Bo Hopkins (Bill Doolin), R. G. Armstrong (Langdon Stanford), Scott Brady (Poker player), Don Collier (Frank Dalton), John Fitzpatrick (Texas Jack), Dennis Fimple (Blackface), James Crittenden (McElhennie), Eric Lawson (Willie), Julie Hill (Julie), Mills Watson (Bill Dalton), Buff Brady (Buffalo Bill Cody). *With* Dick Autry, Johnny Collins, Royal Dano, Jorge Moreno, Elliot Street, Harry Townes, H. M. Wynant, Harris Yulin.

The film is a somewhat tongue-in-cheek look at the Daltons and does not stick strictly with historical fact. Nevertheless, it is entertaining, though overlong.

Belle Starr
(Hanna-Barbera/CBS-TV, April 20, 1980)

The Daltons, Cole Younger, Jesse and Frank James and the titular lady outlaw are among those featured. See full writeup on page 105.

Cattle Annie and Little Britches
(Universal, 1981) 97 min.

Director: Lamont Johnson. Story: Robert Ward. Screenplay: David Eyre and Robert Ward. Producer: Rupert Hitzig and Alan King.

Burt Lancaster (Bill Doolin), John Savage (Bitter Creek Newcomb), Rod Steiger (Tilghman), Diane Lane (Jenny), Amanda Plummer (Annie), Scott Glenn (Bill Dalton), Redmond Gleason (Red Buck), William Russ (Little Dick Raidler), Ken Call (George Weightman), Buck Taylor (Dynamite Dick), John Quade (Morgan), Perry Lang (Elrod), Steven Ford (Deputy Marshal), Mike Moroff (Deputy), John Hock (Bank Teller).

Small town girls Jenny and Annie have romantic notions about riding with an outlaw gang. When the Doolin-Dalton gang, led by aging Bill

Marshal Bill Tilghman (Rod Steiger, left) brings Bill Doolin (Burt Lancaster) to justice in *Cattle Annie and Little Britches* (Universal, 1981).

Doolin, bursts into town and pulls a stick-up, the girls follow them. Annie becomes the lover of a gang member, while Jenny finds a father figure in Doolin. The gang, trailed by lawman Tilghman, continues its bank robbing activities, but eventually breaks up, and Jenny sadly gives up her life with Doolin.

"Taken as just light entertainment the feature is more than passable, especially for Amanda Plummer's work as the strong-willed Annie and Diane Lane's underplayed starry-eyed Jenny. Burt Lancaster is ingratiating as the likable bank robber Bill Doolin, although his characterization has little to do with the reality of the actual outlaw."—James Robert Parish and Michael R. Pitts, *The Great Western Pictures II*, pp. 70–72

"*Cattle Annie and Little Britches* is as cutesy and unmemorable as its title. If oaters were currently being made as regularly as they were in the past, there might be room for this sort of fanciful marginalia. Nowadays, however, this Universal pickup from Hemdale, lensed two years ago, will just give the public one more reason not to go to westerns."—*Variety*, April 29, 1981

The Last Day
(Paramount, February 15, 1984) 120 min.

Director: Vincent McEveety. Story: Steve Fisher and A. C. Lyles. Teleplay: Jim Byrnes and Steve Fisher. Producer: A. C. Lyles. Narrated by Harry Morgan.

Richard Widmark (Will Spence), Christopher Connelly (Dick Broadwell), Robert Conrad (Bob Dalton), Gene Evans (Charlie Connelly), Richard Jaeckel (Grat Dalton), Tim Matheson (Emmett Dalton), Barbara Rush (Betty Spence), Tom Skerritt (Bill Powers), Loretta Swit (Daisy), Morgan Woodward (Ransom Payne), Kathleen Cody (Julie Johnson), Jon Locke (Player), Bryan O'Byrne (Clerk).

The Dalton Gang rides again, forcing a retired gunman to use his weapons in the climactic battle at Coffeyville, Kansas. There is plenty of suspense and action in this telling of the famous Coffeyville bank robbery attempt and it adheres somewhat to historical fact.

The Real West—The Dalton Gang
(Greystone Productions, 1994)

Director: Bill Rosser. Exec. Producer: Craig Hoffman. Narrator: Kenny Rogers.

An excellent documentary of the Dalton brothers who went from being "good guys" to "bad guys."

4

Myra Belle Shirley Starr

The movies have generally depicted a highly romanticized version of Belle Starr and her escapades, *à la* luscious Gene Tierney in *Belle Starr* (1941) and sensuous Jane Russell in *Montana Belle* (1952). In reality she was a hatchet-faced woman with the disposition of a coiled rattlesnake. She had a penchant for appropriating property and livestock belonging to others, and rode the hoot-owl trail with various unsavory characters. She was almost completely lacking in morals and, contrary to *Police Gazette* stories, was no female Robin Hood.

Glenn Shirley in his book *Belle Starr and Her Times* (Norman, University of Oklahoma Press, 1982), in commenting on her death, says:

> She had been elevated to a seat of immortal glory as a sex-crazed hellion with the morals of an alley cat, a harborer and consort of horse and cattle thieves, a petty blackmailer who dabbled in every crime from murder to the dark sin of incest, as female Robin Hood who robbed the rich to feed the poor, an exhibitionistic and clever she-devil on horseback and leader of the most bloodthirsty band of cutthroats in the American West. All this despite the lack of a contemporary account or court record to show that she ever held up a train, bank or stagecoach; or killed anybody; the renegades she supposedly led or kept out of the tangles of the law were only figments of a vivid imagination.

Myra Belle Shirley was born on February 8, 1848, near Carthage, Missouri. Since her death on February 3, 1889, in Oklahoma Indian Territory, a large number of hack writers have created the legend of Belle as the bandit queen, a female Jesse James. However, as far as historians know she never pulled off a bank or train robbery, and most surely she never gave any part of her ill-gotten gains to the poor. Myra Belle's one and only charity was Myra Belle. Apparently her chief sources of income were cattle and horse rustling and a little whoring on the side. Her childhood was spent in Missouri where at one time she was a student in a female academy. The culture failed to rub off on her.

Belle had four brothers and a sister: Edward, Mansfield, John, Cravens and Charlotte. All of the boys were born in Missouri; Charlotte was born in Iowa. Edward, her favorite brother, became a Missouri bushwhacker who rode with Quantrill and was killed during the Missouri-Kansas border war. It was during the turbulent years of the early 1860s that Belle learned to ride and shoot, becoming as proficient in these skills as most men.

Because of the lawlessness in Missouri, the father moved his brood to Texas where in 1866 or 1867 Belle met Cole Younger, on the run from a bank robbery in Liberty, Missouri. Although Cole is generally credited with being the father of Belle's daughter Pearl, there is some evidence to support the contention that Jim Reed, Belle's first husband, was the father and that the baby was first called "Rosie Lee." A manuscript written by Jim's older brother and now owned by a nephew claims that Belle and Jim were married in Decatur, Collins County, Missouri, in 1865, that Baby Pearl was born in Texas in 1867, and that son Edward was born in Rich Hill, Missouri, in 1868.

Author Bill Kelly ("Pearl Younger and the Falling Starrs," *Real West*, November 1976) writes that Jim Reed killed a man in Texas and for that reason he and Belle vamoosed to California for a couple of years. Returning to Texas in 1874, Reed was killed by trusted friend John Morrice, who couldn't resist the temptation of the reward money. Kelly further says that after Reed's death Belle went to live with Bruce Younger, a cousin of Cole, and from this association "Rosie Lee" became known as Pearl Younger.

Eventually Belle took up with an Indian named Blue Duck for a short while. She wasn't very particular about who shared her bed as long as he was a good stud. By this time Belle had returned to the Indian Territory and fallen in with a band of cattle and horse thieves. Blue Duck was just a minor outlaw and had little to offer Belle. Consequently, she cast him aside to marry another Indian, Sam Starr, and settled down on a farm on the Canadian River. The farm, which she named Younger's Bend, was rather isolated and made an ideal stopover for those running from the law.

In 1883 Sam and Belle were convicted of rustling and sentenced to one year and six months respectively by Hanging Judge Parker of Fort Smith, Arkansas.

Belle beat Sam out of prison by six months. When he returned he was a changed man. He figured that he had a few more wild oats to sow and that pickings from robbery or rustling would be good in California. He packed his shooting irons and left in 1885.

With Sam gone, Belle succumbed to the attentions of a man named John Middletown, who moved in with her. Unfortunately for Middletown, Starr decided to come home. Middletown was found shot to death out in the field, but there was no evidence to connect Sam with the slaying. Belle and Sam were soon back at their trade of cattle rustling and horse stealing.

Belle Starr and Blue Duck. (Courtesy Barde Collection, Archives & Manuscript Division, Oklahoma Historical Society.)

Belle was having parental problems with Pearl, now grown, and Edward, who was in his rebellious teens. Leaving home, Pearl went to Arkansas where in time she gave birth to a daughter, Flossie, on April 12, 1887. No one, perhaps not even Pearl herself, knew who the father was. Belle was furious, but she had her hands full keeping Edward under control. When Edward got himself shot up by some whiskey peddlers, it took weeks to recover. Belle wrote Pearl and begged her to come home if she wanted to see her brother alive. Pearl made arrangements for someone to keep Flossie and came back to Younger's Bend. Belle did everything in her power to keep both her children at home, finally convincing Pearl to put her baby up for adoption. Pearl finally relented and did so. Belle never saw her granddaughter (or cared to).

It was towards the end of 1886 that Sam Starr locked horns with Deputy Marshal Frank West at a dance hall called "Aunt Lucy Surratt's." In the shootout, both men died.

Belle had no intentions of remaining a widow for long. Her last relationship was with a Creek Indian named Jim July, 19 years her junior, and under indictment on a larceny charge. In February 1889 Belle convinced Jim that he should give himself up to the marshals at Fort Smith. After all, the government had no hard evidence to support its case. Belle believed that July would beat the rap. She rode halfway to Fort Smith with him, said her goodbye, and started back to Younger's Bend. Nearing home she was ambushed by an unknown assailant. The date was February 3, 1889. A neighbor, Edgar Wallace, was accused of her murder but no charges were filed against him. It was also rumored that she was slain by her son Ed Reed, with whom she had had incestuous relations. He and his mother had fought over his riding her horse without permission. Nothing could be proven, however.

The evidence pointed more to Edgar Wallace, with whom Belle had words on several occasions. They apparently hated each other. A mean man, Wallace subsequently killed a half dozen men before his luck ran out on October 24, 1910. He died at the hands of enraged citizens near Chatham after he had killed two men for no good reason.

Edward Reed was a good-for-nothing who had already served two stretches in the penitentiary for selling booze to the Indians. On one occasion he killed two men who were about to kill the local sheriff, having overheard the men planning to shoot the sheriff in the back. For a while he was a hero with a puffed-up ego.

Federal Judge Isaac C. Parker, believing the young man had turned his life around, appointed him a Deputy U. S. Marshal in 1893. This is the same judge who previously had sent Reed to prison. Surprisingly, Reed became a well-respected and capable marshal. For three years he had a spotless record. The cool manner in which he shot and killed Dick and Zeke Critten, who were shooting up the town of Wagoner, proved his mettle. They were former U. S. deputy marshals who had gone to the bad. However, about a month later, Reed received his comeuppance at the guns of two Claremore bartenders who did not take kindly to being driven out of their own establishment by a cocky, drunk Eddie Starr. At Eddie's funeral, Pearl Starr confessed to Dr. Jesse Mooney, a family friend, that it was Eddie who had killed Belle. Belle had lived just long enough following her assassination to whisper to Pearl her killer's name.

Pearl's marriages (or live-in arrangements) were sordid affairs, but they produced her daughter Flossie and another daughter Ruth, born June 19, 1894. On August 24, 1898, a son, Arthur, was born but died July 28, 1899. Another daughter, Jennette, was born November 8, 1902. All of these children were by different fathers.

Pearl was at a loss after the death of mother Belle and turned to the oldest profession. By 1891 she had saved enough money to open her own whorehouse in Fort Smith. Here she flourished for 23 years before being run out of town in 1916. She kicked around a few years, finally winding up as a resident of the Savoy Hotel in Douglas, Arizona. Her daughter was with her when she suffered a stroke and died on July 8, 1925. Before hitching up with Sam Starr, Belle worked as an entertainer, piano player and faro dealer in a saloon there. She had also operated a livery stable as a front for fencing stolen horses for the Tom Starr gang in Indian Territory.

Belle Starr probably read her own publicity and imagined herself a female Jesse James, as she was known to strut about at times. In reality, however, she hardly deserved the title of bandit queen. The Belle Starr legend was started by a newspaper writer named Alton B. Myers, who had a fertile imagination. *The Police Gazette* eagerly printed his stories and soon many hack writers were churning out lurid accounts of Belle for the popular dime novels of the day. Flossie also contributed a few stories about her grandmother, even though she never knew Belle.

Belle was quickly elevated to a status approaching that of Jesse James, Billy the Kid and other notorious outlaws.

BELLE STARR FILMOGRAPHY

Court Martial

(Columbia, 1928) 7 Reels.

Director: George B. Seitz. Screenplay: Anthony Coldeway. Producer: Harry Cohn.

Jack Holt (Captain James Camden), Betty Compson (Belle Starr), Pat Harmon ("Bull"), Doris Hill (General's Daughter), Frank Lackteen ("Devil" Dawson), Frank Lawson (Abraham Lincoln), George Cowl (Gen. Robert Hackathorne), Zack Williams (Negro).

James Camden, a Union officer, is ordered by President Lincoln to break up a band led by Belle Starr. Camden, posing as an outlaw, manages to infiltrate the gang and soon falls in love with Belle. Belle is out to avenge the killing of her father. During an attack by Union forces, Camden manages to save Belle's life. She returns the favor when she finds out his true identity and that her men want to kill him. Camden returns to the Union army and is court-martialed and sentenced to face a firing squad. Belle again saves his life by voluntarily giving herself up. She is killed by one of her disgruntled men.

"Long drawn-out Civil War yarn. It depends upon shots of Lincoln and the Stars and Stripes for approval. Photography, production, direction and cast make it just a so-so release for the daily grinds. Fewer titles and discreet slicing might help." — *Variety*, October 31, 1928

Robinhood of the Pecos

(Republic, 1941) 59 min.

Assoc. Producer/Director: Joseph Kane. Screenplay: Olive Cooper. Story: Hal Long.

Roy Rogers (Vance Corbin), George F. Hayes (Gabby Hornaday), Marjorie Reynolds (Jeanie Grayson), Cy Kendall (Ballard), Leigh Whipper (Kezeye), Sally Payne (Belle Starr), Eddie Acuff (Sam Starr), Robert Strange (Cravens), William Haade (Captain Morgan), Jay Novello (Stacy), Roscoe Ates (Guffy), Jim Corey, Chick Hannon, Ted Mapes, Al Taylor, Frank McCarroll, Art Mix, Bob Burns, Chuck Baldra.

Vance Corbin, young Confederate soldier released from a northern prison at the close of the Civil War, returns to Texas. He joins forces with Gabby Hornaday, who, as "The Night Rider," is organizing the citizens in protest against the misdeeds of northern post-war politicians and carpetbaggers.

Ballard, the adjunct of the county, and his henchman Cravens are the ringleaders. It is to Ballard's advantage to keep the Texans from swearing the Oath of Amnesty, which, in return for their allegiance to the Constitution, will give them the right to govern themselves. As long as Texas remains under martial law, Ballard can exercise a form of dictatorship.

Vance is joined in his fight by Jeanie, Gabby's niece, as well as by Sam and Belle Starr, a young married couple. They are aware of Ballard's double-dealing but are unable to cope with the power he has over the people. Vance succeeds in getting the people to swear the oath, and they are given the right to elect their own lawmakers.

Vance is made sheriff. His tenure is short-lived, as Ballard makes an issue of the mysterious killing of a Colonel Davis to have the election revoked and martial law re-established on the pretext of mob violence. Davis was actually slain by Stacy, Ballard's secretary, who caught him discovering evidence of Ballard's crookedness.

Vance and Gabby are imprisoned and sentenced to death for treason. Belle and Sam rescue them through a secret tunnel into the cell, but Gabby is recaptured.

Ballard, fearful of an uprising because of his determination to hang Gabby, summons a special troop of militia from the governor. Vance knows that if the citizens try to free Gabby, they will be slaughtered by the militia. Because Stacy is a coward and a weakling, he is shot and left for dead by Ballard. Vance finds him hiding in a barn and wrings from him a confession and evidence to convict Ballard. Vance, Sam and Belle risk their own lives to reach the governor, expose Ballard and save Gabby's life. Vance proposes to Jeanie.

"It's another one for the lower half of duals." — *Variety*, January, 22, 1941

Belle Starr

(20th Century–Fox, 1941) 87 min.

Director: Irving Cummings. Screenplay: Lamar Trotti. Story: Niven Busch and Cameron Rogers. Assoc. Producer: Kenneth MacGowan.

Randolph Scott (Sam Starr), Gene Tierney (Belle Starr), Dana Andrews (U. S. Army Major), John Sheppard [Shepperd Strudwick] (Belle Starr's Brother), Chill Wills (Starr's Aide), Elizabeth Patterson (Wife of Starr's Aide), Louise Beavers (Mammy), Olin Howland (Renegade), Joseph

Sam Starr (Randolph Scott) passes the time with a U.S. Army major (Dana Andrews) as Belle (Gene Tierney) talks with her brother (John Sheppard) at table. From *Belle Starr* (20th Century–Fox, 1941).

Sawyers, Joseph Downing (Outlaws). *With* Paul Burns, Howard Hickman, Charles Trowbridge, James Flavin, Charles Middleton, Clarence Muse, George Melford, Mae Marsh, Herbert Ashley, Norman Willis, Billy Wayne, George Reed, Davidson Clark, Hugh Chapman, Clinton Rosemond, Kermit Maynard, Franklyn Farnum.

In this sentimental treatment, Belle Starr is viewed as a patriot, a Southern sympathizer who will not tolerate surrender of her Confederate clansmen in Missouri. When a Northern army major burns her mansion because she has harbored Sam Starr, also a patriot up to this time, Belle joins the outlaws headed by Starr.

When one of the Starr renegades shoots her own brother, Belle comes to the realization that the gang is out for loot. She is killed as she rides to save her husband from a trap by federal soldiers. Starr gives himself up.

There is hardly a grain of truth in this film, but it does make for an enjoyable one if you can overlook historical inaccuracies.

"Twentieth–Fox makes a good job of completely botching up the historical character it pretends to portray. This is a weak-kneed and thoroughly false biography of the southwest's most notorious female bandit."—*Variety*, August 27, 1941

Badman's Territory
(RKO, 1946)

See full writeup on page 81.

Belle Starr's Daughter
(20th Century–Fox, 1948) 87 min.

Director: Lesley Selander. Screenplay: W. R. Burnett. Producer: Edward L. Alperson.

George Montgomery (Peace Officer), Rod Cameron (Main Heavy), Ruth Roman (Belle Starr's Daughter), Wallace Ford (Outlaw), Isabel Jewell (Belle Starr). *With* William Phipps, Edith King, Jack Lambert, Fred Libby, Charles Kemper, Larry Johns, Kenneth MacDonald, J. Farrell MacDonald, Christine Larsen, William Perrott, Frank Darien, Alvin Hammer, Chris-Pin Martin, Charles Stevens, Mary Foran, Paul E. Burns, Lane Chandler.

A feud exists between Belle Starr and a western town. The two forces agree to a truce that is predicated on both groups keeping out of the other's territory. Rod Cameron breaks the truce by killing the sheriff and then disposing of Belle herself. Ruth Roman, Belle's daughter, believes George Montgomery, a peace officer, did the killing and plans her revenge. She plants herself in the enemy camp under a false identity. Eventually her identity is revealed, she comes to recognize the disgusting brutality of Cameron, and learns that Montgomery did not kill her mother. This leads to her regeneration and accounts for a finale in which justice is served by the death of Cameron.

"*Belle Starr's Daughter* offers the exhibitor a provocative title and a tip-top cast on which to center an exploitation campaign. The Edward L. Alperson production ... takes good advantage of the excellent players by giving them an array of intriguing sagebrush characterizations. The story, however, is not quite up to par. It is wanting in action and the preliminary exposition is long and complicated. Lesley Selander's direction imbues the piece with a bit more spirit in the final reels."—*Hollywood Reporter*, October 25, 1948

Montana Belle
(RKO, 1952)

See full writeup on page 126.

Jane Russell was a buxom and beautiful Belle Starr in *Montana Belle* (RKO, 1952). Forrest Tucker (left) and Scott Brady were fellow outlaws.

Son of Belle Starr

(Allied Artists, 1953) 70 min.

Director: Frank McDonald. Screenplay: D. D. Beauchamp and William Raynor. Story: Jack DeWitt. Producer: Peter Scully.

Keith Larsen (The Kid), Dona Drake (Dolores), Peggie Castle (Clara Wren), Regis Toomey (Tom Wren), James Seay (Clark), Myron Healey (Sheriff), Frank Puglia (Manuel), Robert Keys (Bart Wren), I. Stanford Jolley (Rocky), Paul McGuire (Pinkly), Lane Bradford (Beacher), Mike Regan (Earl), Joe Dominguez (Pablo), Alex Montoya (Mexican).

"The Kid" is forced to wear an outlaw label because of his late mother's reputation. A crooked sheriff seeks him out to participate in a gold robbery. The Kid goes along, figuring he might find out who framed him for a similar stickup the year before. The robbery comes off as scheduled, but the sheriff's men try to kill him. The Kid is faster on the draw and kills them. He hides the gold, hoping it will lead him to the mastermind of the dirty work. Eventually he is able to get the right man, Clark, but by that time his killer reputation is responsible for his being shot down by a posse just as he is about to be cleared.

"Allied Artists has an okay program western feature for the smaller situations in *Son of Belle Starr*. There's one flaw for the audiences to which it will play—the hero is killed at the finale, an unnecessarily drastic ending—but up to that point the story and direction keep things moving along an action course that will satisfy the fans of program westerns in color."—*Variety*, July 8, 1953

Tales of Wells Fargo
(Overland Productions, 1957) 30 min.
A segment entitled "Belle Starr"

Dale Robertson

Young Jesse James
(20th Century–Fox, 1960)

The formative years of the outlaw Jesse James are examined in this film from a psychological perspective; Belle Starr (Merry Anders) is featured as an old flame of Cole Younger (Willard Parker). See full writeup on page 98.

The Outlaws Is Coming
(Columbia, 1965)

See full writeup on page 43.

Belle Starr Story
Il Mio Corpo per un Poker

Director/Screenplay: Nathan Wich. Producer: Gianni Varsi. Music: Charles Dumont. Camera: Alessandro D'Eva.

Elsa Martinelli (Belle Starr). *With* Robert Woods, George Eastman, Francesca Righini, Dan Harrison, Bruno Corazzari, Vladmer Nedar.

The famed Italian artsy director Lina Wertmuller hides behind the male pseudonym Nathan Wich. The story is nothing new, just another retelling of the notorious female outlaw's exploits. However, Elsa Martinelli is a very beautiful Belle Starr. Robert Woods and George Eastman, the two men in her love life, introduce Belle to "the wonderful world of crime."

Zachariah
(ABC Pictures–Cinerama, 1971) 91 min.

Producer/Director: George Englund. Screenplay: Joe Massot, Phil Austin, Peter Bergman, David Ossmon and Phillip Proctor.

John Rubenstein (Zachariah), Don Johnson (Matthew), Pat Quinn (Belle Starr), Elvin Jones (Job Cain), Doug Kershow (The Fiddler), William Challee (Old Man). *With* Robert Ball, Dick Van Patten, The New York Rock Ensemble, The James Gang, Country Joe and the Fish, White Lightnin'.

After Zachariah kills a man in a barroom for disliking the length of his hair and referring to him and his friend Matthew as "fags," they leave searching for something. *What*, they don't know. Matthew allies himself with fast gun Job Cain. Zachariah realizes that if they remain with Cain he and Matthew will eventually be forced to shoot it out. He leaves and finds an old man living alone in the mountains. Here he is peaceful for a while. Eventually he leaves for the border town of Camino, where he seduces Belle Starr.

Unsatisfied in Camino, Zachariah returns to the old man and the mountain, where he is at peace until Matthew arrives and attempts to prod him into a gunfight. Matthew sees the light and they become friends again.

"Rubenstein was a perfect selection for the title role. He grows the three segments of his maturity as a youth, a searcher and a man at peace with himself and the world. Johnson, though not given the full transitions as Rubenstein, makes a startling adaptation from youth to power driven young man and is excellently controlled in a furious scene attempting to goad Rubenstein into a gunfight. ... Miss Quinn is luscious as Belle Starr, camping a bit in the tradition of Mae West, but she is delightful and in constant motion."—*Hollywood Reporter*, January 22, 1971

Belle Starr
(Hanna-Barbera/CBS-TV, April 20, 1980) 100 min.

See full writeup on page 105.

The Long Riders
(United Artists, 1980)

Pamela Reed plays Belle Starr in the story of the exploits of the Younger brothers. See full writeup on page 103.

Dr. Quinn, Medicine Woman
An untitled episode
(CBS-TV, February 25, 1995)

A 14-year-old Belle Starr becomes a patient of Dr. Quinn. See full writeup on page 109.

5

Wyatt Berry Stapp Earp

Wyatt Earp fell somewhere in the echelon of such gunslingers as Wild Bill Hickok, Bat Masterson, Billy the Kid, John Wesley Hardin, Bill Tilghman, Clay Allison and Ben Thompson. At least that is what several generations of readers and moviegoers believed. And perhaps they are correct. So much has been written about him that it is difficult to separate fact from fiction.

Wyatt was born in Mannouth, Illinois, on March 19, 1848. He was of Scottish ancestry. Five brothers (of which he was the third born) and several sisters made up the Earp brood. James was the oldest son (born 1841), followed by Virgil (born 1843). The two younger sons were Morgan and Warren. Each would earn a niche in the history of the West.

When Wyatt was only two years old the family uprooted and moved to Pella, Iowa. Wyatt was a good son who never got into any trouble. He remained at home helping his dad on the farm until the age of 16, when the family made another move, this time to San Bernardino, California. Young Wyatt went to work as a stage and wagon driver and at the age of 20 went into the freighting business. In 1868 or early '69 he returned to Illinois to visit his grandfather and there married for the first time; the blissful marriage was short-lived, as Mrs. Earp died during a typhoid epidemic.

After a period of grieving, Wyatt took a job as hunter for an engineering party, which enabled him to journey throughout the Indian country. In 1870 he spent much time in Kansas City, where he met Wild Bill Hickok and other noted frontier characters. In 1872 he was a buffalo hunter but gave up the occupation in 1874 to become deputy marshal of Wichita. He was good at his job, earning the ire of Texas cowboys who became too rambunctious while enjoying a night on the town. Wyatt remained a deputy marshal for about two years before resigning.

Reaching Dodge City in May 1876, he was immediately made the chief deputy marshal at a salary of $250 a month plus $2.50 for each arrest. He remained in the position only until fall, when he and brother Morgan got gold fever and traveled to Deadwood, South Dakota, during the gold rush to that area. Unsuccessful, they returned in 1877 to Dodge City, where

Wyatt became marshal. Morgan and Bat Masterson worked as deputies under Sheriff Charlie Bassett. For various reasons there was considerable opposition to Wyatt, and the days following his appointment were fraught with danger, as a number of gunmen and Texas cowboys were ready to kill him at any opportunity. In fact, there was an offer of $1,000 to anyone who killed him and a guarantee against prosecution. Wyatt never showed fear and handled every situation in a cool-headed way.

Wyatt was on the trail of Dave Rudabaugh and his gang when he first met Doc Holliday, whose help he solicited in locating Rudabaugh. Doc already had a reputation as a gunman and had killed more than once over a saloon gaming table. He had come west to die from consumption. Wyatt did not particularly care for the fastidious Doc at first but they were soon good friends. Normally Doc would be disinclined to associate with a law-man, yet he was drawn to Wyatt as if by a magnet.

In later years Wyatt summed up his impressions of Doc Holliday with these words:

> He was a dentist whom necessity had made a gambler; a gentleman whom disease had made frontier vagabond; a philosopher whom life had made a caustic wit; a long-lean, ash-blond fellow nearly dead with consumption and at the same time the most skillful gambler and the nerviest, speediest, deadliest man with a six-gun I ever knew.—(Stuart N. Lake, *The Life and Times of Wyatt Earp*, page 122)

Wyatt was still marshal of Dodge in the spring of '78. Doc Holliday established himself there also, gambling with considerable success. It was in Dodge that Doc supposedly saved Wyatt's life when he was up against a bunch of Texas cowboys, but that story seems to have been a figment of author Stuart Lake's imagination. No other source confirms it.

Dodge had become so peaceful by September 1890 that Wyatt resigned his marshal job and headed for the new silver mining town of Tombstone, Arizona, to join his brothers in several ventures. Along the way, Holliday caught up with and joined Wyatt in his trek. Wyatt's alcoholic common law wife Mattie accompanied them. The other Earp brothers also took their wives (legal or otherwise) with them to Tombstone.

Tombstone was a hellhole when the Earps got there. The extent and the duration of the violence in and around Tombstone was due largely to wavering, biased law enforcement. The Earps fared well in their first year in Tombstone—gambling and speculating in town lots, mines and other properties. Both Wyatt and Morgan rode shotgun for the Wells Fargo Company, and Wyatt served the company in the capacity of detective. For a while he worked as deputy sheriff of Pima County under Sheriff Charles Shibell. When Cochise County was created, Wyatt expected the governor

Left: Wyatt Earp in 1886. *Right:* Morgan Earp in 1880. (Both courtesy Western History Collections, University of Oklahoma Library.)

to appoint him sheriff but politics entered the picture. Wyatt was a Republican; the governor, a Democrat. The appointment went to Johnny Behan, who was about as corrupt as they come and a womanizer with few peers. Behan promised Wyatt a deputy job but never kept his word. From that point on, the two men had a strong dislike for each other.

Virgil was town marshal for a while in the absence of an elected marshal. James tended bar at a local saloon. Wyatt acquired an interest in the Oriental Saloon, where old friends Bat Masterson, Doc Holliday and Luke Short often worked the gambling tables.

John Behan met a beautiful young lady by the name of Josephine Sarah Marcus while on a trip to San Francisco. Josephine was from a wealthy Jewish family which deplored her ambition to be an entertainer. Nevertheless this beauty went from San Francisco to Tombstone where she became the belle of the honky tonks. Behan showered her with attention and persuaded her to leave the honky tonks by promising to marry her. He set her up as his mistress, but then balked at marriage. Josephine became pregnant by him but, realizing that Behan would never make her Mrs. Behan, she had an abortion. Wyatt stepped in to court her though he was still living with Mattie.

Behan became furious at losing one of his many conquests to Wyatt. It

James D. ("Doc") Holliday in the early 1800s. (Courtesy Western History Collections, University of Oklahoma Library.)

was only one of several reasons for the bad blood between the two men. Eventually Wyatt dumped his alcoholic "wife" Mattie in favor of Josephine.

At the head of the bad element in Cochise County was Old Man Clanton and his sons on the one hand and Curly Bill Brocius and his so-called cowboys on the other. Curly Bill was engaged in cattle rustling and smuggling. Behan looked the other way so long as he got his cut.

Over the objections of Behan, Wyatt was made town marshal and appointed his brothers Virgil and Morgan his deputies. Cooperation between the sheriff and marshal was out of the question.

Ike Clanton's tongue wagging in the Allen Street Saloon during the evening of October 25, 1881, precipitated the most celebrated encounter between outlaws and peace officers in the history of untamed Arizona.

Warren Earp was in California at the time of the O.K. Corral fight and James Earp was physically unable to participate. That left Wyatt and Morgan and Virgil (Wyatt's deputies) to oppose the Clanton bunch, who spread it all over town that they were going to kill the Earps. Although Wyatt wanted Doc Holliday to stay out of any confrontation, he joined the Earps at the last minute—as soon as he found out what was about to happen. Sheriff Behan laughed at the suggestion that he help the marshal, as he wanted Wyatt out of the way for good. The opposing force was made up of Ike Clanton, Frank and Tom McLowery, Billy Clanton and Billy Claiborne. Killed in the approximately 30 seconds of the fight were Frank and Tom McLowery and Bill Clanton. Ike Clanton ducked his tail and ran, refusing to pull a gun. Wounded were Virgil, shot in the leg, and Morgan, hit in the shoulder.

Sheriff Behan wanted to arrest the Earps for murder but didn't have the nerve to stand up against them. Behan and Clanton tried their best to have the Earps and Holliday prosecuted for murder but their testimony was so contradictory that the judge threw the case out of court.

Things only got worse. Virgil was almost killed when ambushed as he

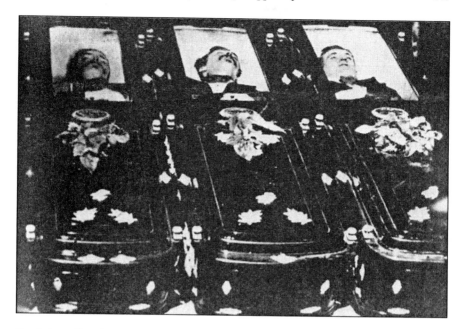

In their coffins: Tom and Frank McLowery and Billy Clanton, after the fight at the O.K. Corral with Wyatt Earp and others. (Courtesy Western History Collections, University of Oklahoma Library.)

was making his nightly rounds of the town. Still later, Morgan was killed by unseen men as he was shooting billiards in the Allen Street Saloon. Wyatt, now a Deputy U.S. Marshal for Arizona, took Virgil and the Earp women to California and upon his return began a bloody vendetta against the Clanton gang. After Clanton was killed in a shootout, Earp and friends clashed with Curly Bill Brocius and his cowboys, who were engaged in various unlawful activities while Sheriff Behan looked the other way. When murder warrants were issued for Wyatt, Holliday and party, they quickly left Arizona.

Wyatt went to California where for a time he raised race horses, then left for the Alaskan gold fields. He was not ready to simply settle down and there was no longer a desire to be a lawman. After about four years in Alaska he returned to the U.S., where for five years he prospected in California and Nevada. Josephine Earp traveled with him wherever he went.

Harry Flood, Jr., a longtime partner of Earp stated that over a period of years Earp filed in excess of 100 mining claims and that he dabbled in real estate and oil operations near Bakersfield.

Although author Stuart Lake liked to take credit as Wyatt's first biographer, he used much material from Flood's unpublished memoirs of Wyatt.

So, too, did Josephine Earp in the book *I Married Wyatt Earp: The Recol-lections of Josephine Sarah Marcus Earp*, edited by Glenn G. Boyer and pub-lished in 1967. She married Wyatt shortly after the O.K. Corral shootout and remained his wife until his death on January 13, 1929. His death at age 80 in Los Angeles was attributed to natural causes. Josie was at his bedside at the end. She died in January 1944. Flood, Earp's business partner, died on March 17, 1958.

Jimmy Cairns, who served as Wyatt's deputy marshal in Wichita in the late 1870s, has stated:

> Wyatt was a wonderful officer; a gamer one never drew breath. He was the most dependable man I ever knew; a quiet, unassuming chap who never drank and in all respects a clean young fellow. He never hunted trouble, but he was ready for any that came his way. There wasn't a bad man in the whole west that Wyatt was afraid of, and some of them came pretty mean. He was always cool and col-lected in the face of danger and never let a threat bother him. His reputation as a dead shot and a man not to be monkeyed with soon spread and the gunmen were few and far between who chose to cross him. The circumstance which made him a Wichita peace officer made him one of the most spectacular figures of the early West.—Stuart N. Lake, *The Life and Times of Wyatt Earp*, Houghton Mifflin, 1956, p. 56

Not everyone shared Cairn's enthusiastic approval of Earp. Paul Andrew Hutton, in his article "Showdown at the Hollywood Corral" (*Montana: The Magazine of Western History*, 1995) quotes noted historian Frank Waters, who characterized Earp as little more than a tin-horn outlaw operating under the protection of a tin badge until he was run out of Arizona. Hutton also took a shot at Stuart Lake's book *Wyatt Earp, Frontier Marshal* (1931) call-ing it the most assiduously concocted blood-and-thunder piece of fiction ever written about the west. In his 1960 *The Earp Brothers of Tombstone*, which was based on Allie Earp's reminiscences, Waters calls Wyatt an itin-erant saloonkeeper, cardsharp, gunman, bigamist, church deacon, policeman, bunco artist and a supreme confidence man.

In the same publication, director Allan Dwan is quoted as saying that Earp was a one-eyed old man in 1915, that he was crooked as a three-dol-lar bill, and that he and his brothers were all racketeers.

Few men knew Earp better than Bat Masterson, who wrote in the Feb-ruary 1907 issue of *Human Life*:

> Wyatt is one of the few men I personally knew in the West in the early days, whom I regarded as absolutely destitute of physical fear.... Wyatt Earp's daring and apparent recklessness in time of danger is wholly characteristic; personal fear does not enter into the equation, and whenever all is said and done, I believe he values his own opinion of himself more than that of others. ... Take it from me, no one has ever humiliated this man Earp, nor made him show the white feather, under any circumstances whatever.

Wyatt Earp like many more men of his character who lived in the West in the early days, has excited by his display of great courage and nerve under trying circumstances, the envy and hatred of those small-minded creatures with which the world seems to be abundantly peopled, and whose sole delight seems to be fly-specking the reputations of real men.

In his book *Burrs Under the Saddle* (1964), author Ramon F. Adams offers another opinion. He says that in the O.K. Corral gunfight the Earps started shooting the opposing force while their hands were in the air and that some in Tombstone called it murder. He states that when Wyatt was run out of Arizona he deserted his common-law wife, and that as late as 1911 Wyatt was arraigned for running a bunco game in Los Angeles, trying to fleece a Mr. Patterson of $25,000.

Adams goes on to state that Wyatt did not perform a single one of the many heroic exploits that he claimed and that he was a pathetic figure who was never respected in his own time. Although a recognized historian, Adams seems to have stretched the truth in making such a statement.

Three books in which Earp was somewhat debunked preceded Stuart Lake's best-selling *Wyatt Earp, Frontier Marshal*. Frederick Bechdolt's *When the West Was Young* (1922), William Breckenridge's *Helldorado* (1928) and William McLeod Raine's *Famous Sheriffs and Western Outlaws* (1929), painted Wyatt and brothers as less than saints. However, Walter Noble Burns' *Tombstone* (1929) was much kinder and presented Wyatt as a hero.

Earp was certainly well-known in his time, especially in the mining camps and on the gambling circuit, and the October 20, 1881, gunfight at the O.K. Corral was widely reported in the national press. But he was never remotely as famous as Wild Bill Hickok, Jesse James or Buffalo Bill. Nor was he particularly identified as a lawman, for men such as Masterson, Bill Tilghman, Chris Madsen, Heck Thomas and for that matter Wyatt's own brother Virgil Earp had longer and more distinguished careers in law enforcement. What Wyatt did have was a literary godfather who through the power of his pen elevated this itinerant gambler and sometime lawman into a towering frontier legend as the incorruptible marshal who tamed the toughest town in the west. The creator of that legend was Stuart Lake.

The movies in which Wyatt Earp has been portrayed appear in the following pages. As usual in dealing with historical characters, the film writers have taken many liberties with the truth. Most of the films have dealt only with the Tombstone segment of his life and have portrayed him as a 100 percent hero based on the O.K. Corral incident. Only in *Tombstone* (1993) and *Wyatt Earp* (1994) has a darker side of Wyatt been shown.

Law and Order (1932), based on W. R. Burnett's novel *Saint Johnson*, is considered to be the first film about Earp and the O.K. Corral shootout, so it is included in the filmography although names were changed in the film so as not to get embroiled in lawsuits. As it was, Josephine Earp protested the film and disliked Burnett's book until he convinced her he considered Wyatt a hero. A friendship then developed between the two. The Burnett script was used twice more as the basis for films. *Law and Order* starring Johnny Mack Brown was a "B" western having little resemblance to the original film. The 1953 *Law and Order* starring Ronald Reagan was more like the 1932 film but on a larger scale. Fictitious names were again used.

Frontier Marshal (1934) and *The Arizonian* (1935) were both based on the exploits of Earp but neither his name or the names of the other actual individuals involved in the Tombstone story were used. However, in *Frontier Marshal* (1939) and *Tombstone—The Town Too Tough to Die* (1942), the name Wyatt Earp was used for the main player. It was also used in subsequent films because by then Wyatt's name had drawing power.

WYATT EARP FILMOGRAPHY

Law and Order
(Universal, March, 1932)

Director: Edward Cahn. Screenplay: John Huston and Tom Reed. Story: W. R. Burnett (*Saint Johnson*)

Walter Huston (Frame Johnson), Harry Carey (Ed Brandt), Raymond Hatton (Deadwood), Russell Hopton (Luther Johnson), Ralph Ince (Poe Northrup), Russell Simpson (Judge Williams), Harry Woods (Walt Northrup), Dick Alexander (Kurt Northrup), Andy Devine (Johnny Kinsman), Alphonz Ethier (Fin Elder). *With* Dewey Robinson, Walter Brennan, Nelson McDowell, D'Arcy Corrigan, George Dixon, Arthur Wanger, Neal Hart, Richard Cramer, Art Mix, Hank Bell.

Marshal Frame Johnson brings law and order to Tombstone but at the cost of his friend Brandt and his own brother. The film has all the usual complications, including the crooked sheriff and the cowardly judge, but Frame fights through at the end.

After the shootout at the O.K. Corral, Frame throws down his badge and rides out of town. Every one of the crooks has been killed as well as Frame's sidekicks and assistants.

"Peace took a holiday in Tombstone and another drama of the wild west was born. With all the cards stacked against him in this picture, Walter Huston manages to crash through for another fine character portrayal, but it's still only a fair to middling horse opera." — *Variety*, March 1, 1932

"*Law and Order* is a first-class production. Huston is seen as deputy marshal of the town and is given an abundance of opportunity. He is the real center of interest. As pals of the marshal are characters portrayed by Harry Carey, Raymond Hatton, and Russell Hopton. Opposed to these four are Ralph Ince, Harry Woods, Dick Alexander, and Alphonz Ethier. Russell Simpson is a well-meaning but at times timid circuit judge." — *International Photographer*, March 3, 1932

Frontier Marshal

(Fox, 1934) 66 min.

Director: Lew Seiler. Screenplay: William Counselman and Stuart Anthony. Story: Stuart N. Lake. Exec. Producer: Winfield R. Sheehan. Producer: Sol M. Wurtzel. Asst. Director: Bert Sebell.

George O'Brien (Michael Wyatt), Irene Bentley (Mary Reid), George E. Stone (David [Abe] Ruskin, Alan Edwards ("Doc" Warren), Ruth Gillette (Queenie La Verne), Berton Churchill (Hiram [Ben] Melton), Frank Conroy (Oscar [George] Reid), Ward Bond (Ben Murchison), Edward Le Saint (Judge Walters), Russell Simpson (Editor Pickett), Jerry Foster (Jerome), Marjorie Seavey, Eleanor Hoagland, Ruth Day (Dance Hall Girls), Ben Hall.

The story is based on Stuart Lake's novel, but the hero's name was changed to Michael Wyatt, to avoid the suits which follow the production of a pseudo-historical play. Otherwise it's the standard plot in which the mysterious stranger brings law and order to a lawless community. In this instance he's not a government official. He spots the mayor as the real mastermind and shows him up, but not until he's in dutch with the girl. The finish goes still more conventional when the dance hall femme boss, who loves him, does the human shield and is killed.

After shooting Queenie with the bullet meant for Wyatt, Melton is then shot by Doc as he tries to escape and falls to his death from a window. Queenie asks Michael to kiss her, and he complies as she dies smiling. Afterward, Michael and Mary embrace in the sunset.

"In addition to O'Brien who is his usual he-man self, good work is turned in by George E. Stone, on comedy, and Alan Edwards as an engaging badman. Irene Bentley is the romance, playing smoothly a negative role, and minor characters are better cast than usual." — *Variety*, February 6, 1934

"Gillette has the audacity to use some of Mae West's lines from *She Done Him Wrong*." — *New York Times*, January 31, 1934

The Arizonian
(RKO, 1935)

Director: Charles Vidor. Story/Screenplay: Dudley Nichols. Assoc. Producer: Cliff Reid. Asst. Director: Dewey Starkey. Photog: Harold Wenstrom.

Richard Dix (Clay Tallant), Margot Grahame (Kitty Rivers), Louis Calhern (Jake Mannan), Preston Foster (Tex Randolph), James Bush (Oren Tallant), Francis Ford (Mayor Ed Comstock), Ray Meher (Frank McCloskey, Joe Sawyer (Shotgun Keeler). *With* J. Farrell Mac-Donald, Edward Van Sloan, Robert Kortman, Ted Oliver, George Lollier, Willie Best, Etta MacDonald, Jim Thorpe, Podner Jones, Hank Bell.

This film is based on Wyatt Earp's exploits in Tombstone but again the film characters have been given fictitious names.

Tallant locks horns with crooked Sheriff Jake Mannen over showgirl Kitty Rivers. Tallant reluctantly decides to accept the job of town marshal of Silver City though he had vowed never again to put on a badge.

Mannen brings in notorious gunman Tex Randolph to kill Tallant. Mannen's plan backfires, however, when Tallant and Randolph become friends. Tallant, his brother and Randolph shoot it out with Mannen and his six henchmen at the Silver City Corral. Randolph and Tallant's brother are killed, as well as Mannen and his men.

Tallant turns over his badge and he and Kitty leave for California for a peaceful retirement.

In Early Arizona
(Larry Darmour Productions/Columbia, 1938) 55 min.

Director: Joseph Levering. Screenplay: Nate Gatzert. Producer: Larry Darmour. Asst. Director: Carl Hiecke. Camera: James S. Brown, Jr.

Bill Elliott (Whit Gordon), Dorothy Gulliver (Alice Weldon), Harry Woods (Bull), Franklyn Farnum (Spike), Art Davis (Art), Charles King (Kaintuck), Frank Ellis (Ben), Edward Cassidy (Tom Weldon), Jack Ingram (Marshal Jeff Bowers), Charles Whitaker (Sheriff). *With* Al Ferguson, Bud Osborne, Lester Dorr, Tom London, Kit Guard, Jack O'Shea, Frank Ball, Tex Palmer, Sherry Tansey, Dick Dorrell, Oscar Gahan, Buzz Barton, Jess Caven, Symona Boniface, Chick Hannon, Bob Card, Cliff Lyons.

Elliott plays a man who is a thinly-disguised Wyatt Earp. Columbia avoided any legal ramifications by not using Earp's name.

Tombstone is terrorized by Bull and his gang. Marshal Jeff Bowers and businessmen join forces to oppose Bull but to no avail. The sheriff and the justice of the peace are in league with the bandits. Marshal Bowers sends for the notorious gunman Whit Gordon, who has just cleaned up Dodge City. Whit arrives in Tombstone in time to save Alice Weldon from bandits who have just held up the stagecoach and killed the driver. Because of his courageous act he is deputized as assistant marshal. When Whit recognizes Bull and his men as the bandits, he accuses them of murder and orders them to get out of Tombstone. They ignore his orders and later return to shoot up the town. Marshal Bowers is killed when he tries to stop the gang and Whit takes his place as marshal. Later Bull and his men are tried before a crooked judge and released. Whit vows to find out who Bull's boss is. An upcoming election to decide the future of the Arizona Territory and who will be the next sheriff becomes the next target of the bandits, as they plan to terrorize Tombstone and frighten the citizens away from the polls.

Bull posts a $5,000 reward for anyone who kills Gordon and makes preparations to stuff the ballot boxes. Buzz, a young boy who likes Whit, secretly disarms the gang. Bull suspects him of informing on them and orders the boy killed. After learning that the early voting results indicate that Whit will be elected sheriff and that Arizona will attain statehood, Bull and his gang approach Tombstone and attempt to scare the citizens away. Whit is able to keep the ballot boxes from being stolen and replaced by Bull's boxes.

When Whit learns of Buzz's death he hunts down Bull and his men and, after a fight, captures the bandit leader. Weldon confesses that it was he who backed the outlaws. Election results indicate that Arizona will become a state. Whit, although elected sheriff, declines the job to take on a bigger one as U.S. Marshal for Arizona.

"Gordon Elliott now comes to the screen as 'Bill' Elliott apparently because Columbia starred him as Wild Bill Hickok in a recent serial. Tombstone's story has been told in pieces in many westerns, never well, and *In Early Arizona* doesn't contribute much either, other than being a western which will get along fairly well. With Tombstone as the avowed subject, it falls away short, however." — *Variety*, December 28, 1938

Frontier Marshal

(20th Century–Fox, 1939) 72 min.

Director: Allan Dwan. Screenplay: Sam Hellman. Source: Based on the book *Wyatt Earp, Frontier Marshall* by Stuart N. Lake. Exec. Producer: Sol M. Wurtzel. Asst. Director: Gordon Cooper, Aaron Rosenberg and Tom Dudley. Photography: Charles Clarke. Film Editor: Fred Allen. Music Director: Samuel Kaylin.

Randolph Scott (Wyatt Earp), Nancy Kelly (Sarah Allen), Cesar Romero (Doc Halliday [*sic*]), Binnie Barnes (Jerry), John Carradine

(Ben Carter), Edward Norris (Dan Blackmore), Eddie Foy, Jr. (Eddie Foy), Ward Bond (Town Marshal), Lon Chaney, Jr. (Pringle), Chris-Pin Martin (Pete), Joe Sawyer (Curly Bill), Del Henderson (Dave Hall), Harry Hayden (Mayor John Henderson), Ventura Ybarra (Pablo), Charles Stevens (Indian Charlie), Harry Woods, Dick Alexander (Curly Bill's Men), Tom Tyler (Buck Newton), Fern Emmett (Hotel Maid), Margaret Brayton (Mother), James Aubrey (Cockney), Pat O'Malley (Customer), Dick Elliott, Cy Kendall (Mine Owners), Harlan Briggs (Editor), John Butler (Harassed Man), Ferris Taylor (Doctor), Kathryn Sheldon (Mrs. Garvey), Henry Clive (Gambler), Arthur Aylesworth, Eddie Dunn (Card Players), William Pawley (Cowardly Man), Jack Stoney (Drunk Man), Jimmie Dundee (Bully), Post Parks (Driver), Philo McCullough, Ethan Laidlaw (Tough Guys). *With* Tom London, Hank Bell, John Bleifer, Hank Mann, Heinie Conklin, Edward Le Saint, George Melford, Jack C. Smith, Walter Baldwin, Harry Strang, Don Hamilton.

The working title for this film was *Wyatt Earp, Frontier Marshal*. However, Josephine Earp threatened to sue because of her dissatisfaction with the script.

Ben Carter, owner of the Palace of Pleasure saloon, complains that his chief competitor, the Belle Union, has brought in saloon girls from Chicago to take away his business. He gets his man Indian Charlie drunk and Charlie shoots up the Belle Union. When the town's marshal refuses to step in, Wyatt Earp, an ex-army scout, steps forward and beats Charlie to the draw. When offered the job of town marshal, Earp turns it down.

Curly Bill and other Carter men take Earp out on the mesa and beat him badly for being a volunteer marshal. Angry, Earp accepts the town marshal job and begins to clean up Tombstone. Gunslinger Doc Halliday arrives to defend the honor of Jerry, owner of the Belle Union. As the result of a series of events Halliday becomes a friend of Earp.

An old girlfriend of Halliday arrives in town looking for Doc. Though unhappy about her finding him, he allows her to stay. When a young Mexican boy is shot, Halliday, with the assistance to Sarah, operates to save his life. Upon leaving the bar, Doc is ambushed and killed by Curly Bill and his men. Earp meets the gang at the O.K. Corral and kills all but Curly Bill, who escapes into town.

When Curly Bill tries to shoot Earp in the back, he is killed by Jerry with Halliday's gun. Sarah decides to stay in the cleaned-up Tombstone but Jerry decides to leave.

"Produced as a lower A in budget, *Frontier Marshal* just misses hitting requirements for general top billing in the major houses, and stand on its own in the subsequents. A fast shooting, six-gun type of melodrama, it carries particular appeal for general audiences."—*Variety*, July 26, 1939

Marshal of Mesa City
(RKO, 1939) 60 min.

Director: David Howard. Screenplay: Jack Lait, Jr. Producer: Bert Gilroy. Prod. Executive: Lee Marcas. Asst. Director: Eddie Donahue.

George O'Brien (Cliff Mason), Virginia Vale (Virginia King), Leon Ames (Sheriff Jud Cronin), Henry Brandon (Duke Allison), Harry Cording (Bat Cardigan), Lloyd Ingraham (Mayor Sam Bentley), Slim Whitaker (Jake Morse), Joe McGuinn (Pete), Mary Gordon (Mrs. Dudley), Frank Ellis (Slim Walker), Cactus Mack (Deputy Marshal), Carl Stockdale (Judge Wainwright), Wilfred Lucas (Marshal Thompson). *With* Monte Montague, Gaylord Pendleton, Spade Cooley, Bob Burns, Rube Schaefer, Edward Piel, Harry Tenbrook, Jack Cheatham, Bill Patton, Ed Brady, Speed Hanson, Ben Corbett.

Schoolteacher Virginia King endures the advances of Sheriff Jud Cronin until she can take it no more. She takes the stage out of Mesa City with the intention of not returning. Cronin sends his gang to hold up the stage. His plan is thwarted by the appearance of Cliff Mason, a retired lawman. He orders the outlaws back to town. The stagecoach has been disabled in the raid. Cliff accompanies Virginia back to Mesa City, where he learns that the town is at the mercy of Cronin. When Pete Henderson, one of Cronin's men, shoots Marshal Thompson in cold blood, Mayor Sam Bentley offers Cliff the marshal job. Cliff accepts and arrests Pete, but after the local judge releases him with a minimal fine, Cliff returns the badge. Cronin's threats prompt Cliff to reconsider, and he urges the citizens to pass an ordinance banning all firearms.

To eliminate Cliff, Cronin sends for Duke Allison, a notorious gunfighter, but his plan backfires when Duke joins forces with the new marshal. After appointing Duke his deputy, Cliff rides after Henderson and brings him back to town. As he turns Henderson over to Cronin, Cliff accuses the sheriff of being a crook. Cronin is able to frame Cliff and Duke for Henderson's murder. Cronin kills Henderson and arrests the lawmen. When the mayor sends for the U.S. Attorney to investigate, Cronin sets fire to the jail to prevent Cliff from testifying, but Cliff and Duke escape the burning building and engage Cronin and his men in a shootout. Duke is killed in the fight but before dying he kills Cronin. With law and order restored, Cliff and Virginia leave Mesa City heading south together.

This film is a remake of RKO's 1935 film *The Arizonian.*

"This is a good George O'Brien western, an edge better than his previous ones, and he has always maintained a good average for the saddle opuses. — *Variety,* December 27, 1939

Tombstone—The Town Too Tough to Die (Paramount, 1942). Richard Dix wore the star as Sheriff Wyatt Earp. Left to right, foreground: Don Curtis (?), Victor Jory, Edgar Buchanan, player, Dick Curtis, Richard Dix; remaining players unknown.

Tombstone—The Town Too Tough to Die
(Paramount, 1942) 76 min.

Director: William McGann. Screenplay: Albert Shelby LaVino and Edward E. Paramore. Story: Dean Franklin, Charles Beisner. Producer: Harry Sherman.

Richard Dix (Wyatt Earp), Kent Taylor (Doc Holliday), Edgar Buchanan (Curly Bill), Frances Gifford (Ruth Grant), Don Castle (Johnny Duanne), Clem Bevans (Tadpole), Victor Jory (Ike Clanton), Rex Bell (Virgil Earp), Charles Halton (Dan Crane), Harvey Stephens (Morgan Earp), Chris-Pin Martin (Chris), Dick Curtis (Frank McLowery), Paul Sutton (Tom McLowery), Donald Curtis (Phineas Clanton), Wallis Clark (Ed Schieffelin), James Ferrara (Billy Clanton). *With* Jack Rockwell, Hal Taliaferro, Charles Stevens, Roy Barcroft, Charles Middleton, Beryl Wallace.

Wyatt Earp arrives in Tombstone with his two younger brothers, Virgil and Morgan. He pays little attention to Curly Bill, the town's gang leader, until a child is killed in the dusty street. At that point Wyatt accepts the marshal's badge and pledges to bring law and order to Tombstone. He cools down Curly Bill and his gang, circumvents plans to get him jailed, reforms young drifter Johnny Duanne and pretty well gets the town quieted down. In the climax, Curly Bill is snagged for holding up a wagon carrying mail. This finale is one of the most rousing gunfights that has come to the screen.

"The violent baptism of a hellroaring western town is told in bold, exciting melodrama in *Tombstone*. It is made to order for a multitude of customers familiar with the Harry Sherman product. Also, the picture's ferocious action and its general quality set it up for solid competition with the war-slanted films, alongside which it will be billed in a wide range of situations."—*Hollywood Reporter*, June 15, 1942

My Darling Clementine
(20th Century–Fox, 1946) 97 min.

Director: John Ford. Screenplay: Samuel G. Engel and Winston Miller. Story: Sam Hellman, from the book by Stuart Lake. Producer: Samuel G. Engel.

Henry Fonda (Wyatt Earp), Victor Mature (Doc Holliday), Cathy Downs (Clementine Carter), Walter Brennan (Old Man Clanton), Linda Darnell (Chihuahua), Ward Bond (Morgan Earp), Tim Holt (Virgil Earp), John Ireland (Billy Clanton), Don Garner (James Earp), Grant Withers (Ike Clanton), Alan Mowbray (Thorndyke), Roy Roberts (Mayor), Jane Darwell (Kate), Russell Simpson (John Simpson), Francis Ford (Town Drunk), Ben Hall (Barber), Arthur Walsh (Hotel Clerk). *With* J. Farrell MacDonald, Jack Pennick, Louis Mercier, Mickey Simpson, Fred Libby, Harry Woods, Charles Stevens, Hank Bell.

When his younger brother is murdered by cattle rustlers, Wyatt Earp takes a job as marshal of Tombstone. An unlikely friendship develops between Wyatt and Doc Holliday, a consumptive gambler. Wyatt falls in love with Clementine, the Eastern fiancée whom Doc has rejected. The Clantons are revealed to be the rustlers, leading to an early morning showdown at the O.K. Corral.

"Remember *Stagecoach*? Well, [Ford] has taken *Clementine* back to the same magnificent country—the stunning beauties of the Monument Valley on the Utah-Arizona border. Here he rebuilt the town of Tombstone, with its O.K. Corral. Here he staged the famous gunfight to the death between the Earps and the Clanton families. Here his skill surpassed that most often remembered Western suspense scene—the Virginian's hunt of Trampas through the fear-emptied streets in *The Virginian*. Really, nothing as splendid as *My Darling Clementine* has come our way since Ford made *Stagecoach.*"—*Hollywood Reporter*, October 9, 1946

"*My Darling Clementine*, though you might not guess it from the title, reproduces vividly and excitingly on the screen the melodramatic life and atmosphere of one of the toughest and wildest towns of the old West. ... The film is tops in acting, direction and authenticity of background. Much of the drama is the sort that gives an audience a solar plexus shiver and sets them on the edge of the seats. If this one misses at the boxoffice, then both westerns and melodrama are out.—*Variety*, October 9, 1946

Gun Belt
(United Artists, 1953) 77 min.

Director: Ray Nazarro. Screenplay: Richard Schayer and Jack DeWitt. Story: Arthur Orloff.

George Montgomery (Billy Ringo), Tab Hunter (Chip Ringo), Helen Westcott (Arlene Reach), John Dehner (Matt Ringo), William Bishop (Ike Clanton), Douglas Kennedy (Dixon), Jack Elam (Kelloway), Joe Hayworth (Hoke), Hugh Sanders (Frazer), Willis Bouchey (Endicott), James Millican (Wyatt Earp), Bruce Cowling (Virgil Earp), Boyd Morgan (Texas Jack), Boyd Stockman (Turkey Creek), William Phillips (Curly), Chuck Roberson (Oliver), Jack Carry (Mort). *With* Rex Lease.

The title comes from a story twist that has Billy Ringo, ex-outlaw, buckling on his gunbelt again to clear himself of a bank robbery frame and to teach his nephew Chip that ranching life isn't as tough as outlawing. Since the frame was set up by Billy's brother Matt, it's a family affair, with the end an audience pleaser.

"The Ringos and the Earps ride again in Global's *Gun Belt*, making for a fast-moving Technicolor Western crammed with action. With George Montgomery and fast-rising Tab Hunter as draw, it should stack up strong as support on a twin bill. Ray Nazarro's megging is topgrade, setting a lively tempo and staging the exciting action in rousing style."—*Hollywood Reporter*, July 1, 1953

"Western action fans will find this United Artists release good entertainment. Action has suspense, plotting and playing bring it off logically, and Technicolor tints are excellent."—*Variety*, July 8, 1953

Law and Order
(Universal-International, 1953) 80 min.

Director: Nathan Juran. Screenplay: John and Gwen Bagni, D. D. Beauchamp. Story: W. R. Burnett (*Saint Johnson*). Producer: John W. Rogers.

Ronald Reagan (Frame Johnson), Dorothy Malone (Jeannie), Preston Foster (Kurt Durling), Alex Nicol (Lute Johnson), Ruth Hampton (Maria), Dennis Weaver (Frank Durling), Russell Johnson (Jimmy Johnson), Chubby Johnson (Denver Cahoon), Barry Kelley (Fin Elder), Walter Cassell (Durango Kid), Richard Garrick (Judge Williams). *With* Buddy Roosevelt, Tris Coffin, Tom Brown, Valarie Jackson, Gregg Barton, William O'Neal.

Frame Johnson, having cleaned up Tombstone, is persuaded by his fiancée, Jeannie, to retire as U.S. Marshal and goes to Cottonwood with his two brothers, Lute and Jimmy, to start a new life as a rancher. Cottonwood is a wide open town run by Frame's old enemy Kurt Durling. The respectable citizens ask Frame to take over as marshal and clean up the town.

Frame refuses and his brother Lute takes the job, but is killed by Durling's son, Frank Durling. Jimmy Johnson, who has fallen in love with Frank's sister Maria, kills Frank in a gun duel. The situation draws Frame into taking over the marshal's job and spearheading the cleanup, after which romance resumes its course.

"*Law and Order* contains some law and almost no order. It has Ronald Reagan as a harried Arizona marshal of the '70s, first in Tombstone then in Cottonwood, and any number of hombres who are quick on the draw. Among these are Alex Nicol and Russell Johnson, Reagan's gunplayful kid brothers. The strife that results from this combination is something awful."— Los Angeles *Times*, May 14, 1953

"*Law and Order* is a good western shaped to the demands of the Universal action market where it should prove a satisfactory grosser. Oater story will find favor with fans of outdoor subjects, as will the familiar cast names, headed by Ronald Reagan, and the Technicolor tests that dress up the presentation."—*Variety*, April 8, 1953

"*Law and Order* is a brisk, fast-moving western that marks an auspicious producing debut for John W. Rogers. Story is well-developed with good, sardonically amusing dialogue that gives the film an added appeal extending far beyond the usual action market. Rogers has gathered together a fine cast that turns in solid performances, with the name value of Ronald Reagan adding to the prospects of strong grosses on this Technicolor oater."—*Hollywood Reporter*, April 3, 1953

Masterson of Kansas
(Columbia, 1954) 72 min.

Director: William Castle. Screenplay/Story: Douglas Heyes. Producer: Sam Katzman.

George Montgomery (Bat Masterson), Nancy Gates (Amy Merrick), James Griffith (Doc Holliday), Jean Willis (Dallas Corey), Benny

Rubin (Coroner), William A. Henry (Charlie Fry), David Bruce (Clay Bennett), Bruce Cowling (Wyatt Earp), Gregg Barton (Sutton), Donald Murphy (Virgil Earp), Gregg Martell (Mitch), Sandy Sanders (Tyler), Jay Silverheels (Yellow Hawk), John Maxwell (Merrick), Wesley Hudman (Gage), Leonard Geer (Lt. Post).

The story stresses the antagonism between Holliday and Masterson, and the friendship of Earp for both. This element provides several scenes of tense excitement. The plot is somewhat involved as a group of crooked cattlemen strive to secure rich Indian grazing lands by framing a peace commissioner. It has no or little historical accuracy, but is true to the character of the three noted gunmen. The gunfights are exciting and the fictional incidents hold interest.

"...a better than average Western, due to three well-thought-out impersonations of three famous gunman. Bruce Cowling, appearing with quiet authority and a believable southern accent, is well cast as Wyatt Earp, and George Montgomery gives what is more than a routine characterization as Bat Masterson. James Griffith is probably the best of the three in the showy role of Doc Holliday."—*Hollywood Reporter*, July 17, 1954

"The characterizations come over well under William Castle's direction of the screen story by Douglas Heyes, and Sam Katzman backs the presentation with suitable outdoor action values."—*Variety*, July, 1954

Wichita

(Allied Artists, 1955) 80 min.

Director: Jacques Tourneur. Story/Screenplay: Daniel B. Ullman. Producer: Walter Mirisch.

Joel McCrea (Wyatt Earp), Vera Miles (Heroine), Lloyd Bridges (Gunslinging Cowpoke), Wallace Ford (Editor/Publisher), Peter Graves, John Smith (Earp's Brothers), Edgar Buchanan (Badman), Mae Clarke (Banker's Wife), Keith Larsen (Bat Masterson), Carl Benton Reid (Mayor), Walter Coy (McCoy), Walter Sande (Wallace), Robert J. Wilke (Ben Thompson). *With* Kermit Maynard, I. Stanford Jolley, Rayford Barnes, Jack Elam, Gene Wessen, Voice of Tex Ritter.

Wyatt Earp pins on the marshal's badge and brings order to Wichita. When he bans pistol toting for townspeople and trail-weary cowpokes alike, and jails without discrimination those who break his strict rules, the town leaders are as upset as they were before law and order came to Wichita. Earp proves his point, however, after several attempts on his life and the death of the wife of the town banker during one wild rampage by vengeful cowboys. With order established there's nothing to prevent his marriage to the heroine, who has stood by him all the time.

"Under the well-paced direction by Jacques Tourneur, the Daniel B.

A friendly horse drops into the newspaper office, greeting (left to right) Joel McCrea as Wyatt Earp, Keith Larsen as Bat Masterson, and Wallace Ford as the newspaper editor in *Wichita* (Allied Artists, 1955).

Ullman screen story is expertly slanted towards the outdoor action fan, who should find this new film version of the career of Wyatt Earp generally interesting."—*Variety*, June 23, 1955

"Many good movies, played by many fine actors, have been made concerning certain portions of his [Earp] career. None have succeeded better than this Allied Artists production in CinemaScope and Technicolor which enables Joel McCrea to deliver a memorable portreait of this deadly peace-loving man."—*Hollywood Reporter*, June 23, 1955

"The film, in CinemaScope and color, is a mixture of fact and fancy—mostly, I suspect, the latter. But with Joe McCrea imparting a sure touch in the role of Earp, and with the excellent assistance of Vera Miles, Wallace Ford, Lloyd Bridges, Edgar Buchanan and Peter Graves, the picture has its interesting moments."—*Los Angeles Examiner*, August 11, 1955

The Life and Legend of Wyatt Earp
(ABC, 1955–1962) 30 min.
228 episodes

Although actors stepped in and out of the series the following actors are most closely identified with the character shown.

Hugh O'Brian (Wyatt Earp), Douglas Fowley (Doc Holliday), Mason Dinehart (Bat Masterson), John Anderson (Virgil Earp), Dirk London (Morgan Earp), Randy Stuart (Nellie Cashman), Lash LaRue, Steve Brodie (Sheriff John Behan), William Phipps (Curly Bill Brocius), Stacy Harris (Mayor John Clum).

In this popular series there was no attempt at giving the television Wyatt Earp the same characteristics or appearance of the real Wyatt Earp.

Gunfight at the O.K. Corral
(Paramount, 1957), 122 min.

Director: John Sturges. Screenplay: Leo Uris. Story: From an article by George Scullin. Producer: Hal B. Wallis.

Burt Lancaster (Wyatt Earp), Kirk Douglas (Doc Holliday), Rhonda Fleming (Laura Denbow), Jo Van Fleet (Kate Fisher), John Ireland (Johnny Ringo), Dennis Hopper (Billy Clanton), Lyle Bettger (Ike Clanton), Lee Van Cleef (Ed Bailey), John Hudson (Virgil Earp), DeForrest Kelley (Morgan Earp), Martin Milner (Jimmy Earp), Joan Camden (Betty Earp), Frank Faylen (Cotton Wilson), Earl Holliman (Charles Bassett), Ted De Corsia (Shanghai Pierce), Kenneth Tobey (Bat Masterson), Whit Bissell (John P. Clum), Tony Merrill (Barber), Harry B. Mendoza (Frank Loving), Charles Herbert (Tommy Earp), Jack Elam (Tom McLowery). *With* Olive Carey, Brian Horton, Nelson Leigh, Don Castle, Dennis Moore, Ethan Laidlaw, William N. Bailey, Dorothy Abbott, Morgan Lane, Roger Creed, Gregg Martell.

Gunfight at the O.K. Corral fits the classic formula of the Western in that it presents a conflict between civilization and anarchy in which there is some ambivalence, expressed in the characters of Earp and Holliday. Although the actual shootout at the end of the film apparently took only a few seconds, it is extended on the screen to several minutes. Ultimately of more interest than the victory of the good guys over the bad guys are Doc Holliday's ambivalent relationships with both Wyatt Earp and Kate Fisher.

"Hall Wallis' *Gunfight at the O.K. Corral* is certainly the best Western of the year and to say this is to say the least you can about this terrific Paramount production starring Burt Lancaster and Kirk Douglas."—*Hollywood Reporter*, May 10, 1957

Hugh O'Brian played the title role in *The Life and Legend of Wyatt Earp*, **a popular ABC-TV series. Any resemblance to the real-life Earp stopped with the name.**

Badman's Country
(Warner Bros., 1958) 68 min.

Director: Fred F. Sears. Screenplay: Orville Hampton. Producer: Robert E. Kent.

George Montgomery (Pat Garrett), Neville Brand (Butch Cassidy), Buster Crabbe (Wyatt Earp), Karin Booth (Lorna), Gregory Walcott (Bat Masterson), Malcolm Atterbury (Buffalo Bill Cody), Russell Johnson (Sundance), Richard Devon (Harvey Logan), Morris Ankrum (Mayor Coleman), Dan Riss (Marshal McAfee). *With* Lewis Martin, Steve Drexel, Fred Graham, John Harmon, Al Wyatt, Fred Krone, William Bryant, Jack Kinney, Tim Sullivan, LeRoy Johnson, Jack Carol.

Badman's Country puts together a group of famous lawmen led by Pat Garrett. They attempt to avert a train robbery by trapping a band of outlaws headed by Butch Cassidy. The outlaws gather outside Abilene to hold up a train carrying gold worth a half million dollars. Garrett wants to entice the outlaws into town where they can more easily be subdued. The townspeople are opposed to Garrett's plan because there will be much gunplay, even though the town will be cleaned up. They eventually give in, however, and the town is freed of Cassidy and his gang.

"The picture does a good job of laying in the threads of the conflict so they can be knotted for a sharp, tight climax and then in prolonging the outcome until the final shootout. Suspense is achieved and so is excitement."—*Variety*, June 4, 1958

The Reluctant Witness
(NBC, 3-31-60) 30 min.
An episode of TV's "Bat Masterson"

Gene Barry (Bat Masterson), Harry Lauter (Sheriff Conners), Donald Murphy (Charles Ryan), Allison Hayes (Ellie Winters), Ronald Hayes (Wyatt Earp).

When the only one who can prove a woman's innocence of murder fails to show up, Bat, knowing she needs a good lawyer, gets Wyatt Earp to pose as one.

The Fatal Garment
(NBC, 5-25-61) 30 min.
An episode of TV's "Bat Masterson"

Gene Barry (Bat Masterson), Ronald Hayes (Wyatt Earp), Ed Nelson (Browder), Lisa Gaye (Elena), Lee Hillman.

Bat takes a job as guard and bouncer in a saloon. Bat runs into serious trouble when a hoodlum uses his weakness for fine clothes to lure him away from his post. Dodge City's famed Wyatt Earp makes himself handy in the ensuing fracas.

Cheyenne Autumn
(Warner Bros., 1964) 170 min.

Director: John Ford. Screenplay: James R. Webb. Suggested by Mari Sandoz's *Cheyenne Autumn*. Producer: Bernard Smith.

Richard Widmark (Captain Thomas Archer), Carroll Baker (Deborah Wright), James Stewart (Wyatt Earp), Edward G. Robinson (Carl Schurz, Secretary of the Interior), Karl Malden (Captain Wessels), Sal Mineo (Red Shirt), Dolores Del Rio (Spanish Woman), Ricardo Montalban (Little Wolf), Gilbert Roland (Dull Knife), Victor Jory (Tall Tree), Arthur Kennedy (Doc Holliday), Patrick Wayne (Second Lieutenant Scott), Elizabeth Allen (Miss Guinevese Plantagenet), John Carradine (Major Jeff Blair), Mike Mazurki (Sergeant Wichowsky), George O'Brien (Major Braden), Harry Carey, Jr. (Trooper Smith), Ben Johnson (Trooper Plumtree), Denver Pyle (Senator Henry). *With* Sean McClory, Judson Pratt, Carmen D'Antonio, Ken Curtis, Shug Fisher, Walter Baldwin, Nancy Hsueh, Chuck Roberson, Jimmy O'Hara, Chuck Hayward, Lee Bradley, Frank Bradley, Walter Reed, Willis Bouchey, Carleton Young, John Qualen, Dan Borzage, Nanomba "Moonbeam" Morton, Dean Smith, David H. Miller, Bing Russell.

Cheyenne Autumn is often described, even by Ford himself, as his apology to the Indians he presented so one-dimensionally in his previous Westerns. It is based on the true story of the grueling 1,800-mile march that the Cheyenne Nation took from a barren Oklahoma reservation to their native Yellowstone. Betrayed by the United States government and decimated by disease and starvation, the Indians set out for Wyoming, joined by Deborah Wright, a Quaker woman who teaches their children. They are pursued by the cavalry and forced into battles along the way.

Cold, hunger, the cavalry and white settlers finally force the Cheyenne Nation to divide, with half going to Fort Robinson for the promise of food and shelter. When these Indians are again betrayed, they make an almost suicidal escape. Archer pleads with Washington on behalf of the Indians, and the Secretary of the Interior agrees that they can remain on their ancestral land; however, only a fraction of the Indian Nation reached the Yellowstone alive.

"*Cheyenne Autumn* is a strange and unusual picture at three hours with an intermission. Its entertainment path is often arduously long and tortuous."—*Hollywood Reporter*, October 7, 1964

Gunmen of the Rio Grande

(Allied Artists, 1964) 86 min.

Jennie Lee Ha Una Huova Pistola (Italian Title)

Director/Screenplay: Tullio Demichelli. Camera: Aldo Ricci. Filmed in Spain, Italy, and France.

Guy Madison (Wyatt Earp), Madeleine Lebeau (Jennie Lee), Gerard Tichy (Zack Williams), Fernando Sancho (Pancho Bogan), Carolyn Davys (Clementine Hewitt), Olivier Hussenot (Judge), Massimo Serato (Leo), Benyt Deus. *With* Dario Michnelis, E. Mern, H. Morrow, Xam Dan Bolas, Alvaro de Luna, Juan Mejan, Natividad Zero.

Jennie Lee, who owns a mine in Mexico, prevails upon Wyatt Earp to help her, as she is threatened by bandit Zack Williams, known as "The Snake." Earp agrees to help her and, assuming another name, thwarts the Snake's attempts to get the mine. Pancho Bogan, a bandit leader, is hired by the Snake to kill Earp but instead most of the bandit's men are killed. The Snake shoots Pancho in the back to silence him, but as Pancho lays dying he asks Earp to avenge his death. Earp kills the Snake and rides away after peace is restored.

Sure it's illogical, but the direction is swift and Madison turns in another enjoyable performance.

The Outlaws Is Coming

(Columbia, 1965)

See full writeup on page 43.

Hour of the Gun

(United Artists, 1967) 101 min.

Director/Producer: John Sturges. Screenplay: Edward Anhalt. Story: Douglas D. Martin (*The Tombstone Epitaph*).

James Garner (Wyatt Earp), Jason Robards, Jr. (Doc Holliday), Robert Ryan (Ike Clanton), Albert Salmi (Octavious Roy), Charles Aidman (Horace Sullivan), Steve Ihnat (Andy Warshaw), Michael Tolan (Pete Spence), Frank Converse (Virgil Earp), Sam Melville (Morgan Earp), Austin Willis (Anson Safford), Richard Bull (Thomas Fitch), Larry Gates (John P. Clum), Karl Swenson (Dr. Goodfellow), Bill Fletcher (Jimmy Ryan), Robert Phillips (Frank Stilwell), William Schallert (Herman Spicer), Jon Voight (Curly Bill Brocius), Lonny Chapman (Turkey Creek Johnson), Monte Markham (Sherman McMasters), William Windom (Texas Jack Vermillion), Edward Anhalt (Denver Doctor), Walter Gregg (Billy Clanton), David Perna (Frank McLowery), Jim Sheppard (Tom McLowery), Jorge Russell (Latigo).

This story takes up where *Gunfight at the O.K. Corral* ended. Ike Clanton arranges to have the Earp brothers and Doc Holliday arrested for murder. The murder charge is dismissed, however, and young Virgil consents to run for city marshal, but Clanton's men ambush and badly wound him. Morgan Earp is killed when he agrees to take his brother's place on the ballot. Wyatt and Doc Holliday escort Virgil and Morgan's body back to California. Wyatt receives a telegram informing him that he has been appointed Federal Marshal. Doc assists in forming an authorized posse, and they set out to find Clanton. On the trip, Wyatt picks off Clanton's men one by one with cold-blooded indifference to human life. Suffering a hemorrhage, Doc is forced to admit himself to a sanitorium but Wyatt continues to Mexico where Clanton is engaged in cattle rustling. Eventually Wyatt traps Ike in a small village and kills him. Having evened the score, he returns for a farewell visit with Doc. As Wyatt leaves, he removes his gun belt and gun. He stores them under his saddle but vows never to use them again.

"As Earp, James Garner performs stoically, with little indication of any inner perturbation, providing Robards with the opportunity to steal much of the film as the consumptive Doc Holliday. Writer Edward Anhalt has not only provided Robards with substantial sardonic wit, but Robards also informs us with most of what we learn of Garner's moral conflict. His are the lines which draw the comparison between his own opportunistic laws of survival and Garner's betrayal of that dedication and who provides constant warnings and reminders lest Garner sacrifice his principles. Given this choral advantage, Robards makes the most of it, scoring the picture's major interest and entertainment."—*Hollywood Reporter*, October 4, 1967

"Genuine zip and interest in first half eventually dissipates into talky, telescoped resolution, perhaps from final editing. A sell based on *Corral* is being used, and wisely so. Fast playoff by United Artists should produce good b.o. returns."—*Variety*, October 4, 1967

Doc

(United Artists, 1971) 95 min.

Director/Producer: Frank Perry. Screenplay: Pete Hamill.

Stacy Keach (Doc Holliday), Faye Dunaway (Kate Elder), Harris Yulin (Wyatt Earp), Mike Witney (Ike Clanton), Denver John Collins (The Kid), Dan Greenberg (Editor). *With* Penelope Allen, Hedy Sontag, Bruce M. Fischer, James Green, Richard McKenzie, John Scanlon, Antoria Ray, John Bottoms, Philip Shafer, Ferdinand Zogbaum, Marshall Efron, Fred Dennis, Mart Hulswit, Gene Collins, Gene Reyes, Lucy Tiller, Vivian Allen, Sharon Frutin, Louis Bar Boo, Per Barclay, Werner Van Husen.

Doc is an intellectual Western about the legendary Doc Holliday and Wyatt Earp, who are portrayed as two eccentric sharpshooters seemingly more interested in each other than in law and order. Doc joins forces with prostitute Kate Elder and the two end up siding with Earp in his battle with the Clanton clan.

"*N. Y. Post* columnist Pete Hamill's debuting screenplay and Perry's direction-production succeed to a large extent, but it takes time to get into, with some fumbling along the way. Stacy Keach, Faye Dunaway and Harris Yulin star in good performances which may shock the naive, outrage the super-patriotic, offend those who prefer the cliches of the nineteenth century American West, but satisfy the well-adjusted."—*Variety*, August 11, 1971

"*Doc* was filmed in Almeria, Spain, where production designer Gene Callahan did an impressive job of recreating Tombstone in the 1880s. Despite its size and apparent authenticity, however, it's the set for a standard Western—crowded streets full of used-up myths."—*Hollywood Reporter*, August 11, 1971

"*Doc* has little to recommend it. It is not an appealing Western, either visually or in its protagonists. The heroes are shown to be worse than the villains and, while Stacy Keach and Faye Dunaway are fair as Doc and Kate, Harris Yulin gives a vague performance as the introspective and hard-as-nails Wyatt Earp."—*The Great Western Pictures II*

I Married Wyatt Earp
(NBC-TV, January 10, 1983) 120 min.

Director: Michael O'Herlihy. Teleplay: J. C. Rapoport. Producer: Richard E. Lyons.

Marie Osmond (Josephine Marcus), Bruce Boxleitner (Wyatt Earp), John Bennett Perry (John Behan), Ross Martin (Jacob Speigler), Alison Arngrim (Amy), Jeffrey DeMunn (Doc Holliday), Joe Ranier (Morgan Earp), Ron Manning (Virgil Earp), Dee Maaske (Mattie Earp), Earl Smith (Frank Stillwell, Randy Wells (Frank McLaury), Joe Corcoran (Tom McLaury), Charles Benton (Ike Clanton), Tom Assalons (Billy Clanton), Elayne Stein (Mamo Speigler), Donna Brown (Allie Earp), Linda Jergens (Louise Earp), Ron Chapman (Marsh Williams), Claud Hereford (Bud Philipot), Kirk Koskells (McMasters), Joseph Bottoms (Driver).

Marie Osmond is Old West singer/actress Josephine Marcus in this dramatization of her memoirs chronicling how a middle-class Jewish teenager from San Francisco joined a travelling opera company at age 19, ran into Marshal Wyatt Earp in Tombstone, became part of a love triangle that included Earp's rival Sheriff John Behan, and ultimately settled down with Wyatt for the next 47 years. The film was made in early 1981, and marked Ross Martin's final role.

Sunset
(Tri-Star, 1988) 107 min.

Director/Screenplay: Blake Edwards. Story: Rod Amateau. Producer: Tony Adams.

Bruce Willis (Tom Mix), James Garner (Wyatt Earp), Malcolm McDowell (Alfie Alperin), Mariel Hemmingway (Cheryl King), Kathleen Quinlan (Nancy Shoemaker), Jennifer Edwards (Victoria Alperin), Patricia Hodge (Christine Alperin), Richard Bradford (Captain Blackworth), M. Emmet Walsh (Chief Dibner), Joe Dallesandro (Dutch Kieffer), Andreas Katsulas (Arthur), Dermot Mulroney (Michael Alperin).

Cowboy star Tom Mix is hired by movie mogul Alfie Alperin to play the lead role in an upcoming film based on the life of Wyatt Earp. In a convoluted mishmash of subplots, Tom and Wyatt team up to solve a case involving the murder of the owner of a swank brothel.

"Mr. Edwards has always had a way of mixing flops in among his hits, but, in the past anyway, even his biggest flops have had some redeeming nuttiness. *Sunset* is such a mess that, when I saw it, I thought the projectionist had misplaced a reel, though he hadn't."—*New York Times*, April 29, 1988

"James Garner's dazzling lead performance is this affectionally acerbic movie's strongest suit, and should result in some respectable boxoffice gold for Tri-Star."—*Hollywood Reporter*, April 29, 1988

The Gambler Returns: The Luck of the Draw
(Kenny Rogers Productions, 1991) 200 min.

Producer/Director: Dick Lowery. Assoc. Producer: Christopher Rich.

Kenny Rogers (Brody Hawks), Reba McIntire (Burgandy Jones), Ric Rossovich (Ethan Cassidy), Dion Anderson (Diamond Jim Brady), Claude Akins (Theodore Roosevelt), Gene Barry (Bat Masterson), Paul Brinegar (Cookie), Jeri Burns (Cade Dalton), David Carradine (Kwai Chang Cane), Chuck Connors (Lucas McCain), Johnny Crawford (Young McCain), Juli Donald (Ruby Roy Dean), Park Overall (Melody O'Rourke), James Drury (Jim), Linda Evans (Kate Muldoon), Brian Keith (The Westerner), Jack Kelly (Bart Maverick), Patrick Macnee (Sir Colin), Doug McClure (Doug), Christopher Rich (Lute Cantrell), Mickey Rooney (Film Director), Brad Sullivan (Judge Roy Bean), Clint Walker (Cheyenne Bodie), Hugh O'Brian (Wyatt Earp), Kent Broadhurst (Sailor), Kevin Furlough (Johnny Loughlin),

Christopher Cody Rogers (Street Urchin), Marianne Rogers (Miss Larosa), Zelda Rubenstein (Butterfly O'Malley). *With* Dub Taylor.

This is the third in *The Gambler* series with Kenny Rogers as the professional gambler who flits from one adventure to another. In this one he is out to engage in the biggest poker game of his life. Tagging along is Reba McIntire, who has money tied up in the game. Hugh O'Brian has a cameo as Wyatt Earp, shooting men down as he and the Gambler stroll along the street.

The Life and Times of Wyatt Earp, Legendary Lawman
(Rhino Home Video, 1993) 53 min.

Producer: Lanny Lee.

Documentary. A factual account of the life of Wyatt Earp, warts and all. Stripped from his head is the halo usually adorning it in the films about him. It is true that Earp was a good lawman, though sometimes stepping outside the law, and at one time or another he was a freight driver, buffalo hunter, card sharp, saloon keeper, womanizer, gold seeker in Alaska, realtor, etc.

Tombstone
(Hollywood Pictures, 1993) 127 min.

Director: George P. Cosmotas. Screenplay: Kevin Jarre. Producer: James Jacks, Sam Daniel and Bob Misiorowski.

Kurt Russell (Wyatt Earp), Val Kilmer (Doc Holliday), Michael Biehn (Johnny Ringo), Powers Boothe (Curly Bill), Robert Burke (Frank McLaury), Dana Delany (Josephine), Sam Elliott (Virgil Earp), Stephen Lang (Ike Clanton), Terry O'Quinn (Mayor Clum), Joanna Pakula (Kate), Bill Paxton (Morgan Earp), Jason Priestley (Billy Breckenridge), Michael Rooker (Sherman McMasters), Jon Tenney (Behan), Dana Wheeler-Nicholson (Mattie Earp), Billy Zane (Mr. Fabian), Buck Taylor (Turkey Creek Jack Johnson), Harry Carey, Jr. (Marshal Fred White), Pedro Armendariz, Jr. (The Priest), Charlton Heston (Henry Hooker), Robert Mitchum (Narrator).

A retelling of Wyatt Earp's experiences in Tombstone following his resignation as marshal of Dodge City. This time Wyatt's darker side is shown as well as his better side. Determined to settle down in Tombstone and go into business with his brothers, he soon is forced to drop his ideology of non-involvement as the town is terrorized by the Clanton and McLaury gangs. There is more killing in this film than in any western of recent memory. The film ends with Wyatt Earp leaving Tombstone.

Tombstone (Hollywood Pictures, 1993) attempted to restore some dimension to Wyatt Earp's character. Kurt Russell (right) was Earp, accompanied by Val Kilmer as Doc Holliday.

"A decent addition to the current cycle of screen and TV Westerns, *Tombstone* is a tough-talking but soft hearted tale that is entertaining in a sprawling, old-fashioned manner."—*Variety*, December 23, 1993

Wyatt Earp—Return to Tombstone
(CBS, July 22, 1994)

Director: L. L. Tarter. Narrator: Buddy McGregor.

Hugh O'Brian (Wyatt Earp), Harry Carey, Jr. (Old Timer), Bruce Boxleitner (Sheriff), Bo Hopkins (Bartender), Bob Steele (Deputy), Trevor Bardette (Ike Clanton), Douglas Fowley (Doc Holliday).

This was a "cheater" film hastily made to capitalize on the current popularity of Wyatt Earp. A minimum of new scenes with Hugh O'Brian were filmed to tie together colorized segments of the old Wyatt Earp television series of the '50s. The result was frustration for the audience. Continuity was lacking. The only good thing about the film was the opportunity to once again see a lot of the character actors of the 1950s.

Another '90s resurrection, this time with Kevin Costner (left) as Earp and Dennis Quaid as Holliday in *Wyatt Earp* (Warner Bros., 1994).

Wyatt Earp
(Warner Bros., 1994) 189 min.

Director: Lawrence Kasdan. Screenplay: Gordon Kasdan. Producer: Jim Wilson, Kevin Costner and Lawrence Kasdan.

Kevin Costner (Wyatt Earp), Dennis Quaid (Doc Holliday), Gene Hackman (Nicholas Earp), Jeff Fahey (Ike Clanton), Mark Harmon (Johnny Behan), Michael Madsen (Virgil Earp), Catherine O'Hara (Allie Earp), Bill Pullman (Ed Masterson), Isabella Rossellini (Big Nose Kate), Tom Sizemore (Bat Masterson), JoBeth Williams (Bessie Earp), Mare Winningham (Mattie Blaylock), David Andrews (James Earp), Linden Ashby (Morgan Earp), Joanna Going (Josie Marcus). *With* James Gammon, Rex Linn, Randle Mell, Adam Baldwin, Annabeth Gish, Lewis Smith, Ian Bohen, Betty Buckley.

Wyatt Earp tells of the life story of the famed lawman, beginning with his boyhood on a Midwest farm. There he learned from his father that blood is what counts—the family must stick together regardless of the circumstances.

After losing his pregnant wife to typhoid, Earp hits the skids for a long period of time. Eventually he becomes a buffalo hunter, winding up in

Wichita where by chance he becomes a lawman. Thereafter the story is a more familiar one. The friendship of Wyatt and Doc Holliday is well presented, as in the fight at the O.K. Corral, which is staged with a brutal and realistic quickness.

Unlike previous Earp films, with the exception of *Tombstone*, attention is given to the Earp brothers' relationships with their women. Wyatt's long-time mistress was an alcoholic whom he abandoned for Josie Marcus, a showgirl who had been the fiancée of Wyatt's enemy, Sheriff Johnny Behan. Wyatt is presented as a cold, implacable man who ruled the Earp clan with an iron hand. Unlike most Earp films, this one brings out his darker side too.

Well-told are the events following the O.K. Corral incident, Behan's attempt to have the Earps prosecuted for murder, and the Earps' roundup or killing of the Clanton gang.

"If you're going to ask an audience to sit through a three-hour, nine minute rendition of an oft-told story, it would help to have a strong point of view on your material and an urgent reason to relate it. Such is not the case with *Wyatt Earp*. ... Everything here that could be expressed in short-hand instead is elaborated on, and everything that could be implied is underlined, especially by the bombastic, faux-ennobling score."—*Daily Variety*, June 20, 1994

"Visually and thematically, this version of Wyatt Earp's life may be the darkest ever put on screen ... but the film's literal-minded approach to the hero's dark soul is one of its terrible problems. *Wyatt Earp* labors to turn this mythic figure into a complex man; instead it makes him a cardboard cutout and his story a creepingly slow one."—*New York Times*, June 24, 1994

Wyatt Earp: Walk with a Legend
(CBS-Television, 1994)

Narrators: Kevin Costner, Lawrence Rasdan and Dan Gordon.

This approximately 20-minute film was made to increase interest in the forthcoming *Wyatt Earp*, a high-budget theatrical film. However, the Kevin Costner starrer turned out to be a box office disaster.

6

James Butler (Wild Bill) Hickok

James Butler (Wild Bill) Hickok owed his early fame not so much to his heroic deeds but to the fact that he was a first-class liar and had found a gullible writer named George Ward Nichols who swallowed his tall tales and half-truths hook, line and sinker. Nichols sold his stories of Hickok to *Harper's Monthly*. His first piece appeared in February 1867 and it introduced Hickok to the multitudes of people east of the Mississippi and west of the Rockies. Until then, he had a reputation only in the Great Plains region.

Wild Bill poured it on thick in describing his adventures to Nichols. To hear him tell it, and as *Harper's* and pulp magazines printed it, he killed hundreds of men (counting Indians). Telling of one Civil War incident, he stated matter-of-factly that he fired 50 times and felled 50 Confederate men.

Wild Bill was born in 1837. As a boy he learned to shoot. Though he didn't kill 200 men, he did, in his lifetime, kill somewhere between eight and 20. Leaving home at an early age, he became a stagecoach and wagon driver. During the Civil War he served as a Union scout; before that, in 1856, he rode with General Jim Lane's Free State forces in Kansas against the Border Ruffians. He tried several occupations in these early years but he could never settle down to a humdrum life.

Hickok was a striking, memorable figure of a man: Six-feet-two, 175 pounds, sinuous, graceful, cool, long wavy brown hair worn shoulder-length, flowing mustache, delicate hands, eyes as gentle as a woman's, almost feminine feet, low-voiced, impeccably dressed in picturesque buckskin clothes, nerveless, thin waist adorned by two ivory-handled Colts worn ostentatiously with the butts thrust forward, dignified bearing. Suffice it to say, he was not your ordinary-looking fellow. He was known to have a liking for the ladies, too.

Nichols was first attracted to Hickok as the result of what has been termed the "McCanles Affair." It happened at Rock Creek, Nebraska, on

Wild Bill Hickok. Photo by E. E. Henry. (Courtesy Amon Carter Museum, Forth Worth, Texas.)

July 12, 1861. Hickok was recuperating from a fight with a bear and was temporarily acting as stablehand. McCanles had sold property to Russell, Majors and Waddell's overland stage company. He, his 12-year-old son, and two men named M. R. Gordon and James Woods rode to the station managed by Horace Wellman. It has been suggested that the purpose of the visit was either to collect money owed McCanles or to kill those at the station, for whatever reason. A more plausible reason might have been to face up to Hickok, as they were both sweet on the same girl. Storekeeper J. W. Brinks was also with Hickok and Wellman at the time. McCanles had told the girl that he was going to "clean up" on those at the station. At any rate, when they got inside the station, Hickok (from behind a curtain) shot McCanles, and Wellman helped in killing Woods. Gordon made a run for the woods and was killed there by one of the three men at the station. The boy was unharmed.

Hickok later bragged that ten men had been killed. Whatever the circumstances were, Hickok, Wellman and Brinks were tried and acquitted. McCanles' son swore none of their party were armed. Hickok and friends claimed self-defense; evidently the jury believed them. Following the McCanles affair, Hickok served as an army scout and engaged in some of the Indian campaigns.

Though Wild Bill was given credit by the pulp writers for cleaning up Abilene, it was actually Marshal Tom Smith who mostly tamed the town. When he was fatally wounded by a shot in the back, the job was offered to Hickok, who had briefly served as marshal of Hays City, Kansas. The year was 1871.

Horan and Sann (*Pictorial History of the Wild West*, 1954) have written an excellent account of Wild Bill during this period:

> In Abilene during his lifetime, he was something less than a six-foot tower of virtue. He didn't wear down the two-inch heels on his $60 boots patrolling the streets to make law 'n' order stick. He spent most of his time bucking the cards in the saloons, or lolling around the cribs where the town's fallen women sold what was left of their charms....
>
> In Abilene a rather expensive error in judgment—suggesting that the "beau ideal" of the Western gunfighters could get as nervous as any dude—tarnished Wild Bill's one display of marksmanship. The marshal shot Mike Williams, another lawman, when he came on the run to help out as Bill was throwing lead at gambler Phil Coe. It happened outside the Alamo, Wild Bill's hangout, and it came down in history in the usual two versions, pro and con. Hickok had just shot Phil Coe when he heard Williams coming and, thinking him to be a friend of Coe, shot him dead.

Wild Bill was allowed to serve out his term, but he was not rehired. He had lasted eight months in Abilene. Later he became a member of Buffalo Bill's Wild West Show, where he was a draw thanks to the purple prose written about him.

William MacLeod Raine (*Famous Sheriffs and Western Outlaws*, 1929) has described Marshal Hickok of Abilene thusly:

> Supreme self-confidence, more than a hint of arrogance, was in his pose. He walked as lightly and as proudly as a buck in the rutting season. Why not? He

was not only the most renowned fighting man of the West but by the testimony of dozen of contemporaries, including General Custer, Henry M. Stanley, and Colonel Little, he was voted one of the most handsome men who ever swung a lithe body to the saddle. Colonel Nichols wrote that he was handsomer in face and form that he thought it possible for a man to be.

In 1876, after floating for a while, Wild Bill wound up in Deadwood. He had been married to a widow, Agnes Thatcher, that spring. After taking her back East to see her kinfolk, Wild Bill decided he was not meant for marriage and cut a trail to the West. His wife never saw him again.

Bill's eyesight was failing to the point where he needed assistance in walking the streets at night. He was no longer the "Prince of Pistoleers." He had lost the respect and awe of those who knew him. His time was spent playing cards and visiting the whores. He is reputed to have had a love affair with Calamity Jane.

Though Wild Bill was no paragon of virtue, he was nevertheless fearless and a dead shot. Few men cared to go up against him in a face-to-face confrontation.

By the time of his death at age 39, the life of Wild Bill Hickok was already the stuff of legend. The pulps had seen to that, along with Hickok's caustic skill as a liar. Bill felt that he was going to die and that Deadwood would be his final resting place. On August 2, 1876, he was playing poker in one of Deadwood's saloons. Normally he played with his back to the wall, but on this occasion the other chairs were taken. There was a door behind Bill and out of that door slipped Jack McCall. Easing up behind Hickok, he put a revolver to Hickok's head and fired. Hickok died instantly, his hands holding what became known as the dead man's hand—a pair of aces and a pair of eights.

The movies have tended to portray Hickok as a tough, upright marshal, the epitome of righteous manhood—except for a few exceptions, that is. Most critics lean toward William S. Hart's *Wild Bill Hickok* and Gary Cooper's *The Plainsman* as being the best Hickok films. Yet these films, too, failed to stick with the truth and portray the real Hickok—warts and all. The 1995 *Wild Bill* is a film to be forgotten as soon as possible. It does depict some of the warts but is not at all a factual account of Hickok's later years.

The B-Western series starring Bill Elliott was a good one by B-Western standards, but Columbia merely used the Hickok name. He might as well have been called Bill Jones or David Smith. But the Hickok name had drawing power. The same was true of the television series starring Guy Madison as Hickok. Madison played as cleancut a Hickok as one can imagine—slender, full of youth, reasonable, possessing a sense of humor, quick with a smile, and quick with his guns and fists. Gone were the long hair, mustache and fancy dress. The series "The Adventures of Wild Bill Hickok" was nothing more than B-Western heroics transferred to the small tube. The series was popular with the younger set and lasted for 113 30-minute episodes (74 in black and white and 39 in color).

WILL BILL HICKOK FILMOGRAPHY

The Pioneer Peacemaker
(Hugh McDonald, 1913) Two reels

Story: Harry Young

Two episodes in the life of J. B. Hickok, known throughout the middle west as "Wild Bill."

Wild Bill Hickok
(Famous Players Lasky/Paramount, 1923) Seven reels

Director: Clifford S. Smith. Screenplay: J. G. Hawks. Producer/Story: William S. Hart.

William S. Hart (Wild Bill Hickok), Ethel Grey Terry (Calamity Jane), Kathleen O'Connor (Elaine Hamilton), James Farley (Jack McQueen), Jack Gardner (Bat Masterson), Carl Gerard (Clayton Hamilton), William Dyer (Horatio Higginbotham), Bert Sprotte (Bob Wright), Leo Willis (Joe McCord), Naida Carle (Fanny Kate), Herschel Mayall (Gambler).

Following the Civil War famed gunfighter Wild Bill Hickok retires to Dodge City where he hangs up his guns and becomes a card dealer. However, when the officials of the town ask him to help rid the community of its bad element, he consents to do so. He does away with the bad element headed by Jack McQueen but, having fallen in love with a married woman, he leaves Dodge City with a broken heart.

"A corking vehicle for William S. Hart's re-entrance into screen prominence. Although another western, it has much to compensate that fact through its ability to sustain interest and suspense, while the action is abundant."—*Variety*, November 22, 1923

The Iron Horse
(Fox Film Corp., 1924) 11 reels

Director: John Ford. Screenplay: Charles Kenyon. Based on an original screen story by John Russell and Charles Kenyon. Presented by William Fox.

George O'Brien (Davy Brandon), Madge Bellamy (Miriam Marsh), Cyril Chadwick (Jesson), Fred Kohler (Deroux), Gladys Hulette (Ruby), James Marcus (Judge Haller), J. Farrell MacDonald (Corporal Casey), James Welch (Private Schultz), Walter Rogers (General Dodge), George Waggner (Buffalo Bill), Jack Padjan (Wild Bill Hickok), Charles O'Malley (Major North), Charles Newton (Collis P. Huntington), Charles Edward Bull (Abraham Lincoln), Colin Chase (Tony), Delbert Mann (Charles Crocker), Chief Big Tree (Cheyenne Chief), Chief White Spear (Sioux Chief), Edward Peil (Old Chinaman), James Gordon (Davy Brandon, Sr.), Winston Miller (Davy as a child), Peggy Cartwright (Miriam as a child), Thomas Durant (Jack Ganzhom), Stanhope Wheatcroft (John Hay), Frances Teague (Polka Dot), Will Walling (Thomas Marsh).

The Iron Horse begins sometime before the Civil War in Springfield, Illinois, where the audience is introduced to young Davy Brandon and Miriam Marsh, childhood sweethearts. Davy Brandon, Sr., dreams of crossing the Western wilderness and he and his son set off for the West. They soon discover an important pass through the mountains but the elder Brandon is killed in cold blood by a two-fingered white man leading a band of Indians. Young Davy witnesses the killing from a hiding place and is later rescued by a scouting party. At this point the film jumps forward several years. During the Civil War, President Lincoln signed a bill that authorizes the construction of a transcontinental railroad. When the war ends, Davy Brandon joins the Union Pacific as a surveyor and meets Miriam, whose father is in charge of construction. Davy and Peter Jesson fight over Miriam; subsequently Miriam refuses Davy's offer of marriage. When a band of Indians led by the renegade Deroux attacks a construction train, Davy recognizes Deroux as his father's killer and kills him in a hand-to-hand fight. Davy then joins the Central Pacific, which is racing the Union Pacific to the center of the continent. The joining of the two railroads is accompanied by the union of Davy and Miriam.

"Just as *The Covered Wagon* was an epic of the plains, so *The Iron Horse* is an epic of the rails. It shows the terrible handicaps under which the first great transcontinental was completed ... wherever Americans live, this one will be waited for. It's great entertainment for the kids, splendid interesting time-passing amusement for the older folk and a lasting and noble contribution to the screen. There's a love story, of course, and lots of comedy."— *Film Daily*, February 7, 1924

The Last Frontier
(Metropolitan, 1926) Eight reels

Director: George B. Seitz. Screenplay: Will M. Ritchie. Story: Courtney Ryley Cooper.

William Boyd (Tom Kirby), Marguerite De La Motte (Beth Halliday), J. Farrell MacDonald (Wild Bill Hickok), Jack Hoxie (Buffalo Bill Cody), Junior Coghlan (Buddy), Mitchell Lewis (Lige Morris), Frank Lackteen (Pawnee Killer), Gladys Brockwell (Cynthia Jaggers).

The story opens shortly after the Civil War with an impoverished Southerner starting for the great West, accompanied by his wife and daughter. Their wagon train is attacked and both of the parents are killed. In her grief, the girl, who was coming out to meet her fiancé Tom Kirby, blames him for the death of her folks.

This gives Lige, a hypocritical trader who is shipping and selling rifles to the Indians, a chance to take the girl to his home and later try to lure her away under the pretext that he is going to take her back east. In reality, he is running away from the town because his dealings with the natives have been discovered and he is in danger of being lynched.

In the big scene a buffalo stampede is organized by the Indians to cover their attack on the town. In this stampede the double-crossing Lige and his mistress meet their death, while the young hero rescues the girl.

"*The Last Frontier* was originally destined to be an epic of the west of proportions to rival *The Covered Wagon*. It was conceived in the mind of the late Thomas H. Ince as a picture that should be a splendid record of the last days of the west, but before Ince could carry out the production of the picture he died. ... The result is an ordinary western that just about ranks as a program production. ... As a western in the spots where westerns are popular it will get the money and please the audiences, but it does not rank in the class for which it was originally intended."—*Variety*, October 27, 1926

The Last Frontier
(RKO, 1933) 12 Chapters

Director: Spencer Bennet. Screenplay: George Plympton and Robert F. Hill. Story: Courtney Riley Cooper. Producer: Fred McConnell.

CHAPTER TITLES

1. The Black Ghost Rides
2. The Thundering Herd
3. The Black Ghost Strikes
4. A Single Shot
5. Clutching Hands
6. The Terror Trail
7. Doomed
8. Facing Death

9. Thundering Doom
10. The Life Line

11. Driving Danger
12. The Black Ghost's Last Ride.

Creighton Chaney [Lon Chaney, Jr.] (Tom Kirby), Dorothy Gulliver (Betty Halliday), Mary Jo Desmond (Aggie Kirby), Francis X. Bushman, Jr. (Jeff Maitland), Joe Bonomo (Blackie), Yakima Canutt (Wild Bill Hickok), Slim Cole (Happy), Judith Barrie (Rose Maitland), Richard Neal (Lige Morris), LeRoy Mason (Buck), Peter Morrison (Hank), Claud Peyton (Colonel Halliday), Ben Corbett (Jake), Fritzi Fern (Maria Morris), Bill Nestell (Tex), William Desmond (General Custer). *With* Walt Robbins, Leo Cooper, Ray Steel, Frank Lackteen, Fred Burns.

Tom Kirby, editor of the Morrisville Paper, suspects Lige Morris, the town's most influential citizen, and newcomer Jeff Maitland, of smuggling firearms to the Indians. In the guise of the Black Ghost, a mysterious range rider, and aided by General Custer, Colonel Halliday, his daughter Betty and Happy and Aggie, Kirby undertakes to prove Morris and his associates guilty of gun smuggling and other villainies. Wild Bill Hickok also aids Kirby in his fight.

While gathering evidence, Kirby is caught with some of the contraband firearms in his possession, and becomes a fugitive. He remains at large seeking to prove his innocence and capture the real culprits. The discovery of gold at Placer City is announced and Morris reveals himself as the arch villain. Reckless with power, he endeavors to capture the rights to the mines. He encounters Kirby, whose faction finally proves victorious. Tom and Betty get married.

Aces and Eights

(Puritan, 1936) 62 min.

Director: Sam Newfield. Story/Screenplay: Arthur Durlan. Producers: Sam Newfield and Leslie Simmonds.

Tim McCoy (Gentleman Jim Madigan/Wild Bill Hickok), Luana Walters (Juanita Hernandez), Rex Lease (Jose Hernandez), Wheeler Oakman (Ace Morgan), Frank Glendon (Amos Harden), Charles Stevens (Capital [Felipe] de Lopez), Earl Hodgins (Marshal), Jimmy Aubrey (Lucky), Joseph Gerard (Don Juillo Hernandez), Frank Ellis (Deputy), Jack Evans, Tom Smith (Spectators), John Merton, Fred Parker (Gamblers). *With* Karl Hackett, Jack Kirk, Oscar Gahan, Milburn Morante, Artie Ortego, Clyde McClary, Robert Walker.

In a prologue, Wild Bill Hickok is shot in the back by Jack McCall while playing cards in a Deadwood saloon. He holds two pair, aces and eights, which come to be known in the West as the "death hand."

Gentleman gambler Tim Madigan is then introduced as Hickok's successor. Madigan, who does not carry a gun, accuses another poker player of cheating. Jose Hernandez overhears Madigan's accusation. Having lost heavily to the accused gambler, Jose Hernandez pulls a gun and demands his money. Later the gambler is shot from behind a tree and Madigan is blamed. The marshal goes after Madigan, who slips across the border into Mexico. Madigan meets Jose, who offers his father's hacienda as a resting place. Madigan finds that Don Juillo and his daughter are in danger of losing the ranch to Ace Morgan and Amos Harden, who have extended much credit to Morgan's saloon, the Gold Dollar, and forces Morgan to give up Jose's IOUs. Morgan and Harden then try to take the ranch by force. While the fight is going on between Madigan and Morgan, the marshal arrives with evidence that Morgan killed the gambler. Madigan and Jose are cleared. The ranch is returned to the Hernandez family, and the Gold Dollar saloon is given to Madigan's sidekick Lucky.

Custer's Last Stand
(Stage and Screen, 1936) 15 Chapters

Director: Elmer Clifton. Screenplay: George A. Durlan, Eddy Graneman and William Lively. Producer: George M. Merrick.

CHAPTER TITLES

1. Perils of the Plains
2. Thundering Hoofs
3. Fires of Vengeance
4. The Ghost Dancers
5. Trapped
6. Human Wolves
7. Demons of Disaster
8. White Treachery
9. Circle of Death
10. Flaming Arrow
11. Warpath
12. Firing Squad
13. Red Panthers
14. Custer's Last Ride
15. The Last Stand

Rex Lease (Kit Cardigan), William Farnum (Fitzpatrick), Lona Andre (Belle Meade), Dorothy Gulliver (Red Fawn), Reed Howes (Tom "Keen" Blade), Jack Mulhall (Maj. Trent), Creighton Hale (Hank), Milburn Moranti (Buckskin), Ruth Mix (Mrs. Elizabeth Custer), Bobby Nelson (Bobby), Frank McGlynn, Jr. (Gen. Custer), Helen Gibson (Calamity Jane), Allan Greer (Wild Bill Hickok), William Desmond (Wagon Boss), Nancy Caswell (Barbara Trent), Chief Thunder Cloud (Young Wolf), Marty Joyce (Buzz), George Chesebro (Lt. Roberts), Ted Adams (Buffalo Bill/Barney), George Morrell (Sgt. Flannigan), Howling Wolf (Sitting Bull), Robert Walker (Pete), Walter James (Judge Hooker), Cactus Mack (Lt. Weir), Budd Buster (Maj. Ware), Carl Mathewa (Maj. Reno), Lafe McKee (Capt. Benteen), Mabel Strickland (Mabel), Barney Fury (Sgt. Peters), James Sheridan

(Jim), Chick Davis (Rain-in-the-Face), Ken Cooper (Spike), Chief Big Tree (Medicine), Iron Eyes Cody (Brown Fox), Patter Poe (Crow Scout), Carter Wayne (Striker Martin), Ed Withrow (Blue Crow). *With* Whiten Sovern, Buddy Fisher, Charles Hunter, William Hunt, Walter Gable, Bill Thompson, William Bartlett, Humming Bird, Swift Eagle, Tall Tree, Little Eagle, Lone Pine, Herb Jackson, J. Spencer, White Feather, Red Star Cody.

A sacred golden arrow is lost during one of the skirmishes between red man and whites and is recovered by Major Trent, who is unaware that it carries the secret of the location of an Indian cavern of gold. Knowing its secret, renegade Tom Blade seeks to steal the arrow. To achieve this purpose, he finds it necessary to keep hostilities going. Scout Kit Cardigan suspects Blade and fights to prevent all-out war, but the stage is set for Custer's Last Stand.

Although the independent serials (those produced by small firms other than Republic, Universal or Columbia) are general criticized as being of inferior quality, they nevertheless have their charm. One of their attractions is the use of many familiar character actors. *Custer's Last Stand* is a prime example. No less than ten members of the cast had once been stars in their own right, and the rest of the cast was composed primarily of familiar actors with whom serial fans were comfortable.

The Plainsman
(Paramount, 1937) 115 min.

Producer/Director: Cecil De Mille. Screenplay: Waldemar Young, Harold Lamb and Lynn Riggs. Based on stories by Courtney Ryley and Frank J. Wilstach.

Gary Cooper (Wild Bill Hickok), Jean Arthur (Calamity Jane), James Ellison (Buffalo Bill), Charles Bickford (John Lattimer), Helen Burgees (Louise), Porter Hall (Jack McCall), Paul Harvey (Yellow Hand), Victor Varconi (Painted Horse), John Miljan (Gen. George Custer), Frank McGlyn (Abraham Lincoln), Granville Bates (Van Ellyn), Frank Albertson (Young Trooper), George F. Hayes (Breezy), Anthony Quinn (Indian), George Cleveland (Van Ellyn Associate), Irving Bacon (Hysterical Trooper), Francis Ford (Old Veteran), Fuzzy Knight (Miner Dave), Purnell Pratt (Capt. Wood), Frank Kohler (Jake), Pat Moriarty (Sgt. McGinnis), Charles Judels (Tony, the Barber).

The film traces the story of Wild Bill Hickok and Calamity Jane. When Calamity is abducted by Indians, Bill tries to free her but is also captured himself. Rather than see Bill burned at the stake, Calamity gives her captors information that leads to General Custer's Last Stand.

"*The Plainsman* reveals Cecil De Mille as the master melodramist. Less stylized, better balanced, obviously not concerned with uppercase art, attractive simply as the narrative of plains men and women conquering the wilderness with blood and iron, this will probably prove De Mille's most prosperous picture. ... Spectacle, mass movement, beautiful pictorial composition, although impressively used, is subordinated to intimate human concerns of conflicting characters:. The picture builds with mounting emotional tension through colorful romance and savage battle holding attention every moment."—*Variety*, November 21, 1936

"De Mille may have romanticized his history as well as condensed it but he has done it to exceedingly good purpose. The picture makes no claims to be documentary and it does introduce such romantic figures as Wild Bill Hickok, Calamity Jane, Buffalo Bill Cody and General Custer with sufficing accuracy. It even sacrifices a happy ending to follow history in ending Wild Bill's career with a bullet in a finale that is the one draggy sequence."—*The Hollywood Reporter*, November 21, 1936

Frontier Scout

(Grand National, 1938) 61 min.

Director: Sam Newfield. Story/Screenplay: Frances Guihan. Producer: Franklyn Warner.

George Houston (Wild Bill Hickok), Al St. John (Whiney Roberts), Beth Marion (Mary Ann), Dave O'Brien (Steve), Jack Ingram (Folsom), Guy (Alden) Chase (Bennett), Slim Whitaker (King), Ken Duncan (Davis), Carl Mathews (Crandall), Kit Guard (Slim), Bob Woodward (Shorty), Jack Smith (General Grant), Walter Byron (Adams), Budd Buster (Jessup). *With* Jim Thorpe.

Intrepid Union spy Wild Bill Hickok, after a series of successful sorties with his pals Whiney and Steve, is entrusted by General Grant with a message which counteracts a planned Confederate attack which might delay the end of the Civil War. After the war Steve is host at a big ball at which Wild Bill meets Steve's sister Mary Ann and Bennett, Steve's partner in a new cattle shipping depot at the Kansas end of a new railroad. Bill is invited to join them, but prefers to follow a life of adventure with Whiney.

Several years later, Steve and Bennett are facing failure because a gang of desperadoes has blockaded the main pass from Texas to the station and are charging ten dollars per head toll and seizing the herds of those who refuse to pay. Bill and Whiney trap the outlaws, and prove that the real leader was Bennett, who has been doublecrossing his partner. Mary Ann urges Bill to settle down as Steve's partner, but Whiney arrives with news of much trouble at a settlement beyond the railroad. Wild Bill and Whiney ride off to further adventures.

"*Frontier Scout* will take its place among the rank and file westerns which pour from poverty row and the California landscape in generous quantities. It's no whiz, and Houston doesn't mean anything on the marquee to the 10-15-20 patronage. Anything better than average will be surprising."—*Variety*, January 11, 1939

The Great Adventures of Wild Bill Hickok
(Columbia, 1938) 15 Chapters

Director: Mack Wright and Sam Nelson. Screenplay: George Rosenor, Charles Arthur Powell, G. A. Durlam, Dallas Fitzgerald and Tom Gibson. Producer: Harry S. Webb. Story: John Peere Miles.

CHAPTER TITLES

1. Law of the Gun
2. Stampede
3. Blazing Terror
4. Mystery Canyon
5. Flaming Brands
6. The Apache Killer
7. Prowling Wolves
8. The Pit
9. Ambushed
10. Savage Vengeance
11. Burning Waters
12. Desperation
13. Phantom Bullets
14. The Lure
15. Trail's End

Bill Elliott (Wild Bill Hickok), Monte Blue (Cameron), Frankie Darro (Jerry), Dickie Jones (Bud), Sammy McKim (Boots), Kermit Maynard (Kit Lawson), Chief Thunder Cloud (Gray Eagle), Ray Mala (Little Elk), Roscoe Ates (Snake Eyes), Monty Collins (Danny), Carole Wayne (Ruth Cameron), J. P. McGowan (Scudder), Eddy Waller (Stone), Walter Wills (Bruce), Kenneth Duncan (Blackie), Lee Phelps (Catty), Reed Hadley (Blakely), Robert Fiske (Morrell), Earle Hodgins (Kimball), Ed Brady (Wilson), Earl Dwire (Jenkins), George Chesebro (Metaxa). *With* Alan Bridge, Budd Buster, Dick Cramer, Ray Jones, Carl Mathews, Walter Miller, Jack Rockwell, Slim Whitaker, Art Mix, Blackjack Ward, Bud McClure, Jack Montgomery, Frank Ellis, Jack Perrin, Steve Clark, Artie Ortego, Curly Dresden, Budd Buster, Jack Rockwell, Tom London, Edmund Cobb, Ernie Adams, Hank Bell, Carl Mathews, Ray Henderson, Francis Walker, Al Haskell, Iron Eyes Cody, Herman Hack, Bill Patton, Frank Lackteen, William Gould, Jack Evans, Ethan Laidlaw, Gene Alsace (Rocky Camron), Charles Brinley, Bob Burns, Lew Meehan, Al Thompson, Chuck Hamilton, Dick Boteler, Horace B. Carpenter, A. R. Haysee, Bruce Lane, Buck Connors, Jesse Graves, David McKim, George Morrell, Edward Hearn, Robert Walker, Allan Cavan.

The story concerns the efforts of Wild Bill Hickok to enforce the law in Abilene, protect a cattle herd being driven from Texas, and to clear the way for the railroad, construction of which has been prevented by the "Phantom Raiders." Bill Elliott plays "Wild Bill." His is a personality that fits the plainsman and he plays the part to the hilt. The film is full of familiar faces and names for those who frequent Westerns quite often.

This serial is considered by most serial buffs as perhaps the best of Columbia's chapterplays. Both the budget and production values were above par for Columbia. Its popularity led to Elliott becoming a major Western star and gave him a name change of "Bill."

Deadwood Dick
(Columbia, 1940) 15 Chapters

Director: James W. Horne. Producer: Larry Darmour. Screenplay: Wymdham Gittens, Morgan B. Cox, George Morgan, John Cutting.

CHAPTER TITLES

1. A Wild West Empire
2. Who Is the Skull?
3. Pirates of the Plains
4. The Skull Baits a Trap
5. Win, Lose, or Draw
6. Buried Alive
7. The Chariot of Doom
8. The Secret of Number Ten
9. The Fatal Warning
10. Framed for Murder
11. The Bucket of Death
12. A Race Against Time
13. The Arsenal of Revolt
14. Holding the Fort
15. The Deadwood Express

Don Douglas (Dick Stanley/Deadwood Dick), Lorna Gray [Adrian Booth] (Anne Butler), Lane Chandler (Wild Bill Hickok), Marin Sais (Calamity Jane), Harry Harvey (Dave), Jack Ingram (Buzz Ricketts), Charles King (Tex), Edward Cassidy (Drew/The Skull), Robert Fiske (Ashton), Lee Shumway (Bentley), Edmund Cobb (Steele), Ed Peil, Sr. (Sears), Edward Hearn (Sharp), Karl Hackett (Jack McCall), Roy Barcroft (Jim Bridges), Bud Osborne (Stagecoach Driver), Fred Kelsey (Bartender), Edward Cecil (McCall's Defender), Joseph W. Glart (Judge), Tom London, Kit Guard, Al Ferguson (Henchmen). *With* Constantine Romanoff, Yakima Canutt, Franklyn Farnum, Kenneth Duncan, Charles Hamilton, Eddie Featherstone, Jim Corey, Joseph Girard.

As statehood seems imminent for the Dakota Territory, The Skull, a grotesquely masked criminal, seeks to create an outlaw empire and gain control of rich mineral lands. *Dakota Pioneer Press* publisher Dick Stanley adopts the disguise of Deadwood Dick, a masked figure, to battle the outlaws, with Wild Bill Hickok giving assistance.

Beyond the Sacramento
(Columbia, 1940) 58 min.

Director: Lambert Hillyer. Screenplay: Luci Ward. Producer: Jack Fier.

Bill Elliott (Wild Bill Hickok), Evelyn Keyes (Lynn Perry), Dub Taylor (Cannonball), John Dilson (Jason Perry), Bradley Page (Cord Crowley), Frank LaRue (Jeff Adams/Shark Lambert), Norman Willis (Nelson), Steve Clark (Curly Wallson), Jack Clifford (Sheriff), Don Beddoe (Warden McKay), Harry Bailey (Storekeeper), Bud Osborne (Joe), George McKay (Bartender), Tex Cooper (Stage Driver Tex), Ned Glass (Bank Teller), Art Mix, Blackjack Ward, Olin Francis (Outlaws), Clem Horton (Townsman).

Recognizing Jeff Adams, Lodestone newspaper publisher, and Cord Crowley, Lodestone saloonkeeper, as notorious swindlers, Wild Bill Hickok's pal Cannonball rides to alert the famous foe of lawbreakers. A few days later Hickok rides into town, where Adams sees him. The newcomer calls upon Jason Perry, town banker, and his pretty daughter Lynn to enlist their aid, but discovers Perry is in cahoots with Crowley.

In Crowley's saloon, the swindler pleasantly suggests Wild Bill leave town; when he refuses to do so, a terrific fight ensues. Bill wins and leaves the saloon before he is arrested for disturbing the peace, as Crowley had planned. Again visiting the Perry home, Bill discovers he can expect no help whatsoever in smashing the crime ring.

Letting it be known that he and Cannonball will ride out to the Bronson mine that night, Bill and Cannonball break into Adams' printing office when Crowley's men ride out to waylay them. Working by candlelight, they reset the next day's front page to include a story about Adams' past frauds.

Adams, confronted the next day by his own past deeds, kills himself. Not yet exposed, Crowley tries to loot the Lodestone Bank. Lynn is wounded in the attempt. Perry, doubly vengeful, goes gunning for Crowley and is himself killed.

Unexpectedly breaking in upon the gunmen through a side window, Bill precipitates a terrific gunfight which ends with Crowley killed and his men in custody.

"A standard giddyapper boasting one unique twist, this will get by for satisfactory results with the cowhand and junior trade. Like others out of the Columbia barn starring Bill Elliott as Wild Bill Hickok, it's patterned on the 'Lone Ranger' mold, which in turn gets inspiration from 'Robin Hood,' etc."—*Variety*, May 7, 1941

Young Bill Hickok
(Republic, 1940) 59 min.

Director: Joseph Kane. Screenplay: Olive Cooper and Norton S. Parker. Roy Rogers (Bill Hickok), George F. Hayes (Gabby Whittaker), Jacqueline Wells [Julie Bishop] (Louise Mason), John Miljan (Nicholas Tower), Sally Payne (Calamity Jane Cannary), Archie Twitchell (Phillip), Monte Blue (Marshal Evans), Hal Taliaferro [Wally Wales] (Morrell), Ethel Wales (Mrs. Stout), Jack Ingram (Red), Monte Montague (Majors), Iron Eyes Cody (Big Bear), Fred Burns (Waddell), Frank Ellis (Stage Driver), Slim Whitaker (Raider), Jack Kirk (Hays), Hank Bell (Hank). *With* Henry Wills, William Desmond, Dick Elliott, John Elliott, Jack Rockwell, Bill Wolfe, Tom Smith.

Young Bill Hickok, scarcely out of his teens, is a relay station attendant for one of the freighting companies. After a series of stage raids that appear to be highly organized, he is assigned to personally escort a shipment of gold.

To doubly insure the safe delivery of the gold, Bill entrusts it to his old friend Gabby Whittaker, who is to secretly take it across the California line with a pack of horses he is herding. He is accompanied by his niece Calamity Jane Cannary, who is in love with Hickok. But Hickok is engaged to marry Louise Mason, daughter of a Southern officer, to whom he confides his plans for the secret shipment of gold.

Louise is concerned over her lover's safety, in spite of his reassurance, and confides her misgivings to Nicholas Tower, one of the leading citizens of the town. She tells him that Bill is conveying decoy gold and the real gold is being sent with Gabby and Calamity Jane.

Tower, who is really a European agent sent to America to seize western territory and gain the control of California's gold supply, is also the brains behind the stage raids. He arranges for his guerrillas to waylay Gabby and seize the gold, and then convinces the citizens that Hickok is the instigator of the raids.

Bill is thrown into jail and it is only through the efforts of Calamity Jane, the girl whose love he could not return, that he is set free in an exciting climax which involves the assassination of President Lincoln.

"Rogers plays the historical hero with a somewhat staccato effect, but his tenoring has some measure of compensation as he tosses off a couple of western standards. Since, history tells us, Hickok didn't actually come into his own for some years after the Civil War, it's to be supposed that the yarn has been fictionalized from what the authors pictured to be his first prominence during the war between the states and immediately thereafter, which accounts for the title."—*Variety*, October 2, 1940

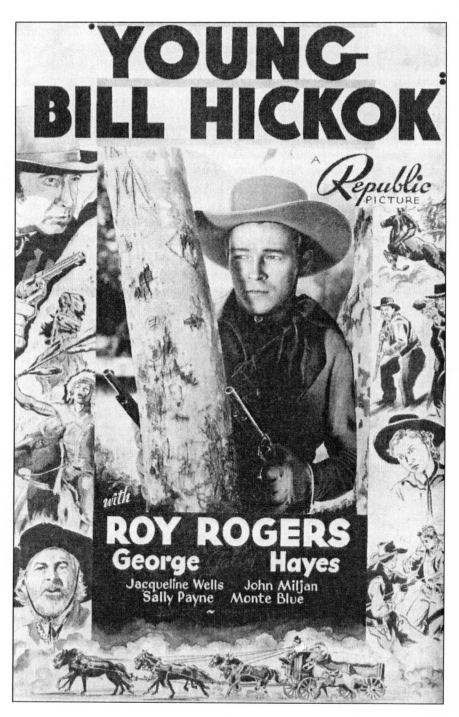

Roy Rogers as *Young Bill Hickok* (Republic, 1940).

Prairie Schooners
(Columbia, 1940) 58 min.

Director: Sam Nelson. Screenplay: Robert Lee Johnson and Fred Myton. Story: George Franklin.

Bill Elliott (Wild Bill Hickok), Evelyn Young (Virginia Benton), Dub Taylor (Cannonball), Kenneth Harlan (Dalton Stull), Ray Teal (Wolf Tanner), Bob Burns (Jim Gibbs), Netta Packer (Cora Gibbs), Richard Fiske (Adams), Edmund Cobb (Rusty), Jim Thorpe (Chief Sanche), George Morrell (Townsman), Merrill McCormack (Farmer), Sammy Stein (Henchman). *With* Ned Glass, Lucien Maxwell.

Wild Bill arrives in a small Kansas town just in time to stop the enraged farmers from lynching Dalton Stull, an unscrupulous money lender who is foreclosing all their mortgages. Bill offers to try to arrange a peaceful settlement, but when he fails, he suggests that they give up their land and go out to Colorado to search for gold.

Hickok is leading the procession of covered wagons when a band of Indians attacks the prairie schooners. During the attack, Virginia Benton is kidnapped. In a thundering climax, Wild Bill and his friend Cannonball devise a scheme whereby the girl and the wagon train are saved after a desperate battle.

"Latest Wild Bill Hickok thriller gives Bill Elliott a break, showing him up as a comer in the horse opera ranks. As much can't be said for the rambling, implausible yarn. Consequently, the comparatively elaborate production outlay seems wasted. Only meager returns appear in prospect."—*Variety*, November 13, 1940

Badlands of Dakota
(Universal, 1941) 75 min.

Director: Alfred E. Green. Screenplay: Gerald Geraghty. Story: Harold Shumate. Producer: George Waggner.

Robert Stack (Jim Holliday), Ann Rutherford (Anne Grayson), Richard Dix (Wild Bill Hickok), Frances Farmer (Calamity Jane), Broderick Crawford (Bob Holliday), Hugh Herbert (Rocky Plummer), Andy Devine (Spearfish), Fuzzy Knight (Hurricane Harry), Lon Chaney, Jr. (Jack McCall), Addison Richards (General Custer), Bradley Page (Chapman), Samuel S. Hinds (Uncle Wilbur). *With* Jane Farley, Edward Fielding, Willie Fung, Emmett Vogan, Glenn Strange, Carleton Young, Dwight Latham, Walter Carlson, Guy Bonham.

The story, set in 1876, is centered on the romance between Jim Holliday and Anne Grayson, with a secondary love affair between Calamity Jane and Bob Holliday. A Sioux Indian night attack on the village brings the yarn

Anne Grayson (Ann Rutherford) embraces her fallen lover, Jim Holliday (Robert Stack), as Wild Bill Hickok (Richard Dix) kneels to comfort her in *Badlands of Dakota* (Universal, 1941).

to an exciting climax as Calamity Jane halts the robbery of the town's bank and ends the outlawry of her sweetheart with a bullet.

"Gold boom days of the Dakotas background this moving melodrama of the west in Wild Bill Hickok's era. It's about the most actionful feature to come out of this studio in months. Not intended as an 'epic,' it's best fitted to the programmer category. Production looks like a real money-getter for Universal."—*Variety*, September 10, 1941

Across the Sierras

(Columbia, 1941) 52 min.

Director: D. Ross Lederman. Screenplay: Paul Franklin. Producer: Leon Barsha.

Bill Elliott (Wild Bill Hickok), Richard Fiske (Larry), Luana Walters (Alice), Dub Taylor (Cannonball), Dick Curtis (Mitch), Milt Kibbee (Sheriff), LeRoy Mason (Stanley). *With* Ralph Peters, Tex

Cooper, Eddie Laughton, Carl Knowles, Tom London, Edmund Cobb, Art Mix, Jim Pierce, Curley Dresden, Ed Coxen, Rube Dalroy.

This film loses no time getting underway. Mitch, a baddie, gets out of the clink and comes gunning for the two people responsible for his six-year stay in prison. One is an old storekeeper and the other is Wild Bill. Of course Wild Bill is victor in the last-reel gun duel with Mitch.

"Elliott's Hickok would have settled down long ago, had it not been for his writers. In every pic he expresses the wish to remain a peaceable man, but that is never allowed. In this one he almost marries the girl (Luana Walters), but the scriptors developed in her a terrific animosity toward any man who packs a gun, so he is forced to ride away on the fade as usual — matrimonially scot-free." — *Variety*, April 16, 1941

Hands Across the Rockies
(Columbia, 1941) 57 min.

Director: Lambert Hillyer. Screenplay: Paul Franklin. Story: Norbert Davis. Producer: Leon Barsha.

Bill Elliott (Wild Bill Hickok), Dub Taylor (Cannonball Taylor), Eddy Waller (Circuit Judge), Kenneth MacDonald (Juneau Jessup), Mary Raily (Marsha Crawley), Stanley Brown (Johnny Peale), Slim Whittaker (Sheriff). *With* Art Mix, Harrison Greene, Hugh Prosser, Tex Cooper, Ethan Laidlaw, George Morrell, George Chesebro, Curley Dresden, Steve Clark, Edmund Cobb, Kathryn Bates, Eddie Laughton, Buck Moulton.

Wild Bill Hickok and Cannonball come to the town of Independence, seeking the murderer of Cannonball's father. They find that the family of Marsha Crawley is forcing her to marry Juneau Jessup. Marsha was a witness to the killing of Cannonball's father and Jessup knows that if she is his wife, then she can't testify against him. Marsha is in love with Johnny Peale and tries to run away with him to get married. However, her family stops her, and Johnny is arrested on a kidnapping charge.

Bill goes to see Johnny in jail, posing as his lawyer. Jessup is furious and plans to dispose of Bill and hang Johnny by mob rule before he can testify. Bill, however, forces the trial and clears Johnny, who is then able to marry Marsha. Bill goes gunning for Jessup, whom he has proved murdered Taylor. In the melee, he gets his man.

The film is a first-rate western, even though it carries less riding and shooting footage than the average cowboy opera. There's a corking comedy courtroom scene which is carried off by Eddy Waller, Bill Elliott, Dub Taylor and an aggregation of primitive-looking jurors. Eddy Waller's impersonation of the rough-and-ready circuit judge who holds court with a double-barreled musket on the bench is a hilarious burlesque from beginning to end. It shifts into high gear, a yarn that for a time threatened to trail off conventionally.

"Getting its greatest story values from a richly amusing courtroom sequence, *Hands Across the Rockies*, in final analysis, stacks up pleasingly with the average Bill Elliott western product. The picture starts slowly, and there is a minimum of fist and gun fighting; absolutely no riding, the action being confined to a single uneventful stagecoach journey. Not until the unorthodox frontier judge—splendidly played for comedy sock by Eddy Waller—makes his entrance for the climaxing trial do proceedings really come to life. But the judge is worth waiting for."—*Hollywood Reporter*, June 3, 1941

North from the Lonestar
(Columbia, 1941) 58 min.

Director: Lambert Hillyer. Screenplay: Charles Francis Royal. Producer: Leon Barsha.

Bill Elliott (Wild Bill Hickok), Richard Fiske (Clint Wilson), Dorothy Fay (Madge Wilson), Dub Taylor (Cannonball), Arthur Loft (Flash Kirby), Jack Roper (Rawhide Fenton), Chuck Morrison (Spike), Claire Rochelle (Lucy Belle), Al Rheia (Slats), Edmund Cobb (Dusty Daggett). *With* Lane Bradford, Francis Walker, Jack Evans, Ray Jones.

Wild Bill Hickok becomes a town marshal in order to clean out an unscrupulous clique. The usual results are achieved two minutes before the fadeout, which gives Wild Bill the opportunity to ride away from two clutching maidens and give the film a comedy ending.

"*North from the Lonestar* contains more fist fights and roaring six-shooter battles than others built around the famed western gunman and 'peaceful man.' Chockful of swift action that oats opera patrons go for; hence, well suited in lower section of duals in houses where they appreciate cactus capers."—*Variety*, June 25, 1941

King of Dodge City
(Columbia, 1941) 59 min.

Director: Lambert Hillyer. Screenplay: Gerald Geraghty.

Bill Elliott (Wild Bill Hickok), Tex Ritter (Tex Rawlings), Dub Taylor (Cannonball), Judith Linden (Janie Blair), Guy Usher (Morgan King), Rick Anderson (Judge Lynch), Pierce Lyden (Reynolds), Francis Walker (Carney), Harrison Greene (Steve Kimball), Jack Rockwell (Martin). *With* Edmund Cobb, George Chesebro, Tris Coffin, Jack Ingram, Kenneth Harlan, Steve Clark, Tex Cooper, Russ Powell,

Frosty Royce, Ed Coxen, Lee Prather, Jay Lawrence, Ned Glass, Herman Hack, Ted Lorch, Horace B. Carpenter, George Morrell, Tom Smith, Jack Evans, Carl Mathews, Ted Mapes.

Morgan King is the open ruler of Abilene when Tex Rawlings rides into town in search of a stolen horse. Tex finds the horse, driven by Cannonball, the local blacksmith, drawing the funeral hearse of the town sheriff, who was killed by King gunmen. Cannonball insists he bought the horse from Bill Lang, a suspected thief, and Judge Lynch names Tex the new sheriff so he can kill Lang "according to law." Lawyer Kimball heads a citizens' committee in the state capitol, seeking means of driving King from the state. Kimball insists that Wild Bill Hickok is the man for the job, but learns that Hickok has turned outlaw in order to avenge the death of a friend. Kimball finds Hickok in Dodge City and, without the committee's knowledge, gives Bill a letter to prove the clean-up assignment.

Under a different name Bill rides into Abilene and immediately encounters Tex. Their chief disagreement, however, is lovely Janie Blair. Bill, as distrustful of Tex as Tex is of him, sees the sheriff talking to King's men and decides that he is in league with them. Suspicious of King and the town banker, Bill and Cannonball break into the bank to inspect the books. They find proof the bank is crooked. Tex, attempting to arrest them, is handcuffed to a post while Bill starts a run on the bank.

For his own protection, Tex, now loose, arrests the banker, along with Bill, and puts them in adjoining cells. King orders the banker killed, and Bill is found with the murder gun and charged with the crime. Cannonball helps Bill to escape. Tex finds him, the situation is explained and the two return together to wipe out King's gang. Tex and Bill ride off together while Cannonball is made the town sheriff.

"This is the first of a new series of westerns in which Columbia intends to team Bill Elliott and Tex Ritter, latter recently completing a monogram ticket. In endeavoring to split footage and importance of the two westerners equally, scripter Gerald Geraghty hit a stone wall—and Ritter suffers by comparison in the acting line against the better performance of Elliott. Picture is an average shoots-and-saddles actioner that will find booking spots with the juvenile trade."—*Variety*, August 13, 1941

Roaring Frontiers
(Columbia, 1941) 60 min.

Director: Lambert Hillyer. Screenplay: Robert Lee Johnson. Producer: Leon Barsha.

Bill Elliott (Wild Bill Hickok), Tex Ritter (Tex Rawlings), Ruth Ford (Reba Bailey), Frank Mitchell (Cannonball), Hal Taliaferro (Link

Twiddle), Bradley Page (Hawk Hammond), Tris Coffin (Flint Adams), Francis Walker (Boot Hill), Joe McGuinn (Knuckles), George Chesebro (Red Thompson), Charles Stevens (Moccasin), Charles King, Lew Meehan (Outlaws), Hank Bell, George Eldredge, Fred Burns, Ernie Adams.

Marshal Wild Bill Hickok arrives in Goldfield to arrest Tex Rawlings, who has been accused of murdering the sheriff. Hawk Hammond, the man behind the sheriff's murder, sends his men to lynch Tex before the trial. Wild Bill and Tex escape to a stagecoach rest station run by Reba Bailey. In a showdown battle at Hammond's saloon, both Hammond and the real murderer are killed. Tex becomes mayor with Reba at his side and Wild Bill moves on to his next assignment.

The Lone Star Vigilantes
(Columbia, 1941) 58 min.

Director: Wallace Fox. Screenplay: Luci Ward. Producer: Leon Barsha.

Bill Elliott (Wild Bill Hickok), Tex Ritter (Tex Martin), Frank Mitchell (Cannonball), Virginia Carpenter (Sherry Monroe), Luana Walters (Marcia Banning), Ethan Laidlaw (Benson), Budd Buster (Colonel Monroe), Forrest Taylor (Dr. Banning), Gavin Gordon (Major Clark), Lowell Drew (Peabody), Edmund Cobb (Charles Cobb), Rick Anderson (Lige Miller), George Chesebro (Outlaw), Paul Mulvey, Eddie Laughton, Francis Walker.

At the close of the Civil War, Wild Bill Hickok and Tex Martin arrive in Winchester, Texas, to discover armed bandits, under Major Clark, posing as army troops and holding the city under martial law. Bill notifies the authorities but is refused aid. Returning, he finds Tex held prisoner by the renegades. Hickok frees Tex and, with proof of Clark's guilt, smashes the bandit gang.

"*Lone Star Vigilantes* is the best of the first three Bill Elliott-Tex Ritter western series. Full of action, aimed to satisfy western addicts, and with plenty of gun-pumping and heroics, picture is a good entry in the western field for dating."—*Variety*, September 24, 1941

"Elliott and Ritter handle their roles with the ease of experience, ably abetted by Frank Mitchell, Gavin Gordon, Budd Buster, Forrest Taylor, a charming youngster named Virginia Carpenter, and Luana Walters, a lovely proponent of the double cross who underplays her role admirably."—*Hollywood Reporter*, September 16, 1941

Wild Bill Hickok Rides

(Warner Bros., 1941) 83 min.

Director: Ray Enright. Screenplay: Charles Grayson, Paul Gerard Smith and Raymond Schrock.

Bruce Cabot (Wild Bill Hickok), Constance Bennett (Belle Andrews), Warren William (Harry Farrel), Betty Brewer (Janey), Walter Catlett (Sylvester Twigg), Ward Bond (Sheriff Edmunds), Howard Da Silva (Ringo), Frank Wilcox (Martin), Faye Emerson (Peg), Julie Bishop (Violet), Lucia Carroll (Flora), Russell Simpson (Nolan), J. Farrell MacDonald (Judge Hathaway), Lillian Yarbo (Daisy), Cliff Clark (Kersey), Trevor Bardette (Sam Bass), Elliott Sullivan (Bart Hanns), Dick Botiller (Sager), Ray Teal (Beadle).

The story revolves around Farrel's attempt to grab Powder River Basin pasture lands from homesteaders. He's in cahoots with Chicago stockyard owners and railroad men, but Hickok, friend of the owner of the biggest ranch, repeatedly thwarts him. When Hickok's friend is lynched after conviction on a trumped-up murder charge, Hickok goes on the rampage and almost single-handedly cleans out the mob, including Farrel.

"Big, raucous Western drama of the rootin', tootin', shootin' school.... All of the familiar elements are there—the gun fights, the deep-dyed villains, the fast rides to rescue, cattle roundups, dynamiting a dam that will flood the valley, and that old stalwart, the mortgage that must be paid or else...."—*Hollywood Reporter*, December 23, 1941

"WB exhumed a time-honored sagebrush formula for this latest tale built around the legendary exploits of Wild Bill Hickok, peopled it with well-known names who make up in performances what the script lacks in originality, and result is a pleasantly exciting session of American frontier days that will do a fair amount of business wherever it's played."—*Variety*, February 11, 1942

Wildcat of Tucson

(Columbia, 1941) 59 min.

Director: Lambert Hillyer. Screenplay: Fred Myton. Producer: Leon Barsha.

Bill Elliott (Wild Bill Hickok), Evelyn Young (Vivian), Stanley Brown (Dave), Dub Taylor (Cannonball), Kenneth MacDonald (McKee), Ben Taggert (Judge), Edmund Cobb (Seth), George Lloyd (Marshall), Sammy Stein (Logan).

Wild Bill Hickok has a hothead brother who decides to swing free of his brother's rep and barges into a ring of legal claim jumpers, which gets him over his head in trouble. Wild Bill hears of his trouble and comes to the rescue.

"The lackadaisical honors among action heroes in films, if such classi-
fication is an honor, belong to Bill Elliott, who fronts for Columbia's Wild
Bill Hickok series. What fire there is in this film has to come from somewhere else. Elliott knows he can beat 'em all to the draw and plays his parts
that way. And that isn't b.o."—*Variety*, February 26, 1941

Bullets for Bandits
(Columbia, 1942) 55 min.

Director: Wallace W. Fox. Screenplay: Robert Lee Johnson. Producer:
Leon Barsha.

Bill Elliott (Wild Bill Hickok), Tex Ritter (Sheriff Tex), Frank
Mitchell (Cannonball), Dorothy Short (Dakota Brown), Ralph
Theodore (Clem Jeter), Edythe Elliott (Queen Katey), Forrest Tucker
(Bert Brown), Eddie Laughton (Outlaw). *With* Joe McQuinn, Tom
Moray, Art Mix, Harry Harvey, Hal Taliaferro, John Tyrrell, Bud
Osborne.

Clem Jeter tries to gain control of Queen Katey's ranch and she sends
Cannonball to town to find her wastrel son Prince to aid her. Cannonball
arrives in town just in time to see Wild Bill Hickok fighting members of
Jeter's gang. Mistaking Wild Bill for Prince, Cannonball takes Bill back to
the ranch with him.

Unable to seize control of the ranch as long as Wild Bill is there, Jeter
informs Sheriff Tex that Bill is an imposter, but Tex refuses to help him.
Jeter and his gang ride out to kill Bill, but Tex and a posse get there in time
to capture Jeter and his men.

The Devil's Trail
(Columbia, 1942) 61 min.

Director: Lambert Hillyer. Screenplay: Robert Lee Johnson. Based on
"The Town in Hell's Backyard." Producer: Leon Barsha.

Bill Elliott (Wild Bill Hickok), Tex Ritter (Tex Martin), Eileen
O'Hearn (Myra Willowby), Frank Mitchell (Cannonball), Noah
Beery, Sr. (Bull McQuade), Ruth Ford (Ella), Joel Friedkin (Don Wil-
lowby), Joe McGuinn (Jim Randall), Edmund Cobb (Sid Howland),
Tris Coffin (Ed Scott), Paul Newlan (Blacksmith), Steve Clark (Out-
law).

Federal Marshal Tex Martin, searching for Wild Bill Hickok, who has
been falsely accused of murder, stumbles across the outlaw camp of Bull
McQuade, who advocates slavery in Kansas. Hickok, hiding in the
McQuade camp, is surrendered by the renegade, who wants no trouble with

the Federal Government. Prisoners of McQuade are Dr. Willowby, his daughter Myra and his servant, Cannonball. Willowby heads the Frontier Emigrant Aid Society and McQuade is attempting to wrest from him the names of his co-workers.

Cannonball rescues Hickok and hides with him in the mountains. Tex, disarmed, heads back to McQuade's camp, still not believing Hickok's story about McQuade's other prisoners. Myra escapes and hides in a deserted shack, but she is trailed by Howland, a McQuade henchman.

Ella, McQuade's girl, confirms Hickok's story for Tex, and gives the latter a gun. He immediately goes after Wild Bill, following the train of McQuade's men, who also are hunting the famed gunman. Tex runs across Howland, who is about to shoot Myra, and wounds him after a terrific battle. Myra and Tex head for the cave in which Cannonball and Wild Bill are hiding. When McQuade and his men discover the wounded Howland, they set out in swift pursuit.

The terrific gun battle which follows wipes out most of the bandit gang; the rest surrender. Tex and Hickok, gun buddies, accompany Myra and her father to safety.

Prairie Gunsmoke
(Columbia, 1942) 56 min.

Director: Lambert Hillyer. Screenplay: Fred Myton. Story: Jack Ganzhorn. Producer: Leon Barsha.

Bill Elliott (Wild Bill Hickok), Tex Ritter (Tex Terrell), Frank Mitchell (Cannonball), Virginia Carroll (Lucy Wade), Hal Price (Bill Wade), Tris Coffin (Jim Kelton), Joe McGuinn (Spike Allen), Frosty Royce (Sam), Rick Anderson (Dan), Art Mix (Outlaw), Francis Walker (Outlaw). *With* Glenn Strange, Ray Jones, Steve Clark, Ted Mapes.

To win possession, Jim Kelton stampedes the cattle on the ranches where he holds mortgages. When a rancher is killed, Wild Bill Hickok arrives in town to administer justice. The townsmen, including Tex Terrell, distrust Hickok, but when outlaws kidnap rancher Wade and his daughter Lucy, Hickok comes to the rescue of them, as well as Tex, who has also been caught. Kelton and his men are killed in a furious fight.

Dallas
(Warner Bros., 1950)

Director: Stuart Heisler. Screenplay: John Twist. Producer: Anthony Veiller.

Gary Cooper (Blayde Hollister), Ruth Roman (Tonia), Steve Cochran (Bryant Marlow), Raymond Massey (Will Marlow), Barbara Payton (Flo), Leif Erickson (Martin Weatherby), Antonio Moreno (Felipe), Jerome Cowan (Matt Coulter), Reed Hadley (Wild Bill Hickok), Gil Donaldson (Luis), Zon Murray (Cullen Marlow), Will Wright (Judge Harper), Monte Blue (Sheriff), Byron Keith (Jason Trask), Jose Dominguez (Carlos), Steve Dunhill (Dink). *With* Buddy Roosevelt, Ben Corbett, Fred Kelsey, Charles Watts, Gene Evans, Slim Talbot, Billie Bird, Frank Kreig, Glenn Thompson, Oscar Williams, Ann Laurence, Dave Dunbar, Tom Fadden, Hal K. Dawson, Alex Montoya, Dolores Corvall, Fred Graham, Charles Harveth, Carl Andre, Roy Bucko.

Blayde Hollister, a Southerner, rides into Texas just after the Civil War, seeking revenge on three brothers who destroyed his home and family in Georgia. He switches identities with a U. S. Marshal to find the brothers and, with the help of Tonia, tracks them down, confronts them, and kills them in a fair fight.

"...*Dallas* is something like Christmas; an old, familiar theme that's always new, that has an eternal glamour and a hold upon your imagination. *Dallas* is our old friend, the Western, here done up in Technicolor glamour, terrific photography, and capturing your imagination because it has action, humor, and Gary Cooper."—*Los Angeles Examiner*, December 25, 1950

"*Dallas* is very effective Western entertainment. The name values are readily apparent. Ruth Roman again contributes a pleasing role as the daughter of a rancher who is bedeviled by the actions of Massey. ... The show is worked up well with the action pattern prevailing. There is a good deal of diverting incidents and the audience should derive much satisfaction from the offering."—*Film Daily*, November 22, 1950

Jack McCall, Desperado
(Columbia, 1953) 76 min.

Director: Sidney Salkow. Screenplay: John O'Dea. Story: David Chandler. Producer: Sam Katzman.

George Montgomery (Jack McCall), Angela Stevens (Rose Griffith), Douglas Kennedy (Wild Bill Hickok), James Seay (Bat McCall), Eugene Iglesias (Grey Eagle), William Tannen (Spargo), Jay Silverheels (Red Cloud), John Hamilton (Col. Cornish), Selmer Jackson (Col. Brand), Stanley Blystone (Judge), Gene Roth (Attorney), Alva Lacy (Hiseva), Joe McGuinn (U. S. Marshal).

The story is told in flashback, opening with Jack McCall shooting down Marshal Hickok. On trial for murder, he tells how circumstantial evidence made him seem like a Confederate spy, with a Union court-martial sentencing him to death. He escaped, but his parents were murdered by his cousin, Bat McCall, and Hickok. From there on it is a tale of vengeance, with McCall tracking the two villains in an effort to get evidence to clear himself, breaking up their conspiracy to drive the Sioux off their land, finding romance with Rose Griffith and finally getting the proof he needs.

"Montgomery plays with a rugged sincerity that lends conviction to his role. Miss Stevens is both lovely and competent in the feminine lead. Kennedy is very good as Hickok, with Seay and William Tannen also making convincing heavies. Eugene Iglesias as the Sioux leader, and Jay Silverheels as his son are both good. Technical functions are all effectively carried out."—*Hollywood Reporter*, March 1953

"*Jack McCall, Desperado*, a western with Civil War overtones, has the ingredients to register with outdoor fans. Technicolor tints and a number of action sequences, including three chases, two jailbreaks and a bloody ambush, enhance pic's appeal. Marquee value, however, is limited to George Montgomery. Film should get by as supporting fare."—*Variety*, March 25, 1953

Son of the Renegade
(United Artists, 1953) 57 min.

Producer/Screenplay: John Carpenter. Director: Reg Brown. Narrator: Pat McGeehan. Exec. Producer: Maurice Kosloff. Photography: William Thompson. A Jack Schwartz Presentation.

John Carpenter (Red River Johnny), Lori Irving (Lori), Joan McKellen (Valley), Valley Keene (Dusty), Jack Ingram (Three Fingers), Verne Teters (Sheriff Masters), Bill Goonz (Wild Bill), Ted Smile (Cherokee), Bill Ward (Baby Face Bill), Roy Canada (The Gun Slinger), Whitey Hughes (The Long-Haired Kid), Lennie Smith (Deputy Sheriff), Ewing Brown (Wild Bill Hickok), Freddie Carson (Big Fred), Percy Lennon (The Australian Kid), Jack Wilson (The Texas Kid).

Via flashback we see a killer named Red River Johnny roaming the West, eliminating all who oppose him and robbing all who have money. He is a tough hombre who evidences only a few actions that are of the kindly and human variety. It is this man's reputation that the son has to fight to prove that the son of an outlaw can be an exemplary individual. With a few devoted friends at his side, the hero rides back to his father's old haunts to regain control of the ranch his father held before being run out of the country. The son of the sheriff whom his father killed now wants to run him out of the country, too.

"Produced on a small budget, *Son of the Renegade* is short on story but long on individual action scenes. The slight plot line is frequently lost by the spectator and the film is suitable only for smaller dual oater houses, since the whole thing is crudely turned out."—*Variety*, March 13, 1953

"An abundance of shootings and an aggregation of corpses are this Western's greatest attributes. The story line offers enough to satisfy only the most zealous of outdoor action enthusiasts. Every time the plot begins to drag, someone manages temporarily to revive interest by spraying the area and a number of bystanders with hot lead. If it's plenty of gunplay [you're] looking for, this film might cater to your viewer's tastes."—*Motion Picture Herald*, April 21, 1953

Pony Express
(Paramount, 1953) 101 min.

Director: Jerry Hopper. Screenplay: Charles Marquis Warren. Story: Frank Gruber. Producer: Nat Holt.

Charlton Heston (Buffalo Bill Cody), Rhonda Fleming (Evelyn), Jan Sterling (Denny), Forrest Tucker (Wild Bill Hickok), Michael Moore (Rance Hastings), Porter Hall (Bridger), Richard Shannon (Barrett), Henry Brandon (Cooper), Stuart Randall (Pemberton), Lewis Martin (Sergeant Russell), Pat Hogan (Chief Yellow Hand). *With* Eric Alden, Howard Joslin, LeRoy Johnson, Jimmy H. Burke, Robert J. Miles, Robert Scott, Bob Templeton, Willard Willingham, John Mansfield, Frank Wilcox.

Heston (Buffalo Bill) and Tucker (Wild Bill Hickok) are the male stalwarts responsible for getting the Pony Express through to the West Coast, despite the skullduggery of Henry Brandon, stage line operator, and Stuart Randall, a foreign agent trying to split California from the Union. Fleming is a loyal Californian being used by Randall and Sterling is a hoydenish, Army post–raised girl in love with Heston.

The villains carry their plot against the Pony Express to such extremes as arming the Indians (led by Pat Hogan), ambushes and destruction of Express relay stations. But all of the tricks are to no avail as the heroes come through, linking the East and West with what were then speedy communications.

"*Pony Express* is a well-titled outdoor action feature that should rate an average run through the market that makes the best use of this type of Technicolored subject. [It] features spectacular, tinted scenic footage, some tight western action, good performances and the other standard ingredients that go with release intentions."—*Variety*, March 3, 1953

Calamity Jane
(Warner Bros., 1953) 100 min.

Director: David Butler. Screenplay: James O'Hanlon. Producer: William Jacobs. Photography: William M. Cline.

Doris Day (Calamity Jane), Howard Keel (Wild Bill Hickok), Allyn McLerie (Maid), Philip Carey (Calamity's boyfriend), Dick Wesson (Singer), Gale Robbins (Adelaide Adams), Paul Harvey (Nightclub Owner). *With* Chubby Johnson, Jack Perrin, Rex Lease.

Calamity is a tomboyish, fast-shooting, markswoman with a flair for exaggerating her fantastic exploits. Her bragging gets her into trouble when she agrees to go to Chicago, vowing to bring musical comedy star Adelaide Adams to Deadwood City. She mistakes the star's maid for the star and the maid plays along, hoping to satisfy her own stage aspirations. When the truth comes out, the Deadwood citizens are ready to wreck the local nightclub, but Calamity persuades them to give the imposter a chance.

The girl makes good but complications follow when Calamity's boyfriend falls in love with the imposter. Everything is straightened out after a lot of amusing events, when Calamity discovers that she really loves Wild Bill Hickok. A double wedding follows.

"A rollicking musical filled with humor, vitality and sure-fire song hits. *Calamity Jane* stands out as one of Warners' brightest film musicals to explode on the screen. With Doris Day in the title role delivering what might easily be her most sparkling performance to date, and Howard Keel turning in an excellent job as Wild Bill Hickok, this ... should pep up the box office considerably."—*Hollywood Reporter*, October 28, 1953

"Howard Keel is Wild Bill Hickok—and he hasn't been this purely pleasant and appealing since *Annie Get Your Gun.* When he blends his baritone in with Doris' soprano, it makes your own heart sing. The scenery is lovely, the action never lags, Doris is adorable, Keel is terrific. William Jacobs produced this for Warner Bros., so love and kisses to him, too."—*Los Angeles Examiner*, November 19, 1953

"*Calamity Jane* can best be described as a burlesque on westerns—musical or straight, stage or screen. On that basis, the sophisticate can accept it and the regulation oater fan will not mind the kidding, so it should fare well in the majority of playdates, particularly since the star value of Doris Day, this time teamed with Howard Keel, usually accounts for good ticket sales."—*Variety*, October 28, 1953

The Adventures of Wild Bill Hickok

(Syndicated/MPTV, 1951–1955; Screen Gems, 1955)
113 30-minute Episodes (74 black and white; 39 in color).

Producer: William F. Broidy 1951–1955; Wesley E. Barry 1955–1958. Director: Thomas Carr, Louis King, Seymour Kulik and others.

Guy Madison (Wild Bill Hickok), Andy Devine (Jingles P. Jones).

Following is a list of 98 of the 113 titles showing other actors appearing in the episode in addition to Madison and Devine.

Behind Southern Lines: William McKenzie, Park McGregor, William Ruhl, Rand Brooks, Murray Alper.

The Lady Mayor: Dick Curtis, Frances Morris, Fred Libby, Isa Ashdown, John Carpenter, David Sharpe.

The Dog Collar Story: Lola Hall, Marshall Reed, Tommy Ivo, Gregg Barton, Byron Foulger, William Fawcett.

The Silver Mine Protection Story: Milburn Stone, Lee Phelps, Bill Meade, Duke York, Robert Shayne, Orley Lindgren.

The Indian Bureau Story: Wendy Waldron, Raymond Hatton, Terry Frost, Jack Reynolds, Steve Pendleton, Neyle Morrow.

Indian Pony Express: Carol Henry, Dave Sharpe, Anthony Sydes, Rory Mallinson, Ferris Taylor, Dick Rich.

The Tax Collecting Story: Margery Bennett, Gordon Jones, Sam Flint, Ray Bennett, Mike Ragan.

The Widow Muldane: Christine Larson, Kenne Duncan, Edward Clark, Helen Van Tyle.

Ghost Town Story: Betty Davison, John Doucette, Russell Simpson.

The Yellow Haired Kid: Alice Rolph, David Bruce, Marsha Mae Jones, William Phipps.

Johnny Deuce: Alan Hale, Jr., Riley Hill, Tommy Ivo, Emery Parnell.

Homer Atchison: George J. Lewis, Fred Kohler, Jr., Carol Brannon, Tris Coffin, Larry Hudson.

Border City Election: Lyle Talbot, Gloria Saunders, Fred Hoose, Robert Bice, Zon Murray.

Pony Express vs. Telegraph: Peggy Stewart, Mike Vallon, Don Hayden, Park McGregor, Fred Kohler, Jr., Tom Steele.

The Lady School Teacher: Rory Mallinson, Pat Mitchell, Isa Ashdown, Almira Sessions.

Outlaw Flats: John Crawford, Bill Hale, Kristine Miller, Ed Clark.

The Child Prodigy: Monte Hale.

Silver Stage Holdup: Jane Adams, William Haade, Len Greer, Wade Crosby, Reed Howes.

Mexican Rustlers: Carol Thurston, Roland Varno, Don Harvey, Leonard Penn, Robert Livingston, Chad Mallory, Eddy Kane.

Masked Riders: Tom Steele, Ted Stanhope, John Carpenter, Norman Bishop.

Barstow and Finch: Robert Livingston.

Hepsibah: Alan Hale, Jr., Renie Riano.

Border City: Gloria Talbott, Don Turner, Steve Pendleton, Murray Alper, George J. Lewis.

The Ex-Convict Story: Bruce Edwards, Jo Carroll Dennison, Rex Lease, Gregg Barton.

Papa Antinelli: Pamela Duncan, Mike Vallon, Alan Foster, Francis McDonald, Elizabeth Harrower, Irene Martin.

The Slocum Family: Raymond Hatton, Carole Mathews, Richard Tyler, Frankie Danon, George Meader, Sara Haden.

The Lost Indian Mine: David Sharpe, Don Turner, Anthony Sides, Guy Beach, John Eldredge, James Bush, Bud Osborne.

Civilian Clothes: Norma Eberhardt, John Merton, Pat Mitchell, Leonard Penn, Fred Kelsey, Rick Vallon, Tris Coffin, William Hale.

The Medicine Show: Fred Kohler, Jr., Ralph Sanford, Tom Monroe, Larry Hudson, Peter McCabe, George Sherwood, William Coontz.

The Blacksmith Story: Carole Mathews, Robert Livingston, Dick Alexander, Sam Flint, William McCormack.

Mexican Gun Running: Tom Tyler, Theodora Lynch, Rand Brooks, Sujata, Murray Alper, Bob Woodward, Neyle Morrow, Charles Stevens.

The School Teacher Story: Anne Carroll, Rory Mallinson, Emory Parnell, Gaylord (Steve) Pendleton, Don Harvey, Peter Votrian, Jim Flowers, Isa Ashdown, Nadeen Ashdown.

Vigilante Story: Tom Neal, William Ruhl, George J. Lewis, Shannon O'Neill, Jim Parnell, Roland Varno, Perry Ivins.

The Professor's Daughter: Martha Hyer.

The Photographer's Story: Dorothy Patrick.

Outlaw's Son: Anne Kimball.

Savvy, the Smart Little Dog: Jeanne Dean.

Wild White Horse: Sally Fraser.

Lumber Camp Story: Frances Charles, Kenne Duncan, George Barrows.

The Trapper Story: Jeanne Cagney, Clayton Moore, Hal Gerald, James Bell, Jack Reynolds.

The Boy and the Bandit: Buddy Roosevelt, Edmund Cobb, Henry Blair, John Merton, Mike Vallon, Bruce Edwards.

A Joke on Sir Anthony: Dick Cavendish, Dick Elliott, Gerald O. Smith, I. Stanford Jolley, Guy Teague, Russ Whiteman, Park MacGregor.

The Wrestling Story: Karl Davis, Douglas Fowley, Rand Brooks, Lyle Talbot, House Peters, Jr., Fred Sherman, Henry Kulky.

Jingles Becomes a Baby Sitter: Toni Jerry, Raymond Hatton, Alan Bridge, Riley Hill, Ray Parsons, Effie Laird.

The Fortune Telling Story: Elizabeth Harrower, Charles Halton, Reed Howes, Florence Auer, Marvin Press.

A Close Shave for the Marshals: Robert Filmer, Byron Foulger, Harry Harvey, Steve Brodie, Burt Wenland.

Prairie Flats Land Swindle: Bobby Hyatt, Irving Bacon, Douglas Evans, Fred Libby, Terry Frost, Sam Flint, Fred Kelsey.

Marriage Feud of Ponca City: Anne Carroll, Robert Jordan, Nelson Leigh, Forrest Taylor, Louise Lorimer, Edward Cassidy, Paul McGuire.

Heading for Trouble: Joan Diener.

Chain of Events: Gloria Winters.

The Doctor Story: Pamela Duncan, Tom Hubbard, Nadene Ashdown, William Hale, Rusty Wescoat, William Tannen, Mike Ragan.

The Indians and the Delegates: John Eldredge, Tris Coffin, Henry Kulky, William Wilkerson.

The Sheriff Was a Redhead: Jim Bannon, Veda Ann Borg, Keith Richards, Henry Rowland, Frank Hagney.

Hands Across the Border: Alan Hale, Jr., Steve Pendleton, Denver Pyle, Rory Mallinson, John Crawford, William Fawcett.

The Avenging Gunman: Joan Arnold, Rosa Turich, Carol Henry, Tom Moore, James Millican, Sandy Sanders, Monte Blue.

The Right of Way: Lyle Talbot, Allan Nixon, Guy Teague, Buzz Henry, Frank Jenks, Theodore von Eltz.

The Monster in the Lake: Bill Henry, Tony Hughes, Bobby Wyatt, Boyd (Red) Morgan, Hal Gerald.

The Maverick: Tommy Cook, Sally Mansfield, Gordon Wynn, Bill Crandall, Marshall Reed, George Eldredge, William Tannen.

The Kid from Red Butte: Sam Flint, Charles Fredericks, Murray Alper, Alice Rolph, Isabelle Dwan, Art Dilland, Henry Rowland, Bill Vetching, Gordon Gebert.

Masquerade at Moccasin Flats: Elizabeth Harrower, Ken Alton, Tom Hubbard, Wes Hudman, Robert Bray, Ella Ethridge.

The Stolen Church Funds: Sam Flint, William George, John Eldredge, Rory Mallinson, Louis Lettieri.

Ol' Pardner Rides Again: Raymond Hatton.

The Gorilla of Owl Hoot Mesa: John Carradine, George Barrows, Rand Brooks, Paul McGuire, Reed Howes, Pete Killett, Chad Mallory.

The Sheriff's Secret: Patricia Lynn.

Sagebrush Manhunt: Jill Richards.

The Outlaw's Portrait: Bernadette Withers, Tris Coffin, Robert Hutton, Sandy Sanders, Michael Dale.

Buckshot Comes Home: Paula Kent, Don Harvey, John Damler, Rayford Barnes, Bobby Hyatt, Iron Eyes Cody.

The Music Teacher: Richard Karlan, William Ching, Don Garrett, Kem Dibbs, Ginny Jackson, Burt Wenland.

The Golden Rainbow: Raymond Hatton, Tom Monroe, John Beradino, Lucien Littlefield, Park MacGregor, Lis Slifar.

Old Cowboys Never Die: Dick Foran, Raymond Hatton, Fuzzy Knight, Robert Filmer, Charles Fredericks.

Blake's Kid: Guinn (Big Boy) Williams, Tommy Ivo, Bill Pullen, John Merton, Tim Sullivan, G. Pat Collins, Ann Staunton.

Treasure Trail: Linda Densen, Wayne Mallory, Thom Carney, Harry Lauter, Ray Walker, Keith Richards, Bert Bradley.

Battle Line: Don Mathers, William Haade, Fuzzy Knight, Earle Hodgins, Major J. S. Wilson.

Ambush: Charles Chaplin, Jr., David Cross, Jonathan Seymour, Sam Flint, Robert Bice, Joseph Grenne, John Eldredge.

Ghost Town Lady: Earl Ross, Burt Wenland, Isa Ashdown, John Damler, Jim Alexander, Robert Homans.

The Mountain Men: Claudia Barrett, Bill Bryant, Henry Kulky, Paul Sorenson, Donald Kerr.

The Return of Chief Redhawk: Frank Scannell, George Chandler, Larry Chance, Allan Wells, Don Marlowe.

Wild Bill's Odyssey: Lyle Talbot, Barbara Woodell, Ralph Neff, Wayne Mallory, Alan MacAteer, Scott Morrow, Tom McKee.

Bold Raven Rodeo: Mary Jane Saunders, Elizabeth Harrower, Julia Montoya, Orlando Rodriguez, Gregg Martell, Iron Eyes Cody, Pepe Hern, Cecil Elliott.

The Rainmaker: Frank Fenton, William Haade, Emory Parnell, Morgan Jones, Earle Hodgins.

The Iron Major: Andrey Conti, Irving Bacon, Leonard Penn, Edward Foster, King Donovan.

Jingles Wins a Friend: Philip Ahn, Harry Lauter, King Donovan, Edward Foster, Larry Chance.

The Gatling Gun: Michael Bryant, Joe Breen, Stanley Andrews, Victor Milland, Donald Sullivan, George Baxter.

The Steam Wagon: Lucien Littlefield, Richard Wessel, Don Harvey, Brad Morrow, Donald Kerr, Louis Lettieri, George Eldredge.

Marvin's Mixup: Bill Henry, Donna Drew, Buzz Henry, Bud Osborne, Fred Sherman, Forest Stanley.

Spurs for Johnny: Johnny Crawford, Harry Hickox, Ted Lehmann, Florence Lake, Gil Perkins, Guy Teague.

Monkeyshines: Michael Vallon, Larry Chance, Lela Bliss, Ken Mayer, Rube Schaffer.

The Runaway Wizard: Monte Hale, William Hale, George Ross, William Newell, Paul Hahn.

Meteor Mesa: Bill Catching, Gil Frye, Harry Antrim, Robert Swan, Sam Flint.

Town Without Law: Carol Nugent, Emmett Lynn, Stanley Andrews, George Barrows, Jack V. Littlefield, John Truax.

The Sheriff of Buckeye: Fred Kohler, Jr., Robert Clarke, Dorothy Neumann, Byron Foulger, Patrick Whyte, Baynes Barron, William Benedict.

Clem's Reformation: William Bryant, Gay Goodwin, Lonnie Thomas, Frank Scannell, Duane Grey, William Justice.

Jingles on the Railroad: Richard Karlan, Leonard Penn, Syd Saylor, Roy Erwin, Ben Welden, Bob Stratton, Dick Farnsworth, Robert Jordan.

The Daughter of Casey O'Grady: Jacquelyn Park, Harry Tyler, Mike Lane, Michael Forest, Frank Lackteen.

The Angel of Cedar Mountain: Rosetta Duncan, Gregg Barton, Chuck Courtney, Chuck Callaway, Wayne Davidson.

Good Indian: Charles Stewart, John Reach, Dehl Berti, Lane Chandler, Rush Williams, Joseph A. Vitale, Michael Carr.

The Counterfeit Ghost: Iris Adrian, Earle Hodgins, William Keene, Rusty Wescoatt, Robert Nash.

I Killed Wild Bill Hickok
(Wheeler Company, 1956) 63 min.

Director: Richard Talmadge. Screenplay/Story/Producer: John Carpenter.

John Forbes [John Carpenter], Helen Wescott, Tom Brown, Frank Carpenter, I. Stanford Jolley, Virginia Gibson, Denver Pyle, R. J. Thomas, Roy DeLar, Phil Barton, Bill Mims, Billy Dean, Lee Sheldon.

Wild Bill Hickok is the heavy here, cheating the U. S. government in a horse deal for the cavalry while sporting his sheriff's star. The hero is a former gunman who rounds up wild horses for the cavalry and who shoots it out with Wild Bill on the street in an unexciting climax.

"An exploitation title like this might have sparked a fast-paced western, but this misses on every count. Picture is handicapped by lack of story and continuity, unrealistic performances and unusually poor technical work in every department. John Carpenter, who both wrote and produced, draws heavily on unmatched color stock footage for number of sequences, while starring under name of John Forbes as man who killed Hickok. Tom Brown plays Hickok like an old-fashioned villain, and director Richard Talmadge has an impossible task with script, which he never assists."—*Variety*, January 12, 1956

The Raiders
(Universal, 1964) 75 min.

Director: Herschel Daugherty. Screenplay: Gene L. Coon. Producer: Howard Christie.

Robert Culp (Wild Bill Hickok), Brian Keith (John G. McElroy), Judi Meredith (Calamity Jane Cannary), James McMullen (Buffalo Bill Cody), Alfred Ryder (Captain Benton), Simon Oakland (Sgt. Austin Tremaine), Ben Cooper (Tom King), Trevor Bardette ("Uncle Otto" Strassner), Harry Carey, Jr. (Jellicoe), Richard Cutting (Jack Goodnight), Addison Richards (Hunington Lawford), Clif Osmond (Duchamps), Paul Birch (Paul King), Richard Deacon (Commissioner Mailer), Michael Burns (Jimmy McElroy).

A group of Texas ranchers have their herds rustled as they drive them to the railhead in Kansas. After losing their cattle they proceed on to Hays City, Kansas, and request that railroad officials extend their rails into Texas. Their request is turned down. Angry, they form a group known as "The Raiders" and begin attacks on the railroad. Wild Bill Hickok and Buffalo Bill Cody are working for the army under the command of Captain Benton, who is determined to avenge the railroad's losses and those of Calamity Jane, who is shipping equipment west for the railroad construction. Benton plans an ambush and orders the Raiders killed, but Hickok and Buffalo Bill intervene and take John McElroy and the Raiders into custody. They persuade the ranchers to return to their homes and then convince the Kansas and Pacific officials to push a line through to Abilene, Kansas, which makes it more convenient for the ranchers.

Seven Hours of Gunfire
(Centauro Films [Spain/Italy], 1964)

Director: Jose Hernandez (Joaquin Romero Marchant). Screenplay: Joaquin Romero Marchant. Photography: Rafael Pacheco. Music:

Angelo Francesco Lavagnino. Asst. Director: Rafael Romero Marchant (brother of Joaquin).

Rick Van Nutter (a.k.a. Clyde Rogers) (Buffalo Bill Cody), Adrian Hoven (Wild Bill Hickok), Gloria Milland (Calamity Jane). *With* Elga Sommerfeld, Carlos R. Marchant, Helga Line, Alfonso Rojas, Antonio Molina Rojo, Francisco Sanz, Raf Baldassare, Cris Huerta.

Buffalo Bill, Wild Bill Hickok and Calamity Jane all meet at a wilderness fort where they try to bring peace between the Indians and the pioneers. Eventually they set up quarters in Silver City, which becomes the target of an Apache attack.

The film met with only moderate success.

Deadwood '76

(Fairway International Films, 1965) 100 min.

Director: James Landis. Screenplay: Arch Hall, Jr. and William Watters (Arch Hall, Sr.). Story: William Watters (Arch Hall, Sr.) Producer: Nicholas Merriwether (Arch Hall, Sr.).

Arch Hall, Jr. (Billy May), Jack Lester (Tennessee Thompson), Melissa Morgan (Poker Kate), William Watters (Boone May), Robert Dix (Wild Bill Hickok), LaDonna Cottier (Little Bird), Richard S. Cowl (Preacher Smith), David Reel (Fancy Poggin), Res Marlow (Sam Bass), Gordon Schwenk (Spotted Snake), John Bryant (Hubert), Barbara Moore (Montana), Ray Zachary (Spec. Greer), Willard Willingham (Deputy Harding). *With* Harold Bizzy, Read Morgan, John Cardos, Little Jack Little, Bobby Means, Ray Vegas.

Young Billy May saves Tennessee Thompson from the Indians of the Dakota Badlands and together they travel to Deadwood. The townspeople mistake Billy for Billy the Kid and place bets on an impending fight between Billy the Kid and Wild Bill Hickok. Tennessee and Billy purchase a gold claim but are captured by Indians. At the Indians' camp Billy meets his father, who is allied with the Indians to defeat Custer and hopefully set up a new Confederate state. Billy also meets and falls in love with Little Bird, a young Indian woman. Later he escapes from the camp and kills two outlaws who have raped Little Bird.

By the time he reaches Deadwood, Wild Bill Hickok has arrived. When Hickok learns Billy's true identity he decides not to fight him. A young boy, Hubert, tricks Billy into a gunfight and is killed. Billy is hunted down and lynched. When Preacher Smith tries to intervene, he is also killed.

The Outlaws Is Coming

(Columbia, 1965)

See full writeup on page 43.

The Plainsman

(Universal, 1966) 92 min.

Director: David Lowell Rich. Screenplay: Michael Blankfort. Producers: Richard E. Lyons and Jack Leewood.

Don Murray (Wild Bill Hickok), Guy Stockwell (Buffalo Bill Cody), Abby Dalton (Calamity Jane), Bradford Dillman (Lt. Stiles), Henry Silva (Crazy Knife), Simon Oakland (Black Kettler), Leslie Nielsen (Col. George A. Custer), Edward Binns (Lattimer), Michael Evans (Estrick), Percy Rodriguez (Brother John), Terry Wilson (Sgt. Womack), Walter Burke, (Abe Ireland), Emily Banks (Louisa Cody).

Wild Bill Hickok is ambushed by a band of Cheyenne Indians headed by Crazy Knife. Black Kettle intercedes on Hickok's behalf and he is allowed to go, minus his horse and boots. Hitching a ride on a stage driven by Calamity Jane, he reports to Lt. Stiles that the Indians now have repeating rifles. The inexperienced officer treats the information with indifference. Later, at the saloon, Hickok meets his old friend Buffalo Bill Cody and his bride Louisa. Wild Bill catches Lattimer cheating at cards and forces him to leave. Soon after, Wild Bill and Buffalo Bill are captured by Indians with repeater rifles. Calamity is also taken prisoner by Crazy Knife. During his captivity Wild Bill learns that the rifles are being supplied by Lattimer. When the trio is rescued, Lattimer is arrested and delivered to the sheriff. Col. George Custer arrives to take over the army post. Calamity declares her undying love for Wild Bill.

This film has the same title, and roughly recalls the 1936 Cecil De Mille movie. Once again, it brings in Wild Bill Hickok, Calamity Jane, Buffalo Bill and Gen. George Custer to hunt down the bad guys who have been selling guns to the Indians. This time, there's more emphasis on the good Indian, Black Kettle, as opposed to the bad one, Crazy Knife, and on a by-the-book martinet of a cavalry officer, whose lack of experience nearly gets everyone killed.

"This remake is altogether out of date and so worried about it that it falls to pieces. Don Murray plays Wild Bill Hickok with a charmlessly twisted mouth that might have been meant to bring a note of astringent realism to the myth, and hint that Cody was almost as nasty a character as the usual Audie Murphy hero. But since the film makes no other concessions to realism the detail is totally meaningless. Abby Dalton plays Calamity Jane as if she were the comic relief in a Rodgers and Hammerstein musical; her eyeballs pop out as if she were preparing to burst into song at any moment. Guy Stockwell's Buffalo Bill is a mellow and cozy fellow; told that he's about to become a father he gets all dang-busted embarrassed and smilingly sings "When the Bough Breaks" while blazing away with both six-guns at Red Indians."—*Films and Filming*, April 1967

Little Big Man
(Cinema Center–National General, 1970) 150 min.

Director: Arthur Penn. Screenplay: Calder Willingham. Story: Thomas Berger. Producer: Stuart Millar.

Dustin Hoffman (Jack Crabb), Faye Dunaway (Mrs. Pendrake), Chief Dan George (Old Lodge Skins), Martin Balsam (Snake Oil Merchant Merriwether), Jeff Corey (Wild Bill Hickok), Richard Mulligan (Gen. George Custer), Amy Eccles (Sunshine), Kelly Jean Peters (Olga), Carol Androsky (Caroline), Robert Little Star (Little Horse), Cal Bellini (Younger Bear), Thayer David (Rev. Pendrake), Ray Dimas (Young Jack Crabb), Alan Howard (Adolescent Jack Crabb). *With* Robert Moreno, Steve Shemayne, William Hickey, James Anderson, Jesse Vint, Alan Oppenheimer, Philip Kenneally, Jack Bannon, Jack Mullaney, Steve Miranda, Lou Cutell, M. Emmet Walsh, Emily Cho, Cecelia Kootenay, Linda Dyer, Dessie Bad Bear, Norman Natham, Helen Verbit, Bert Conway, Earl Rosell, Ken Mayer, Bud Cokes, Rory O'Brien, Tracy Hetchner.

Little Big Man is interesting film fare if nothing else. It was made at a time when Westerns were beginning to explore the legends that surround familiar Western figures, tearing down the folk-hero images that had been built up in earlier days. For example, *Little Big Man* is hardly an endorsement of General George Custer, and Indian culture is depicted as more honorable and dignified than the white man's.

The story is that of Jack Crabb, a perpetual but likable loser who happens to be where history is being made. At age ten he witnessed the killing of his parents and was himself captured by Cheyenne Indians. We follow his life for the next 110 years. A participant in the Little Bighorn massacre, he is the sole surviving white man of that battle. Via flashback the 120-year-old man tells of his friendship with Wild Bill Hickok, his brief marriage, his seduction by the preacher's wife (Faye Dunaway), his gun fighting days and other adventures. His tall tales lead one to question the authenticity of some of them.

At 150 minutes, the film seems interminable. Apart from the first and last segments, the reels could be mixed up without exciting much comment.

The film is not artistically successful. Its commercial chances were heightened by the talent involved, but the picture was one of those occasional offbeat items that must either be a smash success or a major disappointment.

"Thomas Berger's novel was adapted by Calder Willingham into an episodic screenplay which tries very hard to be socially significant and meaningful but at the same time as cool and detached as the current generation is said to be."—*Variety*, Friday, December 11, 1970

"On one level, we have the autobiography of Jack Crabb, 121-year-old sole white survivor of Custer's Last Stand, frontiersman, Indian fighter, Cheyenne-by-adoption, gunslinger, storekeeper,and, possibly, the biggest liar to have roamed the West. ... On another we have a satiric retrospective on every facet of the Wild West mythology.... On its most important level we have the story of Human Beings, as the Cheyenne called themselves, believers in life but a minority doomed by the 'white' man's belief in death."—*New York Times*, December 21, 1970

"Fairly conventionally, the film opens and closes with a close-up of the ancient mythomaniac; once establishing its contemporary vantage point, it flashbacks the story of Crabb with frequent voice-over comments by the wry and elderly Hoffman. We witness the somewhat incredible aspects of his tall tale."—*The Hollywood Reporter*, December 16, 1970

This Was the West That Was

(Universal, December 17, 1974) 90 min.

Director: Fielder Cook. Teleplay: Sam H. Rolfe. Producer: Jo Swerling. Exec. Producer: Roy Huggins. Narrator: Roger Davis.

Ben Murphy (Wild Bill Hickok), Kim Darby (Calamity Jane), Jane Alexander (Sarah Shaw), Anthony Franciosa (J. W. McCanles), Stuart Margolin (Blind Pete), Stefen Gierasch (Carmedly), Matt Clark (Buffalo Bill Cody), Bill McKinney (Oscar Wellman), W. L. LeGult (Hearts). *With* Roger Robinson, Luke Askew, Woodrow Parfrey, Milton Selzer, Bruce Glover, Dimitra Arliss, Ronnie Clair Edwards.

This telefeature is a lighthearted look at the saga of Wild Bill Hickok and his relationship with Calamity Jane. Gunmen are out to get even with Wild Bill, who also must contend with Calamity Jane who is romantically inclined toward him. There really isn't much to recommend this satire of the Wild Bill Hickok–Calamity Jane–Buffalo Bill Cody legends.

The White Buffalo

(United Artists, 1977) 97 min.

Director: J. Lee Thompson. Screenplay: Richard Sale. Producer: Dino De Laurentis and Pancho Kohners.

Charles Bronson (Wild Bill Hickok/James Otis), Jack Warden (Charley Zane), Will Sampson (Crazy Horse), Kim Novak (Poker Jenny), Clint Walker (Kileen), Stuart Whitman (Coxy), Slim Pickens (Pinkney), John Carradine (Briggs), Cara Williams (Cassie), Shay Duffin (Brady), Douglas V. Fowley (Bixby), Cliff Pellow (Holt), Ed Lauter (Capt. Tom Custer).

Chief Crazy Horse goes on the hunt for the white buffalo, as does Wild Bill Hickok, each for different reasons. The buffalo trackdown is actually more of a cheap writing hook on which to hang a lot of dubious sociological gab than an outdoor adventure. Republic could have done a better job with the special effects than United Artists did.

"*The White Buffalo* obviously didn't turn out the way producer Dino De Laurentiis intended. Despite extensive mounting plus a weighty production team and cast, something failed to spark between the drawing board and its final commitment to celluloid. ... Richard Sale's script seems designed so the picture can be watched just as a straight adventure outing, or as a deeper psychological study. Take your pick."—*Hollywood Reporter*, October 12, 1977

"*The White Buffalo* is a turkey. ... Charles Bronson stars as Wild Bill Hickok, returned to the West to hunt down an albino buffalo that haunts his dreams. Will Sampson is an Indian who also must purge himself of some dishonor. Pancho Kohner's production features arch scripting by Richard Sale (from his novel), stilted acting by the cast and forced direction by J. Lee Thompson."—*Variety*, September 14, 1977

The Legend of the Lone Ranger

(Universal, 1981) 98 min.

Director: William A. Fraker. Screenplay: Ivan Goff, Ben Roberts, Michael Kane and William Roberts. Producer: Walter Goblenz.

Klinton Spillsbury (The Lone Ranger), Michael Horse (Tonto), Christopher Lloyd (Cavendish), Matt Clark (Sheriff Wiatt), Juanin Clay (Amy Stricker), Jason Robards (Pres. Grant), John Bennett Perry (Dan Reid), David Howard (Collins), John Hart (Lucas Striker), Richard Farnsworth (Wild Bill Hickok), Lincoln Tate (Gen. Custer), Ted Flicker (Buffalo Bill Cody), Mark Gilpin (Young John Reid), Patrick Mantoya (Young Tonto), David Bennett (Gen. Rodriguez), Rick Traeser (German), James Bowman (Gambler), Kit Wong (Chinese), Daniel Dunez (Agent), R. L. Tolbert (Stage driver), Clay Boss (Shotgun), Ted White (Reid), Chere Bryson (Mrs. Reid), James Lee Crite (Waiter), Min Burke (Stephenson), Jeff Ramsey (Alcot), Bennie Dobbins (Lopez), Henry Wills (Little), Greg Walker (Rankin), Mike Adams (Palmer), Ben Bates (Post), Bill Hart (Corner), Larry Randels (Stacy), Robert Hoy (Perimutter), Ted Gehring (Stillwell), Buck Taylor

(Gatlin), Rom R. Diaz (Eastman), Chuck Hayward (Wald), Tom Laughlin (Meeley), Terry Leonard (Valentine), Steve Meador (Russell), Joe Finnegan (Westlake), Roy Bonner (Richardson), John M. Smith (Whitloff).

A young Texan, whose family and fiancée are killed by the Cavandish gang assumes the identity of the Lone Ranger in his quest for justice.

"The less said about *The Legend of the Lone Ranger*, the less pain Lone Ranger fans will suffer. The film is a wretched affair, made more so by an inept Klinton Spillsbury as the masked hero. Having seen this young man as the Lone Ranger, one can only think more highly of Clayton Moore and wish that the then 65-year-old actor had been astride Silver."—*The Shoot-Em-Ups Ride Again*

Calamity Jane
(CBS Entertainment, March 1984) 120 min.

Director: James Goldstone. Story/Screenplay: Suzanne Clauser. Exec. Producer: Bernie Sofronski. Producer: Herbert Hirschman and Jane Alexander.

Jane Alexander (Martha Jane Cannary [Calamity Jane]), Frederic Forrest (James Butler Hickok [Wild Bill]), David Hemmings (Capt. O'Neil), Talia Balsam (Jean), Ken Kercheval (Buffalo Bill Cody), Walter Scott (Jane's Second Husband). *With* Walter Olkewicz, Isabell Monk, Jack Murdock, Larry Cedar, Doug Toby, Laurie O'Brien.

Calamity Jane meets Wild Bill Hickok and marries him during a drinking spree. Hickok later rides away not knowing that Calamity is pregnant. He marries again. Calamity has her baby, whom she gives the name Jean, alone in the forest.

Jane sadly gives up the baby to a Capt. O'Neill and his wife, an English couple wanting to adopt a baby. She takes up stagecoach driving, drinking, cigar-smoking, poker and another husband. In later years she meets her daughter, who is traveling with Buffalo Bill's Wild West show. Jean never finds out that Calamity is her mother.

"Alexander strides through *Calamity Jane* with nary a false step. Her leading men, except for Forrest, are offhandedly introduced. Director James Goldstone gives the production plenty of energy and enthusiasm, but there are lots of questions unanswered about this American enigma who ended up buried next to Hickok."—*Variety*, March 14, 1984

Set in 1860, "The Young Riders" was a television series featuring six wet-behind-the-ears recruits for the Pony Express. Left to right: Yvonne Suhor as Lou McCloud, Gregg Rainwater as Buck Goss, Josh Brolin as James Butler (Wild Bill) Hickok, Ty Miller as "The Kid," Stephen Baldwin as William (Buffalo Bill) Cody, and Travis Fine as Ike McSwain.

The Young Riders

(ABC, September 1989) A weekly one-hour series

Producer: Ogiens/Kane Productions/MGM-UA Television.

Ty Miller (The Kid), Anthony Zerbe (Teaspoon/Marshal), Brett Cullen (Marshal [dropped after first season]), Yvonne Suhor (Lou), Josh Brolin (James Hickok), Stephen Baldwin (Bill Cody), Gregg Rainwater (Buck), Travis Fine (Ike), Melissa Leo (Way Station Cook [dropped after first season]), Don Franklin (Noah Dixon), Claire Wren (Rachel Dunne [added second season]), Don Collier (Store Keeper [added second season]).

"A grizzled old plainsman named Teaspoon Hunter emerged from his bath ... in a horse trough! He's addressing six raw recruits none older than 18, as prospective Pony Express Riders. ... The riders that Teaspoon was talking to were Billy Cody, who will grow up to become Buffalo Bill; Jimmy Hickok, the future marshal better known on the frontier as Wild Bill; the Indian, Little Buck; the bald headed Ike and one rider with a blazing six-gun known simply as The Kid. The last of the six was Lou. She was a female rider masquerading as a young boy to get and keep her job as a Pony Express Rider....

"'The Young Riders' debuted on the ABC Network on September 20, 1989. The show was shot in color at an hour in length and ran from 8–9 P.M. Saturday nights. The series was filmed at Mescal and Old Tucson, Arizona, where the cast routinely had to endure 100 degrees-plus heat." — *Official TV Western Book*, Vol. 4

Buffalo Girls

(CBS four-hour miniseries, April 30 and May 1, 1995)
(de Passe Entertainment and CBS Entertainment)

Director: Rod Hardy. Teleplay: Cynthia Whitcomb. Story: Larry McMurtry. Exec. Producer: Suzzane de Passe.

Anjelica Huston (Martha [Calamity Jane] Canary), Melanie Griffith (Dora DuFran), Sam Elliott (Wild Bill Hickok), Tracey Walter (Ragg), Jack Palance (Bartle Bone), Floyd Red Crow (No Ears), Gabriel Byrne (Blue), Liev Schreiber (Ogden), Peter Coyote (Buffalo Bill Cody), Reba McEntire (Annie Oakley), Russell Means (Chief Sitting Bull). *With* Chalayne Woodard, John Diehl, Andrew Bicknell, Paul Lazar, Geofrey Bateman, Julie Beven, Peter Birch, Michael Eiland, David Garver, Jane Goold, Robert Harnesberger, Jerry King, Daphne Neville, Robin Nicholas, J. Michael Olivia, Richard Simpson, Hanley Smith, Boots Southerland, Hannah Taylor-Gordon.

The story chronicles the last days of the west, when famous frontier figures found homes touring in wild west shows.

Martha (Calamity Jane) Canary and madam Dora DuFran are the key figures in this panorama of the West. The narrative spans a decade in which the two women learn to survive in the male-dominated frontier. Although Dora deals in the world's oldest profession she is every bit as strong as Calamity. Calamity, although dressing and acting like a man, is very much a woman and in love with Wild Bill Hickok, who makes her pregnant shortly before biting the dust in a Deadwood saloon. When a baby girl is born, Calamity gives it to an English couple who promise to raise her properly.

Years pass. Calamity longs to see her daughter. When Buffalo Bill takes his Wild West show to England she goes along as a performer. In England she finally locates her daughter Janey. Calamity realizes that the girl is much better off where she is, and thus does not reveal her own identity. Calamity returns to America with peace of mind.

Dora and Blue carry on a doomed love affair for years. Dora refuses to marry Blue because she knows that he would not be happy living in town and that she would not be happy living on Blue's ranch. She finally marries a young man who loves her dearly. When she becomes pregnant she does not know if her husband or Blue is the father. Dora dies in childbirth, but not before handing the infant girl to Calamity, who promises to raise her.

"First three quarters of the four-hour opus, Cynthia Whitcomb's teleplay struggles to amuse, but the dialogue's pedestrian, the people insistent on being outlandish, while Jesus is dropped in twice as an expletive. Director Rod Hardy doesn't summon up much life until Buffalo Bill lands in London. Part one's Western hijinx ricochet between silliness and determinedly odd characters; in part two, the opus wisely shuttles between action in London and the West, and a becoming sentiment takes over as characters are disposed of."—Tony Scott, *Daily Variety*, April 26, 1995

"Griffith, who frequently looks and sounds as if she has just rolled out of bed, makes a touching, if stubborn, Dora. Appropriately, however, it is Huston, Griffith's real-life friend of more than two decades, who carries most of the movie's emotional weight."—John Crook, *TV Outlook and Entertainment Guide, The Sunday Oklahoman*, April 30, 1995

Wild Bill Hickok: Gentleman of the Old West
(A&E *Biography*, July 24, 1996) One hour

Narrator: Jack Perkins.

Joseph G. Rosa, Hickok biographer; Dr. Paul Fees, curator of the Buffalo Bill Historical Center; Dr. Roger McGrath, Professor of History, UCLA; Dr. Paul A. Hutton, Professor of History, University of New Mexico; and Leon Metz, writer/historian/biographer of Pat Garrett participate in telling the story of Hickok.

Miscellaneous Television Episodes

The following actors have portrayed Wild Bill Hickok on individual episodes of the indicated TV series:

Rhodes Reason, *Death Valley Days*; Jack Cassidy, *Bronco*; Lloyd Bridges, *The Great Adventure*; Charles Cooper, *Bronco*; Ben Murphy, *The West That Was*; L. Q. Jones, *Wild Times*; Frederick Forrest, *Calamity Jane*.

Wild Bill
(MGM/UA, 1995) 97 min.

Director/Screenplay: Walter Hill. Producer: Richard D. Zanuck and Fifi Zanuck. Based on play *Fathers and Sons* by Thomas Babe and the novel *Deadwood* by Pete Dexter.

Jeff Bridges (Wild Bill Hickok), Ellen Barkin (Calamity Jane), John Hurt (Charley Prince), Diane Lane (Susannah Moore), David Arquette (Jack McCall), Christina Applegate (Lurline), Bruce Dern (Will Plummer), James Gammon (California Joe), Marjoe Gortner (Preacher), James Remar (Donnie Lonigan), Karen Lule (Song Lew), Steve Reevies (Sioux Chief Whistler), Robert Knott (Dave Tutt), Pato Hoffmann (Cheyenne Leader), Patrick Gorman (Doctor), Lee DeBroux (Carl Mann), Stoney Jackson (Jubal Pickett), Keith Carradine (Buffalo Bill Cody).

Wild Bill spent his last days in Deadwood Gulch recalling his violent past, shown in flashback, and resuming his old quasi-romance with Calamity Jane.

The story begins with a 20-minute montage that works against any sympathy for the aging poker-playing gunman, who comes off as an ornery, sore-headed s.o.b. not opposed to partaking of opium to ease his tortured mind. Jack McCall, his killer, is presented as more than likely Hickok's son. That should be a tip-off as to the historical reliability of this film. There is very little factual material in it. There is lots of action and killing but none of it puts a halo over Hickok's head.

7

William Barclay
(Bat) Masterson

Bat Masterson was peace officer of Dodge City when it was the most lawless and disorderly town in America. Forceful and fast with a six-gun, he established his reputation in Kansas and later became a terror to law-breakers in Tombstone, Arizona, Deadwood, South Dakota, Trinidad, Colorado, Denver and Creede, Colorado. As deadly as he was dapper, he became one of the greatest legends of the old West.

Although most writing about Masterson credits him with being born in Illinois, he was born the second of seven children to Thomas Masterson and Catherine McGuirk on November 26, 1853, in the parish of St. George, Henryville County of Iberville, province of Quebec, Canada. His baptismal name was Bartholomew but, not liking his name, he changed it to William Barclay Masterson. Historian and writer Robert K. DeArment (*Bat Masterson: The Man and the Legend*, University of Oklahoma, 1979) pain-stakingly dug back into old records to correct the place-of-birth data.

Bat's father, a farmer, moved his family to Sedgwick County, Kansas, in June 1871 and put down roots there. Bat's formal educational was minimal, forcing his education to be mostly self-acquired. Luckily he was an apt pupil who loved books and persevered in acquiring a considerable amount of knowledge.

In 1871 young Bat, not yet 18, joined his older brother Edward in signing on with a buffalo hunting party as skinners and stock tenders. At this time there were literally millions of buffalo on the plains and there was a huge market for buffalo hides. Bat soon learned to fire with accuracy the "Big Fifty" buffalo guns and personally felled hundreds of buffalo a day. At this time Wyatt Earp, four or five years older than Bat, was also a buffalo hunter, liked the kid and taught him much.

Bat never dressed like the typical cowboy; rather, he looked more like a dude with his neatly pressed clothes and derby hat. Robert DeArment has described him as standing about five-foot-nine, compactly constructed, with

William Barclay (Bat) Masterson. (Courtesy Western History Collections, University of Oklahoma Library.)

broad shoulders, a deep chest, muscular arms, dark brown hair and distinctive heavy black eyebrows that were more inclined to arch upward in laughter than to knit in anger. His eyes were pale gray blue.

In the spring and summer of 1872 Bat and Edward went to work for the subcontractor of the Atchison, Topeka and Santa Fe grading a five-mile section between Fort Dodge and Buffalo City (Dodge City). A little later Bat was one of the gunmen hired by the railroad during a dispute for a right-of-way through the Royal Gorge. However, the dispute was settled without bloodletting.

Bat had courage, loyalty, resourcefulness and cool-headedness. Once in the buffalo camps he quickly learned the "art of the bent elbow—drinking. However, he was always able to control his drinking and knew when to quit. Gambling became his favorite pursuit and he was good at it, following it as a profession most of his life. Interestingly, no one ever accused him of cheating.

When Bat came to Dodge City in 1872 he had behind him experience as a buffalo hunter, a scout and a railroad worker. He had become a dandified gunman and an even more foppish dresser than Wild Bill Hickok. His suit was usually of the latest cut. He wore a pearl-gray bowler hat and a diamond stickpin. Often he carried a cane. But his mannerisms were overlooked by those who knew him to be one of the deadliest gunmen of the frontier.

In the early 1870s Bat became a member of Dodge's law enforcement. The "minions of the law" stood a notch above gamblers from whose ranks many of them were recruited. Robert Haywood wrote in *Victorian West: Class and Culture in Kansas Cattle Towns* (University Press of Kansas, 1991), "A man like Masterson rated well with folks—as long as he kept to the haunts of the criminal and the havens of celebrating cowboys. Bat and others like him in law enforcement rarely moved from Front Street status to Gospel Ridge respectability. ... At the peak of his power and supported by the ruling political clique, his power to control behavior on Front Street was nearly limitless."

Dodge prospered during the 1870s and 1880s as thousands of Texas Longhorns reached the railroad shipping point there. Dodge was pretty much a wide-open town. With the saloons, gambling and dance halls and whorehouses operating to capacity, Dodge offered plenty of excitement for cow hands who had just received their trail wages and wanted to celebrate. The town's business people prospered in this Golden Age while they catered to the cowboys' cravings for pleasure and at the same time economically and efficiently served the cattlemen and cattle buyers.

In 1874 Bat distinguished himself in the battle of Adobe Walls, a settlement located across the Cimarron and deep in the Texas Panhandle. This region was the hunting grounds of the Kiowa, Cheyenne and Comanche tribes, and they did not take the intrusion into their territory lightly. The tribes combined under the leadership of Quanah and vowed to kill all buffalo hunters in the Panhandle country. The white men were not killing a few buffalo in order to sustain life; rather, the buffalo were being slaughtered for the hides. Left behind them were the decaying carcasses of thousands of buffalo.

At Adobe Walls, which the whites had built deep in Indian country, the siege began. After a week of fighting, in which Bat proved his mettle, the white hunters were rescued by a party of whites from Dodge.

Later that year Bat joined a detachment of scouts to guide a military force called the Indian Territory Expedition, given orders to subdue the hostiles in the Indian Territory and the Texas Panhandle.

Bat's reputation as a gunfighter began on the night of January 24, 1876, in a Sweetwater dancehall named the Lady Gay. A soldier by the name of Cpl. Melvin King was vying with Masterson for the affections of Mollie Brennan, employed by the Lady Gay. King caught the two together alone in the dancehall after closing hours. Drunken and jealous, King tried to kill Bat. However, his bullet went through Mollie, killing her and lodging in Bat's pelvis. On his way to the floor, half-blinded with shock and pain, Bat drew his gun and shot King squarely in the heart. It is from this incident that the legend "Bat Masterson, deadly swift-handed man killer" sprang.

When Wyatt Earp was made chief deputy marshal of Dodge in 1876, he began to gain control of Front Street with the help of Bat, his other deputies and Marshal Deger.

Bat got gold fever in July 1876 after hearing tales of the gold to be found in the Black Hills. It was a common malady. He resigned his deputy job to head for the Black Hills. However, he stopped off in Cheyenne and, on a winning streak at faro, stayed several weeks, never making it to Deadwood. Gold seekers making their way back south painted dark pictures of Bat's chances of staking a good claim. Deadwood was overrun with gold seekers; all the potentially good claims had already been staked.

Back in Dodge, and at Wyatt Earp's urging, he ran for sheriff of Ford County. Although he was not yet 24, he won the November 1877 election and was sworn into office January 14, 1878. Wyatt dropped out of Dodge politics, whether by his own hand, or by failure of the mayor and city council to re-appoint him.

Masterson lost his bid for re-election as sheriff of Ford County, gave up his badge on January 12, 1880, and headed for the new gambling town of Leadville, Colorado, where he spent several months doing what he liked to do—gamble. While there he got a message from Ben Thompson asking for help for Bill "Bully" Thompson, his brother, who was jailed in Ogallala over a shooting affair. Bat did not like Bully Bill but he did like Ben, so he went to Ogallala. There he was convinced that a necktie party was in store for Bully Bill as soon as he was able to get out of bed from his wounds. Bat exercised his ingenuity and snatched Bill from the law with the help of a bartender friend who slipped Thompson's guard a "Mickey Finn." Bill had to be assisted because of his weakened condition but they headed toward North Platte and hid out on the ranch of Col. Buffalo Bill Cody and later on the Keith spread some 25 miles south of North Platte, on the way to Dodge.

The Ogallala escapade behind him, Bat made it on to Kansas City, which was at its peak as a gambling town. Here he spent several months before returning to Dodge. Early in 1881 Bat received a telegram from Wyatt Earp urging Bat to come to Tombstone where trouble was brewing. Wyatt felt that he was going to need all the help he could muster. Wyatt was deputy sheriff for the Tombstone District. His brother Virgil was Tombstone city marshal and his brother Morgan still rode shotgun for Wells Fargo.

Wyatt owned a part of the swanky Oriental saloon and gambling house, along with Lou Rickabaugh, Dick Clark and Bill Harris, three of the best gamblers in the West (and friends of Earp from his Dodge days). Bat and Luke worked as dealers and things generally remained civilized within the Oriental.

An organized band of outlaws from the Sam Simon Valley used Tombstone as their own private playground between rustling, stage holdups and smuggling. John Behan, sheriff of Cochise County, and Harry Woods, editor of the *Tombstone Nugget*, sided with the Outlaws. The gang was made up of such gunslingers and frontier riffraff as Curly Bill Brocius, Tom and Frank McLaury, Billy Claiborn, Johnny Ringo, Frank Stillwell, Pony Deal, Pete Spence, Jim Crane, Bill King, Luther King and Harry Head.

When needed, Wyatt's friends would join his posses. The gunfight at the O. K. Corral was fast approaching, but Bat was not destined to aid his old friend in that historic encounter. He had left Tombstone headed for Dodge upon receiving a telegram that his brother Jim, marshal of Dodge, was in trouble.

Arriving in Dodge, Bat was immediately embroiled in what was later dubbed the "Battle of the Plaza." No one was killed but sentiment ran against Bat and Jim. Bat decided in the summer of 1885 that it was in his best interest to leave Dodge.

In 1882 Bat was appointed city marshal of Trinidad, Colorado, by the city council. Bat was indefatigable in his effort to ferret out and arrest persons committing crimes. By the force of his personality and his remarkable ability at the quick draw, Bat was able to subdue the rowdy.

In 1883 the position became an elective one. Although a candidate for the job, Bat was defeated, mainly due to political shenanigans and the fact that Bat had stepped on some important toes.

Bat took up more-or-less permanent residence in Denver in the early 1880s, though he traveled a great deal seeking the good gambling spots. He took an avid interest in sports, especially boxing and politics and journalism. In the summer of 1885 he was voted the most popular man in Dodge, as well as being dubbed the best gambler in the West. Throughout the decade he accepted jobs as guard at polling places and as temporary city marshal. His mere presence in the saloons of Creede, Denver, Trinidad, Dodge and other towns kept red-hot tempers from erupting into shooting affairs.

He also became a promoter, referee and judge of boxing events. In fact, he was conceded to be one of the best judges in America.

In 1902 Bat became sports writer for the new *Morning Telegraph*. President Theodore Roosevelt appointed him deputy federal marshal in 1905, but he gave up the job when it started to interfere with his newspaper work.

Tom Masterson, Jr., wrote that Bat married Emma Walters, a blonde song and dance gal, in Denver on November 21, 1891. There does not seem to be any evidence to back up his statement. Other writers suggest that they were married as early as 1884. The marriage certificate is apparently missing.

Alfred Henry Lewis in his article "The King of the Gun-Players, William Barclay Masterson," (*Home Life*, November 1907) quotes Wyatt Earp as saying, "Bat Masterson was a brave man. As a peace officer he deserved all the celebrity he ever had, but as a killer his reputation has been greatly exaggerated. Old stories credit Bat with having killed 27 men. The truth is, he never killed but four in his life."

On Tuesday, October 25, 1921, Masterson was at work in his office at the *Telegraph* when he suffered a fatal heart attack. He was 67 years old. Funeral services were held on October 27, with burial in Woodlawn Cemetery.

William Barclay Masterson was one of the most colorful figures of the late nineteenth century West. He was a peace officer, professional gambler, fight promoter and newspaperman. At one time he was said to have been the best known man between the Mississippi and the Pacific coast, and his exploits and his ability as a fighter became part of the tradition of the West.

BAT MASTERSON FILMOGRAPHY

Wild Bill Hickok

(Famous Players Lasky/Paramount, 1923)

Masterson is featured in this post–Civil War story of Hickok's adventures in Dodge City. See full writeup on page 181.

"That [William S.] Hart convinces in his interpretation should suffice as to the merit of his personal performance wherein there is ample opportunity for overacting, which he neatly side-stepped."— *Variety*, November 22, 1923

The Woman of the Town

(United Artists, 1943) 90 min.

Director: George Archainbaud. Screenplay: Aeneas MacKenzie. Producer: Harry Sherman.

Claire Trevor (Dora Hand), Albert Dekker (Bat Masterson), Barry Sullivan (King Kennedy), Percy Kilbride (Reverend Small), Clem Bevans (Buffalo Burns), Porter Hall (Dog Kelly), Henry Hull (Inky Wilkinson), George Cleveland (Judge Blackburn), Herbert Rawlinson (Dr. Sears), Arthur Hohl (Robert Wright), Marion Martin (Dancehall Girl), Marlene Mains (Annie Logan), Beryl Wallace (Louella O. Parsons). *With* Hal Taliaferro, Teddie Sherman, Tom London, Charley Foy, Claire Whitney, Russell Simpson, Eula Gay, Frances Morris.

The Woman of the Town takes its title from an editorial written by Bat Masterson. The woman of the title is Dora Hand, and in flashback her story is told.

A shooting in Dog Kelly's saloon results in the killing of the town marshal. Masterson has the badge of authority thrust upon him. In church he meets Dora Hand and subsequently writes the article defending her when the female busybodies of the town complain about her employment as an entertainer in Dog Kelly's saloon.

Dora eventually wins the tolerance of the "fine" ladies of the town by her participation in numerous charities. Bat falls in love with her and competes with King Kelly for her affections.

Code of the Prairie
(Republic, 1944) 56 min.

Director: Spencer Bennet. Screenplay: Albert DeMond and Anthony Coldeway. Story: Albert DeMond.Assoc. Producer: Louis Fray. Photography: Bud Thackery. Music: Joseph Dubin.

Smiley Burnette (Frog Millhouse), Sunset Carson (Sunset Carson), Peggy Stewart (Helen Matson), Weldon Heyburn (Jess Thorpe), Tom Chatterton (Bat Matson), Roy Barcroft ("Professor" David Larson Graham), Bud Geary (Lem), Tom London (Loomis), Jack Kirk (Boggs), Tom Steele (Burley), Bob Wilke, Frank Ellis (Outlaws in Office), Rex Lease, Henry Wills (Outlaws on Trail), Ken Terrell (Outlaw in Brawl), Charles King (Election Informer), Nolan Leary (Rancher), Hank Bell (Stage Driver Jim), Karl Hackett (Deputy Sheriff), Jack O'Shea (Townsman), Horace B. Carpenter (Townsman Jim).

Republic wished to produce a film in which Bat Masterson's later life is fictionalized. By changing Masterson to Matson, the studio felt they were within the law in going ahead with the script it had.

Bat Matson, former marshal, is known throughout the West as a man of courage. He is beloved by men who are honest and forthright, and feared by those who settle arguments at the point of a gun. Despite the fact that Matson has grown older, and has only one arm, he is as respected as ever, for he now uses the most effective weapon known to man—the power of the press.

Bat and his daughter Helen, riding into Canyon City, are held up by two heavies who try to prevent their wagon from reaching town. Sunset and Frog, old friends of Bat, arrive just in time, however, and rescue Bat and Helen. Sunset's clean-cut wholesome qualities have always impressed Bat, and he promises Sunset he will support him for sheriff of the town in the newspaper he plans to set up.

In Canyon City, Professor Graham is a smooth jack-of-all trades who fronts as a barber and has a long record of throat-cutting in one way or another. He has been planning on making Jesse Thorpe sheriff of Canyon City, and thereby hopes to gain a free hand for his crooked dealings. Jesse is a former protégé of Bat Matson's, however, and when he meets up with Bat again, he vacillates between his desire to gain power and the honest teachings of Bat.

It is decided that the two candidates, Sunset (supported by Bat) and Jesse (backed by the professor) will run against each other for sheriff. Unknown to Bat, the Professor's henchmen are using threats of violence to win votes for Jesse. On the day of the election, Bat receives a poster showing a photograph of the Professor and describing his criminal record. When

Bat accuses the Professor of influencing the election, the Professor kills him and drags his body to the back of the barber shop. Frog, meanwhile, has left his camera near the back window of the shop. When he tries to retrieve it, he gets into a tussle with the Professor's men. During the fracas, a photograph is accidentally taken of the Professor and Bat's body. Frog, of course, is unaware of both the murder and the picture's existence. The Professor develops the picture and brings Bat's body to the newspaper office.

Jesse wins the election, becomes sheriff and hires the Professor's henchmen as deputies. When a shipment of gold is sent via stagecoach, Sunset and Frog intercept the deputies in the act of stealing the gold. Jesse arrives on the scene, but his deputies accuse Sunset and Frog of the theft, and Jesse can do no more than arrest the two. When Jesse accuses the Professor of staging the robbery, the Professor decides that now Jesse must be disposed of.

He produces a doctored photograph of Bat's murder showing Jesse (instead of the Professor) standing over the body. When Sunset sees the photo, he is enraged. He manages to get out of jail and confront Jesse and a furious battle ensues. Finally, however, Jesse's innocence is proven, the Professor is revealed as the culprit, and he and his gang get their just punishment. Sunset and Jesse set out to prove themselves worthy protégés of the famous Bat Matson.

Trail Street
(RKO, 1947) 83 min.

Director: Ray Enright. Screenplay: Norman Houston and Gene Lewis. Story: William Corcoran. Producer: Nat Holt.

Randolph Scott (Bat Masterson). *With* Robert Ryan, George (Gabby) Hayes, Anne Jeffreys, Harry Woods, Steve Brodie, Madge Meredith, Billy House, Virginia Sale, Phil Warren, Harry Harvey, Jason Robards, Sr., Forrest Taylor, Kit Guard, Stanley Andrews, Sarah Padden, Frank McGlynn, Jr., Ernie Adams, Roy Butler, Jessie Arnold, Guy Beach, Warren Jackson, Billy Vincent, Frank Austin, Betty Hill, Larry McGrath, Chris Willowbird.

This is one of the few films that has presented Bat Masterson as the main character. Bat rides into the town of Liberal, Kansas, and winds up as the town's peace officer. The main problem confronting the residents is the antagonism between cattlemen and farmers. Bat has to take a hand to protect the farmers and see to it that justice prevails.

"It all adds up to a big-scale pioneer melodrama produced by Nat Holt for the Jack J. Gross unit. It is due to pull its weight at the boxoffice, thanks to the lusty direction by Ray Enright, and the performances of Randolph

Randolph Scott (right) played Bat Masterson, Robert Ryan (left) was a land agent, and George (Gabby) Hayes was Masterson's sidekick in *Trail Street* (RKO, 1947).

Scott, Robert Ryan and George (Gabby) Hayes, particularly the scene-swiping comedy by Hayes, whose bearded character runs away with the show."— *Hollywood Reporter*, February 20, 1947

Prince of the Plains
(Republic, 1949) 60 min.

Director: Philip Ford. Screenplay: Louise Rousseau and Albert Demond. Assoc. Producer: Melville Tucker.

Monte Hale (Bat Masterson), Paul Hurst, Shirley Davis, Rory Mallinson, Roy Barcroft, Harry Lauter, George Carleton, Lane Bradford, Eddie Cobb, Holly Bane.

This B-Western purports to tell why the fabled Masterson turned to law and order but it soon becomes a standard low-budget shoot-'em-up in which Masterson enters the fracas when a bank president is killed by outlaws who also killed Bat's parents. The banker's son is believed dead when the bandits force his stage over a cliff. He is not drowned, however, and the sheriff asks Masterson, just arrived in town, to impersonate the young banker.

The stage hold-up, fights and gunplay are all that keep the film from being dull. Director Philip Ford handles the action effectively and does everything possible with the material. The film stacked up as okay fare for the giddyap trade.

Winchester '73
(Universal, 1950) 92 min.

Director: Anthony Mann. Screenplay: Robert L. Richards and Borden Chase. Story: Stuart N. Lake. Producer: Aaron Rosenberg.

James Stewart (Lin McAdam), Shelley Winters (Lola Manners), Dan Duryea (Waco Johnny Dean), Stephen McNally (Dutch Henry Brown), Millard Mitchell (Johnny "High Speed" Williams), Charles Drake (Steve Miller), John McIntire (Joe Lamont), Will Geer (Wyatt Earp), Jay C. Flippen (Sergeant Wilkes), Rock Hudson (Young Bull), John Alexander (Jack Riker), Steve Brodie (Wesley), James Millican (Wheeler), Abner Biberman (Latigo Means), Anthony [Tony] Curtis (Doane), James Best (Crater), Gregg Martell (Mossman), Edmund Cobb (Target Watcher), Bud Osborne (Man), Guy Wilkerson (Virgil), Chief Yowlachie (Indian), Carol Henry (Dudeen), Chuck Roberson (Long Tom), Frank Chase (Cavalryman), Larry Olsen (Boy), Bob Anderson (Bassett), Bonnie Kay Eddy (Benny Jameson), John War Eagle (Indian Interpreter), Ethan Laidlaw (Station Master), Steve Darrell (Bat Masterson).

As can be gleaned from the cast of characters, Bat Masterson has only a very brief bit part. He does not figure into the story at all. The film begins on a Fourth of July when scores of hopeful marksmen descend upon Dodge City for a rifle match. The winner gets a rifle of unexcelled precision, nearly perfect in its workmanship. Lin McAdam wins the rifle but Dutch Henry Brown steals it. From this point on the film depicts its passage from one character to another. McAdam is obsessed with finding Brown, not so much because of the rifle but, as the viewer learns in the end, because they are brothers and Brown has killed their father. The gun finally finds its way to Brown just before the two men engage in their final battle, alone upon a barren escarpment.

Santa Fe
(Columbia, 1951) 89 min.

Director: Irving Pichel. Screenplay: Kenneth Hamet. Story: Louis Stevens, from the novel by James Marshall. Producer: Harry Joe Brown.

Randolph Scott, Janis Carter, Jerome Courtland, Peter Thompson, John Archer, Warner Anderson, Olin Howlin, Billy House, Frank Ferguson, Roy Roberts, Allene Roberts, Jock O'Mahoney [Mahoney],

Harry Cording, Sven Hugo Borg, Irving Pichel, Harry Tylor, Chief Thundercloud, Paul E. Burns, Charles Evans, Chuck Hamilton, George Sherwood, Roy Butler, Louis Mason, Edgar Dearing, Art Loeb, Blackie Whiteford, Bud Fine, Al Kunde, Richard Fortune, Lane Chandler, Reed Howes, Charles Meredith, Paul Stanton, Richard Cramer, William Haade, Francis McDonald, Frank O'Connor, Harry Tenbrook, James Mason, Guy Wilkerson, Frank Hagney, William Tannen, James Kirkwood, Stanley Blystone, Ralph Sanford, William McCormack.

Santa Fe is an action-packed bigtime Western, a bit fuzzy in the story department, but otherwise vigorous, convincing adventure fare. Scott works for the Santa Fe railroad and fights to repel his brothers' attempts to interfere with the railroad's construction.

Masterson of Kansas
(Columbia, 1954)

The story stresses the antagonism between Holliday and Masterson, and the friendship of Earp for both. See full writeup on page 161.

Wichita
(Allied Artists, 1955)

Bat Masterson is seen as a likable frontier reporter. See full writeup on page 162.

The Life and Legend of Wyatt Earp
(ABC-TV, September 6, 1955—September 26, 1961)
30-minute episodes, 266 episodes

Hugh O'Brian (Wyatt Earp), Alan Dinehart Jr. (Bat Masterson), Douglas Fowley (Doc Holliday). *With* Damian O'Flynn, Steve Brodie, Myron Healey, Lloyd Garrison, Morgan Woodward, Dirk London, Lash LaRue, John Anderson, Carol Thurston, Stacy Harris.

Badman's Country
(Warner Bros., 1958)

See full writeup on page 166.

Joel McCrea as Bat Masterson and Julie Adams as Pauline in *The Gunfight at Dodge City* (United Artists, 1959).

The Gunfight at Dodge City
(United Artists, 1959) 81 min.

Director: Joseph M. Newman. Screenplay: Daniel B. Ullman and Martin M. Goldsmith. Story: Daniel B. Ullman. Producer: Walter Mirisch.

Joel McCrea (Bat Masterson), Julie Adams (Pauline), John McIntire (Doc), Nancy Gates (Lily), Richard Anderson (Dave), Jim Westerfield (Rev. Howard), Walter Coy (Ben), Don Haggerty (Regan), Wright King (Billy), Harry Lauter (Ed), Myron Healey (Forbes), Mauritz Hugo (Purley), Henry Kulky (Bartender).

Bat Masterson is drifting and hoping to stay out of the trouble he and his reputation always seem to bring. But he rides into wide-open Dodge City, presided over by crooked sheriff Regan. When his brother is killed, Bat runs for sheriff. His thirst for revenge and the cleaning out of Dodge are the basic story motivations. He doesn't get the girl he wanted but winds up with another one.

"Characterizations are slight and emotional interaction practically nonexistent. Photography by Carl Guthrie, however, is good, the title of the picture itself is an exploitation asset, and direction by Joseph M. Newman is reasonably actionful." —*Film Daily*, May 15, 1959

"McCrea can do this sort of thing with his left hand, and he even has a few chances in *The Gunfight at Dodge City* to give a reminder that when he wants to be, and has the chance, he is one of the most accomplished light comedians around." —*Variety*, May 13, 1959

The Outlaws Is Coming
(Columbia, 1965)

Ed T. McDonnell portrays Bat Masterson in a bit as Larry, Moe and Curly Joe, printers, go west with the editor of a magazine (Adam West) interested in saving America's wildlife. See full writeup on page 43.

The Gambler Returns: The Luck of the Draw
(Kenny Rogers Productions, 1991)

This is the third in *The Gambler* series with Kenny Rogers as the professional gambler who flits from one adventure to another. Bat Masterson, portrayed by Gene Barry, also does his bit to keep the action lively. See full writeup on page 171.

Wyatt Earp
(Warner Bros., 1994)

See full writeup on page 174.

Bat Masterson Television Series

The author acknowledges Stephen W. and Diane L. Albert, from whose fanzine, *The TV Collector*, September/October 1988 much of the following credits were assembled. As of 1997, a one-year, six-issue subscription to *The TV Collector* (P.O. Box 1088, Easton PA 02334) is $21; issues #37 and #38, which feature the "Bat Masterson" episode guide, are available for $8 postpaid. For more information and a back issue list, send a self-addressed, stamped envelope.

Double Showdown
(10-8-58)

Gene Barry (Bat Masterson), Robert Middleton (Big Keel Roberts), Elisha Cook (Pete Sheeley), Jean Willes (Lucy Slater). *With* Adele Mara, King Donovan, Charles Maxwell.

Bat goes to a lucrative Arizona town to help a friend, a saloonkeeper being crushed by Big Keel Roberts, a gambler and saloonkeeper who "owns" the town. Big Keel suggests they solve the problem by a hand of showdown poker. This historical legend has been passed down from the 1870s with two different endings, both shown here.

Dynamite Blows Two Ways
(10-22-58)

Gene Barry (Bat Masterson), Reed Hadley (Raoul Cummings), Tyler McVey (Thompson), Bill Hale (Bill), Susan Cummings (Valerie Mitchell), Tom McKee (Swede), Richard Warren (Crane). *With* Jeff De Benning, Wes Hudman.

Bat wins a herd of cattle in a poker game and finds that a ruthless rancher has been blocking neighboring ranchers' herds from reaching the Cheyenne stockyards, with their lives being threatened. Bat joins the other ranchers in a drive to market.

Stampede at Tent City
(10-29-58)

Gene Barry (Bat Masterson). *With* William Conrad, James Burt, Joan Marshall.

An ex-girlfriend of Bat's begs for his help; the man she loves has been accused of shooting a man in the back, and she fears he'll be lynched.

The Fighter
(11-5-58)

Gene Barry (Bat Masterson), Marie Windsor (Polly Landers), Patrick Waltz (Jim Bemis), Robert Wilke (Bull Kirby). *With* Ray Kellogg.

Bat admires a promising young boxer and, seeing him mishandled, entices his unscrupulous manager into a poker game and wins the fighter's contract.

Bear Bait
(11-12-58)

Gene Barry (Bat Masterson), James Westerfield (Shapley Howell), Patricia Donahue (Joyce), Milton Frome (Sheriff Clark).

Bat accepts an offer to guide a bear hunting party, and during the trip he discovers that three of his companions are wanted in the East for murder and robbery.

A Noose Fits Anybody
(11-19-58)

Gene Barry (Bat Masterson), Robert Swan (Ben Thompson), Murvyn Vye (Big Ed Bacon), Les Hellman (Ray Clinton), Gary Vinson (Billy Thompson), Bill Henry (Griff Handley), Jack Wagner (Deputy). *With* Max Palmer, George C. Jones.

During a gunfight over a card game, a man is wounded saving Bat's life, and is unable to go through with a plan to help his younger brother, who he claims is innocent, to escape from jail. Grateful, Bat takes over.

Dude's Folly
(11-26-58)

Gene Barry (Bat Masterson), Nancy Hadley (Jan Larkin), Leo Gordon (Joe Quince), Joe Turkel (Woodrow Larkin).

A ruthless man threatens to run Jan and Woody Larkin out of town unless they agree to sell him the hardware store they inherited from their father. Amidst this danger, Bat agrees to teach Woody how to handle a gun.

The Treasure of Worry Hill
(12-3-58)

Gene Barry (Bat Masterson), Audrey Dalton (Abigail Feather), Ross Martin (Caulder Larsen), Harvey Stephens (Isaac Parker), Bob Anderson (Richard Woodman).

Three heirs to an uncle's estate each have one third of a map showing the location of his huge treasures. Distrusting each other they each give Bat their piece of the map and hire him to guide them to the site.

Cheyenne Club
(12-17-58)

Gene Barry (Bat Masterson), Louis Fletcher (Sarah Lou), Dean Harens (Steve Haley), Karl Swenson (Pate), William Tannen (John Conant).

An influential man calls Bat to Cheyenne, to test the rumors that his daughter's fiancé is a poker cheat. Bat finds unusual adventure between the tensions of gambling and the excitement of romance.

Sherman's March Through Dodge City
(12-24-58)

Gene Barry (Bat Masterson), John Gallaudet (General Sherman), Michael Whalen (Marshal), Joe Hamilton (President Hayes), Robert J. Stevenson (Luke). *With* William Joyce, Harvey B. Dunn, Phyllis Coughlan.

President Rutherford B. Hayes and General William Tecumseh Sherman, the scourge of Atlanta, come to Dodge City on a campaign tour. With rumors that ex–Confederates threaten violence against Sherman, Bat is given the task of guarding the general.

Trail Pirate
(12-31-58)

Gene Barry (Bat Masterson), Gloria Talbot (Eileen Parish), Barry Atwater (Egan), James Barron (Sheriff).

Bat answers a call for help from a friend in Salome and finds the man has been killed while operating a wagon train, one of many being destroyed in the scorching desert by ruthless trail pirates. The unique method that the pirates use to lure the wagons astray puts Bat on the track of a monstrous conspiracy.

Double Trouble in Trinidad
(1-7-59)

Gene Barry (Bat Masterson), Yvette Vickers (Jessie Simons), Richard Bakalyan (Sam Teller), Lance Fuller (Mornsby), Dick Reeves (George Swift), Johnny Silver (Drummer).

Learning that a man using his name has become sheriff of Trinidad, Bat arrives incognito to investigate, and learns that the man plans to steal a gold shipment and frame him. He decides to impersonate the impersonator, and teaches him that it's not by derby and cane alone that Bat Mastersons make their mark in the world.

Election Day
(1-14-59)

Gene Barry (Bat Masterson), Peter Hansen (Teddy Wright), Dan Sheridan (Joe Rankin), Kasey Rogers (Kitty Meadows).

Hired as trail boss on a cattle drive, Bat runs into a strong man in Protection, Kansas, who demands a special, illegal cattle toll before allowing him to move on. Refusing to pay, Bat investigates and finds corruption in civic circles.

One Bullet from Broken Bow
(1-21-59)

Gene Barry (Bat Masterson), H. M. Wynant (Chief Stone Calf), Joan O'Brien (Dolores Clark), Donna Martell (Barbara Rafferty).

At a general's request, Bat challenges a renegade Indian chief in an effort to rescue a pair of sisters from their kidnappers, the chief's war party.

A Personal Matter
(1-28-59)

Gene Barry (Bat Masterson), Alan Hale (Bailey Harper), Raymond Hatton (Adam Fairbanks), Peggy Knudsen (Louise Carey), Don Eitner (Stage Driver), Robert Lynn (Inn Clerk).

Bat tests his great skill at trailing fugitives after a boastful outlaw steals his gun, money and horse and brags that Bat will never find him. At the end of the line he runs into sudden, explosive action.

License to Cheat
(2-4-59)

Gene Barry (Bat Masterson), Douglas Kennedy (Jeb Crater), Allison Hayes (Ellie), William Phipps (Ken Wills).

Bat stops off at Mason City to set up the only honest game in town. The sheriff insists he join the Protective Gamblers' Association, a group which Bat finds unsavory. He refuses and is thrown behind bars by the sheriff, who controls the organization.

Sharpshooter
(2-11-59)

Gene Barry (Bat Masterson), Conrad Nagel (Harry Varden), Lisa Gaye (Lori Dowling), Paul Dupov (Danny Dowling), Harry Fleer (Darby Cole), Ann Dore (Jezebel).

Bat unwittingly makes an enemy of the owner of Dodge City's largest saloon, who fears that he plans to relieve him of some of his property and hires a gunman to eliminate him.

River Boat
(2-18-59)

Gene Barry (Bat Masterson), Patricia Powell (Nora), Jacques Aubuchon (King Henry), Walter Barnes (Paulson), Clark Howat (Murdock).

On a Mississippi riverboat, Bat goes into the captain's cabin to deposit $10,000 in the safe, and has his money stolen by an outlaw gang holding the captain prisoner. After the clever robbers work their way systematically through the entire passenger list, Bat goes into action.

Battle of the Pass
(2-25-59)

Gene Barry (Bat Masterson), Wayne Morris (Mace Pomeroy), Roy Engel (Maloney), Will Wright (Billy Willow), Emile Meyer (Gen. Moran), Leo Needham (Bartender).

A ruthless man racing frantically to be first to lay railroad tracks through a canyon offers Bat a small fortune to help, but Bat decides to help his rival and ends up in a historic gang fight in the wilds of canyon country.

Marked Deck
(3-11-59)

Gene Barry (Bat Masterson), Cathy Downs (Amelia Roberts), Denver Pyle (Morgan), Phil Chambers (Sheriff). *With* Richard Emory.

In a card game Bat is cheated out of a lot of money by Morganville's strong man. Aiming to recover it, he learns that the man also swindled a brother and sister, and sets out to settle scores for his other victims as well as for himself.

Incident at Leadville
(3-18-59)

Gene Barry (Bat Masterson), Kathleen Crowley (Jo Hart), John Cliff (Jess Santola), Jonathan Hole (Mart), Edward C. Platt (Roy Evans), Jack Lambert (King Fisher), Helen Jay (Jennie), Terry Rangno (Denny).

Furious at a newspaper article labeling him as a gunman and scoundrel who should be eliminated, Bat goes to have a talk with the author, a charming lady editor, who exercises a woman's prerogative of changing her mind.

The Tumbleweed Wagon
(3-25-59)

Gene Barry (Bat Masterson), Fay Spain (Julie Poe), Paul Lambert (Luke Steiger).

When one of Bat's friends is murdered, he's deputized as a federal officer to escort the suspect to Fort Smith for trial. But the night before they're to leave, the outlaw disappears.

Brunette Bombshell
(4-1-59)

Gene Barry (Bat Masterson), Rebecca Welles (Isabel Fowler), Gene Nelson (Whit Morrison), Charles Fredericks (Marty).

Bat buys the Denver Athletic Club, only to have it condemned by the fire commissioner as a fire hazard.

Deadline
(4-8-59)

Gene Barry (Bat Masterson), Ken Lynch (Tim Minton), Eve Brent (Loma Adams), Dean Stanton (Jay Simms). *With* Nick Nickoll, Ralph Moody.

Heading to the state capitol, Bat's happy that his stagecoach companion is a lovely lady. She is rushing to bring evidence that will clear an innocent man who's condemned to hang. They end up racing against time and the executioner after being held up and stranded en route.

Man of Action
(4-22-59)

Gene Barry (Bat Masterson), Harold J. Stone (Jess Hobart), Joan Elam (Deborah Jenkins), Gavin Muir (Oliver Jenkins). *With* Mickey Simpson, Mike Ragan.

Bat calls on his tailor in Junction, New Mexico to order new clothes, but the craftsman, newly chosen head of a special citizens' committee, is too busy to serve him. This leads to an unusual adventure for Bat, the man's most famous customer.

A Matter of Honor
(4-29-59)

Gene Barry (Bat Masterson), Paula Raymond (Millie Wilkins), John Vivyan (Chip Grimes), Stephen Bekassy (Anton von Landi).

Hurrying to buy into a new casino, Bat stops for a roulette game, during which an Austrian nobleman, temporarily without funds, pulls a holdup.

Lottery of Death
(5-13-59)

Gene Barry (Bat Masterson), Constance Ford (Gwenn Parsons), Myron Healey (Jack Latigo), Len Hendry (Manager), John Sutton (Andrew Stafford), Warren Oates (Sonny Parsons), Bill Erwin (Teller).

During a poker game in Tucson, a player stakes half a lottery ticket, which Bat wins and finds it's worth a great deal of money. But the owner of the other half is found dead and the ticket missing.

The Death of Bat Masterson
(5-20-59)

Gene Barry (Bat Masterson), Claude Akins (Jack Fontana), Ruta Lee (Nellie Fontana), Willard Waterman (Bank Manager). *With* Cliff Edwards, Sam Buffington.

Bat is pleased to announce that reports of his death are much exaggerated. But when he tries to withdraw some money from his Bonanza, Colorado bank account, he finds the account is closed and he's "deceased."

The Secret Is Death
(5-27-59)

Gene Barry (Bat Masterson), John Larch (Garrickson), George Neise (Calhoun), Allison Hayes (Ellie). *With* Joel Ashley, William Boyett.

When a crime wave sweeps Cheyenne, the territorial administrator calls on the one man he knows can handle and solve the problem—Bat Masterson.

Two Graves for Swan Valley
(6-3-59)

Gene Barry (Bat Masterson), Marcia Henderson (Molly Doyle), Broderick Crawford (Sgt. Foley), Patrick McVey (Angus McLarnin).

Passing through Swan Valley, Bat becomes interested in a dance hall beauty, the girlfriend of hot-tempered Sgt. Foley, who orders him out of town. Though his life is threatened, Bat refuses to leave.

[Note: This episode may have first aired on 10-15-58.]

Promised Land
(6-10-59)

Gene Barry (Bat Masterson), Carol Ohmart (Linda Beaudine), Gerald Mohr (Courtney Shepherd), Arthur Space (Doc Ferguson).

Bat is waylaid and taken to a community of reformed outlaws trying to lead decent lives. He reluctantly becomes their bank president, entrusted with their savings and their right to continue their new way of life.

The Conspiracy—Part One
(6-17-59)

Gene Barry (Bat Masterson), Diane Brewster (Lynn Harrison), Arthur Shields (Ruggles), Paul Richards (Ned Ruggles), Jerome Cowan (Jasper Salt).

Fifteen years after Lincoln's assassination, the niece of acquitted suspect John Surratt begs Bat to prevent publication of a scurrilous, untrue story signed by Surrett, who she claims is dead, concerning his involvement in the conspiracy.

The Conspiracy—Part Two
(6-24-59)

Bat discovers that a bartender posed as another man to sell the scandal-ridden story to the newspaper. Revealing him as the scoundrel, Bat almost immediately finds the man dead, which points to his own mortal danger.

The Black Pearls
(7-1-59)

Gene Barry (Bat Masterson), Jacqueline Scott (Carol Otis), James Coburn (Polk Otis), Gerald Milton (Sheriff Gowdy). *With* Emile Meyer, Jack Hogan, Carlos Romero, Wayne Mallory.

Accused of cheating at cards, Bat is thrown into jail and finds his cellmate is a murderer who masterminded a train robbery and stole priceless black pearls.

The Desert Ship
(7-15-59)

Gene Barry (Bat Masterson), Karen Steele (Elsa Dorn), John Wengraf (Anders Dorn). *With* Jack Kruschen.

The legendary Santa Lucia, a fabulous ship rumored lost in the Colorado River, filled with Spanish gold and pearls, lures many treasure hunters to destruction in the Colorado Territory. Bat tries to dissuade a man and his niece who have come from Holland on the hazardous expedition.

The Romany Knives
(7-22-59)

Gene Barry (Bat Masterson), Ray Denton (Tonio), Chana Eden (Leda), Frank Silvera (Grasia), Robert Carricart (Mitka).

Bat comes to the rescue of an old gypsy woman who has angered a hot-tempered Dodge City rancher. Never has his chivalry been so sorely tested as when she rewards him with a number of valuable gifts, including a beautiful girl.

Buffalo Kill
(7-29-59)

Gene Barry (Bat Masterson), Lisa Gaye (Susan Carver), John Doucette (Luke Simes), Ted Jacques (J. J. Carver), Tom Greenway (Charlie Bowman).

Incensed over some uncomplimentary remarks about his style of dress, Bat temporarily puts a man out of commission, and then takes on the assignment that the man is unable to carry out—risking his scalp on an expedition to hunt buffalo hides in dangerous Indian country.

To the Manor Born
(10-1-59)

Gene Barry (Bat Masterson), Audrey Dalton (Abby Chancellor), Myron Healey (Col. Marc James), Ernestine Barrier (Mrs. Dwight Chancellor), Jack Hogan (Stuart Chancellor).

When her daughter becomes involved with a cousin of dubious reputation, a woman friend asks Bat's help. He resorts to duelling pistols to expose the cowardice of a self-styled "Colonel," a Confederate deserter, and ends his career of blackmailing and terrorizing the woman's daughter.

Wanted—Dead
(10-15-59)

Gene Barry (Bat Masterson), John Dehner (Sheriff), John Archer (Blacksmith), Don Kennedy (Fred Sanders), Bethel Leslie (Mildred Conrad), John Maloney (Irish Comedian), Dennis Moore (Tom), Dabbs Greer (Will).

A gunman trying to reform borrows money from Bat, who later learns he's killed a man and is on the lam. Bat goes after him, but ends up battling for justice against a trigger-happy sheriff who wants to deny the man his day in court.

No Funeral for Thorn
(10-22-59)

Gene Barry (Bat Masterson), Elisha Cook (Thorn Loomis), Ray Teal (Vergil Gardiner), Joi Lansing (Sapphira).

Hearing that a friend is dying, Bat rushes to his side and is caught in the crossfire of two towns battling to be named county seat. Bat and his "dying" friend try to outgun the Wichita Kid, and Bat writes his name in the history of the state of Kansas.

Shakedown at St. Joe
(10-29-59)

Gene Barry (Bat Masterson), Bruce Gordon (Jason Medford), Joan O'Brien (Dora Miller), Harvey Stephens (Judge Thatcher).

Visiting an old girlfriend at the local opera house in St. Joseph, Bat comes to the rescue when a local merchant is attacked.

Lady Luck
(11-5-59)

Gene Barry (Bat Masterson), Pamela Duncan (Rachel), Don Haggerty (Jess Porter), Dyan Cannon (Mary Lowry), Charles Maxwell (Ron Davis).

In one of Sacramento's gayest casinos, the owner blackmails two beautiful girls and their father. Playing detective, Bat comes to their aid.

Who'll Buy My Violence?
(11-12-59)

Gene Barry (Bat Masterson), Mort Mills (Barney Kaster), Joanna Moore (Sharon Stabler), Sam Buffington (Capt. Fogerty).

When Bat buys one of his famous bowlers in Whistle Valley, he's outraged by the price and learns that the town is in the grip of a men who has a monopoly on riverboat cargo. He devises a plan to break the man's hold on the shipping.

Dead Men Don't Pay Debts
(11-19-59)

Gene Barry (Bat Masterson), Steve Terrell (Hal Clements), Robert J. Wilke (Rod Clements), Jeremy Slate (Bob Clements).

Bat tries to put a stop to a feud between the Clements and Basset families. He has a vested interest—the Bassetts owe him money.

Death and Taxes
(11-26-59)

Gene Barry (Bat Masterson), Richard Arlen, Don Kennedy, Susan Cummings.

When Bat is asked by a sheriff to help collect the county taxes, they learn that some citizens are evading tax assessment by shipping their assets outside of the county.

Bat Plays a Dead Man's Hand
(12-3-59)

Gene Barry (Bat Masterson), Jan Harrison (Belle Simms), Guy Prescott (Phil Hood), Don Harvey (John Mills).

Bat turns lawyer to break the power of a tyrant who uses the law to his own ends, stifling the freedom and lives of his townspeople.

Garrison Finish
(12-10-59)

Gene Barry (Bat Masterson), Frankie Darro (Edward "Snapper" Garrison), Emile Meyer (Gen. Moran), John Gallaudet.

Certain that his Kentucky thoroughbred is faster that Col. Pierce's Western quarterhorse, Gen. Moran bets his railroad on it. But when he begins to have misgivings, he asks for Bat's help.

The Canvas and the Cane
(12-17-59)

Gene Barry (Bat Masterson), John Sutton (Orrin Thackeray), Dean Harens (Sheriff), Jacqueline Scott/Joanna Moore (?) (Teresa Renault).

The Inner Circle
(12-31-59)

Gene Barry (Bat Masterson), Marcia Henderson (Susan Stevens), Jean Willes (Grace Williams), Phillip Baird (John Scott Powers).

Bat fights against the "Inner Circle," a group of men determined to keep women from voting. Fighting for women suffrage, Bat finds himself knee-deep in trouble.

The Pied Piper of Dodge City
(1-7-60)

Gene Barry (Bat Masterson), Donald Barry (Luke Short), Ron Hayes (Wyatt Earp), King Caulder (Mayor Webber), Evan MacNeil (Dolly McGregor).

To help pick up business at a friend's saloon, Bat imports a pretty piano player. A rival saloonkeeper, Mayor Webber, changes city ordinances to outlaw the entertainment. Using Dodge City's bad conditions as leverage, Bat gets the governor to set up a commission, made up of some of the West's most famous lawkeepers. The commission lasts long enough to get rid of Webber and clean up the town.

A Picture of Death
(1-14-60)

Gene Barry (Bat Masterson), Donald Woods (Roger Purcell), Patricia Donahue (Miss Tuesday), Howard Petrie (Hugh Blaine).

Intrigued by the age-old question, Bat believes that a trotting horse's four feet are off the ground at the same time and puts his money where his mouth is, and to prove his assertion tries to take a picture.

Pigeon and Hawk
(1-21-60)

Gene Barry (Bat Masterson), Howard Petrie (Hugh Blaine), Hugh Sanders (Lee Baxter), Rand Brooks (Willard Wynant).

Two would-be tycoons try to corner the Denver mining stock market by using ex–Pony Express riders to rush them advance news of shifting silver values and mine conditions. A broker hires Bat to counter their move and he becomes involved in a "coup" with the valuable stock.

Flume to the Mother Lode
(1-28-60)

Gene Barry (Bat Masterson), Miranda Jones (Nancy Wilkerson), Paul Lambert (Charles Hamilton), Jerome Cowan (Ben Wilson), Stephen Bekassy (Emile Barole).

Bat becomes partner in a gold mine and finds himself party to a timber war, when a millionaire competitor prevents him from bracing any mine tunnels by buying up all the available timber.

Death by the Half Dozen
(2-4-60)

Gene Barry (Bat Masterson), Willard Waterman (Mayor Samuel Goodwin), Ted De Corsia (Hank Griswell), Patrick Waltz (Buck Peters).

Unable to prevent the kidnapping of a young bride, Bat is forced by the kidnappers to deliver a ransom note. He manages to save her and then has the job of rounding up the outlaws.

Deadly Diamonds
(2-11-60)

Gene Barry (Bat Masterson), Kenneth Tobey (Meade Amhurst), Allison Hayes (Ellie Winters), William Schallert (Dr. Hal Dunsmore), William Tannen (Charlie Graves), Bill Catching (Guard), Hank Patterson (Soda Smith).

Bat suspects that a mine owner is putting over a hoax on the people of the boom town of Leadville. To get proof he invests in the questionable mine and wins the gratitude of the entire town.

Mr. Fourpaws
(2-18-60)

Gene Barry (Bat Masterson), Paula Raymond (Linda Wills (Frank Gerstle (Sheriff), Gregory Walcott (Sam Long), Les Hellman (Brad Pierce).

Investigating some shortages uncovered in a small town bank, Bat encounters a dead man and a larcenous stray dog who seems eager to help. Bat is also nearly killed and subsequently meets a charming lady. With the dog's help he retrieves the money, solves a murder, brings the killers to justice, and then reluctantly takes leave of his new lady fair.

Six Feet of Gold
(2-25-60)

Gene Barry (Bat Masterson), James Coburn (Leo Tailey), Carol Ohmart (Lisa Truex), Ronald Foster (Toby Dawson).

A woman settles a debt by giving Bat a parcel of wasteland, which he decides to turn into a cemetery. But the double-dealing woman forces the county clerk to alter the land deed, and Bat's branded a swindler.

Cattle and Cane
(3-3-60)

Gene Barry (Bat Masterson), Joyce Taylor (Jane Taylor), Ken Drake (Colby), Dan White (Ben Taylor).

It's a cane against guns when Bat steps into a feud between ranchers and cattle barons. Once he chooses sides, he's not at all responsive to being urged at gunpoint to become a "turncoat."

The Disappearance of Bat Masterson
(3-10-60)

Gene Barry (Bat Masterson), Erin O'Brien (Genie Landry), Robert Karnes (Landry), Liam Sullivan (Pronto), Oscar Beregi (Herman the Great), Doris Fesette (Herman's Assistant), Chuck Roberson, Jack Williams (Cowboys).

Herman the Great brings magic to the badlands, using sleight-of-hand to disarm a cowboy. Bandits think they might try the same thing on Bat, but he's able to perform a bit of magic himself.

The Snare
(3-17-60)

Gene Barry (Bat Masterson), Marshall Reed (Alf Hayman), Robert Ivers (The Yaqui Kid), Bill Henry (Sheriff Brady).

When the heartless Yaqui Kid kills Bat's friend, he joins the posse. The sheriff is ambushed and slain, and the posse flees in panic, leaving Bat to ride the trail alone into almost certain death.

Three Bullets for Bat
(3-24-60)

Gene Barry (Bat Masterson), Tris Coffin (Marshal Roy Dunning), Kent Taylor (John Martin), Brett King (Dan Mosely), George Eldredge (Judge), Suzanne Lloyd (Linda), Miguel Landa (Jorge), Stephen Holt (LaTour), Dennis Moore (Barker).

Bat is conned into trailing some nonexistent missing jewelry into Mexico, and by the time he learns he's been duped, he's facing a firing squad.

The Reluctant Witness
(3-31-60)

Gene Barry (Bat Masterson), Harry Lauter (Sheriff Conners), Donald Murphy (Charles Ryan), Allison Hayes (Ellie Winters), Ronald Hayes (Wyatt Earp).

When the only one who can prove a woman's innocence of murder fails to show up, Bat, knowing she needs a good lawyer, gets Wyatt Earp to pose as one.

Come Out Fighting
(4-7-60)

Gene Barry (Bat Masterson), Rhys Williams (Judge Malachi), Joan Granville (Belinda Muldoon), Ken Mayer (Largo Morgan), Connie Buck (Lolita), Steve Warren (Paddy Muldoon).

Arrested on his way to watch a championship boxing match, Bat find himself arraigned before a formidable, vindictive, infamous "fining judge."

Stage of Nowhere
(4-14-60)

Gene Barry (Bat Masterson), James Seay (Parker James), Michael Forest (Noah Gannon), Constance Ford (Ivy Dixon).

Bandits are stealing silver bullion from stagecoaches, and Bat's ingenious plan to thwart them is an early milestone in crime-busting history. When he puts it into effect, not only does the bullion disappear, but the stagecoach vanishes too.

Incident at Fort Bowie
(4-21-60)

Gene Barry (Bat Masterson), Cathy Downs (Julie Giles), Will Wright (Billy Willow), Tyler McVey (Col. Sloane), Robert J. Stevenson (Ben Roper), Dennis Flaherty (Corporal).

Bat turns horse trader to sell cavalry stock to the army, but a horse thief hijacks the herd. He sets out to find and deliver the horses and bring the thieves to justice.

Masterson's Arcadia Club
(4-28-60)

Gene Barry (Bat Masterson), Larry Hudson (Clark Chisum), X Brands (Jeb Mitchell), Morgan Jones (Mace Gunnison), Kasey Rogers (Dixie Mayhew), Lane Bradford (Rod Bradbury).

To lure customers into his casino, a crooked gambler appropriates Bat's identity and takes over the town of Liberal, Kansas, fleecing townsmen with gambling and third-rate liquor. Anyone who squeals is thrown into jail and then out of town. Outraged, Bat aims to clear his name and get the people's money back.

Welcome to Paradise
(5-5-60)

Gene Barry (Bat Masterson), Robert Foulk ("Judge" Peter Perkins), Ralph Taeger (Frank Dexter), James Parnell (Sheriff), Lonnie Blackman (Elsie Snow).

Bat is hit with an exorbitant fine when he rides into Paradise, Colorado, where crooked officials demand money from strangers who unwittingly violate the town law against carrying firearms. But the law puts the man with the cane at a greater advantage.

A Grave Situation
(5-12-60)

Gene Barry (Bat Masterson), Howard Petrie (Hugo Blaine), Lance Ruller (Powers), John Doucette (Carstairs), Peggy Knudsen (Katie), Jack Harris (David Winkler).

A huge herd of cattle dwindles overnight on a ranch bought by Bat's friend. Bat suspects a swindle by the agent who sold the property and baits a trap with more than $15,000, which leads to a fight for his life in which Bat digs his own grave.

Wanted—Alive Please
(5-26-60)

Gene Barry (Bat Masterson), Diana Crawford (Renee), Douglas Dumbrille (Taylor Millard), Joseph Turkel (Fargo), Steve Darrell (Alec Hudson).

Bat performs one of his greatest public services by stopping the smuggling of diseased cattle across the Rio Grande into the United States. Alerted to the danger to healthy American stock, he volunteers for the task of guarding the border single-handedly.

The Elusive Baguette
(6-2-60)

Gene Barry (Bat Masterson), Leslie Parrish (Lucy Carter), Allison Hayes (Ellie), Don O'Kelly (Reed Morgan).

A pretty San Francisco widow hires Bat as her personal escort to prevent thieves from snatching her fabulous diamond, making him prime suspect when the gen disappears. In one of the great demonstrations of his cane's effectiveness as a fighting weapon, he clears himself and catches the culprit.

The Big Gamble
(6-16-60)

Gene Barry (Bat Masterson), Evan Thompson (Steve Fansler), Arch Johnson (Mr. Smith), Morgan Woodward (Kana).

Bat stakes a prospector who sets out for the famous Lost Dutchman Mine and vanishes without a trace, the latest in a long line of disappearing man en route to the mine. Bat sets out to solve the mystery.

Blood on the Money
(6-23-60)

Gene Barry (Bat Masterson), Kaye Elhardt (Eva Rogers), Walter Coy (Andrew Strathmere), Page Slattery (Dane Holloway), Paul Fierro (Ridalgo), Len Lesser (Frank Holloway).

In search of a young man for whom he's holding a bequest, Bat advertises for information, which a cattle baron immediately offers to sell him. Thinking that Bat is out to kill the man, the cattle baron misleads him.

Barbara Castle
(6-30-60)

Gene Barry (Bat Masterson), Gloria Talbott (Mary MacLeod), Jay Novello (Capt. Angus MacLeod), Stuart Cradley (Tracy Crow).

Bat finds that an old Scottish sea captain has smuggled a castle into the U. S. one stone at a time and set it up in San Francisco.

Gold Is Where You Steal It

(date unknown)

Gene Barry (Bat Masterson), Gloria Castillo (Rosita Anselm), Carlos Romero (Juan Torrino), Martin Garralaga (Pio Anselm).

In Southern California Bat becomes involved with a Spanish beauty and a bandit who terrorizes the region.

Debt of Honor

(9-29-60)

Gene Barry (Bat Masterson), Edgar Buchanan (Cactus Charlie Hayden), Paul Langton (U. S. Marshal), Don Haggerty (Gordon Hall).

Bat's prospector friend comes to town to repay a grubstake debt. He gives Bat two sacks of gold, tells the town that Bat's his new partner and disappears. Then Bat learns that the gold is part of a missing shipment.

Law of the Land

(10-6-60)

Gene Barry (Bat Masterson), Barbara Lawrence (Melanie Haywood), Howard Petrie (Hugh Blaine), Leo Gordon (Red Eric Pederson), Ray Teal (Cogswell). *With* Allan Jaffe.

When open range cattlemen strip over 50 miles of barbed wire fence intended to keep the herds off the tracks, the railroad president asks Bat to help. Though his sympathies lie with the cattlemen in their fight against the railroads, he doesn't condone lawlessness and sides against them.

Bat Trap

(10-13-60)

Gene Barry (Bat Masterson), Lon Chaney, Jr. (Rance Fletcher), Frank Ferguson (Dick Pearce), Dick Ryan (Burt Mason), Leslie Parrish (Lisa Anders), Maggie Pierce (Amber Mason), Jack Ging (Billy Webb), Robin Riley (Edie), Art Stewart (Old Man).

Bat has his hands full when he's hired to judge a turkey shoot in Midas Creek to keep it on the up-and-up and prevent the town bully from causing any trouble.

The Rage of Princess Anne
(10-20-60)

Gene Barry (Bat Masterson), Elaine Stewart (Anne Eaton), Paul Lambert (Augustus Ulbrecht), Ron Hayes (Jeremy French), William Hickman (Topaz), Gene Roth, Marx Hartman (Miners).

Bat becomes partners in a mining venture and ends up sorry when he gets a report that the mine is unsafe and the manager is forcing the men to work it anyway. But although he wants none of the blame, Bat doesn't walk out on his responsibility.

The Hunter
(10-27-60)

Gene Barry (Bat Masterson), John Vivyan (Sir Edward Marion), Mickey Simpson (Donovan), Gerald Milton (Middlesworth), Sue Randall (Elizabeth), Brett King (Johnny Hillman), Allan Ray (Jake).

Convinced that range is more vital than speed in shooting, an Englishman gets an unexpected chance to prove it when he accidentally kills a gunman noted for his fast draw. Attaining a certain notoriety, he's brought to the attention of Bat, with whom he exchanges some unusual demonstrations of fancy gunmanship.

Murder Can Be Dangerous
(11-3-60)

Gene Barry (Bat Masterson), Kathleen Crowley (Marri Brewster), Tipp McClure (Shad), Ken Drake (Secret).

Mystified when his gambling hall's profits plummet while business is booming, Bat investigates and finds that his partner's fingers are in the cash drawer—until he slams it shut.

High Card Loses
(11-10-60)

Gene Barry (Bat Masterson), Joan O'Brien (Eileen McDermot), Paul Fierro (Jose Thomas Reilly), Jean Blake (Mildred Vaughn).

Bat's friend is murdered while escorting three mail order brides to Noble Creek. Bat takes over and becomes a target when for some unknown reason a certain "hot gun" doesn't want the ladies to arrive.

Dakota Showdown
(11-17-60)

Gene Barry (Bat Masterson), Tom Gilson (Jocko Dakota), Quentin Sondergaard (Jeb Dakota), Les Hellman (Gus Dakota), James Seay (Harry Cassidy), Kasey Rogers (Francie Wallace).

After three brothers kill the town sheriff so that they can operate their rackets freely, the town council sends for Bat to help select the man's successor. He chooses a saloon girl to help bring some law and order to the frightened community.

Last of the Night Raiders
(11-24-60)

Gene Barry (Bat Masterson), Paula Raymond (Angela Pierce), Don O'Kelly (Jack Doolin), Steve Mitchell (Tulsa Jack), Eugene Martin (Jimmy), William Vaughn (Arkansas Tom).

After being terrorized and escaping from the Doolin Boys, one of the frontier's roughest gangs, a woman and her son seek Bat's protection.

Last Stop to Austin
(12-1-60)

Gene Barry (Bat Masterson), Jan Merlin (Kid Jimmy Fresh), Robert Karnes (U. S. Marshal), Charles Fredericks (Sheriff Ankers), Susan Cummings (Rona Glynn). *With* Charles Reade.

Seeing in a young gunslinger the image of an old friend who died years ago in an Indian battle, Bat sets out to learn if the trigger-happy boy is his friend's orphaned son. He starts by getting legal custody of the boy from another friend, the governor of Texas.

A Time to Die
(12-15-60)

Gene Barry (Bat Masterson), Robert Strauss (Howard Smith), William Tannen (Sheriff Geary), Jack Searl (Desk Clerk).

Bat's an important prosecution witness at the upcoming trial of a man charged with murdering Bat's friend at a card game, and the father of the accused begins making bloody threats against him and other witnesses.

Death by Decree
(12-22-60)

Gene Barry (Bat Masterson), Paul Richards (Marshal Corbett), Raymond Bailey (Justice Bradshaw), Wayne Treadway (Bank Manager), June Blair (Constance Whitney), Robert F. Simon (Harrison Whitney), Allan Jaffe (Bolo).

Bat inherits a casino in Shot Gun Falls from an old gambling rival. The place has a string of debts and when he is suddenly pressed for payment on the mortgage, he finds the property's value has unexpectedly increased. Discovering a conspiracy to swindle him between the town marshal and a "trigger," he goes after them. His net profit: 12 and a half dollars.

The Lady Plays Her Hand
(12-29-60)

Gene Barry (Bat Masterson), Wanda Hendrix (Daphne Kaye), Judith Rawlins (Elsie), Johnny Seven (Burt Comers), William Schallert (George Winston), Robert Lynn (Zach), Pop London (Pop), Dave Cameron (Danny Simms).

A slick Eastern gambler playing blackjack at Bat's casino breaks the bank, putting Bat out of business and a lady dealer out of work.

Tempest at Tioga Pass
(1-5-61)

Gene Barry (Bat Masterson), George Macready (Clyde Richards), Hank Patterson (Soda Smith), John Burns (Hunch).

Helping a road crew cut through mountains to build a road from Nevada to California, Bat deals with bitter cold and conspirators against the railroad. His biggest obstacle is a stubborn miner whose cabin is directly in the path of the proposed road, and who plants dynamite around the place to keep the crew from advancing.

The Court Martial of Major Mars
(1-12-61)

Gene Barry (Bat Masterson), John Anderson (Major Liam Mars), Peggy Knudsen (Lottie Tremaine), Glen Gordon (Jake Sims), John Dule (Magnus).

Bat and a lady passenger arrive at Crazy Creek station along with a major, who finds not comfort and rest but capture and torture. The station master is gone and an Indian and a half-breed have taken his place.

The Price of Paradise
(1-19-61)

Gene Barry (Bat Masterson), Richard Arlen (Sheriff Rainey), Dyan Cannon (Jean Jansen), Lance Fuller (Walker Hayes).

Along with other creditors Bat is thrown out of a Paradise, Colorado saloon when he tries to collect a gambling debt. The saloonkeeper doesn't like to pay bills, but Bat is determined to make an honest man out of him — at least to the extent of what he is due.

End of the Line
(1-26-61)

Gene Barry (Bat Masterson), Liam Sullivan (Dick Jeffers), Thom Carney (Captain Scott), Denver Pyle (Walsh).

In charge of a construction crew building a railroad through the Rockies, Bat's beset by troubles. Rain, fire, hail and Indians have slowed up the work and two wagonloads of expensive equipment just went over a cliff, killing four men. But Bat's determined to get the job done.

The Prescott Campaign
(2-2-61)

Gene Barry (Bat Masterson), John Dehner (Marshal Ben Holt), George Sawaya (Harry Sutton), Philip Ober (Silas Guild), Valerie Allen (Catherine Guild).

Bat arrives in Prescott just in time to stop a marshal from shooting a man who he claims is involved in an illegal land grab. But the man claims it's the marshal who's not on the side of the law.

Bullwhacker's Bounty
(2-16-61)

Gene Barry (Bat Masterson), Jack Lambert (Wancho Tully), Jan Shepard (Jody Reese), Will Wright (Billy Willow).

Bat is hired to guide a wagon train carrying explosives, but the escort who's supposed to take him to the convoy is ambushed. For want of better manpower Bat settles for some not-too-trustworthy renegades and ends up "buying" his life and the major part of the train at the cost of exploding some of his cargo.

A Lesson in Violence
(2-23-61)

Gene Barry (Bat Masterson), Virginia Gregg (Nora Grant), Allan Jaffe (Cross), Jerry Catron (John Grant), Richard Eastham (Orin Dilts), Larry Darr (Page Grant), Al Harvey (Gunman).

In response to an urgent telegram, Bat hurries to a lady's farm in Texas. But the woman greets him standing behind a shotgun. Somehow she has decided that Bat is a hired killer.

Run for Your Money
(3-2-61)

Gene Barry (Bat Masterson), Gerald Mohr (Crimp Ward), Carlyle Mitchell (Theo Stebbins), Jan Harrison (Lori Adams), Bob Swan (Charlie Bassett), Ray Hamilton (Terry Bowen).

Bat turns banker in Denver and learns that having gold isn't enough— you've got to be able to convince people you have it. When an enemy challenges the bank to back up its gold certificates, it starts a stampede of people cashing in their bank notes.

Terror on the Trinity
(3-9-61)

Gene Barry (Bat Masterson), William Conrad (Dick McIntyre), Lisa Lu (Hsich-Lin), Mickey Morton (Bearded Giant).

Bat wins a mining claim in a lottery. En route to the site he's attacked by a huge bearded man, leading to his discovery of a beautiful Chinese girl held captive by outlaws.

Episode in Eden
(3-16-61)

Gene Barry (Bat Masterson), Bek Nelson (Martha Yale), Dan White (Sheriff Bart Sloane), Ken Drake (Ron Daigle), Robert Bice (Sam Shanks).

Bat stakes his life to establish justice in the desert town of Eden, New Mexico, where a gangleader has started a reign of terror. Arriving there more dead than alive, he finds a murder trial in progress and the guilty man's friends using strong-arm tactics to silence witnesses.

The Good and the Bad
(3-23-61)

Gene Barry (Bat Masterson), Jeanette Nolan (Sister Mary Paul), Anna Navarro (Teresa Martinez), Robert Ivers (Charley Boy), Grace Lee Whitney (Louise Talbot).

Masked bandits loot the stage to Tombstone, taking the most priceless possession of the widow of a national hero—the medal of honor for which her husband gave his life. Bat produces a roll of hidden bills and offers to buy it back, but the heartless bandits leave with the money and the medal. Bat sets out to get it all back.

No Amnesty for Death
(3-30-61)

Gene Barry (Bat Masterson), Robert Blake (Bill), R. G. Armstrong (Marshal MacWilliams), DeForest Kelley (Brock Martin), Betty Barry (Mrs. Kendall).

On the way to Las Tables, Bat finds the marshal's son hiding in the graveyard, playing his guitar. The young man points out that the cemetery is less macabre than the town itself, where three men are about to hang.

Ledger of Guilt
(4-6-61)

Gene Barry (Bat Masterson), Jean Allison (Lorna), Barry Kelley (Frank Williams), Jack Hogan (Johnny Dillon).

The mountain town of Meeker, Colorado, is terrorized by the invasion of three men bent on killing a woman. Late one night Bat is summoned from a poker game by the terrified lady, but before she can explain her problem, a shot is fired, an old man is killed and she disappears.

Meeting at Mimbers
(4-13-61)

Gene Barry (Bat Masterson), Harry Shannon (Jobe Crail), Warren Oates (Cats), John Burns (Warren Oates).

Two men try to trigger a war between two Indian tribes so that they can steal the redmen's horses while the tribes are at each others' throats. Sent by the army, Bat rides in to put an end to the hostilities.

Dagger Dance/Valley of Death
(4-20-61)

Gene Barry (Bat Masterson), Ken Mayer (Major Whitsett), William Tannen (Doc), Marya Stevens (Nione), George Eldredge.

Bat, an army civilian scout, rushes a message to a cavalry major that Indians plan an ambush and becomes involved in an affair of Colorado politics. In 1876 the newly-created state is engulfed in a wave of high military sentiment, putting one army man after another into office, including Grant as president. The major, whose political career had been blocked by Colonel Downey, fails to deliver the message to the colonel, who has left Fort Logan for a peace talk with the redmen, and Bat has to extricate himself from a capital charge that arises.

The Fourth Man
(4-27-61)

Gene Barry (Bat Masterson), George Kennedy (Zeke Armitage), Mickey Finn (Hunk Bass), Dehl Berti (Gant Barth), Audrey Dalton.

Arriving in Lordsburg to meet a friend, Bat finds that three power-hungry ranchers and the town's top lawman ganged up on him and killed him. Bat sets out to square accounts.

Dead Man's Claim
(5-4-61)

Gene Barry (Bat Masterson), Charles Maxwell (Harvey Mason), Taffy Paul (Ann Elkins), Craig Duncan (Clay Adams), Chuck Webster (Judd Elkins).

The ghost town of Monument City, once the scene of a historic silver mine, springs back to life when a new silver strike is made. Bat returns there with an old claim and is roadblocked by a pair of interlopers who accuse him of claim jumping.

The Marble Slab
(5-11-61)

Gene Barry (Bat Masterson), Marvin Miller (John Kelso), Patrick Waltz (Sheriff), Robert Bice (Deb Bledsoe), Erin O'Brien (Marie).

The Pinkerton Detective Agency, baffled in attempts to expose a crime chieftain, hires Bat to get evidence to put the man behind bars permanently.

Pretending to be a marble salesman, Bat plays upon the man's ego with the idea of erecting a statue of him in the town square.

Farmer with a Badge
(5-18-61)

Gene Barry (Bat Masterson), John Agar (Marshal Sam Phelps), Gregory Walcott (Lou), King Calder (Dinny Cave), Jackie Loughery.

En route to Tombstone, Arizona, Bat is bushwhacked by outlaws and left for dead. Rescued by a marshal, Bat soon finds the chance to repay him when the lawman asked for help; a killer is waiting to murder him in Rawhide.

The Fatal Garment
(5-25-61)

Gene Barry (Bat Masterson), Ron Hayes (Wyatt Earp), Ed Nelson (Browder), Lisa Gaye (Elena). *With* Les Hillman.

Bat takes a job as guard and bouncer in a saloon. The most frequent invaders are bandit raiders; before Bat can earn his keep, he runs into serious trouble when a hoodlum uses his weakness for fine clothes to lure him away from his post. Dodge City's famed Wyatt Earp makes himself handy in the ensuing fracas.

Jeopardy at Jackson Hole
(6-1-61)

Gene Evans (Bat Masterson), Larry Pnnell (Cal Beamus), Ron Foster (Sheriff Simpson), Harry Fleer (Harvey Field), Joan Tabor (Kate Gannon), Paul Dubov (Tom Fulton), Nick Pawl (Al Stowe).

Bibliography

Abilene (Kansas) *Chronicle*, Various issues 1870 and 1871.

Adams, Jeff. "Hellacious Young Hellion." *Old West*, Spring 1965, p. 38; *Badman*, Summer 1971, p. 21.

Adams, Ramon F. "Billy the Kid's Last Years." *The Texas Monthly*, Vol. 4, no. 2, September 1929.

_____. *Burrs Under the Saddle: A Second Look at Books and Histories of the West.* Norman: University of Oklahoma Press, 1964.

_____. *A Fitting Death for Billy the Kid.* Norman: University of Oklahoma Press, 1960.

_____. *More Burrs Under the Saddle: Books and Histories of the West.* Norman: University of Oklahoma Press, 1979.

_____. *Six-Guns and Saddle Leather: A Bibliography of Books and Pamphlets on Western Outlaws and Gunmen.* New York: Doubleday, Page, 1927 and 1954; revised edition, Norman: The University of Oklahoma Press, 1969.

_____. *Western Words: A Dictionary of the American West.* Norman: University of Oklahoma Press.

_____. "With Our Rocking Chair Historians." *Denver Westerners Brand Book*, 1952.

Adler, Alfred. "Billy the Kid: A Case Study in Epic Origins." *Western Folklore*, Vol. 10, no. 2, April 1951.

Adrean, Tony. "The Life of Belle Starr, from Civil War Spy to Bandit Queen and Death." *Muskogee* [Oklahoma] *Times-Democrat*, April 21, 1921.

Aikman, Duncan. *Calamity Jane and the Lady Wildcats.* New York: Henry Holt, 1927.

Alliance Courier, Ardmore, Indian Territory, March 22, 1894.

Alvarez, N. *James Boys in Missouri.* Ames Publishing, 1906.

Anaya, A. F. "I Hid Out Billy the Kid." *Personal Adventure Stories*, Vol. 1, no. 2, September 1937.

Anderson, Charles, ed. *Outlaws of the West.* Los Angeles: Mankind, 1973.

Anderson, La-Vere Shoenfeit. "A Hill Perpetuates Belle Starr's Memory." *Tulsa World*, August 20, 1933.

_____. "Site of Belle Starr's Lookout Tower on Bald Hill Still Mecca for Tourists." *Tulsa World*, February 3, 1936.

Andress, A. T., and W. G. Cutler. *History of the State of Kansas.* Chicago: 1893.

Anez, Nicholas. "Wyatt Earp." Part I: June–July 1990, pp. 323–33. Part II: August–September 1990, pp. 395–406.

"Another Dalton Battle." *Alliance Courier*, May 3, 1894.

Appell, George C. *Belle's Castle.* New York: Macmillan, 1959.

Applegate, Frank G. "New Mexico Legends." *Southwest Review*, Vol. 17, no. 2, Winter 1932.

Appler, Augustus. *Guerillas of the Border.* Saint Louis: John Appler, 1875.

_____. *Guerrillas of the West; or, The Life, Character, and Daring Exploits of the Younger Brothers.* Saint Louis: Eureka, 1877.

"Arizona Affairs: An Interview with Virgil W. Earp." *Real West*, January 1982, p. 26.

Arnold, Oren. *Thunder in the Southwest: Echoes from the Wild Frontier.* Norman: University of Oklahoma Press, 1937.

Arnott, Richard D. "Bandit Queen Belle Starr." *Wild West*, Vol. 10, no. 2, August 1977, pp. 34–38, 85–87.

Atchison [Kansas] *Daily Champion*, February 5, 1867.

Atchison [Kansas] *Weekly Free Press*, March 2, 1867.

Austin [Texas] *Democratic Statesman*, October 12, 1867.

Austin [Texas] *Weekly State Journal*, October 26, 1871.

Bailey, Lynn R., ed. *A Tenderfoot in Tombstone: The Private Journal of George Whitwell Parsons. The Turbulent Years, 1880–1882.* Tucson AZ: Westernlore, 1996.

Bailey, Tom. "The Fight That Finished Tombstone." *Frontier Times*, Vol. 1, no. 1, September 1968, p. 44.

_____. "King of Cards." *New Magazine for Men*, May 1958, p. 12.

_____. "Wyatt Earp's Last Gun Fight." *The Western Adventures*, no. 1, 1957, p. 2.

Bainright, Frank. "The Truth About Wyatt Earp's Mystery Marriage." *The West*, January 1965, p. 42.

Ball, Eve. "Billy Strikes the Pecos." *New Mexico Folklore*, 1950.

Ball, Larry D. *Desert Lawman: The High Sheriffs of New Mexico and Arizona 1846–1912.* Albuquerque: University of New Mexico Press, 1992.

_____. *The United States Marshals of New Mexico and Arizona Territories 1846–1912.* Albuquerque: University of New Mexico Press, 1978.

Ballantyne, Bill. *Bat Masterson's Last Regular Job.* Playwrights Canada Press, 1989.

Ballenger, Dean W. "The Day Wyatt Earp Tamed 100 Men." *Pioneer West*, November 1978, p. 36.

Bankes, James. "Wild Bill Hickok." *Wild West*, August 1996, p. 50.

Barabas, SuzAnne, and Gabor Barabas. *Gunsmoke: A Complete History and Analysis of the Legendary Broadcast Series with a Comprehensive Episode-by-Episode Guide to Both the Radio and Television Programs.* Jefferson NC: McFarland, 1990.

Barde, Frederick S. "How Belle Starr Died." *Kansas City Star*, August 14, 1910.

_____. "Says Belle Starr's Ghost Still Rides." *Saint Louis Republic*, August 21, 1920.

_____. "The Story of Belle Starr." *Sturn's Oklahoma Magazine*, Vol. 2, no. 1, September 1910.

Barkdull, Tom. "There Never Was a Fight at the O. K. Corral." *Wild West*, July 1972, p. 8.

Barker, Allen. "I Refound Stinking Springs." *True West*, February 1989, p. 14.

Barndollar, Lve. *What Really Happened on October 5, 1892?: An Attempt at an Accurate Account of the Dalton Gang and Coffeyville.* Coffeyville Historical Society.

Bartholomew, Ed. *The Biographical Album of Western Gunfighters.* Houston: Frontier Press of Texas, 1958.

_____. *Famous Gunfighters of the Western Frontier.* Toyahvale TX: Frontier, 1968.

_____. *Wyatt Earp 1848 to 1880: The Untold Story.* Toyahvale TX: Frontier, 1963.

_____. *Wyatt Earp 1879 to 1882: The Man and the Myth.* Toyahvale TX: Frontier, 1964.

Bat Masterson. Dell Publishing Co., 1959.

"Bat Masterson Dies at Editor's Desk." *New York Morning Telegraph*, October 26, 1921.

"Bat Shows White Feather." *Santa Fe Magazine*, July 1909.

"The Battle of Adobe Walls." *Hunter-Trader-Trapper.*

Bayston, Phillip E. "They Called Him 'Wild Bill.'" *Great West*, February 1969, p. 44.

Beadle, J. H. *Western Wilds and the Men Who Redeem Them.* Cincinnati: 1878.

Bechdolt, Frederick R. *Tales of the Old Timers.* New York and London: Century, 1924.

_____. *When the West Was Young.* New York and London: Century, 1922.

Becker, Bill. "Wyatt Earp's Own Vice Madam." *Man's Western*, August-September 1959, p. 10.

Beebe, Lucius, and Charles Clegg. *The Saga of Wells Fargo.* New York: 1949.
Bell, Bob Boze. *The Doctor Will See You Now.* Phoenix: Tri-Star–Boze, 1994.
_____. *The Illustrated Life and Times of Billy the Kid.* Phoenix: Bell, 1995.
_____. *The Illustrated Life and Times of Doc Holliday.* Phoenix: Tri-Star–Boze, 1995.
_____. *Wyatt Earp.* 3d ed. Phoenix: Tri-Star–Boze.
"Belle Starr Rides Again." In *A Collection of Cash Steven's Poems, Including Beel Meezon.* Shawnee OK: Shawnee American, 1948.
Belle Starr, the Bandit Queen, or the Female Jesse James: A Full and Authentic History of the Dashing Female Highwayman, with Copious Extracts from Her Journal; Handsomely and Profusely Illustrated. New York: Police Gazette, 1889.
Benay, Larry. "Old Man Clanton Cashes In." *The West,* January 1971, p. 29; reprinted, *The West,* January 1974, p. 31; reprinted *Western Frontier,* July 1978, p. 41.
Bendall and Wronsky. *Calamity Jane and Belle: Cowgirl's Memories and Correspondence.* Virginia City NV: Sun Mountain.
Benedict, Mrs. J. D. "Belle Starr, the Bandit Queen." *Twin Territories,* Vol. 2, no. 9, October 1900.
Bennett, Estelline. *Old Deadwood Days.* New York: J. H. Sears, 1928; reprint, New York: Charles Scribner, 1935; reprint, Lincoln: University of Nebraska Press.
Biggers, Don R. (Lan Franks pseud.) *History That Will Never be Repeated.* EnosTX: 1902.
"Billy LeRoy, the Bandit." *National Police Gazette,* Vol. 38, no. 195, June 18, 1881.
"Billy the Kid." *Deadwood,* Vol. 1, December 1970, pp. 4–7.
"Billy the Kid." *National Police Gazette,* Vol. 38, no. 203, August 13, 1881.
"Billy the Kid." *True Western Adventures,* ("Gallery of Gunmen"), no. 2, June 1960, p. 49.
"Billy the Kid—In Two Films About Him, Hollywood Fakes History." *Life,* Vol. 2, no. 5, August 4, 1941.
Billy the Kid—Killed in New Mexico—Died in Texas. DeSota TX: Valdez, 1993.
Billy the Kid: Las Vegas Newspaper Accounts of His Career, 1880–1881. W. N. Morrison, 1938.
Billy the Kid: Legends of the American West. TV video. Cave Creek AZ: Pieces of History.
"Billy the Kid's Exploits." *National Police Gazette,* May 21, 1881.
"Billy the Kid's Friend Tells for the First Time of Thrilling Incidents." *Arizona's Daily Citizen,* March 28, 1931.
Bird, Roy. "The Custer-Hickok Shootout at Hays City." *Real West,* May 1979, p. 28.
_____. "Those Dirty Little Cowards." *Real West,* May 1988, p. 32.
Biscup, Walter. "Dashing Belle Starr Was Called 'Lily of the Cimarron.'" *The American Indian,* Vol. 1, no. 4, January 1927.
Black, A. F. "The End of the Long Horn Trail." *Selfridge Journal,* 1936[?].
Black, Hugh E. "Did Jesse Play Poker in Brownsville Saloon?" *WOLA Journal Quarterly,* Vol. 1, no. 2, Fall-Winter 1991, p. 2.
Blake, H. Cody. "The Old .45 Peacemaker." *Frontier Times,* August-September 1968, p. 49.
Blanchard, Leola Howard. *The Conquest of Southwest Kansas.* Wichita: Wichita Eagle, 1931.
Blanton, Kelsey. "The Killer of Belle Starr." *All-Florida Magazine, Pensacola News Journal,* July 17, 1960.
Blazer, Almer N. "The Fight at Blazer's Mill in New Mexico." *Frontier Times,* August 1939, Vol. 16, no. 11.
Blewitt, Andrew. "Calamity Jane." *English Westerners Brand Book,* Vol. 2, no. 2, January 1963.
Bluestone, George. "The Changing Cowboy! From Dime Novel to Dollar Film." *Western Humanities Review,* Vol. 14, Summer 1960.
Boatright, M. C. "The American Myth Rides the Range." *Southwest Review,* Vol. 33, Summer 1951.

Boessenecker, John. "Grat Dalton's California Jailbreak." *Real West*, August 1988, p. 14.
Bogdanovich, Peter. *John Ford*. Berkeley: University of California Press, 1970, pp. 84–85.
Bolds, George. *Reminiscences as a Frontier Deputy Under Wyatt Earp, Bat Masterson, Bill Tilghman and Participant in the County Seat Wars of Kansas*. Letters, newspaper clippings, etc. The James D. Horan Civil War and Western Americana Collection.
"Book Recounts the Tale of Bill Dalton." *The Ada* [Oklahoma] *Sunday News*, May 28, 1995, p. 6C.
Booker, Anton S. *Wildcats in Petticoats: A Garland of Female Desperadoes—Lizzie Merton, Zoe Wilkins, Flora Quick Mundis, Bonnie Parker, Katie Bender, and Belle Starr*. Girard KS: Hildeman-Julius, 1945.
Border, Bartlett. "Belle Starr—and Her Times." *Museum Graphic*, Vol. 5, no. 2, Spring 1953.
Boswell, Charles. "Belle of the Six-Gun." *True Western Adventure*, August 1961, p. 16.
Botkin, B. A., ed. *Folk-Say, Regional Miscellany*. Norman: University of Oklahoma Press, 1930.
_____. *A Treasury of Western Folklore*. Raton TX: Bennett-Walls, 613 pp.
_____. *A Treasury of Western Folklore*. New York: Crown Publishers, 1951.
Boucher, Leonard Harold. "How Wild Bill Lost His Head." *True West*, June 1959, p. 17.
Bourke, Francis. *Great American Train Robberies*. New York: 1909.
Bowen, Sanford. "End of the Trail for Red Buck." *Frontier Times*, July 1970, p. 26.
Bowyes, Edith M. (Edith M. Nicholl, pseud.). *Observations of a Ranchwoman in New Mexico*. London: Macmillan, 1898.
Boyer, Glenn C. "Curly Bill Has Been Killed at Last." *Real West*, June 1984, p. 32; reprinted, *Real West Yearbook*, Winter 1986, p. 29.
_____. "Johnny Behan: Assistant Folk Hero." *Real West Annual*, Spring 1983, p. 6.
_____. "Johnny Behan of Tombstone." *Frontier Times*, July 1976, p. 6.
_____. "Morgan Earp: Brother in the Shadow." *Old West*, Winter 1983, p. 16.
_____. "On the Trail of Big Nosed Kate." *Real West*, March 1981, p. 14; reprinted, *Real West Yearbook*, 1961, p. 24.
_____. "Postscripts to Historical Fiction About Wyatt Earp in Tombstone." *Arizona and the West*, Vol. 18, Autumn 1976, pp. 217–36.
_____. "The Secret Wife of Wyatt Earp." *True West*, June 1983, p. 12.
_____. *The Suppressed Murder of Wyatt Earp*. San Antonio: Naylor, 1967.
_____. "Those Marryin' Earp Men." *True West*, April 1976, p. 14.
_____. "Trailing an American Myth." *Real West*, January 1981, p. 14; reprinted, *Real West*, Special Issue, Spring 1982, p. 10.
_____. "Wyatt Earp: Guns on Fire." *True West*, June 1994, p. 16.
_____. "Wyatt Earp: Legendary American." *True West*, Vol. 41, no. 5, May 1994.
_____. "Wyatt Earp: Luke McGlue." *True West*, March 1994.
_____. "Wyatt Earp: Tombstone's Helen of Troy." *True West*, July 1994.
_____. "Wyatt Earp Legendary American: Part XIII, a Proposition Both Monstrous and Startling." *True West*, Vol. 41, no. 8, Whole No. 316, August 1994, pp. 14–20.
_____. *Wyatt Earp's Tombstone Vendetta*. Honolulu: Talei Publishers, 1993.
_____, ed. *I Married Wyatt Earp: The Recollections of Josephine Sarah Marcus Earp*. Tucson: University of Arizona Press, 1976.
Bradley, Tom. "Dead Man's Hand." *Man's Western*, August-September 1959, p. 24.
Bragow, Michael. "A Wild Bunch of Good Ol' Boys." Review of the film *The Long Riders*. *Los Angeles Herald-Examiner*, Friday, May 19, 1980.
Branch, Douglas. *The Cowboy and His Interpreters*. New York: Appleton, 1926.
Brant, Marley. "Cole Younger, Confederate at Large." *Old West*, Fall 1997, p. 18.
_____. "John Younger: James Gang Member?" *True West*, March 1987, p. 45.
_____. "John Younger, the Forgotten Brother." *Old West*, Spring 1995, p. 12.

_____. *The Outlaw Youngers, a Confederate Brotherhood.*

_____. "Outlaws' Inlaws in California." *Frontier Times*, February 1985, p. 18.

_____. "Whatever Happened to the Russelville Bank?" *True West*, March 1987, p. 42.

Brauer, Ralph. "Who Are Those Guys? The Movie Western During the TV Era." *The Journal of Popular Film*, Vol. 2, no. 3, Fall 1973, p. 389.

Braun, Matt. *Doc Holliday the Gunfighter.* New York: St. Martin's Paperbacks, 1997.

_____. *Outlaw Kingdom.* New York: St. Martin's, 1996.

_____. *Tombstone.* New York: Pocket Books, 1981; St. Martin's Paperback, 1995.

_____. *Wyatt Earp.* New York: St. Martin's, 1994.

Breakenridge, William M. *Helldorado: Bringing the Law to the Mesquite.* 1928; reprint, Lincoln: University of Nebraska Press.

_____. "Alias Jesse James." Part I: *Real West*, January 1971, p. 22. Part II: *Real West*, February 1971, p. 48.

Breihan, Carl W. "Alias Jesse James" (Part I). *Real West*, January 1971, p. 22; (Part II) *Real West*, February 1971, p. 48.

_____. "Bad Belle Starr." *Western Action*, Vol. 22, no. 5, March 1959.

_____. *Badmen of the Frontier Days.* New York: McBride, 1957.

_____. "Bat Masterson, Law Man." Part I: *Real West*, November 1969, p. 44; Part II: *Real West*, December 1969, p. 17. Reprinted as one-part article *Real West*, Special Issue, Fall 1973, p. 8.

_____. "Belle Starr: Oklahoma Whirlwind." *The West*, March 1967, p. 30; reprinted, *The West*, August 1972, p. 28; reprinted, *Western Frontier*, July 1977, p. 28.

_____. "Bill Ryan, Worst of the James Gang." *Real West*, July 1967, p. 24.

_____. "Bill Tilghman: Last of the Old-Time Lawmen." *Oldtimers Wild West*, June 1978, p. 14.

_____. "Billy the Kid's Date with Destiny." *Pioneer West*, Part I, May 1977, p. 6; Part II, July 1977, p. 6.

_____. "Blood on the Queen of Hearts." *Golden West*, May 1967, p. 16; *The West*, December 1971, p. 14.

_____. "Bob Ford Did Kill Jesse James." *Real West*, May 1959, p. 28.

_____. "Chris Madsen: The Fighting Dane." Part I: *Real West*, December 1970, p. 24. Part II: *Real West*, January 1971, p. 38. Repeated as one-part article, *Real West*, Fall 1973, p. 24.

_____. "Clay Allison, Psychopathic Killer." *Western Frontier*, 1995 Annual no. 1, p. 40.

_____. "Cole Younger of Lee's Summit." *Real West*, December 1973, p. 14.

_____. *Complete and Authentic Life of Jesse James.* New York: Frederic Fell, 1953, 1970.

_____. "The Daltons and Bill Doolin." *Western Frontier*, July 1979, p. 14.

_____. *A Date with Destiny: Life of Billy the Kid.*

_____. "The Day Billy the Kid Was Killed." *Real West*, March 1962, p. 38.

_____. "The Day Jesse James Attempted Suicide." *NOLA Quarterly*, Vol. 1, no. 4, Winter 1975-76, p. 11.

_____. "The Day Quantrill Burned Lawrence." *The West*, January 1967, p. 14; rpt., *The West*, January 1972, p. 14; rpt., *Western Frontier*, September 1976, p. 34; rpt., *Western Frontier*, May 1979, p. 34; rpt., *Western Frontier*, August 1985, p. 34.

_____. "The Death of Bob Ford." *Real West*, March 1970, p. 20.

_____. "The Death of Frank James." *Real West*, Vol. 18, no. 136, March 1975, p. 38.

_____. "The Death of Jesse James." *Denver Westerners Brand Book*, 1956.

_____. "The Death of John Younger." *Real West*, September 1974, p. 36.

_____. "Desperate Man, Desperate Guns." *Real West Annual*, Winter 1977-78, p. 16.

_____. "Did Cole Younger Rob the Bank at Corinth?" *Real West*, November 1971, p. 17.

_____. "Did the James Boys Take Part in the Muscle Shoals Robbery?" *Real West*, March 1972, p. 40.

_____. *The Escapades of Frank and Jesse James.* New York: Frederic Fell, 1974.

_____. "Exit Bill Doolin and Bill Dalton." *Real West*, June 1975, p. 45.

_____. "The Glendale Train Robbery." *Real West*, May 1972, p. 29.

_____. *The Great Gunfighters of the West.* London: John Jong, 1961; reprint, New York: NAL, 1977.

_____. "The Hickok-McCanles Affair." *Real West*, September 1967, p. 10.

_____. "The James Gang and the Huntington Bank Robbery." *Real West*, June 1973, p. 38.

_____. "The James Gang at Bardston." *Real West*, June 1975, p. 28.

_____. "The James Gang in California." *Real West*, February 1975, p. 36.

_____. "Holdup of the Omnibus at North Lexington." *Real West*, March 1979, p. 32.

_____. "Jesse James and the Gallatin Bank Robbery." *Real West*, May 1974, p. 43.

_____. "Jesse James and the Liberty Bank Robbery." *Real West*, August 1972, p. 40.

_____. "Jesse James and the Winston Train Robbery." *Real West*, October 1972, p. 53.

_____. "Jesse James in Mexico." *Real West*, January 1968, p. 24.

_____. "Jesse James' Attempted Suicide." *True West*, November 1982, p. 21.

_____. "Jesse James' First Train Robbery." *Real West*, March 1969, p. 40; reprinted, *Real West Annual*, Summer 1970, p. 20.

_____. "Jesse James: The King of Bandits." Part I: *Oldtimers Wild West*, April 1978, p. 16. Part II: *Pioneer West*, May 1978, p. 12.

_____. "Jesse James: The Russelville Bank Robbery." *Real West*, October 1969, p. 16.

_____. "Jessie's Trouble Maker." *Frontier Times*, Fall 1959, p. 24.

_____. "King of Bandits." *The West*, May 1967, p. 10; reprinted, *Golden West*, April 1972, p. 34; reprinted, *Western Frontier*, July 1976, p. 34; reprinted, *Western Frontier*, November 1982, p. 34.

_____. *Lawmen and Robbers.* Virginia City NV: Sun Mountain.

_____. "The Man Who Killed Pat Garrett." *Westerner*, January-February 1970, p. 24; reprinted, *Old Trails*, Spring 1978, p. 56.

_____. "The Night They Bombed 'Castle James.'" *Oldtimers Wild West*, April 1980, p. 22.

_____. "The Northfield Raid." *The West*, November 1966, p. 10; reprinted, *The West*, June 1972, p. 26; reprinted, *Western Frontier*, September 1980, p. 34.

_____. "The Real Billy the Kid." *Double-Action Western*, June 1959.

_____. *Ride the Razor's Edge.* Gretna, LA: Pelican, 288 pp.

_____. *The Saga of Jesse James.* College Station TX: The Early West, 1996.

_____. "Saga of Patrick Floyd Garrett." *Golden West*, January 1968, p. 16; reprinted, *Golden West*, May 1974, p. 12; reprinted, *Western Frontier*, September 17, p. 12.

_____. "They Called Him Bat." *Oldtimers Wild West*, October 1978, p. 17.

_____. "The Truth About Jesse James' Death." *Real West*, December 1971, p. 21.

_____. "The Twelve Greatest Gunslicks." *Real West*, Vol. 19, p. 38, January 1976.

_____. "'Whiskey Head' Bill Ryan." *Pioneer West*, September 1979, p. 22.

_____. "Who Robbed the Store at Westport, Missouri?" *Real West*, July 1975, p. 44.

_____. "William Clark Quantrill and His Lieutenants." *The West*, May 1969, p. 10; reprinted, *Western Frontier*, November 1977, p. 34; reprinted, *Western Frontier*, November 1982, p. 40.

_____. *Younger Brothers.* San Antonio: Naylor, 1962.

_____, and Charles A. Rosamound. *The Bandit Belle.* Seattle: Hanman, Superior, 1970.

Brent, Lynton. *The Bird Cage: A Theatrical Novel of Early Tombstone.* Philadelphia: Dorrance, 1945.

Breshears, Claudia. "The Outlaw Was a Lady." *Big West*, August 1967, p. 22.

Brininstool, E. A. "Billy the Kid." *Wide World Magazine*, November or December 1919.

Bronaugh, Warren A. *The Youngers Fight for Freedom.* Columbia MO: Stephens, 1906.

Broome, Bertram C. "Nuff Said." *New Mexico Highway Journal*, Vol. 9, no. 4, April 1931.

Brothers, Mary Hudson. *Billy the Kid*. Farmington NM: Hustler, 1969.

_____. "Meeting of Gun Fighters." *New Mexico*, Vol. 16, no. 2, February 1938.

Brown, Dee. *Gentle Tamers: Women of the Old Wild West*. Lincoln: University of Nebraska Press.

_____, and Mort Kunstler. *Images of the Old West*. Park Lane, 1996.

_____, and Martin F. Schmitt. *Trail Driving Days*. New York: Charles Scribner, 1952.

Brown, Florence V. "The Legend of Belle Starr, Courtesan." *Great West*, April 1967, p. 26.

Brown, Jesse, and A. M. Willard. *The Black Hills Trails*. Edited by John T. Milek. Rapid City SD: Rapid City Journal, 1924.

Brown, Richard Maxwell. "Historiography of Violence in the American West." In *Historians and the American West*. Edited by Michael P. Malone. Lincoln: University of Nebraska Press, 1983. Pp. 234–69.

Browning, James A. *Violence Was No Stranger: A Guide to the Grave Sites of Famous Westerners*. Stillwater OK: Barbed Wire.

_____. *The Western Reader's Guide: A Selected Bibliography of Nonfiction Magazines, 1953–1991*. Stillwater OK: Barbed Wire, 1992.

Brownlow, Kevin. *The War, the West, and the Wilderness*. New York: Alfred A. Knopf, 1979. p. 280.

Buel, James William. *Heroes of the Plains*. St. Louis: 1882.

_____. *The True Story of Wild Bill Hickok*. Edited by J. Brussel. New York: 1946.

Buel, T. W. *Heroes of the Plains*. St. Louis: 1881.

Buell, James W. *The Border Outlaws, the Younger Brothers, Jesse and Frank James, and Their Comrades in Crime*. St. Louis: Dan, Linahan, 1882.

_____. *James and Youngers*. Baltimore: I & Q Ottenheimer.

Buetler, Randy L. "'Red Buck': An Unknown Oklahoma Outlaw." *NOLA Quarterly*, Vol. 7, no. 1, Spring 1982, p. 4.

"Buffalo Bill and Billy the Kid; or, The Desperadoes of Apacheland." *The Buffalo Bill Stories*, no. 268, June 30, 1906.

Bulloch, Nolan. "Tourists Take Robber's Trail." *Tulsa Tribune*, June 26, 1951.

Burke, John. "The Wildest Woman in the West." *True Frontier*, June 1967, p. 12; reprinted, *True Frontier*, Special Issue no. 7, Fall 1973, p. 10.

Burkey, Rev. Blaine. *Wild Bill Hickok: The Law in Hays City*. Hays City KS, 1973.

Burkholder, Edwin V. "Bat Masterson." *Real West*, Americana Series, Fall 1965, p. 13.

_____. "Bat Masterson: Gunslinging Dude from Dodge." *Western Action*, September 1960, p. 28.

_____. "Belle Starr—Petticoat Desperado." *Argosy*, Vol. 343, no. 2, August 1956.

_____. "I Knew the Real Bat Masterson." *Real West*, May 1960, p. 12. Reprinted *Real West*, Annual, Summer 1966, p. 6.

_____. "Who Killed Jesse James?" *The English Westerners Brand Book*, Vol. 6, no. 4, April 1964.

Burnett, W. R. *Bitter Ground*. New York: Alfred A. Knopf, 1958.

_____. "Nobody's All Bad." *Collier's*, June 7, 1930, Vol. 85, no. 23.

_____. *Saint Johnson*. New York: Dial, 1930.

Burns, Walter Noble. "Billy the Kid." *Frontier*, December 1925.

_____. *The Saga of Billy the Kid*. Garden City NY: Doubleday, Page, 1926.

_____. *Tombstone: An Iliad of the Southwest*. New York: Doubleday, Page, 1927.

Burrows, Jack. *John Ringo: The Gunfighter Who Never Was*. Tucson: University of Arizona Press, 1987.

_____. *Johnny Ringo*. College Station, TX: The Early West Books, 242 pp.

_____. "The Story of a Western Myth." *Montana: The Magazine of Western History*, Vol. 30, October 1980, pp. 2–15.

Buscombe, Edward, ed. *The BFI Companion to the Western.* New York: Atheneum, 1988.

Byrd, Larry. "Billy the Kid." *Classic Images,* no. 157, July 1988, p. 20.

Callon, Milton W. "Billy the Kid's Last Christmas." *Frontier Times,* January 1968, p. 34.

Cannary, Martha Jane. "Autobiography of Calamity Jane." *Gunslingers of the West,* Winter 1966.

Cantrell, Dallas. *Youngers' Fatal Blunder at Northfield, Minnesota.* San Antonio: Naylor.

Carle, Edwin. "Billy the Kid in Arizona." *Arizona Highways,* February 1954.

Carlyle, Thomas. *On Heroes, Hero-Worship, and the Heroic in History.* Everyman's Library, 1941.

Carpen, George Blackwell. "Bob Dalton, Renegade Marshal." *True Western Adventure,* October 1958, p. 8.

Carson, John. "Doc Holliday." *True West* ("Backgrounds of Famous Western Badmen") June 1962, p. 25.

_____. "Frank James in Wyoming." *Real West,* March 1967, p. 50.

Carson, Kit. "Billy the Kid's Restless Bones." *Real West,* March 1962, p. 14.

_____. "The Day Billy the Kid Died." *Real West,* March 1964, p. 15.

Carson, William J. "What Was Billy the Kid's Real Name?" *Real West,* May 1969, p. 46.

Carson, Xanthus. "The Riddle of Billy the Kid: Living Phantom or Walking Dead Man?" *Frontier West,* October 1975, p. 40.

_____. "They All Loved Billy the Kid." *True Frontier,* July 1970, p. 30; reprinted, *True Frontier,* Special Issue no. 9, 1974, p. 48.

"The Case of James Butler Hickok, Alias 'Wild Bill.'" *Westerners Brand Book,* Vol. 3, nos. 2–3, April–May 1946.

Casey, Robert. *The Black Hills and Their Incredible Characters.* New York: 1950.

_____. *The Texas Border and Some Borderlines.* New York: Bobbs-Merrill, 1950.

Castel, Albert. "Men Behind the Masks, the James Brothers." *American History,* June 1982.

Castleman, Sean. "Arkansas Tom: Last of the Horseback Outlaws." *Oldtimers' Wild West,* August 1979, p. 10.

Cawelti, John G. "Reflections on the New Western Films." *University of Chicago Magazine,* January-February 1973.

_____. *The Six-Gun Mystique.* Bowling Green OH: Bowling Green University Popular Press, 1971, pp. 38–47.

Ceuse, Thomas. *Apache Days and After.* Caldwell ID: 1941.

Chapman, Arthur. "Billy the Kid, a Man All 'Bad.'" *Outing Magazine,* Vol. 46, no. 1, April 1905.

_____. "A Cowboy War." *Outing Magazine,* Vol. 58, no. 4, July 1911.

_____. "A Cowboy War in New Mexico." *Santa Fe Magazine,* Vol. 6, November 1912.

_____. "Getting the Drop and Living." *New York Herald Tribune Magazine,* January 1932.

_____. *The Pony Express.* New York, 1932. Pp. 173–174.

Chaput, Donald. *The Earp Papers: In a Brother's Image.* Encampment WY: Affiliated Writers of America.

_____. *Virgil Earp, Western Peace Officer.* Norman: University of Oklahoma Press, 1994.

Charbo, Eileen. "Doc Outland and Emmett Dalton." *True West,* August 1980, p. 43.

Charles, Tom. "Those Were the Days in Lincoln County." *New Mexico,* Vol. 10, no. 4, April 1932.

Chatfield, Harry. "Bat Masterson's Railroad War." *Real West,* March 1965, p. 20.

Cheaney, W. D. "I Saw the Daltons Die." *Real West,* May 1964, p. 18; reprinted, *Real West,* Americana Series, Fall 1964, p. 31.

_____. "Who Lies Buried in Jesse James' Grave?" *Real West,* January 1967, p. 32.

Cheyenne Daily Leader. Various issues, 1874–1877.

Chicago Inter-Ocean, August 17, 1876.

Chittendae, William Lawrence. *Ranch Verses.* New York: G. F. Putnam, 1893.

Chrisman, Henry E. *Fifty Years on the Owl Hoot Trail.* Denver: Sage, 1962.

Chrisman, J. Eugene. "America's Most Incredible Nymph." *Glance*, Vol. 3, no. 6, August 1960.

Clark, J. B. "The Hickok-Tutt Duel." *Frontier Times*, Spring 1962, p. 45.

Clark, Mike. "'Wild Bill': A Shot in the Foot." *Show*, 1995.

Clark, Neil M. "Close Call." *American Magazine*, Vol. 107, no. 1, January 1929.

Clark, O. S. *Clay Allison of the Washita.* Attica IN: G. M. Williams, 1920; privately printed, 1922.

Claunch, Zula. "Memories of Belle Starr." *Looking Back*, Vol. 3, no. 3, Fall 1975.

Cline, Donald. *Alias Billy the Kid: The Man Behind the Legend.* Santa Fe: Sunstone, 1986.

_____. *Antrim and Billy.* College Station TX: Early West, 183 pp.

_____. "Battle Over Billy the Kid's Horse." *NOLA Quarterly*, Vol. 12, no. 3, Winter 1988, p. 12.

_____. "Billy LeRoy: The Original Billy the Kid." *Frontier Times*, February 1985, p. 25.

_____. "Billy the Kid and Escape from Jail in Albuquerque." *NOLA Quarterly*, Vol. 10, no. 2, Fall 1985, p. 9.

_____. "Billy the Kid Photos: The Faces, the Places, the Facts." *Old West*, Spring 1986, p. 46.

_____. "Bob Olinger, Killer Deputy." *Golden West*, January 1967, p. 44; reprinted, *Golden West*, February 1972, p. 41; reprinted, *Western Frontier Annual*, Winter 1977, p. 6; reprinted, *Western Frontier*, Special Issue, September 1975.

_____. "The Mystery of Billy the Kid's Home." *NOLA Quarterly*, Vol. 13, no. 2, Fall 1988, p. 16.

_____. "The Secret Life of Billy the Kid." *True West*, April 1984, p. 12.

Clum, John P. *It All Happened in Tombstone.* Flagstaff: Northland, 1965.

Coan, Charles F. *A History of New Mexico.* Chicago and New York: American Historical Society, 1925.

Cockrell, W. S. "A Mild-Eyed Man Who Has Killed Twenty-Six Persons." *Ford County Globe*, November 22, 1881.

Cody, William F. *Life of the Honorable Frederick Cody, Known as Buffalo Bill, the Famous Hunter, Scout, and Guide, an Autobiography.* Hartford: 1879.

Coe, George W. *Frontier Fighter, the Autobiography of George W. Coe.* Boston and New York: Houghton Mifflin, 1934.

_____, and Nan Hillary Harrison. *Frontier Fighter.* Albuquerque, 1934.

Cole, Nancy J. "When Wyatt Earp and Bat Masterson Visited Dodge City, Kansas." *Westerns and Serials*, no. 39, pp. 32–33.

Coleman, Max. "Frontier Sheriffs Played Important Role." *Frontier Times*, Vol. 13, no. 2, November 1935.

_____. "Never Fool with a Fool." *Frontier Times*, Vol. 13, no. 4, January 1936.

Collins, Charles. "Bloody Coffeyville." *Great West*, May 1968, p. 34.

Connelley, William Elsey. *Quantrill and the Border Wars.* Cedar Rapids: 1909.

_____. "Wild Bill—James Butler Hickok: David C. McCanles at Rock Creek." *Kansas State Historical Society Collections*, Vol. 17, 1926–1928.

_____. *Wild Bill and His Era.* New York: Press of the Pioneers, 1933.

Cook, Jim. *Lane of the Llamo.* Boston: Little, Brown, 1936.

Coolidge, Dane. *Fighting Men of the West.* New York: E. P. Dutton, 1932.

Coop, W. E. *Billy the Kid: The Trail of a Kansas Legend.* Kansas City: Kansas City Westerners, 1965.

Corele, Edwin. *Mojave.* New York: Liveright, 1934.

Cortesi, Lawrence. "The Bloody Shootout at Murray's Saloon." *Frontier West*, August 1972, p. 22.

The Cowboy's Career; or, the Daredevil Deeds of Billy the Kid, the Noted New Mexico Desperado. Chicago and St. Louis: Belford and Clarke, 1881.

Cowdrick, J. C. *Billy the Kid from Texas; or, Silver Mask's Claw.* Beadle's Pocket Library, no. 321. New York: Beadle and Adams, 1890.

_____. *Silver Mask, the Man of Mystery; or, The Cross of the Golden Keys.* Beadle's Half-Dime Library, no. 360. New York: Beadle and Adams, June 17, 1884.

Cox, James. *Historical and Biographical Record of the Cattle Industry and the Cattlemen of Texas and Adjacent Territory.* St. Louis: Woodward & Tiernan, 1895.

Cox, William R. *Luke Short and His Era.* New York: Doubleday, 1961.

Crane, Ray. "The Doolin Gang." *Great West*, February 1970, p. 44.

Crichton, Kyle S. *Law and Order, Ltd., the Rousing Life of Elfego Baca of New Mexico.* Santa Fe: New Mexican, 1928.

Cronin, C. "Arizona's Six Gun Classic." *Arizona Historical Review*, Vol. 3, July 1930, pp. 7–11.

Cronyn, George. "Who Really Shot Billy the Kid?" *Real West*, September 1966, p. 42.

Crow, Pat. "Vacationers Follow Outlaws' Footsteps." *Tulsa World*, May 25, 1969.

Crowther, Bruce. *Hollywood Fiction: Reality and Myth in the Movies.* London: Columbus, 1984.

Croy, Homer. "The Book, the Gun, and Jesse James." *True Western Adventure*, October 1959, p. 36.

_____. *He Hanged Them High: An Authentic Account of the Fanatical Judge Who Hanged Eighty-Eight Men.* New York: Duell, Sloan, and Pearce, 1952; Boston: Little, Brown, 1952.

_____. "I Knew Jesse James' Mother." *True West*, Vol. 6, no. 5, May-June 1959.

_____. "Last of the Great Outlaws." *America's Frontier West*, no. 1 (n.d.), p. 44.

_____. *Jesse James Was My Neighbor.* New York: Duell, Sloan, and Pearce, 1949.

_____. *Last of the Great Outlaws: The Story of Cole Younger.* New York: Duell, Sloan, and Pearce, 1956.

Crutchfield, James A. *It Happened in New Mexico.* Helena MT: Falcon, 1995.

Cummin, Jim. *Jim Cummin's Book—By Himself.* 1903.

Cunningham, Eugene. *Famous in the West.* El Paso: Hicks-Hayward/Baptist, 1926.

_____. "Fought with Billy the Kid." *Frontier Times*, Vol. 9, no. 6, March 1932.

_____. "The Kid Still Rides." *New Mexico Magazine*, March 1935.

_____. *Triggernometry: A Gallery of Gunfighters.* New York: Press of the Pioneers, 1934.

Currie, Barton W. "American Bandit; Lone and Otherwise." *Harper's Weekly*, Vol. 52, September 12, 1908.

Cushman, George L. "Abilene, First of the Kansas Cowtowns." *Kansas State Historical Society Quarterly*, Vol. 60, no. 3, August 1940.

Dacus, J. A. *Illustrated Lives and Adventures of Frank and Jesse James and the Younger Brothers: The Noted Western Outlaws.* St. Louis: 1882.

_____. *Life and Adventures of Frank and Jessie James, the Noted Western Outlaws.* San Francisco: N. D. Thompson, 1890.

Daggett, Thomas F. *Billy LeRoy. The Colorado Bandit; or, the King of American Highwaymen.* New York: Police Gazette Library, March 1, 1883.

Daily Oklahoma State Capitol. Guthrie, Oklahoma Territory, September 2 & 4, 1893, and 1895.

Dale, Henry. *Adventures and Exploits of the Younger Brothers, Missouri's Most Daring Outlaws, and Companions of the James Boys.* New York: Street and Smith, 1890.

Dalton, Emmett. "Prison Delivery." *Old West*, Spring 1971, p. 74.

_____, and Jack Jungmeyer. *Last of the Daltons.* New York: 1931.

Dalton, Kit. *Under the Black Flag.* Memphis: Lockhart, 1914.

"Dalton Brothers and Their Astounding Career of Crime." Part I: *Real West,* July 1962, p. 24; Part II: *Real West,* September 1962, p. 24.

The Dalton Gang of the Far West. 1892.

Davis, David B. "Ten-Gallon Hero." *American Quarterly,* Vol. 6, Summer 1954, pp. 111–125.

Davis, Robert Murray. *Playing Cowboys: Low Culture and High Art in the Western.* Norman: University of Oklahoma Press, 1992, pp. 31–57.

Dawson, Charles. *Pioneer Tales of the Oregon Trail and Jefferson County.* Topeka KS: 1912.

"A Day of Carnival." *Ford County Globe,* September 5, 1879.

Deac, Wilfred P. "Outlaws' Deadliest Double-Dare." *Wild West,* April 1989, p. 35.

_____. "Two Minutes in Tombstone." *Wild West,* August 1991, p. 42.

_____. "War Without Heroes." *Wild West,* April 1991, p. 18.

Deadwood Black Hills Pioneer. Various issues, 1876–77.

Deadwood Black Hills Times. Various issues, 1879.

Deadwood Pioneer Times, August 22, 1925.

DeArment, Robert K. *Bat Masterson: The Man and the Legend.* Norman: University of Oklahoma Press, 1979.

_____. "Bat Masterson's Rescue of Bully Bill." *True West,* October 1979, p. 10.

_____. *Knights of the Green Cloth: Saga of Frontier Gamblers.* Stillwater OK: The Book Mart, 1996.

"Death of John Younger." *Real West,* September 1974.

DeGregorio, Armand. "The Death Hoax of Jesse James." *NOLA Quarterly,* Vol. 10, no. 4, Spring 1986, p. 4.

DeMattos, Jack. "Bat Masterson." ("Gunfighters of the Real West" column) *Real West,* February 1985, p. 32. Reprinted *Real West,* Special Issue, Spring 1986, p. 56.

_____. "Bat Masterson Was Colorful Lawman and Sport." *NOLA Quarterly,* Vol. II, no. 4, Winter 1976, p. 4.

_____. "The Daltons." *Real West* ("Gunfighters of the Real West"), December 1983, p. 32; *Real West Yearbook,* Fall 1984, p. 48.

_____. *The Earp Decision.*

_____. "Frank and Jesse James." Part I: *Real West* ("Gunfighters of the Real West"), October 1984, p. 32. Part II *Real West* ("Gunfighters of the Real West"), December 1984, p. 38. Two parts combined when reprinted in *Real West Yearbook,* Fall 1985, p. 28.

_____. "Henry McCarty." *Real West* ("Gunfighters of the Real West"), August 1983, p. 40.

_____. "The Kid." *Real West,* Special Issue, Spring 1984, p. 42.

_____. *Masterson and Roosevelt.* College Station TX: Creative Publishing, 1984.

_____. "The Search for Billy the Kid's Roots." *Real West,* November 1978, p. 12.

_____. "The Search for Billy the Kid's Roots Is Over." *Real West,* January 1980, p. 26.

_____. "Those Guns of Bat Masterson." *Frontier Times,* March 1977, p. 10.

_____. "A Tour of Earp Country." *Real West Annual,* 1981, p. 12.

_____. "Whatever Became of the Dodge City Peace Commission?" *Real West,* Vol. 20, no. 149, January 1977, p. 38.

_____. "Wild Bill Hickok." *Real West* ("Gunfighters of the Real West"), June 1980, p. 30.

Denmark, Harry Van. "Boothill Battle Song." *Big Book Western Magazine,* date unknown.

Denton, Cyclone. "I Danced with Belle Starr." *True West,* August 1970, p. 18.

Department of Missouri. *Special Orders Number 89, District of Southwest Missouri, 1864.* Vol. 269, p. 254.

Derek, Elley. *The Epic Film: Myth and History.* London: Routledge and Kegan Paul, 1984.

Dobie, J. Frank. "Belle Starr in Bed Under Disguise." *Houston Post,* January 1, 1961.

_____. "Billy the Kid." *Southwest Review*, Vol. 14, no. 3, Spring 1929.

_____. "Billy the Kid as Robin Hood." *Austin American Statesman*, May 2, 1948.

_____. "The Kid." *The Nation*, Vol. 126, no. 326, February 15, 1928.

_____. "Vaquero of the Brush Country." *Southwest Review*, Vol. 14, no. 3, April 1929.

_____. "What the Kid Said—Went." *Frontier Times*, Vol. 33, no. 5, Winter 1958-59.

_____, ed. *Southwestern Lore*. Austin TX: Publications of the Texas Folk-Lore Society, no. 9, 1931.

"'Doc' Holliday: He Pulled a Deadly Six-Gun After He Gave Up on Teeth." *Gunslingers of the West*, Winter 1966, p. 28.

Dodd, Susan. *Mamaw: A Novel of an Outlaw Mother*. Rotan TX: Bennett Walls.

Dodge City Globe, various issues.

Dodge City Police Dockets, 1878–1880.

Dodge City Times, various issues.

Donald, Jay. *Outlaws of the Border: A Complete and Authentic History of the Lives of Frank and Jesse James, the Younger Brothers, and Their Robber Companions*. Chicago: Coburn & Newman, 1882.

"Doolin-Dalton Outlaws." *True West*, August, 1968.

Dorson, Richard M. *American Folklore and the Historian*. Chicago: University of Chicago Press, 1971.

Doughty, Francis W. *Old King Brady and Billy the Kid; or, The Great Detective's Chase by a New York Detective*. New York Detective Library, no. 411. New York: Frank Tousey, October 11, 1890.

Drago, Harry Sinclair. *Notorious Ladies of the Frontier*. New York: Dodd, Mead, 1964.

_____. *Outlaws on Horseback: The History of the Organized Bands of Bank and Train Robbers Who Terrorized the Prairie Towns of Missouri, Kansas, Indian Territory, and Oklahoma for Half a Century*. New York: Dodd, Mead, 1964.

_____. *Road Agents and Train Robbers: Half a Century of Western Banditry*. New York: Dodd, Mead, 1973.

_____. *Wild, Wooly and Wicked*. New York: Clarkson N. Potter, 1960.

Dullenty, Jim. "Bombing of the Jesse James Home." *True West*, January 1983, p. 20.

_____. "Was Wyatt Earp a Horsethief?" *NOLA Quarterly*, Vol. 10, no. 2, Fall 1985, p. 38.

Durlington, John C. "Chris Madsen Versus a Hundred Outlaws." *The West*, June 1965, p. 36; reprinted, *Western Frontier*, July 1983, p. 24.

Dyer, Robert. "Billy the Kid: The Photos Face Forensics." *True West*, March 1990, p. 26.

_____. *Jesse James and the Civil War in Missouri*. Columbia: University of Missouri Press.

Dykes, J. C. *Billy the Kid: The Bibliography of a Legend*. Albuquerque: University of New Mexico Press, 1952.

_____. "A 'Billy the Kid' Bibliographic Check List." *Southwestern Historical Quarterly*, Vol. 49, no. 4, April 1946.

_____. "Billy the Kid Was My Friend." *Westerners Brand Book*, Vol. 8, no. 2, April 1951.

_____. *Four Sheriffs of Lincoln County*. Washington DC: Potomac Westerners, 1965.

Dykstra, Robert R. *The Cattle Towns: A Social History of the Kansas Cattle Trading Centers, Abilene, Ellsworth, Wichita, Dodge City, and Caldwell, 1867–1885*. New York: Alfred A. Knopf, 1968; reprint, University of Nebraska Press.

Earle, James H. *The Capture of Billy the Kid*. Early West Series. Denver: Creative, 1988.

Earp, Josephine. "The Earps in Tonopah." Edited by Glenn G. Boyer. *West*, August 1975, p. 14.

_____. "Sinister Shadows from the Past." Edited by Glenn G. Boyer. *True West*, October 1975, p. 20.

_____. "Who Killed John Ringo?" Edited by Glenn G. Boyer. *Real West*, February 1987, p. 14.

Earp, Wyatt. *How I Routed a Gang of Arizona Outlaws.* Reprint of 1891 newspaper accounts. Trail to Yesterday Books.

_____. "How Wyatt Earp Routed a Gang of Arizona Outlaws." *Real West,* May 1978, p. 16; reprinted, *Real West Annual,* Winter 1979, p. 8.

_____. "Wyatt Earp Tells Tale of the Shotgun Messenger Service." *San Francisco Examiner Sunday Magazine,* August 9, 1896.

_____. "Wyatt Earp's Tribute to Bat Masterson, the Hero of 'Dobe Walls." Part I: *Real West,* September 1978, p. 8; Part II: *Real West,* November 1978, p. 36. Reprinted as one-part article *Real West,* Yearbook, Fall 1979, p. 16.

East, Charles. *Memoirs of Old Arizona.* Tucson: Arizona Historical Society.

Eceritt, David. *Legends—The Story of Wyatt Earp.* New York: Knightsbridge, 1990.

Eden, M. C. "Clell Miller and the Corydon Bank Robbery." *English Westerners Brand Book,* Vol. 20, no. 3, April 1978, and no. 4, July 1978 (combined issue).

Editors of Time-Life Books. *The Cowboys.* Text by William H. Forbis. New York: Time-Life, 1973.

Edmondson, Wilson. "Did Jesse James Attend His Own Funeral?" *True Frontier,* March 1968, p. 8; reprinted, *True Frontier,* October 1972, p. 12; reprinted, *True Frontier,* Special Issue no. 17, Winter 1976, p. 40.

Edwards, Harold. *Goodbye Billy the Kid.* College Station TX: Early West.

Edwards, Harold L. "Anthony Dalton, Not a Member of the Dalton Gang." *NOLA Quarterly,* Vol. 13, no. 4, 1989, p. 16.

_____. "The Daltons in California." *NOLA Quarterly,* Vol. 10, no. 1, Summer 1985, p. 18.

_____. "The Man Who Killed Ike Clanton." *True West,* October 1991, p. 24.

_____. "Was Wyatt Earp Cowed?" *True West,* September 1991, p. 51.

Edwards, J. B. *Early Days in Abilene.* Abilene TX: 1940.

Edwards, John Newman. "A Terrible Quintette." *Saint Louis Dispatch,* Special Supplement, November 22, 1873.

El Paso (TX) *Herald,* November 2, 1915.

Elles. "TV Western Craze—How Long Will It Last?" *Look,* Vol. 24, June 24, 1958, p. 70.

Elliott, Captain David. (Title of article unknown.) *Coffeyville Journal,* October 7, 1892.

Elliott, Susan. "Sixguns at Northfield." *Great West,* May 1968, p. 16.

Ellis, Earl H, ed. *1954 Brand Book.* Vol. 10, Denver Posse of the Westerners.

Elman, Robert. *Badmen of the West.* New York: Ridge Press/Pound, 1974.

Elsele, Wilbert E. *The Real Wild Bill Hickok, Famous Scout and Knight Chivalric of the Plains.* W. H. Andre, 1931.

Emery, J. Gladstone. *Court of the Damned: Being a Factual Story of the Court of Judge Isaac C. Parker and the Life and Times of the Indian Territory and Old Fort Smith.* New York: Comet, 1959.

Erdoes, Richard, ed. *Tales from the American Frontier.* Rotan TX: Bennett Walls.

Erwin, Allen A. Letter. *True West,* August 1957, p. 44.

Erwin, Richard E. *The Truth About Wyatt Earp.* Norman: University of Oklahoma Press.

Esselman, Kathlyn C. "When the Cowboy Stopped Kissing His Horse." *Journal of Popular Culture,* Vol. 6, no. 2, Fall 1972, pp. 387–399.

Etter, Jim. "If Jessie's Not Shot, What?" *The Daily Oklahoman,* Monday, March 25, 1991, pp. 1–2.

Fable, Edmund, Jr. *The True Life of Billy the Kid.* Denver: Creative, 1988.

Faulk, Odie B. *Tombstone's Myth and Reality.* New York: Oxford University Press, 1972.

Fenin, George N., and William K. Everson. *The Western.* New York: Bonanza, 1962.

_____, and _____. *The Western from Silents to Cinerama.* New York: Orion, 1962.

_____, and _____. *The Western from Silents to the Seventies.* New York: Grossman, 1973.

Fergusson, Harvey. "Billy the Kid." *American Mercury*, June 1925, Vol. 5, no. 18.
_____. *Rio Grande*. New York: Alfred A. Knopf, 1933.
Fielder, Mildred. *Wild Bill and Deadwood*. New York: Bonanza, 1963.
_____. "Wild Bill's Guns in Deadwood." *Old West*, Fall 1970, p. 14.
Fisher, Truman Rex. "The Lion of Tombstone's Ghost." *Old West*, Vol. 31, no. 31, Spring 1995, p. 50.
Fitzgerald, Ruth C. "Clell and Ed Miller, Members of the James Gang." *NOLA Quarterly*, Vol. 15, no. 3, July–September 1991, p. 29.
Fleischer, Nat. "Crusading Scribes." *Ring Magazine*, June 1941.
Flynn, Claire. "The Children of Belle Starr." *True Frontier*, August 1975, p. 6; *True Frontier*, October 1977, p. 30.
Folsom, James K. "Western Themes and Western Films." *Western American Literature*, Vol. 2, no. 3, Fall 1967, pp. 195–203.
Fontes and Korman. *Wild Bill Hickok and the Rebel Indians*. American Frontier no. 10. Virginia City NV: Sun Mountain.
Forbes, Stanley G. "Fast Gun From Texas." *Golden West*, September 1965, p. 37; reprinted *Western Frontier*, Special Issue, Fall 1974, p. 17; reprinted, *Western Frontier*, January 1983, p. 5.
Ford County Globe, May 14, 1879.
Forrest, Cris, ed. "Wild Bill's First Trail as He Told It." *Dewitt's Ten Cent Romances*, no. 10, December 1867.
Forrest, Earle R. *Arizona's Dark and Bloody Ground*. Introduction by William MacLeod Raine. Caldwell ID: Caxton, Ltd., 1936; reprint: University of Arizona Press, 1953.
_____. "The Killing of Ed Masterson." *The Brand Book of the Los Angeles Corral of the Westerners*. 1949.
Fowler, Gene. *Skyline: A Reporter's Reminiscences of the 1920s*. New York: Viking, 1961.
Fox, Kendra. "Historic Robbers' Cave Great Family Hideout." *The Sunday Oklahoman*, Travel and Entertainment Section, October 13, 1996, p. 5.
Foy, Eddie, and Alvin P. Harlow. *Clowning Through Life*. New York: E. P. Dutton, 1928.
Franz, Joe B., and Julian Ernest Choate, Jr. *The American Cowboy: The Myth and the Reality*. Westport CT: Greenwood, 1981.
Fraser, George MacDonald. *The Hollywood History of the World—From One Million B.C. to Apocalypse Now*. New York: William Morrow, 1988, pp. 206–209.
Frazier, Thomas A. "Jesse James: The Man and the Legend." Part I: *Real West*, May 1970, p. 16. Part II: *Real West*, June 1970, p. 44.
_____. "Wild Bill Hickok, the Man and the Legend." Part I: *Real West*, January 1969, p. 26. Part II, *Real West*, February 1969, p. 28. Republished as one-part article, *Real West*, Special Issue, Fall 1973, p. 42.
Freeman, G. D. *Midnight and Noonday; or, Dark Deeds Unraveled*. Binder's Title: *A True History of Caldwell, Kansas*. Caldwell KS: G. D. Freeman, 1890.
_____. *Midnight and Noonday: The Incidental History of Southern Kansas and the Indian Territory, 1871–1890*. Norman: University of Oklahoma Press, 1984.
French, Joseph Lewis, ed. *A Gallery of Old Rogues*. New York: Alfred H. King, Inc., 1931.
Fulton, Maurice Garland. "Billy the Kid in Life and Books." *New Mexico Folklore Record*, Vol. 4, 1949–1950.
_____. *History of the Lincoln County War*. Tucson: University of Arizona Press, 1986.
_____, and Paul Morgan, eds. *New Mexico's Own Chronicle*. Dallas: Banks Upshaw, 1937.
Gaddis, Robert W. "They Headed North to Death." *True Frontier*, June 1967, p. 32.
Gaddy, Jerry J., comp. *Dust to Dust: Obituaries of the Gunfighters*. San Rafael CA: Presidio, 1977; Fort Collins, CO: Old Army, 1977.
Gagliasso, Dan. "The Shooting of Wyatt Earp." *Western Horseman*, Vol. 59, September 1994, pp. 137–39.

Ganghorn, Jack. *I've Killed Men.* London: Robert Hale, n.d.

Gard, Robert M. *Dodge City, the Cowboy Capital.* Wichita KS: 1919.

Gardner, Raymond Hatfield, and B. H. Montae. *The Old Wild West.* San Antonio: 1944.

Garfield, Brian. "Warlock Revisited: The Vanishing Western." *South Dakota Review,* Vol. 23, Autumn 1985, pp. 72–101.

Garfield, Brian. *Western Films: A Complete Guide.* New York: Rawson, 1982.

Garrett, Pat F. *The Authentic Life of Billy the Kid, Noted Desperado of the Southwest, Whose Deeds of Daring and Blood Made His Name a Terror in New Mexico, Arizona, and Northern Mexico.* Santa Fe: New Mexico Printing and Publishing Co., 1882; revised ed. (edited by Maurice Garland Fulton), New York: Macmillan, 1927; 2d revised ed. (edited and annotated by J. C. Dykes), Norman: University of Oklahoma Press, 1954; reprint, Dorchester, 1977.

Garwood, W. R. *Ringo's Tombstone.* Ann Arbor MI: Bath Street, 1981.

Gatto, Steve. *Wyatt Earp,* Tucson: San Simon, 1997.

Gehrman, B. L. "Charlie Bowdre's Wish." *Frontier Times,* Fall 1958, p. 19.

_____. "Hardened Criminal." *True West,* December 1958, p. 21.

Ghent, W. J. "Jesse James." *Dictionary of American Biography.* New York: Charles Scribner, 1932.

_____. "William Barclay Masterson." *The Dictionary of American Biography.* New York: Charles Scribner, 1933.

Gibson, Marijo. "Jesse James and the Cloth." *The West,* June 1970, p. 20; reprinted, *Western Frontier,* Special Issue, Fall 1974, p. 40.

Giffen, Guy. "Charlie Pitts—RIP." *True West,* April 1965, p. 42.

_____. "De-Gunning the Gun-Man." *Frontier Times,* Vol. 15, no. 12, September 1938.

Gilmore, Donald L. "Showdown at Northfield." *Wild West,* August 1996, p. 36.

Gish, Anthony. *American Bandits: A Biographical History of the Nation's Outlaws—From the Days of the James Boys, the Youngers, the Jennings, the Dalton Gang and Billy the Kid, Down to Modern Bandits of Our Own Day, Including Dillinger, "Pretty" Boy Floyd, and Others.* Girard KS: Haldeman-Julius, 1938.

Glass, Ben, and Jim Wilson. *Wyatt Earp's West: Images and Words.* New York: Newmarket, 1994.

Gluck, Harold. "He Knew Billy the Kid." *Famous Western,* Vol. 13, no. 1, February 1952.

Glynn, Dean. "The Last Fight of the Wild Bunch." *Westerner,* July-August 1970, p. 42.

Good Bye, Jesse James: Six of the Best News Stories from the Kansas City Journal *of 1882 on the Career and Death of Jesse James.* Liberty MS: 1967.

Gord, Wayne. *Frontier Justice.* Norman: University of Oklahoma Press, 1949.

Gordon, Dan. *Wyatt Earp.* New York: Warner, 1994.

"Gossip from Crede." *Colorado Sun,* February 25, 1892.

Gray, William F. "Billy the Kid." *Life,* Vol. 2, no. 7, February 15, 1937.

Green, Carl. *Bat Masterson.* Hillside NJ: Enslow, 1992.

Gregg, Andy. "Who Was the Real Billy the Kid?" *Real West,* November 1963, p. 35.

Grey, Frederick William. *Seeking Fortune in America.* London: Smith, Elder, 1912.

Griffin, Nancy. "Return of the Ride-Back Gang." *Premiere,* Vol. 7, July 1994, p. 54.

Griggs, George. *History of Mesilla Valley, or the Gadsden Purchase.* Las Cruces NM: Bronson, 1930.

Gryden, Harry. Letter to Bat Masterson. *Dodge City Times,* June 9, 1881.

Guinon, J. P. "The Last Days of Billy the Kid." *Real West,* Special Issue, Fall 1964, p. 40.

The Gunfighters. New York: Time-Life, 1974.

Gunfighters of the Old West. Two-tape video set. Cave Creek AZ: Pieces of History.

Guyer, James S. *Pioneer Life in West Texas.* Brownwood TX: Privately printed, 1938.

Hackenberry, Charles. *I Rode with Jesse James.* New York: Harper Paperbacks, 1996.

Hale, Donald R. "Resurrection of Jesse James." *NOLA Quarterly*, Vol. 5, no. 3, April 1980, p. 1.

Haley, J. Evetts. "Horse Thieves." *Southwest Review*, Vol. 15, no. 3, April 30, (?).

Hall, Frank. *History of the State of Colorado*. Vol. 3. Chicago: Blakely. 1891.

Hall, Frank O., and Lindsey H. Whitten. *Jesse James Rides Again*. Lawton OK: LaHoma, 1948.

Hall, Oakely. *Warlock*. New York: Viking, 1958.

Hall-Quest, Olga W. *Wyatt Earp: Marshal of the Old West*. New York: Farrar Straus and Cudahy, 1956.

Hamill, Pete. *"Doc": The Original Screenplay*. New York: Paperback Library, 1971, p. 17.

Hamlin, William Lee. *The True Story of Billy the Kid*. Caldwell ID: Caxton, 1959.

Hammond, John Hayes. "Strong Men of the Wild West." *Scribner's Magazine*, Vol. 77, no. 2, February 1925.

Hancock, J. *In Old Arizona: True Tales of the Wild Frontier*. Virginia City NV: Sun Mountain.

Hane, Louis. "Bloodbath at Coffeyville." *Westerner*, January-February 1972, p. 34.

Hanes. *Bill Doolin, Outlaw O.T.* Norman: University of Oklahoma Press.

Hansen, George W. "True Story of Wild Bill—McCanles Affray in Jefferson County, Nebraska, July 12, 1861." With supporting articles by Addison E. Sheldon and William Monroe McCanles. *Nebraska History Magazine*, Vol. 10, no. 2, April-June 1927.

_____. "The Truth About Wild Bill." *Mail and Breeze*. Topeka, Kansas, December 20, 1901.

Hardcastle, Stoney. "Belle Starr's Piano." *True West*, June 1977, p. 22.

_____. *The Legend of Belle Starr*. New York: Carlyle, 1979.

Hardin. *Raider: Tombstone Territory*. New York: Berkeley, 1990.

Hardy, Phil. *Samuel Fuller*. New York: Frederick A. Praeger, 1970. Pp. 124–28, 142.

_____. *The Western*. New York: William Morrow, 1983.

Harmon, Samuel W. *Hell on the Border: He Hanged Eighty-Eight Men*. Fort Smith: Phoenix, 1898; reprint, Raton TX: Bennett-Walls.

Harper's New Monthly Magazine, February 1867.

Harrel, Melvin. "The Dalton Gang." *Northfork Sparks and Flashes*. 3 Parts: May, June, July, 1953.

Harrington, Fred Harvey. *Hanging Judge*. Norman: University of Oklahoma Press, 1995.

Harrison, John. "Billy Breakenridge, the 'Tenderfoot' Deputy." *Real West*, Vol. 20, no. 149, January 1977, p. 18.

Harshbarger, I. Letter. *True West*, August 1957, p. 46.

Hart, George. "Frontier Enigma." *Real West*, November 1972, p. 18; reprinted, *Real West Yearbook*, Spring 1974, p. 51.

_____. "Hays City Under the Guardian Care of Wild Bill." Part I: *Real West*, April 1971, p. 26. Part II: *Real West*, May 1971, p. 46.

_____. "Hickok: Hero or Heel?" *True West*, June 1956, p. 26.

_____. "Identifying Frank and Jesse James: The Case of the Missing Finger." *NOLA Quarterly*, Vol. 11, no. 1, Summer 1986, p. 14.

_____. "Irvin Walley: The Murder of Cole Younger's Father." *NOLA Quarterly*, Vol. 15, no. 1, 1991, p. 4.

_____. "The Mystery of Wild Bill Hickok's Remains." *Real West*, October 1970, p. 32.

_____. "Stanley Waterloo Meets the Fords." *NOLA Quarterly*, Vol. 14, no. 1, 1990, p. 1.

Hart, Louis. "The Daltons Won Their Fame in Little Coffeyville, Kansas on October 5, 1892, But at Great Cost." *Wild West*, Vol. 9, no. 3, October 1996, p. 68.

_____. "It's Bonney Country—No Kidding." *Wild West*, Vol. 6, no. 5, February 1994, p. 40.

Hattich, William. *Tombstone*. Norman: University of Oklahoma Press, 1981.

Hawgood, John A. *The American West*. London: Eyre and Spottiswoode, 1967; published in U.S.A. by Alfred A. Knopf as *America's Western Frontier*.

Hawkeye, H. *The Dalton Brothers and Their Gang: Fearsome Bandits of Oklahoma and the Southwest.* Philadelphia: Kerner and Gettis, 1908.

Hays City (Kansas) *Railway Advance.* Various issues, 1867–68.

Hays City (Kansas) *Sentinel,* August 1879.

Haywood, E. Robert. *Victorian West: Class and Culture in Kansas Cattle Towns.* Lawrence: University of Kansas, 1991.

"He Preached Sermon for Belle Starr." *The Daily Oklahoman,* April 23, 1939.

Heermans, Forbes. *Thirteen Stories of the Far West.* Syracuse NY: C. W. Bardeen, 1887.

Henderson, Sam. "Tombstone's Adventurous Journalist: John Clum." *Golden West,* November 1969, p. 28; reprinted, *The West,* December 1971, p. 22.

Hendricks, George D. *The Bad-Man of the West.* San Antonio: Naylor, 1941.

Hendron, J. W. "The Old Lincoln Courthouse." *El Palacio,* Vol. 46, no. 1, January 1939.

_____. *The Story of Billy the Kid, New Mexico's Number One Desperado.* Santa Fe: Rydal, 1948.

Hening, H. B., ed. *George Curry: An Autobiography (1938).*

Henn, Nora. "Was a Piano in the McSween House During the Five-Day Battle?" *Real West,* February 1984, p. 26; reprinted, *Real West Annual,* Spring 1985, p. 30.

Henry, Raymond H., to Heinie Schmidt, January 14, 1936. Quoted in Joseph W. Snell, ed., "The Diary of a Dodge City Buffalo Hunter, 1872–1873." *Kansas Historical Quarterly,* Winter 1965.

Henry, Stuart. *Conquering Our Great American Plains.* New York: 1930. P. 288.

Henry, Will. *Jesse James, Death of a Legend.* Stamford CT: Dorchester, 1995.

_____. *Who Rides with Wyatt.* New York: Random House, 1954.

Hermon, Gregory. "Wild Bill's Sweetheart: The Life of Mary Jane Owen." *Real West,* February 1987, p. 21.

Hertzog, Peter. *Little Known Facts About Billy the Kid.* Santa Fe: Press of the Territorian, 1964.

Hervey, James Madison. "The Assassination of Pat Garrett." *True West,* April 1961, p. 16.

Hickey, Michael M. *Los Dos Pistoleros (The Earp Pistoleers).* Honolulu: Talei, 1994.

_____. *John Ringo, The Final Hours: A Tale of the Old West.* Honolulu: Talei, 1995.

_____. *Street Fight in Tombstone Near the OK Corral.* Honolulu: Talei, 1995.

"Hickok: Hero or Heel?" *Badman Annual,* 1971, p. 72.

Hicks, Edwin P. *Belle Starr and Her Pearl.* Little Rock: Pioneer, 1963.

_____. "Who Killed Belle Starr?" *Expose for Men,* Vol. 3, no. 1, June 1959.

_____, and Paul Sann. *Pictorial History of the Wild West: A True Account of the Bad Men, Desperadoes, Rustlers, and Outlaws of the Old West—and the Men Who Fought Them to Establish Law and Order.* New York: Crown, 1954.

Hill, J. L. *The End of the Cattle Trail.* Long Beach: George W. Moyle, 1924.

Hines, James. "Death of Bob Ollinger [sic], Sadistic Jailer." *Real West,* July 1996, p. 40.

_____. "Jesse James' Attempted Suicide." *Real West,* January 1962, p. 52.

_____. "Scandal That Killed Jesse James." *Real West,* May 1965, p. 40.

Hinkle, James F. *Early Days of a Cowboy on the Pecos.* Roswell NM: Privately printed, 1937.

Hinkle, Milt. "The Earp and Masterson I Knew." *True West,* December 1961, p. 25.

Hitt, Jim. *The American West from Fiction 1823–1976 into Film 1909–1986.* Jefferson NC: McFarland.

Hockley, G. W. "Last Days of a Plainsman." *True West,* December 1965, p. 22.

Hoctor, Emmett C. Letter. *WOLA Journal Quarterly,* Vol. 1, no. 2, Fall Winter 1991, p. 2.

_____. "Safe Retreat Found." *NOLA Quarterly,* Vol. 15, no. 4, October–December 1991, p. 20.

Hogan, Ray. *Betrayal in Tombstone.* New York: Popular Library, 1975.
_____. *The Life and Death of Johnny Ringo.* New York: Signet, 1963.
Holbrook, Stewart H. "The Bank the James Boys Didn't Rob." *American Mercury,* 1948.
_____. "Calamity Jane." *American Mercury,* Vol. 64, February 1947.
_____. *Wyatt Earp, U.S. Marshal.* New York: Random House, 1956.
Holder, Gene. Letter. *True West,* August 1957, p. 43.
Hollon W. Eugene. *Frontier Violence: Another Look.* New York: Oxford University Press, 1974.
_____. *The Southwest: Old and New.* New York: Alfred A. Knopf, 1961.
Holloway, Carroll C. *Texas Gun Lore.* San Antonio: Naylor, 1951.
Hoole, Stanley. *The James Boys Rode South.* Tuscaloosa AL, 1955.
Horan, James D. *The Authentic Wild West: The Lawmen's Accounts by Eyewitnesses and the Lawmen Themselves.* New York: Random House, 1996.
_____ "Billy the Kid, the True Story of a Western 'Bad Man.'" *Everybody's Magazine,* Vol. 5, no. 25, September 1901.
_____. *Desperate Men: The James Gang and the Wild Bunch,* Revised and Enlarged Edition, Lincoln: University of Nebraska Press.
_____. *Desperate Women.* New York: G. P. Putnam, 1952.
_____. *The Great American West.* New York: Crown, 1959; revised ed., 1962.
_____. *The Gunfighters.* New York: Gramercy, 1994.
_____. *Lawmen: The Authentic Wild West.* New York: Crown, 1992.
_____. *The Outlaws.* 312 pp.
_____. "The Strange Marriage of Wild Bill Hickok." *The West,* March 1964, p. 21; reprinted, *The West,* August 1974, p. 14.
_____. "When Wild Bill Hickok Wouldn't Fight." *The West,* December 1964, p. 18; reprinted, *Western Frontier,* April 1983, p. 20.
_____, and Paul Sann. *Pictorial History of the Wild West: A True Account of the Bad Men, Desperadoes, Rustlers and Outlaws of the Old West; and the Men Who Fought Them to Establish Law and Order.* New York: Crown, 1954.
Horton, Harvey R. "Horton Favors Homicide Theory for Ringo." *NOLA Quarterly,* Vol. 3, no. 4, Spring 1978, p. 8.
Hough, Emerson. *The Story of the Outlaw.* New York: Outing, 1907.
House, R. C. "'Gramp' Gibson Identifies Jesse." *The National Tombstone Epitaph,* Vol. 14, no. 10, October 1987, p. 16.
Hubbard, George V. "The Lynching of Killer Miller." *True Frontier,* March 1969, p. 12; reprinted, *True Frontier,* Special Issue no. 1, 1971, p. 46.
Huff, Marcus. "The Kid in the Black Hat." Review, Bob Boze Bell, *The Illustrated Life and Times of Billy the Kid,* 2d ed. *True West,* Vol. 43, no. 1, November 1996, p. 54.
Hughes, Albert Hilliard. "Jesse James: Outlaw with a Halo." *Montana,* Vol. 17, no. 4, October 1967, pp. 68–75.
Hunt, Frazier. "The Tall Slayer of Billy the Kid." *Argosy,* Vol. 331, no. 6, December 1950.
_____. *The Tragic Days of Billy the Kid.* New York: Hastings House, 1956.
Hunt, Greg. *When Legends Die.* New York: Dell, 1982.
Hunter, J. Marvin. "Billy the Kid's Captor Dead." *Frontier Times,* Vol. 7, no. 11, August 1930.
_____. "The Bloody Trail of Billy the Kid." *Frontier Times,* Vol. 1, no. 2, November 1923.
_____. "Charles A. Siringo Dead." *Frontier Times,* Vol. 6, no. 3, December 1928.
_____. "Has Billy the Kid Come Alive?" *Frontier Times,* Vol. 27, no. 5, December 1950.
_____. "Pat Garrett, Slayer of Billy the Kid." *Frontier Times,* Vol. 27, no. 5, June 1985.
_____, and Noah H. Rose. *The Album of Gunfighters.* Bandera TX: 1951; 2d ed., Mountain Home TX: Y.D., 1955.
Huntley, A. "Cole Younger." *Real West,* Special Issue, Fall 1964, p. 26.

Huston, Fred. "Death of the Coward Killer." *Real Frontier*, August 1971, p. 19.

_____. "Ed Masterson: He Was More Than Just Bat's Brother." *Golden West*, January 1974, p. 34.

Hutton, Paul. "Billy the Kid as Seen in the Movies." *Frontier Times*, Vol. 57, no. 3, June 1985.

_____. "Celluloid Lawman." *American West*, May-June 1984, pp. 58–65.

Hyde, Albert E. "The Old Regime in the Southwest: The Reign of the Revolver in New Mexico." *Century Magazine*, March 1902.

An Illustrated History of New Mexico Chicago: Lewis, 1895.

Ingraham, Colonel Prentiss. *Wild Bill the Pistol Deadshot*. New York: Beadle's Dime Library, 1882.

Irwin, Helen. "When Billy the Kid Was Brought to Trial." *Frontier Times*, Vol. 14, no. 3, Spring 1929.

Jacobsen. *Such Men as Billy the Kid: The Lincoln County War Reconsidered*. Lincoln: University of Nebraska.

Jahans, Pat. *The Frontier World of Doc Holliday*. New York: Hastings House, 1957.

James, Frank. *The Only True History of the Life of Frank James, Written by Himself*. Pine Bluff AR: Norton, 1926.

James, J. Coleman. "His Legs Are Missing." *Great West*, November 1967, p. 14.

James, Jesse, Jr. *Jesse James, My Father*. Independence MO: Sentinental, 1899.

_____. *The Facsimile Edition of Jesse James, My Father, the First and Only True Story of His Adventures*. New York: Frederick Fell, 1957.

James, Jesse Lee III. "The James Brothers." *History of Clay and Platte Counties, Missouri*. St. Louis: National Historical Company, 1885.

_____. *Jesse James and the Lost Cause*. New York: Pageant, 1961.

James, Stella. "Some Notes on Jesse James." *True West*, August 1962, p. 28.

"The James Boys: Jesse and Frank." *Scholastic Magazine*, January 21, 1939.

Jameson, Henry B. "Lay Off Abilene." *True West*, September 1982, p. 16.

Jeffers, H. Paul. *Tombstone Revenge*. New York: Zebra, 1991.

Jenardo, Don. *Five-Cent Wide Awake Library*. August 1881.

_____. *The True Life of Billy the Kid*. Frank Tousey Publications, August 29, 1881.

Jennewein, Leonard. *Calamity Jane of the Western Trails*. Huron SD: 1953.

"Jesse James." *American Heritage*, Vol. 2, no. 5, August 1960.

"Jesse James." *Kansas City Times*, August 14, 1876.

"Jesse James." *Nashville Banner*, July 10, 1875.

"Jesse James." *True Western Adventures* ("Gallery of Gunmen"), no. 4, August 1960, p. 56.

Jesse James: The Life and Daring Adventures of This Bold Highwayman and Bank Robber. Philadelphia: Barclay, 1882.

"Jesse James Impersonators Had Limited Success." *The Ada* [Oklahoma] *Sunday News*, July 23, 1995.

"Jesse James Reincarnated." *Real West*, April 1973.

Jessey, Kenneth. "Chain of Death Ends in Creede." *NOLA Quarterly*, Vol. 11, no. 3, Fall 1987, p. 15.

Johannsen, Albert. *The House of Beadle and Adams and Its Dime and Nickel Novels: The Story of a Vanished Literature*. 2 vols. Norman: University of Oklahoma Press, 1950.

Johnson, Allen, ed. *Dictionary of American Biography*. Vol. 2. New York: Charles Scribner, 1929.

Johnson, David. *John Ringo*. Stillwater OK: Barbed Wire, 1996.

Johnson, Dorothy M. *Western Badmen*. New York: Dodd, Mead, 1970.

Johnson, E. *Wyatt Earp: Gunfighting Marshal*. New York: Julian Messner.

Johnson, Norman K. "General Joe Shelby and the Trial of Frank James." *Real West*, October 1988, p. 14.

Jones, Archie H. "Cops, Robbers, Heroes, and Anti-Heroines: The American Need to Create." *Journal of Popular Culture*, Vol. 1, no. 2, Fall 1967, pp. 114–18.

Jones, Daryl E. "Clenched Teeth and Curses: Revenge and the Dime Novel Outlaw Hero." In *The Popular Western*. Bowling Green OH: Bowling Green University Press, 1974.

Jones, Kelly. *Wild Western Desire*. Washington DC: Kensington, 1993.

Jordan, Philip. *Cowgirls: Women of the American West*. Lincoln: University of Nebraska Press, 1992.

_____. *Frontier Law and Order: Ten Essays*. Lincoln: University of Nebraska Press, 1970.

_____. "The Pistol Packin' Cowboy: From Bullet to Burial." *Red River Valley Historical Review*, Vol. 2, no. 1, 1975, pp. 65–93.

_____. "The Town Marshal and the Police." In Ray Allen Billington, ed., *People of the Plains and Mountains, Essays in the History of the West Dedicated to Everett Dick*. Westport CT: Greenwood, 1973.

Joseph, Jack L. "Virgil Earp, Western Peace Officer." *Wild West*, October 1995, p. 68.

Junction City (Kansas) *Daily and Weekly Union*. Various issues, 1866–71 and 1876 (including November 4, 12, and 19, 1870).

Kadlec, Robert F., ed. *They Knew Billy the Kid: Interviews with Old Time New Mexicans*. Ancient City Press, 1987.

Kansas City (Missouri) *Star*, November 18, 1928.

Kantor, Seth. "Time October 26, 1881—Place OK Corral." *Western Action*, December 1960, p. 10.

Kasdan, Lawrence, and Jake Kasdan. *Wyatt Earp: The Film and the Filmmakers*. New York: Newmarket, 1994.

Keleher, William A. *The Fabulous Frontier: Twelve New Mexico Items*. Albuquerque: University of New Mexico Press, 1945; revised ed., 1962.

_____. "In Re' Billy the Kid." *New Mexico Folklore Record, 1949–1950*, Vol. 4. Albuquerque: 1950.

_____. *Violence in Lincoln County, 1889–1891*. Albuquerque: University of New Mexico, 1957.

Kelland, Clarence Budington. *Tombstone*. New York: Harper, 1952.

Kelleton, Ives. "Get Away Ridge." *True Frontier*, Special Issue no. 1, 1971, p. 6.

Kelley, Charles. *The Outlaw Trail*. New York: 1939, 1959.

Kelley, Thomas P. *Jesse James*. New York: Export, 1950.

Kelly, Bill. *Encyclopedia of Gunmen*. New York: Printer's Devil, 1976.

Kelly, Bill. "Pearl Younger and the Falling Starrs." *Real West*, Vol. 19, no. 148, November 1976.

Kemp, Ben W. "Ride for Mexico, Billy." *Frontier Times*, March 1980, p. 6.

Kerr, William Ray. "In Defense of Ingalls, Oklahoma." *True West*, October 1964, p. 6.

Ketchum, Philip. *Wyatt Earp*. Racine WI: Whitman, 1996.

_____. "Wyatt Earp's Million Dollar Shotgun Ride." *True West*, August 1958, p. 16.

Kildare, Charley. "Bullet Swapout in Oklahoma." *Real West*, October 1973, p. 48.

Kildare, Maurice. "Six Gun Justice Took Strange Turns in Cimarron." *Frontier West*, December 1973, p. 26.

Kilpatrick, Jack F. "Belle Starr's Medicine Man Boyfriend." *Real West*, 1967, p. 38.

King, A. M. "The Last Man." *True West*, June 1959, p. 28.

King, Frank M. *Wranglin' the Past*. Los Angeles: Raynes, 1935.

Kirkpatrick, J. B. "Doc Holliday's Missing Grave." *True West*, October 1995, p. 16.

Kirpatrick, Fred. "The Kid's Escape." *New Mexico*, Vol. 14, no. 9, September 1936.

Knoles, Thelma. "Curly Bill." *Old West*, Summer 1980, p. 23.

Knowles, Edward. "The Lost Love of Jim Younger." *Old West*, Spring 1967, p. 18.

Knowles, Thomas W., and Joe R. Lansdale, eds. *The West That Was*. Ovenel NJ: Outlet.

Koller, Joe. "Bloody Ingalls Under Siege." *The West*, August 1972, p. 38; reprinted, *Western Frontier*, July 1976, p. 6.

Koop, W. A. "Billy the Kid: The Trail of a Kansas Legend." *The Trail Guide*, September 1964.

Kutas, Mildred. Letter. "Life of Wild Bill." *Wild West*, August 1976, p. 8.

Lake, Stuart N. "Brush Poppers." *Saturday Evening Post*, Vol. 203, no. 41, April 11, 1931.

_____. "Buffalo Hunters." *Saturday Evening Post*, October 25, 1930.

_____. "The Frontier Marshal." *Saturday Evening Post*, November 15, 1930.

_____. "Guns and Gunfighters." *Saturday Evening Post*, November 1, 1930.

_____. *The Life and Times of Wyatt Earp*. Boston, Houghton Mifflin, 1956.

_____. "Straight-Shooting Dodge." *Saturday Evening Post*, March 8, 1930.

_____. "Tale of the Kansas Cow Towns." *Saturday Evening Post*, November 8, 1930.

_____. "Tales of the Kansas Cow Towns." *Saturday Evening Post*, 1930.

_____. *Wyatt Earp, Frontier Marshal*. Boston: Houghton Mifflin, 1931.

Lamar, Howard R. *The Far Southwest 1865–1885*. New Haven CT: Yale University Press, 1966.

_____, ed. *Reader's Encyclopedia of the American West*. New York: T. Y. Crowell, 1977.

Langford, N. P. *Vigilante Days and Ways*. 2 vols. New York and St. Paul: 1893.

Lansdale, Joe R. "When Bill Dalton Hit the Longview Bank." *Old West*, Summer 1978, p. 6.

Laramie (Wyoming) *Daily Sentinel*, 1873.

Laredo Texas Times, Wednesday, August 10, 1881.

Las Cruces Thirty Four. Various issues, 1880–1881.

Las Vegas Daily Gazette. Various issues, 1880–1881.

Las Vegas Daily Optic. Various issues, 1880–1881.

Las Vegas Morning Gazette. Various issues, 1880–1881.

Latta, Frank F. *Dalton Gang Days*. Santa Cruz CA: Bear State, 1976.

Lavash, Don. *Wilson and the Kid*. College Station TX: Early West.

Lavash, Donald R. *William Brady: Tragic Hero of the Lincoln County War*. Santa Fe NM: Sunstone, 1986.

"Law Man or Bad Man: Wild Bill Hickok." *Gunslingers of the West*, Winter 1966, p. 2.

Lawrence (Kansas) *Daily Tribune*. Various issues, 1868–69.

Lazaru, Leon. "Deadliest Dentist of the West." *Man's Western*, January 1960, p. 10.

Leavenworth (Kansas) *Daily Bulletin*, February 13, 1867.

Leavenworth (Kansas) *Daily Commercial*. Various issues, 1867–69.

Leavenworth (Kansas) *Daily Conservative*. Various issues, 1867–72.

Lee, Paul. "Bill Doolin: King of Oklahoma Outlaws." *Pioneer West*, June 1972, p. 16.

Lee, Wayne C. *Bad to the Bone*, Caldwell, Idaho: Caxton Printers, 1994.

Legends of the American West 5-vol. video set: "Billy the Kid," "Jesse James," "Wyatt Earp," "The West Remembered," and "Cowboys and Indians." Country Club Hills IL: Fusion Video.

Lehman, M. P. "Terror of the Territorial Outlaws." *Golden West*, January 1966, p. 42; reprinted, *The West*, March 1972, p. 34; reprinted, *Western Frontier*, May 1980, p. 46.

Legends of the Wild West, Lincolnwood, IL: Publications International, 1997.

Lentz, Harris M. III. *Western and Frontier Film and Television Credits: 1903–1995*. Jefferson NC: McFarland, 1996. 2 vols.

Lester, D. C. "Belle Starr, Oklahoma's Woman Outlaw: She Died as She Had Lived 'with Her Boots On.'" *The Daily Oklahoman*, August 21, 1921.

Letter to the Editor. *Outdoor Life*, Vol. 17, no. 6. June 1906.

Lewis, Alfred Henry. "How Mr. Hickok Came to Cheyenne: An Epic of an Unsung Ulysses." *The Saturday Evening Post*, Vol. 176, no. 37, March 12, 1904.

_____. "The King of the Gun-Players, William Barclay Masterson." *Human Life*, November 1907.

_____. *The Sunset Trail*. New York: A. S. Barnes & Co., 1905.

Lewis, John Woodruff (Don Jenardo, pseud.). *The True Life of Billy the Kid*. Wide Awake Library, no. 451. New York: Frank Tousey, August 29, 1881.

Lewis Lloyd. *It Takes All Kinds*. New York: Harcourt, Brace, 1947.

Life and Tragic Death of Jesse James. 1883.

The Life of Billy the Kid, a Juvenile Outlaw. Morrison's Sensational Series, no. 3. New York: John W. Morrison, 1881.

Lincoln County Leader, January 15, 1890.

Linn, William C. "The James-Younger Gang: Murderers." *NOLA Quarterly*, Vol. 3, no. 4, Spring 1977, p. 7.

_____, and Carl W. Breihan. "Two Views of Jesse James: Ruthless Killer and Tender Love." *NOLA Quarterly*, Vol. 4, no. 3, March 1979, p. 6.

"Little Game of Money with Billy the Kid." *Literary Digest* ("Personal Glimpses"), Vol. 90, no. 7, August 14, 1926.

Lockwood, Frank C. *Pioneer Days in Arizona*. 1937.

Logue, Roscoe. *Under Texas and Border Skies*. "By Way of Explanation" by Horace M. Russell. Amarillo: Russell Stationery Company, 1935.

Lombroso, Cesar, and Guglielmo Ferrero. *The Female Offender*. New York: D. Appleton, 1903.

Lord, John. *Frontier Dust*. Edited with introduction by Natalie Shipman. Hartford CT: Edwin Valentine Mitchell, 1926.

_____. "Picturesque Road Agents of the Early Days." *Overland Monthly*, 2d Series, Vol. 70, November 1917.

Love, Nat. *The Life and Adventures of Nat Love, Better Known in the Cattle Country as "Deadwood Dick."* Los Angeles: Wayside, 1907.

Love, Robertus. "Rise and Fall of Jesse James." *Kansas City Star*, July 19, 1926.

_____. *The Rise and Fall of Jesse James*. New York: G. P. Putnam, 1926. 446 pp.

Lynch, John T. "Devil's Grin." *True West*, April 1955.

Lynd, Ralph A. "Billy the Kid." *Glendale* (California) *News Press*, December 2, 1930.

Lyon, Peter. "The Wild Wild West." *American Heritage*, Vol. 11, no. 5, August 1960, pp. 33–48.

_____. *The Wild, Wild West*. New York: Funk and Wagnalls, 1969.

Lyons, Robert, ed. *My Darling Clementine*. New Brunswick: Rutgers University Press, 1984.

Magill, Frank, ed. *Magill's Survey of Cinema, Second Series*. Englewood Cliffs NJ: Salem, 1981.

Mahon, Howard. "Bob Ford Did Not Kill Jesse James." *Real West*, November 1958, p. 22.

Mallory, Charles. "Younger Family Reunion." *Frontier Times*, February 1985, p. 54.

Malocsay, Zoltan. "Bat." *Westerner*, November-December 1972, p. 13.

_____. "Defiance in the Street." *Westerner*, September-October 1972, p. 28.

_____. "OK Corral: 100 Years of Lies." *Westerner*, July-August 1973, p. 34.

Malone, Michael P., ed. *Historians and the American West*. Lincoln: University of Nebraska Press, 1983. Pp. 234–69.

Mangum, William P. "Frank and Jesse James Raced Horses Between Their Holdups." *NOLA Quarterly*, Vol. 13, no. 2, Fall 1989, p. 8.

_____. "Frank James' Secret Travels Authenticated." *NOLA Quarterly*, Vol. 9, no. 4, Spring 1984, p. 18.

_____. "Near Disaster at Bradenburg." *NOLA Quarterly*, Vol. 12, no. 4, Spring 1988, p. 14.

Mann, Edward. *Gamblin' Man*. New York: William Morrow, 1934.

Marks, Paula Mitchell. *And Die in the West: The Story of the O. K. Corral Gunfight.* New York: William Morrow, 1989.

Markson, Dave. "The Secret Life of Billy the Kid." *Male Magazine,* July 1957.

Martin, Chuck. "Emmett Dalton's Six-Shooter." *True West,* February 1956, p. 12; reprint, *Badman,* Fall 1972, p. 32.

Martin, Cy. "The Lincoln County War." *Real West Yearbook,* Summer 1978, p. 12.

Martin, Douglas D. *Tombstones' Epitaph.* Albuquerque: University of New Mexico Press, 1951.

Martinez, Roberto. Letter. *True West,* August 1957, p. 3.

Maslin, Janet. "Emilio Estevez in Reprise of Billy the Kid Role." *The New York Times,* Wednesday, August 1, 1990.

_____. "Hickok Did Not Go Gentle into That Good Sunset." *The New York Times,* Friday, December 1, 1995.

Masohn, Richard. *The Last Gunfighter: John Wesley Hardin.*

Mason, Frank. "What Really Happened at the O. K. Corral?" *True West,* October 1960, p. 35.

Mason, John. "Belle Starr, Bandit Queen." *Real West Annual,* Summer 1966, p. 22.

_____. "Belle Starr, Sister of Sin." *Real West,* Vol. 2, no. 6, February 1959, p. 38.

Masterson, William Barclay. "Famous Gunfighters of the Western Frontier." *Human Life,* Vol. 4, February 1907.

_____. *Famous Gunfighters of the Western Frontier.* Ruidoso NM: Frontier, 1957.

_____. "Famous Gunfighters of the Western Frontier: Ben Thompson." *Human Life,* January 1907, p. 9.

_____. "Famous Gunfighters of the Western Frontier: Doc Holliday." *Human Life,* May 1907.

_____. "Famous Gunfighters of the Western Frontier: Luke Short." *Human Life,* April 1907, p. 10.

_____. "Famous Gunfighters of the Western Frontier: William F. Cody." *Human Life,* March 1908, p. 9.

_____. "Famous Gunfighters of the Western Frontier: Wyatt Earp." *Human Life,* February 1907.

_____. Letter to Frank Baldwin, February 4, 1890. William Carey Brown Collection, University of Colorado, Boulder.

_____. Letter to H. H. Raymond, July 23, 1899. Manuscript Division, Kansas Historical Society, Topeka.

_____. "Masterson's Views on Timely Topics." *New York Morning Telegraph,* October 20, 1921.

Mattis, W. "Emmett Dalton's Bold Stroke." *Westerner,* November-December 1973, p. 42.

Maynard, Richard A. *The American West on Film: Myth and Reality.* Rochelle NJ: Hayden, 1974.

Mays, Carelton. "Angel from Hell." *Real West,* January 1961, p. 8; reprinted, *Real West Annual,* Spring 1968, p. 34.

_____. "The Cattle Baron Who Wouldn't Fight." *Real West,* August 1958, p. 6.

_____. "Greatest of the Daltons." *Real West,* March 1960, p. 18.

_____. "Jesse James." *Real West,* Special Issue, Fall 1964, p. 22.

_____. "What Really Happened at the OK Corral?" *Real West,* January 1958, p. 14; reprinted, *Real West Annual,* Summer 1966, p. 28.

_____. "Wild Bill Was No Hero." *Real West,* March 1962, p. 8.

_____. "Wyatt Earp." *Real West,* Americana Series, Fall 1965, p. 6.

McBee, G. Fred. "Don't Wake the Neighbors." *Golden West,* June 1971, p. 20; reprinted, *Western Frontier,* Special Issue, Fall 1974, p. 38.

McCarty, John L. Letter. *True West,* August 1957, p. 48.

_____. *Maverick Town: The Story of Old Tascosa.* Norman: Univ. of Oklahoma Press, 1946.

McCarty, Lea F. "Billy the Kid's Funeral." *True West*, December 1960, p. 6.

McClelland, Marshall K. "The Day the Daltons Died." *True West*, February 1956, p. 10; *Badman*, Fall 1972, p. 32.

McCreight, M. I. "Hickok: Hero or Heel?" *True West*, June 1956, p. 27.

McCright, Grady F. "Who Sleeps in Billy the Kid's Tomb?" *True Frontier*, April 1978, p. 12.

_____, and James H. Powell. *Jesse Evans: Lincoln County Badman*. College Station TX: Early West.

McCubbin, Robert G. "Pat Garrett at His Prime." *NOLA Quarterly*, Vol. 15, no. 2, April-June 1991, p. 1.

McCullough, Harrell. *Selden Lindsey U. S. Deputy Marshal*. New York: Paragon, 1990.

McDonald, A. B. *Hands Up*. Indianapolis: Bobbs-Merrill, 1927.

McGrath, Roger. *Gunfighters, Highwaymen and Vigilantes: Violence on the Frontier*. Berkeley, CA: 1984.

McIntire, Jim. *Early Days in Texas: A Trip to Hell and Heaven*. Kansas City MO: McIntire, 1902.

MacLean, Angus. "The Ghosts of Frank and Jesse James." *Golden West*, November 1965, p. 22; reprinted, *Western Frontier*, January 1978, p. 16; reprinted, *Western Frontier*, May 1985, p. 26.

McLeod, Norman. "The Northfield Raid and Whiskey." *NOLA Quarterly*, Vol. 13, no. 3, Winter 1989, p. 25.

McLintock, John S. *Pioneer Days in the Black Hills*. Deadwood SD: 1939.

McMurtry, Larry. *Anything for Billy*. New York: Simon & Schuster, 1988.

McNeal, T. A. *When Kansas Was Young*. New York: Macmillan, 1922.

McVey, William D. "Wyatt Earp at Ellsworth." *Chicago Westerners Brand Book*, Vol. 10, no. 9, November 1953, p. 1.

_____, and R. N. Mullen. "Wyatt Earp: Frontier Peace Officer." *Chicago Westerners Brand Book*, Vol. 6, no. 9, November 1949, p. 1.

Mecate, Jim. "S.C.P.A. to Honor Morgan Earp." *Westerns and Serials*, no. 37, p. 40.

Medical History of Camp Carlin, Wyoming. War Records, National Archives, Washington, DC.

Meketa. *From Martyrs to Murderers: The Old Southwest's Saints, Sinners, and Scalawags*. Yucca Tree Press.

Mendota (Illinois) *Bulletin*, March 18, 1869 and April 11, 1873.

Merlock, Raymond J. "Billy the Kid in Films." *Favorite Western*, no. 10, April 1983.

Metz, Leon. *John Selman, Gunfighter*. Norman: University of Oklahoma Press.

_____. *John Wesley Hardin: Dark Angel of Texas*. El Paso TX: Mangan, 1996.

_____. "My Search for Pat Garrett and Billy the Kid." *True West*, August 1983, p. 35.

_____. "Pat Garrett: Another Look at a Western Gunman." *Montana: The Magazine of Western History*, Vol. 21, no. 4.

_____. *Pat Garrett: The Story of a Western Lawman*. Norman: University of Oklahoma Press, 1974.

_____. *The Shooters*. Vienna WV: Old West Shop.

Millard, J. M. "Heck Thomas, Lawman Who Tamed the 'Most Wanted.'" *True Frontier*, September 1969, p. 8.

Miller, George Jr., ed. *The Trial of Frank James for Murder*. Columbia MO: E. W. Stephens, 1898.

Miller, Leo. "The Man Who Killed Billy the Kid." *Man's Action*, July 1958.

Miller, Lora. Letter. *NOLA Quarterly*, Vol. 15, no. 3, July–September 1991, p. 2.

Miller, Nyle H. *Some Widely Publicized Western Police Officers*. Topeka: Kansas Historical Society.

_____, and Joseph W. Snell. *Great Gunfighters of the Kansas Cowtowns, 1867–1886*. Lincoln: University of Nebraska Press, 1967.

Miller, William Alexander. "Early Days of the Wild West." *Bulletin of the District of Columbia, Dons of the American Revolution*, February 8, 1943.

Mitchum. *Stagecoach Station Tombstone*. New York: Bantam, 1983.

Monaghan, Jay, ed. *The Book of the West*. New York: Bonanza, 1963.

Montgomery, Wayne. "More Unpublished Writings of Frank James." *Westerner*, July-August 1973, p. 26.

_____. "Revealed: The Secret Writings of Frank James." *Westerner*, May-June, p. 26.

_____. "The Secret Diary of Frank James." *Westerner*, January-February 1973, p. 26.

_____. "Was Jesse James Really Murdered?" *Big West*, February 1968, p. 28.

Mooney, Charles W. "Belle Starr as Her Doctor Knew Her." *True Frontier*, April 1973, p. 12; reprinted, *True Frontier*, April 1976, p. 38.

_____. "Belle Starr's Killer Revealed." *True West*, February 1969, p. 12.

_____. *Doctor in Belle Starr Country*. Oklahoma City: Century Press, 1975.

_____. "The Secret Belle Starr Took to Her Grave." *Western Frontier Annual*, no. 1, 1975, p. 6.

Morey, Jeffrey J. "The Curious Vendetta of Glenn C. Boyer." *Quarterly of the National Association for Outlaw and Lawman History*, Vol. 18, October–December 1994, pp. 22–28.

Morgan, Speer. *Belle Starr*. Boston: Little, Brown, 1979.

Morrison, John W. *Billy the Kid and His Girl*. Morrison's Sensational Series, no. 20. New York: 1881.

_____. *Billy the Kid and the Cowboys*. Morrison's Sensational Series, no. 2. New York: 1881.

Morsberger, Robert E. *Lew Wallace: Militant Romantic*. New York: McGraw-Hill, 1980.

Morton, Arnold M. "That Good Dalton Boy." *The West*, December 1965, p. 24; reprinted, *The West*, April 1974, p. 42; reprinted, *Western Frontier Annual*, no. 5, 1977, p. 26.

Mote, Wayne D. "The Wildest Woman of the West." *Man's Exploits*, Vol. 1, no. 4, January 1958.

Mulgannon, James H. "Aftermath at Coffeyville and San Fernando." *Real West Annual*, Winter 1977-78, p. 22.

Mullin, Robert H. *A Chronology of the Lincoln County War*. Santa Fe: Press of the Territorian, 1966.

_____. "The Key to the Mystery of Pat Garrett." *Los Angeles Westerners Corral*.

_____. "Pat Garrett: Ten Forgotten Killings." *Password*, Vol. 12, Summer 1965.

_____. *The Strange Story of Wayne Brazel*. Canyon: Palo Duro, 1969.

_____, and Philip J. Rasch. "New Light on the Legend of Billy the Kid." *New Mexico Folklore Record*, Vol. 2, 1952–53.

Mumery, Nolie. "Belle of the Ozarks." *Frontier Times*, Vol. 29, no. 8, May 1952.

_____. *Creede*. Denver: Artcraft Press, 1948.

Mumsell, Marion Ebenezer. *Flying Sparks, as Told by a Pullman Conductor*. Kansas City: Tiernan-Dart, 1914.

Murbarger, Nell. "Battle of Blazer's Mill." *The Cattleman*, Vol. 36, no. 8, January 1950.

Murray, Jim. "The 'Reel' Jesse James." *Western Revue*, Vol. 6, no. 1, June 1980, p. 13.

Myers, John. *The Last Chance: Tombstone's Early Years*. New York: E. P. Dutton, 1950.

Nash, J. Robert. *Encyclopedia of Western Lawmen and Outlaws*. New York: Da Capo.

Naylor, Lee. "The Hated Nickname That Led to Wild Bill Hickok's Murder." *Frontier West*, August 1973, p. 38.

Nebraska Advertiser, July 25, 1861.

New York Westerners Brand Book, Vol. 1, no. 1, Winter 1954, p. 8.

Nichols, George Ward. "Wild Bill." *Harper's New Monthly Magazine*, Vol. 34, no. 201, February 1876, pp. 273–385.

Nieberding, Velma, and Harold Preece. "The West's Outlaws Found No Peace Even in Death." *Frontier West*, December 1971, p. 42.

Nix, Evett Dumas. *Oklahombres*. Raton TX: Bennett-Walls. Originally published in 1929.
"No-Frills 'Wild Bill' Headed to Boot Hill." *Variety*, 1995. (Movie review.)
Noel, Mary. *Villains Galore*. New York: Macmillan, 1954.
Nolan, Frederick W. "The Horse Thief War." *Old West*, Vol. 30, no. 4, Summer 1994, pp. 16–23.
_____. *The Life and Death of John Henry Tunstall, the Letters, Diaries, and Adventures of a Remarkable Young Englishman Who Was Murdered in 1878 During New Mexico's Lincoln County War*. Albuquerque: University of New Mexico Press, 1965.
_____. *The Life and Times of the Horrell Brothers*. Stillwater OK: Barbed Wire, 1995.
_____. *The Lincoln County War: A Documentary History*. Norman: University of Oklahoma Press.
Nolan, Richard. "Gunfight in Gomorrah." *Westerner*, September-October 1972, p. 10.
Nolan, Warren, and Owen P. White. "The Bad Man from Missouri." *Colliers*, January 14, 1928.
"Northfield Bank Raid." *Northfield News*, September 7, 1876.
Nye, Nelson C. *Pistols for Hire*. New York: Macmillan, 1941.
Nye, Nolan C. *Gunfight at the O. K. Corral*. New York: Hillman, 1960. (Novelization of the Leon Uris screenplay.)
O'Connor John E., ed. *American History/American Television: Interpreting the Video Past*. New York: Frederick Ungar, 1983.
O'Connor, John E., and Martin A. Jackson, eds. *American History/American Film: Interpreting the Hollywood Image*. New York: Frederick Ungar, 1979.
O'Connor, Richard. *Bat Masterson*. New York: Doubleday, 1957.
_____. *Pat Garrett: A Biography of the Famous Marshal and the Killer of Billy the Kid*. New York: Doubleday, 1960.
_____. *Young Bat Masterson*. New York: McGraw-Hill, 1967.
O'Liam, Dugal. "Cole Younger: Outlaw King." *True Western Adventures*, February 1960, p. 40.
Omaha (Nebraska) *Daily Bee*, March 31, 1876, p. 2, cols. 3 and 4.
Omaha (Nebraska) *Daily Republican*, July 1873.
O'Neal, Bill. "Aftermath of the OK Corral." *True West* ("Great Western Gunfights"), May 1991, p. 60.
_____. "Bill Dalton Killed." *True West*, June 1994, p. 12.
_____. "Bill Dalton's Last Raid." *Real West*, June 1983, p. 6; reprinted, *Real West Annual*, Spring 1984, p. 10.
_____. "Bill Doolin vs. Heck Thomas." *True West* ("Great Western Gunfights"), September 1971, p. 60.
_____. "'Duck Bill' Hickok vs. the McCanles Gang." *True West* ("Great Western Gunfights"), April 1991, p. 56.
_____. *Encyclopedia of Western Gunfighters*. Norman: University of Oklahoma Press, 1979.
_____. "First National Bank Robbery." *True West* ("Great Western Gunfights"), October 1991, p. 58.
_____. "John and Jim Younger vs. Pinkertons." *True West* ("Great Western Gunfights"), February 1991, p. 56.
_____. "Wild Bill vs. Phil Coe." *True West* ("Great Western Gunfights"), March 1988, p. 59.
O'Neal, Harold. "The San Joaquin Train Holdup." *Golden West*, March 1966, p. 44.
O'Neil, B. *They Die But Once, the Story of a Tejano*. New York: Knight, 1935.
Osborne, Shy. "Gun with a Story to Tell." *Badman*, Fall 1972, p. 36.
Otero, Miguel Antonio. *My Life on the Frontier, 1864–1882*. New York: Press of the Pioneers, 1935.
_____. *The Real Billy the Kid with New Light on the Lincoln County War*. New York: Rufus Rockwell Wilson, 1936.

Overly, William W. Letter. *True West*, August 1957, p. 48.

Paddock, Mary. "Queen of the Outlaws Lived, Loved and Died Beyond the Law." *The Daily Oklahoman*, August 23, 1959.

Palmquist, Robert F. "A Busy Season: Virgil Earp in Prescott, 1877." *Real West*, December 1980, p. 32; reprinted, *Real West Annual*, 1981, p. 60.

_____. "Good Bye Old Friend." *Real West*, May 1979, p. 24.

Panell, Walter. *Civil War on the Range*. Los Angeles: Welcome News, 1943.

Park, Robert A. "Colorful Belle Starr: Immortal Hoyden's Life Full of Twists, Turns." *Muskogee* (Oklahoma) *Daily Phoenix*, November 17, 1940.

Parker, James. "It Don't Hurt Much, Ma'am." *American Heritage*, Vol. 22, no. 2, February 1921, pp. 66–69.

Parker, Watson. *Deadwood: The Golden Years*. Lincoln: University of Nebraska Press.

Parkhill, Forbes. *The Wildest of the West*. New York: Henry Holt, 1951.

Parsons, Chuck. "Bitter Creek." *Frontier Times* ("Answer Man"), May 1991.

_____. "The Boy Who Turned in the Younger Gang." *True West* January 1984, p. 24.

_____. "Charlie Bawdre: Lincoln County Regulator" *True West* ("Answer Man"), December 1991, p. 12.

_____. "Companion of Billy the Kid" *True West* ("Answer Man"), March 1988, p. 12.

_____. "Doolin Gang Lookout." *True West* ("Answer Man"), July 1984, p. 38.

_____. "Hero of the Northfield Raid." *True West* ("Answer Man"), November 1990, p. 12.

_____. "In Pursuit of the Northfield Robbers." *NOLA Quarterly*, Vol. 4, no. 4, June 1979, p. 14.

_____. "It's Wild Bill." *True West*, July 1989, p. 42.

_____. "Jim Reed and Belle Starr." *True West*, March 1988, p. 12.

_____. *Phil Coe: The Texas Gambler*. Wolfe City TX: Henington, 1984.

_____. "'Wild Bill' Hickok Killed Two Men in Abilene." *NOLA Quarterly*, Vol. 1, no. 1, 1975, p. 9.

_____. "Who Was the Fastest Gunman, James B. 'Wild Bill' Hickok or John W. 'Little Arkansas' Hardin?" *NOLA Quarterly*, Vol. 1, no. 3, 1975, p. 8.

Patterson, W. "Calamity Jane." *Wide World Magazine*, Vol. 2, August 1903.

Peck, Ann Merriman. *Southwest Roundup*. New York: Dodd, Mead, 1950.

Peet, Creighton. "Billy the Kid." Review of the motion picture. *Outlook Magazine*, Vol. 156, no. 9, October 29, 1930.

Pendleton, Albert S., Jr., and Susan McKey Thomas. *In Search of the Holliday: The Story of Doc Holliday and His Holliday and McKee Families*. Valdosta GA: Little River, 1973.

Penfield, Thomas. *Western Sheriffs and Marshals*. New York: Grosset & Dunlap, 1955.

Penn, Chris. "Edward J. Masterson, Marshal of Dodge City." Part I: *The English Westerners Brand Book*. July 1965; Part II, *The English Westerners Brand Book*, October 1965.

Penn, Chris. "A Note on Bartholomew Masterson." *The English Westerners Brand Book*, April 1967, p. 11.

Pennill, Mark S. "Roy Dalton: The Son Emmett Never Had." *NOLA Quarterly*, Vol. 15, no. 2, April–June 1991, p. 13.

Perek, Elley. *The Epic Film: Myth and History*. London: Routledge and Kegan Paul, 1984.

Phelps, Barton K. "Who Killed Bill Doolin?" *Real West*, January 1958, p. 40.

Philadelphia Evening Bulletin, January 29, 1910.

Phillips, C. J. "The Battle of Adobe Walls." *Hunter-Trader-Trapper*, December 1928.

Phillips, Robert W. "Looking Back at Wild Bill Hickok." *Classic Images*, no. 230, August 1994, p. 30.

Pierce, D. *Wild West Characters: Unique Fascinating People of the Wild West*. Virginia City NV: Sun Mountain.

Pizzelo, Stephen. "Heading West with Wyatt Earp." *American Cinematographer*, Vol. 75, June 1994, pp. 37–46.

Place, J. A. *The Western Films of John Ford.* New York: Citadel, 1974, pp. 58–73.

Place, Marian. *Bat Masterson.* J. Messner, 1960.

Poe, John W. "Death of Billy the Kid." *True West*, June 1962, p. 6.

_____. *The Death of Billy the Kid!* Introduction and Epilogue by Maurice Garland Fulton. Boston and New York: Houghton Mifflin, 1933.

_____. *The True Story of the Killing of Billy the Kid.* Los Angeles: Privately printed, 1922.

Ponroy, E. B., to Wayne MacVeigh, June 23, 1881. National Archives, Legislative, Judicial, and Diplomatic Division, Records of the Department of Justice concerning Wyatt Earp, 1881–1882. Record Group 60, microcopy 701, roll 6.

Potter, Pam. "Murdered on the Street of Tombstone." *NOLA Quarterly*, Vol. 5, no. 1, October 1979, p. 9.

Powers, Mark. "The Doolin Gang's Last Shootout." reprinted, *True Frontier*, March 1968, p. 22; *True Frontier*, Special Issue no. 1, 1971, p. 42.

Prassel, Frank Richard. *The Great American Outlaw: A Legacy of Fact and Fiction.* Norman: University of Oklahoma Press.

_____. *The Western Peace Officer: The Legacy of Law and Order.* Norman: University of Oklahoma Press, 1972.

Preece, Harold. "Adeline Dalton, Outlaw Mother." *Real West*, September 1965, p. 10.

_____. "Bob Dalton's Bandit Bride." *Real West*, March 1965, p. 10.

_____. "The Day the Daltons Died." *Frontier West*, April 1971, p. 10.

_____. "Grat Dalton's Fatal Looking Glass." *The West*, December 1964; *Western Frontier*, November 1982, p. 32.

_____. "The Incredible Bill Dalton." *Real West*, January 1964, p. 36.

_____. "The Sorry Saga of Charley Pierce." *Real West*, November 1967, p. 18.

_____. "The Truth About Emmett Dalton." *Real West*, March 1966, p. 30.

Preston, Paul. "Wild Bill, the Indian-Slayer: A Tale of Forest and Prairie Life." *DeWitt's Ten Cent Romances*, no. 3. July 1867.

Price, G. G. *Death Comes to Billy the Kid.* Greensburg KS: Signal, 1940.

Priestley, Lee. *The Good Side of a Badman: Billy the Kid.* Arroyo, 1979.

Proett, Patrice North. "The Parson's Pants." *Rocky Mountain Life*, June 1949.

Pryor, Rafelita. "Siege of the McSween House." *Frontier Times*, May 1969.

Pryse, Dorothy. "Bill Hickok's Friends." *True West*, April 1978, p. 14.

Quale, J. L. "The Strange Love Affair Between Big Nose Kate and Doc Holliday." *Real West*, September 1964, p. 36.

Qualey, J. S. "How Doc Holliday Died." *Real West*, February 1959, p. 11; reprinted, *Real West Annual*, Summer 1966, p. 76.

_____. "The Legend of Belle Starr." *Famous Outlaws of the West*, American Library Book no. 2, Fall 1964.

Qualey, Jake. "Little Dick, the Terrible." *Real West*, November 1960, p. 24.

Raine, William MacLeod. *Famous Sheriffs and Western Outlaws.* Garden City NY: Doubleday, Doran, 1929.

_____. *45 Caliber Law, the Way of Life on the Frontier.* Evanston IL: 1941.

_____. *Guns of the Frontier.* New York: Houghton Mifflin Co., 1940.

_____. *The Story of the Outlaw: A Study of the Western Desperado.* New York: Outing, 1907.

_____, and Will C. Barnes. *Cattle, Cowboys, and Rangers.* New York: Grossett and Dunlap, circa 1930.

Raines, Lester G. "Billy the Kid." *The Pacific Monthly*, Vol. 20, no. 1, July 1908.

_____. *More New Mexico Writers and Writing.* Las Vegas: Department of English and Speech, New Mexico Normal University, 1935.

_____. *Writers and Writings of New Mexico.* Las Vegas: Department of English and Speech, New Mexico Normal University, 1934.

Rand, Phillip. "Frank Dalton." *Real West,* Fall 1965, p. 22.

Randisi, Robert J. *The Ham Reporter: Bat Masterson in New York.* Garden City NY: Doubleday, 1986.

Randolph, Vance. *Gun-Fighters of the Old West.* Girard KS: Haldeman-Julius, 1943.

Rasch, Philip J. "A Billy the Kid Incident." *NOLA Quarterly,* Vol. 4, no. 1, Fall 1978, p. 8.

_____. "The Bonney Brothers." *Frontier Times,* January 1965, p. 43.

_____. "Clues to the Puzzle of Billy the Kid." *English Westerners Brand Book,* Vol. 4, December 1957-January1958, p. 1.

_____. "Dave Rudabaugh, Gunman." *Real West,* November 1979, p. 18; reprinted, *Real West,* Special Issue, 1981, p. 46.

_____. Did Billy the Kid Kill Bronco Jake?" *NOLA Quarterly,* Vol. 8, no. 2, Autumn 1977, p. 12.

_____. "Farewell to the Clantons." *New York Westerners Brand Book,* Vol. 5, 1958, p. 43.

_____. "Five Days of Battle." *Denver Westerners Brand Book,* 23, 1963, p. 150.

_____. "The Governor Meets the Kid." *English Westerners Brand Book,* Vol. 8, April 1966, p. 5.

_____. "Gunfire in Lincoln County." *English Westerners Brand Book,* Vol. 9, no. 3, April 1967, p. 6.

_____. "How the Lincoln County War Started." *True West,* April 1962, p. 30.

_____. "The Hunting of Billy the Kid." Part I: *English Westerners Brand Book,* January 1969. Part II: *English Westerners Brand Book,* April 1969.

_____. "Jesse James in New Mexico Folklore." *New York Westerners Brand Book,* Vol. 4, 1957, p. 62.

_____. Letter. *True West,* August 1957, p. 45.

_____. "A Man Called Antrim." *Los Angeles Westerners Brand Book,* Vol. 6, 1956.

_____. "More on the McCartys." *English Westerners Brand Book,* Vol. 3, April 1957.

_____. "New Light on the Legend of Billy the Kid." *New Mexico Magazine,* Vol. 31, May 1953.

_____. "The Olingers, Known Yet Forgotten." *Potomac Westerners Corral Dust,* Vol. 8, no. 1, February 1963.

_____. "Prelude to War: The Murder of John Henry Tunstall." *English Westerners Brand Book,* Vol. 12, January 1970.

_____. "A Second Look at the Blazer's Mill Affair." *Frontier Times,* January 1969, p. 30.

_____. "The Short Life of Tom O'Folliard." *Potomac Westerners Corral Dust,* Vol. 5, July 1960, p. 20.

_____. "Sidelights on Billy the Kid." *NOLA Quarterly,* Vol. 8, no. 2, Fall 1983, p. 2.

_____. "Trailin' Billy the Kid, *Western Publications.* 220 pp.

_____. "The Trials of Billy the Kid." *Real West,* November 1987, p. 12.

_____. "The Twenty-One Men He Put Bullets Through." *New Mexico Folklore Record,* Vol. 9, 1954–1955.

_____. "The Violent Life of Warren Earp." *NOLA Quarterly,* Vol. 14, no. 1, 1990, p. 3.

_____. "War in Lincoln County." *English Westerners Brand Book,* Vol. 6, July 1964.

_____, and Robert N. Mullin. "Dim Trails: The Pursuit of the McCarty Family." *New Mexico Folklore Record,* Vol. 3, 1954.

Rascoe, Burton. *Belle Starr, the Bandit Queen.* New York: Random House, 1941.

Ray, Clarence E. *The Dalton Brothers: A Tale of Adventure in the Indian Territory, Together with the Desperate and Startling Criminal Career of the Gang.* Van Buren AR: Ryan, n.d.

Ray, Grace Ernestine. "Wiley Women of the West." *Real West,* Vol. 17, no. 128, July 1974.

_____. *Wild Women of the West.* San Antonio TX: Naylor, 1972.

Raymond, Charles. "The Man Who Killed the Man Who Killed Billy the Kid." *Real West*, March 1969, p. 48.

Raymond, Henry H. "Notes on Diary of H. H. Raymond of 1873." *Kansas Historical Quarterly*, Winter 1965, p. 360.

"The Real Wyatt Earp." *TV Guide*, May 2, 1959.

Recipes Used by Belle Starr Still Popular." *The Daily Oklahoman*, June 5, 1938.

Redfield, Georgia B. "Billy the Kid Rides the Chisum Trail." *The Cattleman*, Vol. 32, no. 10, March 1946.

Reed, Linda. "The Pulp Heroics of a Bandit King." *NOLA Quarterly*, Vol. 5, no. 4, April 1980, p. 9.

Reedstrom, E. Lisle. "Free the Youngers." *True West*, February 1991, p. 14.

_____. "Of Mines and Men." *Wild West*, Vol. 6, no. 5, February 1994, p. 34.

Reilly, Anthony. "Wyatt on the Set." *Premier*, January 1994, p. 28.

Reported Early Photo of Jesse James Discovered in Texas." Associated Press, December 30, 1996.

Repp, Ed Earl. "Belle Starr Saved My Life." *Real West*, Vol. 13, no. 79, February 1970.

_____. "Gun-Toting Female Killer." *Pioneer West*, Vol. 5, no. 2, April 1971, p. 36; reprinted, *Old Timers Wild West*, August 1973, p. 46; reprinted, *Pioneer West*, July 1976, p. 16.

_____. "Home Made Hero." *True Frontier*, December 1974, p. 19.

_____. "Last of the Old Time Outlaws." *True Frontier*, January 1974, p. 24; reprinted, *True Frontier*, Special Issue no. 17, Winter 1976, p. 6.

_____. "Massacre at Rock Creek." *The West*, April 1970, p. 38.

_____. "Who Was Bill Chadwell?" *Golden West*, November 1973, p. 38; reprinted, *Western Frontier*, September 1976, p. 2.

Resciora, Richard. "Killing Jim Miller." *Golden West*, November 1969, p. 16; reprinted, *The West*, December 1971, p. 10; reprinted, *Western Frontier*, Special Issue, Fall 1974, p. 32; reprinted, *Western Frontier*, January 1985, p. 12.

Rhodes, Eugene Manlove. "In Defense of Pat Garrett." *Sunset*, Vol. 59, no. 3, September 1927.

_____. *Once in the Saddle and Pasó por Aqui.* Boston: Houghton Mifflin, 1927.

_____. "Pasó por Aqui." Part I: *Saturday Evening Post*, Vol. 198, no. 34, February 20, 1926. Part II: *Saturday Evening Post*, Vol. 198, no 35, February 27, 1926.

Rice, Carolyn. "Lincoln, New Mexico: War and Peace in the Heart of Billy the Kid Country." *Historic Traveler*, October-November 1995, p. 14.

Rice, Mike. *Reminiscences of Early Tombstone.* Arizona Historical Society.

Richards, Jeffrey. *Visions of Yesterday.* London: Routledge and Kegan Paul, 1973.

Richardson, Leander P. "A Trip to the Black Hills." *Scribner's Monthly*, Vol. 13, February 1877.

Richardson, Rupert N. "The Comanche Plains History at the Adobe Walls Fight." *The Panhandle Plains Historical Review*, Vol. 1, 1931.

Rickards, Colin. "Bob Ford Tells 'How I Killed Jesse James.'" *Real West*, January 1970, p. 15.

_____. "Bones of the Northfield Robbers." *Real West*, January 1979, p. 28.

_____, Colin. "Pat Garrett Tells 'How I Killed Billy the Kid.'" *Real West*, Special Issue, Fall 1973, p. 30.

_____. "Wyatt Earp Tells About the Gunfight at the O. K. Corral." *Real West*, February 1970, p. 36; reprinted, *Real West*, Americana Series, Fall 1973, p. 39.

Rickell, Water. "Found: The Revolver Frank James Used." *Westerner*, July-August 1974, p. 41.

Rieupeyrout, Jean-Louis. *À grande aventur du western.* Paris: Editions du Cerf, 1964.

Ringgold, Jennie Parks. *Frontier Days in the Southwest.* San Antonio TX: Naylor, 1952.

Ripple, Sam. "Billy's Murderous Deed." *Westerner*, November-December 1973, p. 37.

_____. "Doc Holliday's Girl." *Westerner*, November-December 1971, p. 48.

Riske, Milt. "Wild Bill's Women." *Real West*, March 1980, p. 22.

Roberts, Captain Dan W. *Rangers and Sovereignty*. San Antonio TX: Wood, 1914.

Roberts, Gary L. "The Brothers of Bat Masterson." *Frontier Times*, June-July 1963, p. 23.

_____. "Earp Brothers." In Howard R. Lamar, ed., *The Readers Encyclopedia of the American West*. New York: Thomas Y. Crowell, 1977, pp. 327–29.

_____. "The Fight That Never Dies." *Frontier Times*, November 1965, p. 48.

_____. "The Freemont Street Fiasco." *True West*, July 1988, p. 14.

_____. "The Gunfight at the O. K. Corral: The Wells Spicer Decision, 1881." *Montana the Magazine of Western History*, Vol. 20, January 1970, pp. 62–74.

_____. "The Night Wyatt Earp Almost KO'ed Boxing." *The West*, April 1966, p. 14; reprinted, *The West*, November 1971, p. 10.

_____. "Was Wyatt Earp Really a U. S. Deputy Marshal?" *True West*, February 1961, p. 30.

Roberts, J. B. Letter. *Real West*, April 1980, p. 6.

Roberts, J. R. *The Gunsmith—Three Guns for Glory*. New York: Ace Charter, 1982.

_____. *The Gunsmith—Trouble in Tombstone*. New York: Jove, 1993.

Robertson, Ruth T. *Famous Bandits; Brief Accounts of the Lives of Jesse James, Cole Younger, Billy the Kid and Others*. Washington DC: 1928.

Robinson, Ruth. "Belle Starr Dramatized." *Oklahoma News*, April 25, 1937.

Roemer, Joseph. "The Third Man: Wyatt Earp." *True Western Adventures*, February 1960, p. 15.

Rolt-Wheeler, Francis. *The Book of Cowboys*. Boston: Lothrop, Lee & Shepard, 1921.

Rosa, Joseph G. *Age of the Gunfighter: Men and Weapons on the Frontier 1840–1900*. Norman: University of Oklahoma Press, 1995.

_____. *Alias Jack McCall*. Kansas City: 1967.

_____. "George Ward Nichols and the Legend of Wild Bill Hickok." *Arizona and the West*, Vol. 19, no. 2, Summer 1977.

_____. "The Girl and the Gunfighter: A Newly Discovered Photograph of Wild Bill Hickok." *Real West*, December 1984, p. 18.

_____. *The Gunfighter: Man or Myth?* Norman: University of Oklahoma Press, 1969.

_____. "How Mr. Hickok Really Came to Cheyenne." *Kansas and the West*. Kansas State Historical Society, 1976.

_____. "J. B. Hickok, Deputy U. S. Marshal." *Kansas History*, Vol. 2, no. 4, Winter 1979.

_____. *The Taming of the West*. New York: Smithmark, 1993.

_____. *They Called Him Wild Bill: The Life and Adventures of James Butler Hickok*. 2d ed. Norman: University of Oklahoma Press, 1974.

_____. "Was Wild Bill Photo Taken Here?" *Mendora* (Illinois) *Reporter*, July 13, 1977.

_____. *The West of Wild Bill Hickok*. Norman: University of Oklahoma Press, 1982.

_____. "Wild Bill and the Timber Thieves." *Real West*, April 1982, p. 12; reprinted, *Real West*, Special Issue, Spring 1983, p. 54.

_____, and Robin May. *Gun Law: A Study of Violence in the Wild West*. Chicago: Contemporary, 1977.

Rosca, Burton. *Belle Starr: The Bandit Queen*. New York: 1947.

Roy, Robert. "Oklahoma's Bandit Hideout." *Real West Yearbook*, Summer 1978.

_____. "The True Story of Wyatt Earp." *Real West Yearbook*, Summer 1977, p. 36.

Rozar, Lily B. "Inside the Dalton Legend." *The West*, August 1972, p. 32; reprinted, *Western Frontier*, Special Issue September 1975, p. 8; reprinted, *Western Frontier*, July 1977, p. 32; reprinted, *Western Frontier*, Special Issue, November 1982, p. 22.

Rozar, Lily B. "Quantrill's Bloody Trail." *Western Round-Up*, May 1970, p. 16.

Russell, C. M. "Some Incidents of Western Life." *Scribner's Magazine*, Vol. 37, no. 2, February 1902.

Russell, Don. *The Wild West: or, A History of the Wild West Shows.* Fort Worth: Amon Carter Museum, 1970.

_____. *Life of the Honorable William Frederick Cody, Known as Buffalo Bill.* Norman: University of Oklahoma Press, 1960.

Rybolt, Robert. "Wild Bill Murder Plot." *True West*, July 1985, p. 42.

Sabin, dmund Legrand. *Wild Men of the Wild West.* New York: Thomas Y. Crowell, 1929.

Sailor, John Noble. "Untold Facts About the Daltons." *Real West*, August 1958, p. 18.

St. George, Tim. "Were the Daltons Guilty?" *Real West*, January 1962, p. 18.

St. John, Harvey. "Wyatt Earp As I Knew Him." *Real West*, November 1965, p. 22.

St. Johns, Adela Roberts. "I Knew Wyatt Earp." *American Weekly*, May 22, 1960, p. 10.

St. Joseph Daily Gazette, Saint Louis, Missouri, April 9, 1882.

Saint Louis (Missouri) *Weekly Missouri Democrat.* Various issues, 1867 and 1873.

Samuelson, Nancy B. "The Dalton Gang Family: Geneological Study of the Daltons and Their Family Connection." Pamphlet, August 1989.

_____. *The Dalton Gang Story*, Shooting Star Press. 183 pp.

_____. "Emmett and Julia: A Dalton Myth." *NOLA Quarterly*, Vol. 14, no. 2, Summer 1990, p. 6.

Sanchez, Lynda A. "They Loved Billy the Kid: To Them He Was "Billito.'" *True West*, January 1984, p. 12.

Sandell, Jay. "The Tragic Story of Wild Bill Hickok." *Real West*, August 1959, p. 30; reprinted, *Real West Annual*, Summer 1966, p. 34.

_____. "Whistling Bill: Nemesis of the Youngers." *Real West*, May 1960, p. 32.

_____. "Wild Bill Hickok." *Real West*, Americana Series, Fall 1965, p. 10.

Sanders, John R. "Faro: Favorite Gambling Game of the Frontier." *Wild West*, Vol. 9, no. 3, October 1996, p. 62.

Sanders, William Peery. *Days That Are Gone.* Los Angeles: Grafton, 1918.

Sandoz, Mari. *The Buffalo Hunters.* New York: 1954.

Sarf, Wayne Michall. *God Bless You, Buffalo Bill: A Layman's Guide to History of the Western Film.* East Brunswick NJ: Cornwall Book/Fairleigh Dickinson Press, 1983. Pp. 45–61.

Savage, William W., Jr. "Western Literature and Its Myths: A Rejoinder." *Montana the Magazine of Western History*, Vol. 22, October 1972.

Sawyer, Eugene T. *Buffalo Bill and Billy the Kid; or The Desperadoes of Apache Land.* The Buffalo Bill Stories, no. 268. New York: Street and Smith, June 30, 1906.

Scanland, J. M. "Lurid Trails are Left by Olden Day Bandits." *Los Angeles Times*, March 12, 1922.

Scanland, John Milton. *Life of Pat Garrett and the Taming of the Border Outland.* El Paso: Southwestern, 1908.

Scates, Roy J. "Famous Gun Fighters I Knew." *Great Guns*, Vol. 4, no. 3, March 1955.

Scheide, Frank. "Mythicized Gunfighters of the Old West." *The Velvet Light Trap*, no. 8, 1973, pp. 29–33.

Schillingberg, William B. "Wyatt Earp and the Buntline 'Special' Myth." *Kansas State Historical Quarterly*, Summer 1976.

_____. *Wyatt Earp and the Buntline Special Myth.* Tucson AZ: Blaine, 1976.

Schoenberger, Dale T. *The Gunfighter.* Caldwell ID: Caxton, 1971.

Schofield, Henry W. "Dead Man's Hand." *Trails End*, Vol. 2, no. 2, August-September 1996, p. 67.

Schuessler, Raymond. "Bill Langley: Thirty Notch Gunman." *Real West*, February 1969, p. 17.

Scullin, George. "The Killer." *Holiday*, August 1954.

Secrest, William B. "Bill Hickok's Girl on the Flying Trapeze." *Old West*, Winter 1967, p. 26.

_____. "Wild Bill Hickok: On Shooting." *True Frontier*, March 1971, p. 32; reprinted, *True Frontier*, Special Issue no. 11, Winter 1974-75, p. 26.

_____. "Wild Bill's Wild Women." *True Frontier*, May 1969, p. 8.

Settle, William A., Jr. *Jesse James Was His Name: Or, Fact and Fiction Concerning the Careers of the Notorious James Brothers of Missouri.* Columbia: University of Missouri Press, 1966.

Shackelford, Jake. *Jesse, the Outlaw: A Narrative of the James Boys.* New York: Street and Smith, April 1883.

Shackelford, William Yancey. *Belle Starr, the Bandit Queen: The Career of the Most Colorful Outlaw the Indian Territory Ever Knew.* Girard KS: Haldeman-Julius, 1943.

_____. *Gun-Fighters of the Old West.* Girard KS: Haldeman-Julius, 1943.

Shannon, Malone. "Those Bumptious Custers." *Golden West*, Vol. 9, no. 12, November 1973, p. 10.

Sherman, Jory. "Death Dealing Dentist." *Big West*, October 1967, p. 38.

Shipman, Jack (Mrs. O. L. Shipman). "Brief Careers of Tom O'Follard, Billy the Kid's Partner." *The Voice of the Mexican Border*, January 1934.

Shirley, Glenn. *Belle Starr and Her Times: The Literature, the Facts, and the Legends.* Norman: University of Oklahoma Press, 1982.

_____. *Guardian of the Law: The Life and Times of William Matthew Tilgehman.* Austin TX: Eskin, 1988.

_____. *Heck Thomas.* Norman: University of Oklahoma Press, 1981.

_____. "How Belle Starr Got to Be a Desperate Woman." *True West*, September 1982, p. 10.

_____. *Law West of Fort Smith: A History of Frontier Justice in the Indian Territory, 1834–1896.* New York: Henry Holt, 1957.

_____. "Outlaw Queen." *Old West*, Spring 1965, p. 26; reprinted, *Badman*, Summer 1971, p. 8.

_____. *Outlaw Queen.* Derby CT: Monarch, 1960.

_____. *Shotgun for Hire: The Story of "Deacon" Jim Miller, Killer of Pat Garrett.* Norman: University of Oklahoma Press, 1970.

_____. *Six-Gun and Silver Star.* Albuquerque: University of New Mexico Press, 1995.

_____. *Toughest of Them All.* Albuquerque: University of New Mexico Press, 1953.

_____. *West of Hell's Fringe: Crime, Criminals, and the Federal Peace Officer in Oklahoma Territory.* Norman: University of Oklahoma Press, 1978.

Short, K. R. M., ed. *Feature Films as History.* Knoxville: University of Tennessee Press, 1981.

Short, Wayne. *Luke Short: A Biography,* Tombstone: Devil's Thumb Press, 1997.

Shouse, T. R. "Origin of Plan Which Resulted in Jesse James' Death." *Missouri Historical Review*, Vol. 34, no. 1, October 1939.

Shull, Dana. "Losers' View of the O. K. Corral." *Wild West*, October 1995, p. 50.

Silva, Lee. "The Wyatt Earp/Buntline Special Controversy." *Quarterly of the National Association for Outlaw and Lawmen History*, Vol. 18, October–December, 1994, pp. 44–50.

Silver City Mining Life, September 19, 1874.

Simmons, M. *Ranchers, Ramblers, and Renegades: True Tales of the Southwest.* Virginia City, NV: Sun Mountain.

_____. *When Six Guns Ruled: Outlaw Tales of the Southwest.* Virginia City NV: Sun Mountain.

Simpson, H. O. "Early Day Gunmen Gave Color to Picturesque Setting of Dodge City." *Topeka Daily Capital*, December 9, 1934.

Siringo, Charles A. "The Capture of Billy the Kid." *Big West*, December 1969, p. 12.

_____. *A Cowboy Detective.* Chicago: W. B. Conkey, 1912.

_____. *History of Billy the Kid.* Santa Fe: Privately printed, 1920.

_____. *A Lone Star Cowboy.* Santa Fe: Privately printed, 1919.

_____. *A Texas Cowboy, or Fifteen Years on the Hurricane Deck of a Spanish Pony—Taken from Real Life.* New York: William Sloane, 1950; University of New Mexico Press, 1981.

_____. *Riata and Spurs.* Boston and New York: Houghton Mifflin, 1927.

Slatta, Richard W. "Old West Outlaws." *Cowboys and Indians,* Winter 1996, p. 96.

Slight, J. E. "Billy-the-Kid." *Overland Monthly,* Vol. 52, no. 1, July 1908.

_____. "The Lincoln County War—A Sequel to the Story of 'Billy-the-Kid.'" *Overland Monthly,* Vol. 52, no. 1, August 1908.

Slotkin, Richard. *Gunfighter Nation: The Myth of the Frontier in Twentieth-Century America.* New York: Atheneum, 1992, pp. 379–390.

_____. *Regeneration Through Violence, the Mythology of the American Frontier 1600–1860.* Middleton CT: 1974.

Smith, Donald C. *In Defense of Billy; the Truth About Billy the Kid and His Participation in the Lincoln County War and Its Aftermath.* Brushy Bill, 1991.

Smith, Joe Heflin. "The Tragic Life of Pat Garrett." *Real West,* January 1968, p. 10.

Smith, Paul. "The Kid." *Westerner,* November-December 1971, p. 16.

Smith, Robert Barr. "Dalton Gang's Mystery Rider at Coffeyville." *Wild West,* October 1995, p. 64.

_____. *Daltons! The Raid on Coffeyville, Kansas.* Norman: University of Oklahoma Press, 1996.

_____. "No God West of Fort Smith." *Wild West,* October 1991, p. 46.

_____. "The Short, Short Nasty Life of Dave Rudabaugh." *Wild West,* August 1996, p. 40.

Smith, Wilbur. "The Amigo of 'Billy the Kid.'" *New Mexico,* April 1933, Vol. 2, no. 4.

Smith, William R. "Death in Doña Ana County." Part I: *English Westerners Brand Book,* Vol. 9, no. 2, January 1967, p. 12. Part II: *English Westerners Brand Book,* Vol. 9, no. 3, April 1967, p. 1. Part I reprinted, *Western Frontier,* September 1977, p. 12. Part II reprinted, *Golden West,* May 1974, p. 12.

Snell, Joseph P., ed. "The Diary of a Dodge City Buffalo Hunter, 1872–1873." *Kansas State Historical Quarterly,* Winter 1965.

Snyder, Robert M., Jr. "The Kansas City Days of Wild Bill." *Kansas City Star Magazine,* Vol. 3, no. 4, August 15, 1926, p. 3.

Sommer, Robert Langley. *The History of the U. S. Marshals, the Proud Story of America's Legendary Lawmen.*

Sonnichsen, C. L. "Pat Garrett's Last Ride." *True West,* December 1958, p. 4.

_____. *Tombstone: The Private Life of an Arizona Boom Town.* Tucson: University of Arizona Press, 1972.

_____. *Tularosa: Last of the Frontier West.* Albuquerque: University of New Mexico Press.

_____. "The Wyatt Earp Syndrome." *The American West,* Vol. 7, May 1970, pp. 60–62.

_____, and William V. Morrison. *Alias Billy the Kid.* Albuquerque: University of New Mexico Press, 1955.

Sooner, Norman. "Hickok: Longhaired Rebel or National Hero?" *Westerner,* August 1971, p. 14.

Sooner, Paul. "Earp: The Man Who Invented His Own Legend." *Westerner,* October 1971, p. 41.

Sparks, Elmer W. Letter. "Hickok: Hero or Heel?" *True West,* June 1956, p. 28.

Speer, Bonnie Stahlman. *Portrait of a Lawman: U. S. Deputy Marshal Heck Thomas.* Norman OK: Reliance, 1996.

Spivey, Louis E. "James Home Restoration." *Frontier Times,* February 1985, p. 62.

Stanley, F. (pseud. of Stanley Crocchiola). *Dave Rudabaugh: Border Ruffian.* Denver: 1961.

_____. *Desperadoes of New Mexico,* aka *The Las Vegas Story.* Denver: 1951.

Stanley, Henry M. [Title Unknown.] *Weekly Missouri Democrat*, April 4, 1867.

Stanley, Samuel. "Bill Tilghman Was the Toughest Lawman of Them All." *Frontier West*, October 1973, p. 14.

Stansbery, Lon R. "Early Oklahoma Outlaws Contributed by Many States." *Tulsa World*, February 7, 1937.

Starnes, Lee. "The Legend of Jesse James." *Museum Graphic*, Vol. 4, no. 2, Spring 1952.

State Herald (Ardmore Indian Territory), May 24, 1894.

Steckmesser, Kent Ladd. *The Western Hero in History and Legend*. Norman: University of Oklahoma Press, 1965.

Steele, Philip W. "Belle Starr Museum Dedicated." *True West*, November 1991, p. 9.

———. "The Bullet That Killed Jesse James." *True West*, October 1987, p. 50.

———. "The Dalton Family Found in California." *NOLA Quarterly*, Vol. 9, no. 3, July–September 1991, p. 2.

———. "The Daltons After Coffeyville." *NOLA Quarterly*, Vol. 9, no. 1, Summer 1984, p. 2.

———. "James Brothers' Death Hoax." *NOLA Quarterly*, Vol. 8, no. 3, Winter 1983, p. 14.

———. "Jesse James Slept Here." *True West*, June 1986, p. 40.

———. "Jesse James' Tombstone." *True West*, December 1988, p. 46.

———. "Jim Reed, Outlaw." *NOLA Quarterly*, Vol. 14, Nos. 3 and 4 (combined issue), 1990, p. 4.

———. *Starr Tracks: Belle and Pearl Starr*, Gretna, LA: Pelican, 112 pp.

———. "The Woman Red Buck Couldn't Scare." *The West*, April 1971, p. 20; reprinted, *Western Frontier*, Special Issue, Fall 1974, p. 12.

———, and George Warfel. *The Many Faces of Jesse James*. 128 pp.

Steinke, Rick. Letter. *True West*, August 1957, p. 46.

Stevens, Ray W., Jr. "Hickok the Hero." *True West*, December 1955, p. 12; reprinted, *Badman Annual*, 1971, p. 30.

Stevenson, Phillip. "Prelude to Murder." *Southwest Review*, Vol. 14, no. 3, Spring 1929.

Stiles, Bill. "I Was Hanged by Jesse James." *The West*, November 1973, p. 34.

———. "I Was the Last of the James Gang." *True Frontier*, June 1972, p. 18.

———. "The James Gang and the Bounty Hunters." *Real Frontier*, August 1970, p. 16; reprinted, *True Frontier*, Special Issue no. 1, 1971, p. 24.

———. "Who Was Bill Chadwell?" *Golden West*, Vol. 9, no. 12, November 1973, p. 38; reprinted, *Western Frontier*, September 1976, p. 2.

Stillman, W. K., and Cy Martin. "Was Billy the Kid a Psychopathic Killer?" *Golden West*, December 1965, p. 30; reprinted, *Western Frontier*, January 1978, p. 12; reprinted, *Western Frontier*, November 1982, p. 28.

Stillwater (Oklahoma) *Gazette*, December 29, 1893.

Street Fight in Tombstone Near the O. K. Corral. Honolulu: Telei.

Streeter, Floyd Benjamin. *Ben Thompson: Man with a Gun*. New York: Frederick Fell, 1957.

———. *Prairie Trails and Cow Towns*. New York: Devin Adair, 1963.

Strong, Zachary. "Tombstone's Billy the Kid." *Real Western*, Vol. 16, no. 6, April 1951.

Stuart, N. *The Life and Times of Wyatt Earp*. New York: Houghton-Mifflin, 1956.

Sufrin, Mark. "Desperate Manhunt in the Oklahoma Territory." *Frontier West*, June 1971, p. 10.

———. "The Massacre at Adobe Walls." *Frontier West*, October 1972, p. 12.

Sullivan et al. *Gunfight at the O. K. Corral and Other Western Adventures*. New York: Avon, 1957.

Summers, Neil. "Robert Taylor, the Handsomest Billy the Kid." *Favorite Western*, no. 17, 1984.

Sutton, Felix. *The Picture Story of Wyatt Earp.* New York: Simon and Schuster, 1958.

Sutton, Fred E. "Belle Starr, Queen of Outlaws." *The 101 Magazine*, Vol. 2, no. 4, June 1926.

_____. "Fill Your Hand." *Saturday Evening Post*, Vol. 198, no. 41, April 10, 1926.

_____. As written down by A. B. MacDonald. *Hands Up! Stories of the Six-Gun Fighters of the Old Wild West.* Indianapolis: Bobbs-Merrill, 1927.

Swan, Oliver G., ed. *Frontier Days.* Romance of America's History Series. Philadelphia: Macrae-Smith, 1928.

Synar, Joe, and Richard Venator. "Lonely Memorial in Hills Marks Grave of Woman Outlaw, Belle Starr." *Muskogee* (Oklahoma) *Daily Phoenix*, January 5, 1936.

Tallent, Annie D. *The Black Hills; or, The Last Hunting Grounds of the Dakotas.* St. Louis: 1899.

Targ, William, ed. *Western Story Omnibus.* Cleveland and New York: World, 1945.

Tatum, Stephen. *Inventing Billy the Kid: Visions of the Outlaw in America 1881–1981.* Albuquerque: University of New Mexico Press, 1982.

Taylor, Drew Kirksey. *Taylor's Thrilling Tales of Texas.* Privately printed, 1926.

Taylor, Paul. "Wyatt Earp's Town." *Old West*, Spring 1989, p. 60.

Taylor, T. U. *The Chisholm Trail and Other Routes.* San Antonio TX: Naylor, 1936.

_____. "John Simpson Chism and His Kin." *Frontier Times*, December 1937, Vol. 15, no. 3.

Thede, Marion, and Harold Preece. "The Ballad of Jesse James: The Story Behind the Song." *Real West*, September 1973, p. 8.

Thomas, Leva L. "A Family Letter Regarding the Youngers." *True West*, October 1972, p. 34.

Thomas, Robert L. "Gunfight at Iron Springs." *True West*, February 1965, p. 38.

_____. "I Think Earp Took Johnny Ringo." *Old West*, Fall 1972, p. 13.

Thomason, Hugh. "The Dirty Little Coward Who Shot My Howard." *True Western Adventures*, Summer 1958, p. 4.

Thompson, Anne. "Shoot First, Ask Questions Later." *Entertainment Weekly*, December 24, 1993, p. 32.

Thompson, George G. *Bat Masterson: The Dodge City Years.* Language and Literature Series, no. 1. F. B. Streeter, Editor; General Series, no. 6. Topeka: Kansas State Printing Plant, 1943.

Thorndike, Thaddeus. *Lives and Exploits of Frank and Jesse James.* Baltimore: Ottenheimer, 1909.

Thorp, Raymond W. "Mr. Howard of Tennessee." *The Graphic*, Vol. 6, no. 2, February 1925.

_____. "Wild Bill's Famous Bullet." *Real West*, May 1961, p. 18.

_____. "Wyatt Earp: A Triple Acquaintance." *Frontier Times*, March 1963, p. 24.

Thrapp, Dan. *Encyclopedia of Frontier Biography.* 3 vols. Spokane WA: A. H. Clark, 1988.

"Three Officers, Three Bandits, Two Citizens Killed." *Eagle Gazette* (Stillwater, Oklahoma Territory), April 27, 1894.

Tilghman, Zoe A. *Outlaw Days: A True History of Early-Day Oklahoma Characters.* Oklahoma City: Harlow, 1926.

_____. *Spotlight: Bat Masterson and Wyatt Earp as U. S. Deputy Marshals.* San Antonio TX: Naylor, 1960.

Time-Life Editors. *The Wild West.* Alexandria VA: Time-Life.

Times (London), April 20, 1894.

Tippette, Giles. *Tombstone.* Novelization of the Kevin Jarre screenplay. New York: Berkeley, 1994.

Toepperwein, Herman. *Showdown.* Rotan TX: Bennett-Walls.

Tombstone, Arizona, Photo Album: The Town Too Tough to Die. Vienna WV: Old West Shop.

Tombstone Epitaph, October 27, 1881, and November 1, 1881.

Topeka Capital, August 30, 1908.

Topeka Daily Commonwealth, Various issues, 1870–71.

Topeka Mail and Breeze, September–December 1901.

Topeka State Record, Various issues, 1869–70.

Towns, Leroy. "Was Belle Starr Killed by Mistake?" *True West*, April 1971, p. 20.

Townshend, R. B. *The Tenderfoot in New Mexico*. Preface by Dorothea Townshend. London: Bodley Head, 1923.

Traylor, Leslie. "Facts Regarding the Escape of Billy the Kid." *Frontier Times*, Vol. 13, no. 9, July 1936.

Traywick, Ben. "Big Nose Kate and Other Ladies of Tombstone." *True Frontier*, April 1972, p. 8.

_____. "Boothill." *Wild West*, October 1995, p. 57.

_____. *Chronicles of Tombstone*. Tombstone AZ: Red Marie's Bookstore.

_____. *The Clantons of Tombstone*. Tombstone AZ: Red Marie's Bookstore, 1996.

_____. *Ghost Towns and Lost Treasures*. Tombstone AZ: Red Marie's Bookstore.

_____. *Hell's Belles*. Tombstone AZ: Red Marie's Bookstore.

_____. *Historical Documents and Photographs of Tombstone*. Tombstone AZ: Red Marie's Bookstore.

_____. *John Henry*. Tombstone AZ: Red Marie's Bookstore, 1996.

_____. *Legendary Characters of Southeast Arizona*. Tombstone AZ: Red Marie's Bookstore.

_____. "The Lost Grave of Johnny Behan." *True West*, July 1991, p. 48.

_____. "The Murder of Warren Baxter Earp." *Old West*, Winter 1990, p. 53.

_____. "Old Man Clanton Ran Cattle on the Border Until He Ran Out of Luck on the Way to Tombstone." *Wild West*, Vol. 10, no. 3, October 1997, pp. 12–20.

_____. "The Real Doc Holliday." *Wild West*, Vol. 10, no. 3, October 1997, pp. 36–42.

_____. *Tombstone Clippings*. Tombstone AZ: Red Marie's Bookstore.

_____. *Tombstone's Boothill*. Tombstone AZ: Red Marie's Bookstore.

Triplett, Frank. *The Life, Times and Treacherous Death of Jesse James*. Chicago: J. H. Chambers, 1882.

True Tales from Old Tombstone. Audio book available from Bookmart, Stillwater, Oklahoma.

Tunstall, John H. "A Document of the Lincoln County War: John H. Tunstall's Letter to His Parents." *New Mexico Folklore Record*, Vol. 10, 1955–1956.

_____. Letter. *Mesilla Independent*, January 27, 1878.

Turner, Alford E. "Colton's Marshal Earp." *Real West*, March 1981, p. 28; reprinted, *Real West Annual*, Spring 1982, p. 52.

_____. *The Earps Talk*. College Station TX: Creative Publishing, 1980.

_____. "The Florentino-Earp Affair." *Real West*, January 1979, p. 16; reprinted, *Real West Yearbook*, 1980, p. 44.

_____. *The O. K. Corral Inquest*. College Station TX: Early West.

_____. "Wyatt Earp's Unique Faro Game." *Real West*, June 1986, p. 48.

Turner, Brian P. "The James-Younger Gang: Some Profitable Time Spent in Kentucky." *Real West*, December 1982, p. 41.

_____. "The James-Younger Gang in Kentucky." *Real West*, Special Issue, Spring 1985, p. 8.

_____. "The James-Younger Robbery in Columbia." *True West*, February 1982, p. 61.

Turner, Russell M. Letter. *True West*, August 1957, p. 47.

Tuska, Jon. *The American West in Films: Critical Approaches to the Western*. Westport CT: Greenwood, 1985.

_____. *Billy the Kid: A Bio-Bibliography* Westport CT: Greenwood, 1983.

_____. *Billy the Kid: A Handbook*. Lincoln: University of Nebraska Press, 1983.

_____. *A Variable Harvest: Essays and Reviews of Film and Literature*. Jefferson NC: McFarland, 1990.

Twitchell, Ralph Emerson. *The Leading Facts on New Mexico History*, Vol. 2. Cedar Rapids IA: Torch, 1912.

Uhlarik, Carl. Letter. *Real West*, April 1969, p. 75.

United States vs. Belle Starr, Case no. 1180, U. S. District Court, Western District of Arkansas, Fort Smith.

United States vs. Sam and Belle Starr, Case no. 2370, U. S. District Court, Western District of Arkansas, Fort Smith.

Utley, Robert M. *Billy the Kid*. Lincoln: University of Nebraska Press, 1989.

_____. *Four Fighters of Lincoln County*. Albuquerque: University of New Mexico Press, 1986.

_____. *High Noon in Lincoln: Violence on the Western Frontier*. Albuquerque: University of New Mexico Press.

Van Slyke, Sue C. Letter. *Old West* ("Trails Grown Dim"), Spring 1980, p. 60.

_____. "The Truth About the Clantons of Tombstone." *NOLA Quarterly*, Vol. 2, no. 1, Spring 1975, p. 8.

_____, and Dave Johnson. "Kin to the Clantons." *NOLA Quarterly*, Vol. 14, no. 2, Summer 1990, p. 8.

Varga, Jon. "The Davis Tutt—Wild Bill Hickok Showdown had Dramatic Buildup and Face-to-Face Action." *Wild West*, August 1996, p. 22.

Vestal, Stanley. *Queen of Cowtowns, Dodge City: The Wickedest Little City in America, 1872–1886*. New York: Harper, 1952.

Vidal, Gore. *Screening History*. Cambridge: Harvard University Press, 1992.

Virgines, George E. "The Weapons of Wyatt Earp." *Golden West*, January 1970, p. 16; reprinted, *Western Frontier Annual*, Winter 1977, p. 38.

Walker, Henry J. *Jesse James, the Outlaw*. Des Moines: Wallace-Homestead, 1961.

Walker, Wayne T. "The Day the Outlaws Came to Town." *The West*, November 1971, p. 30; reprinted, *Western Frontier*, September 1979, p. 30.

_____. "How Many Bullets Did It Take to Kill Jesse James?" *Frontier West*, January 1976, p. 41.

_____. "To Hell in a Tumble Weed Wagon." *Oldtimers Wild West*, October 1979, p. 22.

_____. "The Truth About the Dodge City War." *Real West*, March 1970, p. 28.

_____. "When the Dalton Brothers Wore the White Hats." *Real West*, July 1981, p. 32; reprinted, *Real West Annual*, Spring 1982, p. 28.

Wallace, William. "How the James Gang Was Wiped Off the Face of the Earth." *Kansas City World*, November 8, 1898.

Walter, Helen Louise. "A Murdering So-and-So." *Motion Picture Classic*, Vol. 31, no. 6, August 1930.

Walters, Lorenzo D. *Tombstone's Yesterdays*. Tucson AZ: Acme, 1928.

Walters, Raymond L. "Jesse James' Double." *True West*, Vol. 31, no. 7, July 1984, pp. 17, 39.

Walton, William. *Life and Adventures of Ben Thompson, the Famous Texan*. Austin TX: Walton, Edwards, and Church, 1884.

Ward, George C. *The West: An Illustrated History*. Introduction by Steven Ives and Ken Burns.

Warner, A. "Western Heroes." *Films and Filming*, Vol. 18, no. 5, February 1972, pp. 34–40.

"Was Jesse James Shot with His Own Gun?" *Great Guns*, Vol. 2, no. 4, April 1953.

Wasserman, Murray. "Another View of the O.K. Corral Shoot-out." *Great West*, April 1967, p. 17.

Waters, Frank. *The Earp Brothers of Tombstone: The Story of Mrs. Virgil Earp*. New York: Clarkson N. Potter, 1960.

Watson, Frederick. *A Century of Gunmen*. London: Ivor Nicholson & Watson, 1931.

Watson, James A. "The Battle of Adobe Walls." *True Western Adventures*, no. 1, 1957, p. 6.

Watts, P. *Dictionary of the Old West.* Virginia City NV: Sun Mountain.

"The Weapons of Wyatt Earp." *Best of the West,* 1973 Annual.

"Weather-Beaten Hut Still Stands, Amid Chat Piles, Monument to Outlaw Days." *The Daily Oklahoman,* August 11, 1918.

Weaver, Barry Roland. "Jesse James in Arkansas: The War Years." *Arkansas History Quarterly,* Vol. 23, no. 4, Winter 1968.

Weekly Oklahoma State Capitol (Guthrie, Oklahoma Territory), February 8, 1894.

Weekly Patriot (Springfield MO), July 27, 1865, p. 3, col. 1.

Weisner, Herman B. "Outlaw Rock." *True West,* March 1982, p. 48.

_____. "Pistol or Shotgun: Which Killed Billy?" *Old West,* Summer 1981, p. 48.

Weisser, Thomas. *Spaghetti Westerns—the Good, the Bad and the Violent: A Comprehensive, Illustrated Filmography of 558 Eurowesterns and Their Personnel, 1961–1977.* Jefferson NC: McFarland, 1992.

Wellman, Paul I. *A Dynasty of Western Outlaws.* Garden City NY: Doubleday, 1961.

_____. *Trampling Herd.* Philadelphia: Lippincott, 1939; NY: Corrick & Evans, 1939.

Wesley, Paul H. "Bandit Samaritan." *New Mexico,* Vol. 17, no. 10, October 1939.

West, Elliott. "The Saloons of Territorial Arizona." *Journal of the West,* Vol. 13, July 1974, pp. 61–73.

_____. "Shots in the Dark: Television and the Western Myth." *Montana: The Magazine of Western History,* Vol. 38, Spring 1988.

West, Jeffrey D. *Custer: The Controversial Life of George Armstrong Custer.* New York: Simon & Schuster, 1996.

West, Richard. *Television Westerns: Major and Minor Series, 1946–1978.* Jefferson NC: McFarland, 1987.

"A Western Desperado." *NOLA Quarterly,* Vol. 15, no. 1, 1991.

Westerners Brand Book, Vol. 3, no. 4, June 1946.

"Westerns: The Six-Gun Galahad." *Time,* Vol. 73, March 30, 1959, pp. 57, 60.

Westwood, Dick. "Secret Meetings with Billy the Kid." *NOLA Quarterly,* Vol. 11, no. 4, Spring 1987, p. 12.

Wheeler, Homer W. *The Frontier Trail.* Los Angeles: Times-Mirror, 1923.

White, Owen P. "Billy the Kid." Part I: *Collier's: The National Weekly,* Vol. 76, no. 20, November 14, 1925. Part II: *Collier's: The National Weekly,* Vol. 76, no. 21, November 21, 1925.

_____. *Lead and Likker.* New York: Minton, Balch, 1932.

White, Richard. "Outlaw Gangs of the Middle Border: American Social Bandits." *The Western Historical Quarterly,* Vol. 12, no. 4, October 1981, p. 384.

Whittlesey, D. H. "He Said 'Hell No' to the Daltons." *Golden West,* May 1974, p. 38.

Wichita Beacon, May 12, 1875.

"Wild Bill's Ride." *True West,* Winter 1953, p. 48.

Williams, Jack. "Goldfield and the Wyatt Earp I Knew." *Frontier Times,* Winter 1959-60, p. 16.

Wilson, Robert L. "Slaughter at Rock Creek Station." *Westerner,* May-June, 1969, p. 48.

Wilstach, Frank J. *Wild Bill Hickok: The Prince of Pistoleers.* New York: Doubleday & Page, 1926.

Wiltsey, Norman B. "Billy the Kid." *True Western Adventure,* February 1959, p. 14.

_____. "Billy the Kid: Ruffian or Robin Hood?" Part I: *Real West,* October 1970, p. 35. Part II: *Real West,* November 1970, p. 46.

_____. "Clay Allison, Laughing Killer." *Real West,* Vol. 17, no. 123, January 1974, p. 32.

_____. "The Hard Road Back." *Real West,* February 1974, p. 38.

_____. "Killer Kid." *True West,* April, 1957.

_____. "A Man Called Bat." *True West,* December 1956.

Winfield, Craig. "The Adventurous Saga of Wyatt Earp." *Pioneer West*, September 1977, p. 6.

_____. "Bill Doolin's Bold Hold-Up," *Westerner*, January-February 1974, p. 43.

_____. "The Blue Cut Train Robbery." *Pioneer West*, July 1977, p. 15.

_____. "Jesse James and the Winston Train Robbery." *Oldtimers Wild West*, August 1977, p. 14.

_____. "Jesse's Bloodiest Escape." *Westerner*, November-December 1974, p. 27.

_____. "The Northfield Bank Job." *Westerner*, January-February 1972, p. 29.

_____. "Raid on the Missouri Pacific." *Westerner*, September-October 1973, p. 24.

Winters, Frank. "The Day the Gangs Were Born." *Golden West*, September 1965, p. 42; reprinted, *Western Frontier*, May 1985, p. 10.

Work, James C., ed. *Gunfight*. Lincoln: University of Nebraska/Bison Books.

Wright, Robert M. *Dodge City: The Cowboy Capital*. Wichita KS: Wichita Eagle, 1913.

Wright, Thomas. Letter. *True West*, August 1957, p. 48.

Wukovits, John F. "Raiders Repulsed by Fire." *Wild West*, October 1988, p. 18.

"Wyatt Earp Is in Town Again." *Dodge City Times*, July 7, 1877.

"Wyatt Earp, Our Old Assistant Marshal Is in Fort Clark, Texas." *Globe*. n.d.

Wyatt Earp's Old West. CD-ROM. Danbury CT: Grolier Electronic Publishing, 1994.

Wybrow, Robert J. "From the Pen of a Noble Robber: Letters from Jesse Woodson James, 1847–1882." *English Westerners Brand Book*, Vol. 24, no. 2, Summer 1987, p. 1.

_____. "The James Gang in Kentucky." *English Westerners Brand Book*, Vol. 15, no. 12, January 1973, p. 1.

_____. "Jesse's Juveniles." Part I: *English Westerners Brand Book*, Vol. 11, no. 3, April 1969, p. 1. Part II: *English Westerners Brand Book*, Vol. 12, no. 1, October 1969, p. 1.

_____. "Ravenous Monsters of Society: The Early Exploits of the James Gang." *English Westerners Brand Book*, Vol. 17, no. 2, Summer 1990, p. 11.

Yankton-Press Dakotaian, December 5 and 7, 1876; March 1, 1884, p. 4.

Yeatman, Ted P. "Bill Ryan, Outlaw." *NOLA Quarterly*, Vol. 5, no. 4, April 1980.

_____. "Jesse James in Tennessee." *True West*, July 1985, p. 10.

_____. "Jesse James' Surrender." *Old West*, Vol. 31, no. 1, Fall 1994, pp. 14–19.

Yoggy, Gary A. *Riding the Video Range: The Rise and Fall of the Western on Television*. Jefferson NC: McFarland, 1995.

Younger, Cole. "A Letter from the Notorious Cole Younger." *St. Louis Republican*, November 30, 1874.

_____. *Monthly Reports to Henry Wolfen, Warden of the Minnesota State Prison, Stillwater*. Archives of the Office of the Warden.

_____. *The Story of Cole Younger, By Himself*. Rupert, ID: Triton Press; first published in 1903.

Zamo, Stan. "They Stole the Parson's Pants." *True West*, April 1955.

Zink, Wilbur A. "Gun Battle at Roscoe." *Frontier Times*, March 1969, p. 6.

Zoglin, Richard. "Back from Boot Hill." *Time*, November 15, 1993, p. 93.

Index

Abbott, Dorothy 164
Aces and Eights (1936) 184
Across the Sierras (1941) 194
Acuff, Eddie 75, 136
Adair, Phyllis 17
Adams, Betty [Julie] 124, 235
Adams, Clifton 96
Adams, Ed 53
Adams, Ernie 33, 188, 198, 231
Adams, Jane 206
Adams, Les 14
Adams, Nick 39
Adams, Ramon F. 151
Adams, Ted 12, 15, 16, 21–23, 27, 30, 185
Adams, Tony 171
Adler, Robert 94
Adobe Walls 225–226
Adreon, Franklin 81–82, 88, 95
Adrian, Iris 210
Adrian, Jane 89
Adventures of Wild Bill Hickok (1951–1955, TV) 205
Agar, John 46, 100, 263
Aguglia, Mime 26
Aidman, Charles 49, 168
Ainslee, Mary 121
Akins, Claude 171, 243
Albeck, J. Frederik 95
Albert, Diane L. 236
Albert, Stephen W. 236
Albertson, Frank 121, 186
Albritton, Louise 125
Albuquerque Journal 4
Alda, Rutayna 51
Alden, Eric 204
Alderson, Erville 73, 121
Alexander, Jane 215, 217
Alexander, Jim 209
Alexander, John 233
Alexander, Richard (Dick) 81, 97, 152, 156, 207
Alford, Phillip 101
Alias Billy the Kid (1946) 33

Alias Jesse James (1959) 97
Allen, Chad 109
Allen, Elizabeth 167
Allen, Fred 155
Allen, Jonelle 109
Allen, Penelope 169
Allen, Valerie 259
Allen, Vivian 169
Allen Street Saloon 148–149
Allison, Clay 145
Allison, Jean 261
Alonza, John A. 105
Alper, Murray 43, 206–208
Alperson, Edward L. 139
Alsace, Gene [Rocky Camron] 188
Alton, Ken 208
Amateau, Rod 171
"Ambush" (TV) 209
American Weekly 84
Ames, Leon 157
Amin, Mark 108
Anders, Merry 98, 127, 141
Anderson, Bloody Bill 58
Anderson, Bob 40, 233, 238
Anderson, Dave 81
Anderson, Dion 171
Anderson, Erville 78
Anderson, James 91, 214
Anderson, John 164, 234, 258
Anderson, Rick 77, 196, 198, 201
Anderson, Richard 235
Anderson, Roger 89
Anderson, Warner 233
Andre, Carl 202
Andre, Lona 185
Andrews 101
Andrews, Dana 39, 137
Andrews, David 174
Andrews, Robert Hardy 35, 90
Andrews, Stanley 82, 122, 126, 209–210, 231
Androsky, Carol 214
"The Angel of Cedar Mountain" (TV) 210

Angustain, Ira 101
Anhalt, Edna 83–84
Anhalt, Edward 168
Ankrum, Morris 96, 166
Anthony, Stuart 120, 153
Antoinette, Marie 47
Antrim, Harry 210
Antrim, Henry [Kid] 3
Antrim, William H. 3
Applegate, Christina 221
Archainbaud, George 229
Archer, John 90, 233, 246
The Arizonian (1935) 154, 157
Arkansas Tom 115, 118–129
Arlen, Richard 87, 248, 259
Arliss, Dimitra 215
Armendariz, Pedro, Jr. 46, 172
Armitage, George 47
Armstrong, Lyle 108
Armstrong, R.G. 51, 102, 128, 261
Armstrong, Robert 33
Arness, James 97
Arngrim, Alison 170
Arnold, Jessie 231
Arnold, Joann [Joan] 91, 208
Arquette, Alexis 108
Arquette, David 221
Arthur, Jean 186
Ashby, Linden 174
Ashdown, Isa 206–207, 209
Ashdown, Nadeen 207–208
Asher, Irving 16
Ashley, Herbert 138
Ashley, Joel 244
Askew, Luke 51, 102, 108, 215
Askew, Mari 108
Assalons, Tom 170
Ates, Roscoe 10, 78, 136, 188
Athena 101
Atherton, William 108
Atterbury, Malcolm 127, 166
Atwater, Barry 94, 239
Auberjonois, Rene 53
Aubrey, Jimmy 21, 23, 25, 28–29, 31–32, 156, 184
Aubuchon, Jacques 241
Auer, Florence 208
Austin, Frank 231
Austin, Phil 142
Autry, Dick 128
"The Avenging Gunman" (TV) 208
Avila, Enrique 45
Aylesworth, Arthur 73, 156

Babe, Thomas 220
Bacon, Irving 76, 186, 208–209
Bad Bear, Dessie 214

Badlands of Dakota (1941) 193
Badman's Country (1958) 166
Badman's Territory (1946) 80–81, 123, 138
Badmen of Missouri (1941) 78
Bagni, John 160
Bailey, Bill 89
Bailey, Harry 190
Bailey, Raymond 258
Bailey, William N. 164
Baird, Phillip 248
Bakalyan, Richard 42, 100, 239
Baker, Carroll 167
Baker, Sunshine 70
Baldassare, Raf 212
Baldra, Chuck 136
Baldwin, Adam 174
Baldwin, Stephen 218
Baldwin, Walter 33, 156, 167
Balendon, Rafael 42
Ball, Frank 154
Ball, Robert 142
Ballard, Lucien 101
Balsam, Martin 214
Balsam, Talia 217
Bancroft, George 121
Bane, Holly 81, 126, 232
Bani, Barta 45
Banks, Emily 213
Bannon, Jack 214
Bannon, Jim 91, 208
Baralla, Orlando 45
"Barbara Castle" (1960, TV) 254
Barbier, George 76
Barclay, Joan 15, 20, 22
Barclay, Per 169
Barcroft, Roy 33, 36, 44, 77, 81, 88, 126, 189, 230, 232
Bardette, Trevor 173, 199, 211
Barker, Jess 122
Barker, Lex 33
Barkin, Ellen 221
Barlow, Jack 107
Barnes, Binnie 155
Barnes, Rayford 98, 100, 162, 209
Barnes, Walter 241
Barnett, Griff 125
Baron, Lita 93–94
Barrett, Claudia 209
Barrett, James Lee 105
Barrett, Robert H. 36, 125
Barrie, Judith 184
Barrier, Ernestine 246
Barron, Baynes 210
Barron, James 239
Barron, Robert V. 52
Barrows, George 207–208
Barry, Betty 261

Barry, Donald 35, 75, 79, 89, 93–94, 124, 249
Barry, Gene 166, 171, 237–263
Barry, Wesley E. 205
Barsha, Leon 194, 196, 197, 199–201
"Barstow and Finch" (TV) 205
Bart, Dennie 108
Barton, Anne 40, 102
Barton, Buzz 154
Barton, Gregg 37, 126, 161–162, 206, 210
Barton, Phil 210
Bassett, Charlie 146
Bat Masterson Television Series (1958–1961, TV) 236
"Bat Plays a Dead Man's Hand" (1959, TV) 248
"Bat Trap" (1960, TV) 255
Bateman, Geofrey 219
Bates, Ben 216
Bates, Granville 186
Bates, Kathryn 195
Battista, Lloyd 46
Battistini, Silvio 45
"Battle Line" (TV) 209
"Battle of Eilson Creek" (TV) 57
"Battle of the Pass" (1959, TV) 241
Battling Outlaws (1941) 18
Baxley, Jack 122
Baxter, Alan 46, 78, 94
Baxter, Eugene 126
Baxter, George 34, 209
Beach, Brandon 33
Beach, Guy 207, 231
Bean, Oscar 109
"Bear Bait" (1958, TV) 237
Beard, Leah 78
Beard, Stymie 76
Beauchamp, D.D. 93, 97, 140, 160
Beaudine, William 43, 100
Beavers, Louise 137
Bechdolt, Frederick 151
Beck, John 10, 51, 73, 121
Beckett, Scotty 75
Beddoe, Don 190
Beebe, Ford 124
Beery, Noah, Jr. 122, 125–126
Beery, Noah, Sr. 200
Beery, Wallace 8–11
Behan, Johnny 147–148, 227
"Behind Southern Lines" (TV) 206
Bekassy, Stephen 243, 249
Bell, Hank 29–30, 32, 77, 126, 154, 156, 188, 191, 198, 230
Bell, James 207
Bell, Rex 158
Bell, Rodney 126
Bellamy, Madge 182
Belle Starr (1941) 131, 137–138

Belle Starr (1980) 105, 128, 142
Belle Starr and Her Times 131
"Belle Starr Story" (1968, TV) 141
Belle Starr's Daughter (1947) 139
Bellini, Cal 214
Ben-Hur 4
Benbow, June 125
Benedict, William (Billy) 77, 210
Bennet, Spencer 183
Bennett, Bruce 83, 84, 86
Bennett, Constance 199
Bennett, David 216
Bennett, Lee 125
Bennett, Mac 107
Bennett, Margery 206
Bennett, Marjorie 44
Bennett, Ray 30–31, 124, 206
Bentley, Irene 153
Benton, Charles 170
Beradino, John 209
Beregi, Oscar 251
Berger, Thomas 214–215
Bergman, Peter 142
Berke, William 35, 89
Berkeley, George 37
Berti, Dehl 210, 262
Best, James 40, 87, 96, 97, 126
Best, Willie 154, 233
Best of the Badmen (1951) 90
Bettger, Lyle 164
Betts, Harry 101
Bevans, Clem 36, 38, 216, 229
Beven, Julie 219
Beyond the Law (1918) 120
Beyond the Sacramento (1940) 190
Biberman, Abner 233
Bice, Robert 88, 206, 209, 260, 262
Bickford, Charles 186
Bicknell, Andrew 53, 219
Biehn, Michael 172
"The Big Gamble" (1960, TV) 254
Big Tree, Chief 182
Bill and Ted's Excellent Adventure (1989) 52
Billy the Bandit (1916) 8–9
Billy the Kid 3–55, 135, 145
Billy the Kid (1911) 8–9
Billy the Kid (1930) 8–10
Billy the Kid (1941) 8, 16–17
Billy the Kid (1962) 42
Billy the Kid (1989) 53
"Billy the Kid" (1957, TV) 40
"Billy the Kid" (song) 6–7
Billy the Kid in Santa Fe (1941) 18
Billy the Kid in Texas (1940) 14
Billy the Kid Outlawed (1940) 12–13
Billy the Kid Returns (1938) 11–12
Billy the Kid Versus Dracula (1966) 43–44

Billy the Kid Wanted (1941) 19
Billy the Kid's Fighting Pals (1941) 17
Billy the Kid's Gun Justice (1940) 15
Billy the Kid's Range War (1941) 15
Billy the Kid's Roundup (1943) 20
Billy the Kid's Smoking Guns (1942) 19
Binns, Edward 213
Birch, Paul 122, 211
Birch, Peter 219
Bird, Billie 202
Bischoff, Samuel 90
Bishop, Julie 199
Bishop, Norman 206
Bishop, William 160
Bissell, Whit 164
Bizzy, Harold 212
"The Black Pearls" (1959, TV) 245
Blackman, Lonnie 253
"The Blacksmith Story" (TV) 207
Blaine, Marla 42
Blair, Henry 207
Blair, June 258
Blair, Robert 81
Blake, Geoffrey 51
Blake, Jack 118
Blake, Jean 256
Blake, Pamela 89, 125
Blake, Robert 261
Blakeney, Olive 16
"Blake's Kid" (TV) 219
Blanco, Tomas 45
Blankfort, Michael 213
Blazing Frontier (1943) 32
Bleifer, John 156
Bliss, Lela 210
Blocker, Dirk 108
"Blood on the Money" (1960, TV) 254
Blue, Monte 75, 83, 188, 190, 202, 208
Blue Duck 132–133
Blumenthal, Richard 78
Blystone, Stanley 79, 121, 202, 234
Boetticher, Budd 101–102, 126
Bohen, Ian 174
Bolas, Xam Dan 168
"Bold Raven Rodeo" (TV) 209
Bolder, Cal 100
Bolton, Joe 43
Bolton, Joy 53
Bonanza: Under Attack (1995) 108
Bond, Ward 86–97, 153, 156, 159, 199
Bonham, Guy 193
Boniface, Symona 154
Bonner, Roy 217
Bonner, William H. 3, 5, 8, 37
Bonomo, Joe 184
Boo, Louis Bar 169
Booth, Karin 166
Boothe, Powers 192

"Border City" (TV) 207
"Border City Election" (TV) 206
Bordine, Mabel 120
Boris, Robert 108–109
Borg, Sven Hugo 234
Borg, Veda Ann 208
Borneo, Phil 47
Borzage, Dan 167
Boss, Clay 216
Boteler, Wade 11, 75, 188
Botiller, Dick 199
Bottoms, John 104, 169
Bottoms, Joseph 170
Bouchey, Willis 160, 167
Bower, Stony 107
Bowers, William 97
Bowman, James 216
Bowman, Jessica 109
Boxleitner, Bruce 170, 173
"The Boy and the Bandit" (TV) 207
The Boy from Oklahoma (1954) 37
Boyd, William 183
Boyer, Glenn G. 150
Boyett, William 244
Bradford, Lane 29, 82, 88, 140, 196, 232, 253
Bradford, Richard 171
Bradley, Bert 209
Bradley, Frank 167
Bradley, Lee 167
Bradley, Leslie 98
Bradshaw, Peter 107
Brady, Buff 128
Brady, Ed 26, 121, 157, 188
Brady, Edwin J. 16
Brady, Scott 37, 87, 126, 128, 140
Brand, Neville 166
Brandon, Henry 96, 157, 204
Brands, X 253
Brannon, Carol 206
Brannon, Fred C. 36, 80, 82, 88
Brauer, Tiny 43
Braunstein, Alan 47
Braxton, Steve 25
Bray, Robert 33, 36, 208
Brayton, Margaret 156
Breakston, George 73
Breckenridge, William 151
Breen, Joe 209
Breihan, Carl W. 69
Brennan, Mollie 226
Brennan, Walter 90, 152, 159
Brent, Eve 242
Brent, George 126
Brent, Lynton 24, 75
Brent, Roy 30
Brewer, Betty 199
Brewster, Diane 244

Bridge, Alan 122, 188, 208
Bridges, Jeff 221
Bridges, Lloyd 162–163, 220
Brien, Edwin 25
Briggs, Harlan 156
Bright, Richard 51
Brimley, Wilfred 53
Brinegar, Paul 171
Brinks, J.W. 179
Brinley, Charles 188
Brissac, Virginia 73, 78, 122, 125
Britton, Barbara 84–85
Broadhurst, Kent 171
Broadwell, Dick 113–114
Brocco, Peter 101
Brocius, Curly Bill 148–149, 227
Brockwell, Gladys 183
Brodie, Steve 33, 42, 80, 164, 208, 231, 233–234
Broidy, William F. 205
Brolin, Josh 218
Bromberg, J. Edward 73, 76, 84
Bromfield, John 126
Bromley, Sheila 98
Bronson, Charles 216
Brooks, Geraldine 83–84
Brooks, Rand 126, 206–208, 249
Brophy, Kevin 103
Brown, Barry 102
Brown, Donna 170
Brown, Ewing 203
Brown, Harry Joe 124, 233
Brown, James 83–84, 91
Brown, James S., Jr. 154
Brown, John 107
Brown, John Mack 8–11
Brown, Reg 203
Brown, Stanley 195, 199
Brown, Tom 161, 210–211
Brown, Wally 40
Brownlee, Frank 79
Bruce, David 162, 206
Bruce, Ed 107
Brueck, Betty 93
Brunell, Juny 42
"Brunette Bombshell" (1959, TV) 242
Bryant, Charles 113
Bryant, John 212
Bryant, Michael 209
Bryant, William (Bill) 46, 166, 209–210
Bryar, Claudia 51
Bryden, Bill 103
Bryson, Chere 216
Buchanan, Edgar 86, 121, 158, 162–163, 255
Buchanan, West 104
Buchanan Rides Alone (1958) 101
Buchs, Julio 45

Buck, Connie 252
Buckington, George 116
Buckley, Betty 174
Bucko, Buck 21
Bucko, Ralph 83, 88
Bucko, Roy 30, 83, 88, 202
"Buckshot Comes Home" (TV) 209
Buetel, Jack 8, 26, 90, 93
Buffalo Girls (1995) 219
"Buffalo Kill" (1959, TV) 246
Buffington, Sam 243, 247
Bull, Charles Edward 182
Bull, Richard 168
Bullet for Billy the Kid (1963) 42
Bullets for Bandits (1942) 200
"Bullwhacker's Bounty" (1961, TV) 259
Bulnes, Quinton 128
Burbridge, Betty 33
Burgess, Helen 186
Burke, Caroline 25–26
Burke, James 107
Burke, Jimmy H. 204
Burke, Mim 216
Burke, Robert 172
Burke, Walter 213
Burnett, W.R. 139, 151–152, 160
Burnett, Smiley 11, 230
Burns, Bob 136, 157, 188, 193
Burns, Forest 88
Burns, Fred 11, 75, 184, 190, 198
Burns, Jeri 171
Burns, John 258, 261
Burns, Michael 211
Burns, Paul E. 73, 134, 138, 139
Burns, Walter Noble 6, 9, 16, 151
Burrs Under the Saddle 151
Burt, James 237
Burt, Nellie 102
Busch, Niven 137
Bush, James 154, 207
Bushman, Francis X., Jr. 184
Buster, Budd 12, 17, 19, 21–22, 24, 27–28, 30, 185, 187–188, 198
Butler, Dan 107
Butler, David 204
Butler, Frank 37
Butler, John K. 95, 156
Butler, Roy 231, 234
Byrd, Tom 53
Byrne, Gabriel 219
Byron, Walter 187

Cabot, Bruce 46, 90, 199
Cagney, Jeanne 207
Cahill, F.P. 3
Cahn, Edward 152
Cain, Christopher 51
Cairns, Jimmy 150

Calamity Jane 180
Calamity Jane (1953) 204
Calamity Jane (1984) 217
Calder, King 263
Calhern, Louis 154
Call, Ken 128
Call, R.D. 53
Callahan, Gene 170
Callaway, Chuck 210
Calloway, Bill 102
Calloway, Tom 51
Cameron, Dave 258
Camden, Joan 39, 164
Cameron, Rod 78, 139
Camfield, Bill 43
Camillerj, Terry 52
Canada, Roy 203
Canalejas, Jose 45
Cannon, Dyan 247
Canutt, Yakima 82, 124, 184, 189
"Canvas and the Cane" (1959, TV) 248
Captive of Billy the Kid (1952) 36
Card, Bob 11, 154
Card, Ken 77
Cardenas, Elsie 128
Cardos, John 212
Carey, Harry, Jr. 44, 103, 167, 172–173, 211
Carey, Harry, Sr. 152
Carey, Macdonald 86
Carey, Olive 44, 164
Carey, Philip 205
Cariff, Robert 47
Carle, Naida 181
Carleton, George 232
Carlin, George 52
Carlson, Walter 193
Carmen, Julie 53
Carney, Thom 209, 259
Carol, Jack 166
Carpenter, Frank 210
Carpenter, Horace B. 20, 188, 197, 230
Carpenter, John 36, 203, 206, 210–211
Carpenter, Virginia 198
Carr, June 34
Carr, Kenneth 47
Carr, Mary 72
Carr, Michael 210
Carr, Thomas 33, 81, 205
Carradine, David 103–104, 171
Carradine, John 43–45, 73, 76, 94, 100,
    155, 167, 208, 216
Carradine, Keith 103–104, 221
Carradine, Robert 103
Carricart, Robert 245
Carroll, Anne 207–208
Carroll, Gordon 49
Carroll, Lucia 199
Carroll, Virginia 201

Carry, Jack 160
Carson, Freddie 203
Carson, Sunset 33, 230
Carter, Alice 51
Carter, Ellis W. 88
Carter, Janis 233
Cartwright, Peggy 182
Caruso, Anthony 37–38
Casaravilla, Carlos 45
Case, Allen 99
Case, Carroll 43, 100
Cash, Johnny 107
Cash, June Carter 107
Casey, Bernie 52
Cason, John 37–38
Cassell, Walter 161
Cassidy, Edward 30, 33, 81, 122, 154, 189,
    208
Cassidy, Jack 220
Cassidy, Mary 122
Castillo, Angel Del 42
Castillo, Gloria 255
Castle, Don 158, 164
Castle, Peggie 93–94, 96, 140
Castle, William 37, 92, 161, 162
Caswell, Nancy 185
Catching, Bill 210, 250
Cates, Phillip 107
Catlett, Walter 78, 199
Catron, Jerry 260
"Cattle and Cane" (1960, TV) 251
Cattle Annie and Little Britches (1981) 128–
    129
Caulder, King 249
Cavan, Allan 188
Cavanagh, Paul 37
Cavanaugh, Michael 106–107
Caven, Jess 154
Caven, Taylor 79
Cavendish, Dick 207
Cecil, Edward 189
Cedar, Larry 217
Centralia, Missouri, Massacre 58
Chadwell, Bill 62
Chadwick, Cyril 182
"Chain of Events" (TV) 208
Challee, William 44, 102, 142
Chambers, Phil 241
Chambers, Wheaton 122
Chance, Larry 209–210
Chandler, David 202
Chandler, George 73, 76, 87, 209
Chandler, John 51
Chandler, Lane 33, 139, 189, 210, 234
Chaney, Lon, Jr. 37–38, 73, 122, 156, 184,
    193, 255
Chanslor, Roy 122
Chapin, Doug 105

Chaplin, Charles, Jr. 209
Chapman, Hugh 138
Chapman, Lonny 168
Chapman, Marguerite 87
Chapman, Ron 170
Charles, Frances 207
Charlita 44
Charters, Spencer 73, 78
Chartrand, Lois 86
Chase, Alden 15
Chase, Borden 233
Chase, Colin 182
Chase, Frank 100, 233
Chase, Guy [Alden] 187
Chatterton, Tom 33, 81, 121, 230
Cheatham, Jack 157
Chesebro, George 12–13, 15–17, 28, 31–32, 38, 79–82, 122, 126, 185, 188, 195–196, 198
Cheshire, Harry 85
Cheyenne Autumn (1964) 167
"Cheyenne Club" (1958, TV) 238
Chicago, Rock Island and Pacific Railroad 60
Chick, Tom 108
"The Child Prodigy" (TV) 206
Ching, William 209
Chisum (1970) 46
Chisum, John 4
Chisum, Sallie 7
Cho, Emily 214
Christie, Howard 211
Christine, Virginia 43, 91
Churchill, Berton 153
The Cimarron Kid (1951) 126
Cisar, George 44
"Civilian Clothes" (TV) 207
Claiborne, Billy 148, 227
Clanton, Billy 148–149
Clanton, Ike ["Old Man"] 148
Clark, Cliff 85, 199
Clark, Davidson 76, 122, 138
Clark, Dick 120, 227
Clark, Edward 206
Clark, Fred 83–84
Clark, Glen 107
Clark, Matt 51, 102, 128, 215–216
Clark, Steve 12–13, 18–19, 22–23, 29–30, 33, 36, 83, 188, 190, 196, 200–201
Clark, Wallis 78, 158
Clarke, Charles 155
Clarke, Mae 162
Clarke, Robert 33, 210
Clauser, Suzanne 217
Clavel, Aurora 51
Claxton, William 98
Clay County Bank 61
Clayton, Melissa 109

Clements, Stanley 38
"Clem's Reformation" (TV) 210
Cleveland, George 186, 229
Cliff, John 37, 92, 242
Clifford, Jack 121, 190
Clifton, Frank M. 71
Cline, William M. 204
Clive, Henry 156
Coates, Franklin B. 70–71
Coates, Tommy 79, 81, 88
Cobb, David 107
Cobb, Edmund 36, 81, 188–189, 193, 195–196, 198–200, 207, 232–233
Coburn, James 9, 49, 51, 53, 98, 245, 250
Cochran, Steve 202
Code of the Plains (1947) 31
Code of the Prairie (1944) 230
Cody, Buffalo Bill 151
Cody, Iron Eyes 126, 188, 190, 209
Cody, Kathleen 130
Coe, David Allen 107
Coe, Fred 40–41
Coffin, Tristram 81, 126, 161, 196, 198, 200–201, 206–209, 251
Coghlan, Junior 183
Cohen, Bennett 33
Cohn, Harry 136
Cokes, Bud 214
Colby, Marion 34
Coldeway, Anthony 136
Cole, Lester 120
Cole, Royal 88
Cole, Slim 184
Cole Younger, Gunfighter (1958) 96–97
Coleman, Don 10
Collier, Don 128, 218
Collins, Denver John 169
Collins, Eddie 76
Collins, G. Pat 209
Collins, Gene 84, 169
Collins, Johnny 128
Collins, Monty 188
Collins, Ray 80
Colt .45 (1950) 42
Comanche Station (1960) 101
Combs, Gary 107
Combs, Gilbert 107
"Come Out Fighting" (1960, TV) 252
The Commonwealth 41
Compson, Betty 136
Compton, John 81
Congdon, James 40
Conklin, Chester 77, 81
Conklin, Hennie 156
Conlin, Frank 16
Conlin, Jimmy 78
Connelly, Christopher 130
Connors, Chuck 171, 188

Connors, Michael 128
Conrad, Robert 42, 130
Conrad, William 260
Conroy, Frank 153
"The Conspiracy—Part One" (1959, TV)
    244
"The Conspiracy—Part Two" (1959, TV)
    245
Conti, Andrey 209
Conti, Steve 89
Converse, Frank 168
Conway, Bert 214
Conway, Morgan 80
Coogan, Richard 98
Cook, Elisha, Jr. 51, 102, 237, 246
Cook, Fielder 215
Cook, Tommy 208
Cooley, Spade 157
Coolidge, Rita 51
Coon, Gene L. 211
Coontz, William 207
Cooper, Ben 91, 211
Cooper, Charles 220
Cooper, Clancy 94
Cooper, Courtney Ryley 183
Cooper, Dee 197
Cooper, Gary 97, 180, 186, 202
Cooper, Gordon 155
Cooper, Jackie 76
Cooper, Jeanne 98
Cooper, Ken 79
Cooper, Leo 184
Cooper, Olive 136
Cooper, Tex 20, 23, 27, 30, 190, 195, 196
Coppola, Talia 47
Coquillion, John 51
Corazzari, Bruno 141
Corbett, Ben 14, 78, 157, 184, 202
Corbett, Glenn 46
Corby, Ellen 91
Corcoran, Joe 170
Corcoran, William 231
Cording, Harry 121, 157, 234
Corey, Jim 11, 79, 136, 189, 214
Corey, Wendell 86, 97
Corman, Roger 47–48
Corrigan, Darcy 152
Corrigan, Lloyd 76
Cort, Bud 47
Corvall, Dolores 202
Corydon Bank (Iowa) 61
Cosgrove, Luke 77
Cosmotas, George P. 172
Costner, Kevin 174–175
Cottier, LaDonna 212
Coughlan, Phyllis 239
Council Bluff, Iowa, Holdup 62
Counselman, William 153

"The Counterfeit Ghost" (TV) 210
Country Joe and the Fish 47–48, 142
"Court Martial of Major Mars" (1961, TV)
    258
Courtland, Jerome 233
Courtney, Chuck 43–44, 210
Courtwright, William 72
The Covered Wagon (1923) 182–183
Cowan, Jerome 202, 244
Cowl, George 136
Cowl, Richard S. 212
Cowling, Bruce 160, 162
Cox, Morgan B. 189
Cox, Victor 81, 83
Coxen, Ed 195, 197
Coy, Walter 162, 235, 254
Coyote, Peter 219
Crabbe, Buster 8, 19, 20–25, 27–32, 42,
    166
Cradley, Stewart 254
Craig, James 38–39
Cramer, Dick 188
Cramer, Gilbert 42
Cramer, Richard 20, 152, 234
Crandall, Bill 208
Crane, Jim 227
Crane, Richard 91
Crawford, Broderick 121, 193, 244
Crawford, Diana 253
Crawford, John 82, 88, 100, 206, 208
Crawford, Johnny 171, 210
Creed, Roger 100, 164
Crehan, Joseph 11
Cripps, Kernan 122
Crite, James Lee 216
Critten, Dick 134
Critten, Zeke 134
Crittenden, James 128
Crittenden, T.T. [Governor] 65
Crook, John 220
Crosby, Bing 97
Crosby, Wade 206
Cross, David 209
Cross, Marcia 107
Crowley, Kathleen 242, 256
Croy, Homer 84
Cullen, Brett 218
Culp, Robert 211
Cummings, Irving 137
Cummings, Susan 237, 248, 257
Cunningham, Sarah 107, 142
Currie, Louise 12, 15
Custer, George [General] 180
Custer's Last Stand (1936) 185–186
Curtis, Alan 122, 123
Curtis, Anthony (Tony) 87, 233
Curtis, Craig 102
Curis, Dick 16, 124, 158, 194, 206

Curtis, Don 158
Curtis, Ken 167
Curtiz, Michael 37–38
Cutell, Lou 214
Cutting, John 189
Cutting, Richard 37, 91, 211

"Dakota Showdown" (1960, TV) 257
Dalbes, Alberto 42
Dale, James 82
Dale, Michael 209
Dallas (1950) 201
Dallesandro, Joe 171
Dalroy, Rube 195
Dalton, Abby 96, 213
Dalton, Adeline Younger 111
Dalton, Audrey 208, 246, 262
Dalton, Bill 113–117, 119
Dalton, Bob 43, 111–114
Dalton, Emmett 111, 113–114, 119–121
Dalton, Emmett (Mrs.) 121
Dalton, Frank 111, 113
Dalton, Grat 111, 113–114
Dalton, J. Frank 69, 70
Dalton, Jennie 116
Dalton, Louis 111
The Dalton-Doolin Gang 111–130
The Dalton Gang (1949) 124
The Dalton Girls (1957) 127
The Dalton That Got Away (1960) 127
The Daltons 128
"The Daltons" (TV) 127
The Daltons Ride Again (1945) 122–123
The Daltons' Women (1950) 125
Damler, John 209
Dane, Karl 9
Daniel, Sam 172
Dano, Royal 102, 128
Danon, Frankie 207
Darby, Kim 215
Darien, Frank 26, 139
Darmour, Larry 154, 189
Darnell, Linda 159
Darnham, Bruce 107
Darr, Larry 154, 189
Darrell, Steve 37, 82, 233, 253
Darro, Frankie 188, 248
Darwell, Jane 73–73, 159
DaSilva, Howard 199
Daugherty, Herschel 211
"The Daughter of Casey O'Grady" (TV) 210
Davenport, Ned 126
David, Clifford 52
David, Thayer 214
Davidson, Wayne 210
Davis, Art 154
Davis, Frank 37

Davis, Gail 97
Davis, Jim 38, 91, 97, 100
Davis, John 40
Davis, Karl 207
Davis, Lisa 127
Davis, Roger 215
Davison, Betty 206
Davys, Carolyn 168
Dawson, Hal K. 202
Day, Doris 205
Day, Lynda 46
Day, Ruth 153
Days of Jesse James (1939) 75
Deacon, Richard 211
"Dead Men Don't Pay Debts" (1959, TV) 247
"Deadline" (1959, TV) 242
"Deadly Diamonds" (1960, TV) 250
Deadwood Dick (1940) 189
Deadwood '76 (1965) 212
Deal, Pony 227
Dean, Billy 210
Dean, Jeanne 207
Dean, Margia 38, 84, 87
Dearing, Edgar 121, 234
"Death and Taxes" (1959, TV) 248
"Death by Decree" (1960, TV) 258
"Death by the Half Dozen" (1960, TV) 250
"The Death of Bat Masterson" (1959, TV) 243
De Benning, Jeff 237
De Broux, Lee 221
"Debt of Honor" (1960, TV) 255
De Carlo, Suzette 101
Decision at Sundown (1957) 101
De Corsia, Ted 164, 250
De Forrest, Kelley 164
Dehner, John 40, 160, 246, 259
Dekker, Albert 36, 229
De Kova, Frank 39
Delaney, Charles 87
Delany, Dana 172
De Lar, Roy 210
De Laurentiis, Dino 215
Delevanti, Cyril 122
Dell, Myrna 35
Del Rio, Dolores 167
Demichelli, Tullio 168
De Mille, Cecil B. 186–187
Demond, Albert 232
De Munn, Jeffrey 170
Dennis, Fred 169
Dennison, Jo Carroll 207
Densen, Linda 209
Denton, Ray 245
Dern, Bruce 221
"Deser Ship" (1959, TV) 245

Desmond, Mary Jo 184
Desmond, William 184–185, 191
Desti, Maria 101
Deuel, Geoffrey 46
Deus, Benyt 168
D'Eva, Alessandro 141
The Devil's Trail (1942) 200
Devine, Andy 121, 126, 152, 193, 205–206
Devon, Richard 166
DeWitt, Jack 140, 160
Dexter, Anthony 39
Dexter, Pete 220
Diaz, Rom R. 217
Dibbs, Ken 209
Dickey, Basil 81–82
Dickinson, Dick 122
Diehl, John 219
Dierkes, John 40
Dierner, Joan 208
Dillard, Bert 23–24
Dillman, Bradford 213
Dillon, Forrester 75
Dilson, John 190
Dimas, Ray 214
Dinehart, Alan, Jr. 234
Dinehart, Mason 164
Di Reda, Joseph 95
Dirty Little Billy (1972) 9, 49–50
"Disappearance of Bat Masterson" (1960, TV) 251
Dix, Richard 158, 193–194
Dix, Robert 98, 212
Dixon, Billy 49
Dixon, Denver 14, 18, 20
Dixon, Eileen 34
Dixon, George 152
Dixon, Glenn 127
Dobbins, Bennie 216
Doc (1974) 169–170
Dr. Quinn, Medicine Woman (1995) 109, 142
"The Doctor Story" (TV) 208
Dodson, Jack 51
"The Dog Collar Story" (TV) 206
Dominguez, Joe 140
Dominguez, Jose 202
Donahue, Patricia 208, 237, 249
Donald, Juli 171
Donaldson, Gil 202
Donlevy, Brian 16, 73, 78, 87, 91, 121
Donner, Robert 46, 101
Donovan, King 209, 237
Doolin, Bill 113, 115, 117–119, 126
The Doolins of Oklahoma (1949) 124–125
Doran, Ann 99
Dore, Ann 241
Dorr, Lester 154
Dorrell, Dick 154

"Double Showdown" (1958, TV) 237
"Double Trouble in Trinidad" (1959, TV) 239
Doucette, John 94, 206, 246, 253
Douglas, Don 189
Douglas, Gordon 85, 124
Douglas, Kirk 164
Downing, Joseph 138
Downs, Cathy 159, 241, 252
Downs, Walter 81
Dragoti, Stan 49
Drake, Charles 233
Drake, Dona 125, 140
Drake, Ken 251, 256, 260
Drake, Oliver 12, 21, 39
Dresden, Curly 14–15, 17–18, 20, 22, 24, 28, 30, 32, 77, 188, 195
Drew, Donna 210
Drew, Ellen 78, 86
Drew, Lowell 198
Drexel, Steve 166
Drury, James 171
DuBrey, Claire 73
"Dude's Folly" (1958, TV) 238
Dudley, Robert 121
Dudley, Tom 155
Duffin, Shay 216
Duffy, Jesse 81
Dugay, Yvette 126
Dule, John 258
Dumbrille, Douglas 122, 253
Dumont, Charles 141
Dunaway, Faye 169–170, 214
Dunbar, Dave 202
Duncan, Bob 34, 40
Duncan, Craig 262
Duncan, Kenne 12, 15, 18–20, 23, 187–189, 206–207
Duncan, Pamela 207–208, 247
Duncan, Rosetta 210
Dundee, Jimmie 156
Dunez, Daniel 216
Dunhill, Steve 202
Dunlap, Jack 53
Dunn, Eddie 84, 156
Dunn, Harvey B. 239
Dunn, Liam 102
Dunn, Ralph 11
Dunn, William 120
Dupov, Paul 241, 263
Durant, Marjorie 102
Durant, Thomas 182
Durlam, G.A. 189
Durlan, Arthur 184
Duryea, Dan 233
Duvall, Robert 102–103
Dvorak, Ann 87
Dwan, Allan 91, 150

Dwan, Isabelle 208
Dwire, Earl 188
Dyer, Linda 214
Dyer, Micah 108
Dyer, Robert L. 61
Dyer, William 181
Dylan, Bob 49, 51
"Dynamite Blows Two Ways" (1958, TV) 237
Dynamite Dick 115, 118

Earp, Allie 150
Earp, James 145, 148
Earp, Mattie 146, 147–148
Earp, Morgan 145–149, 227
Earp, Virgil 145, 147–149, 151, 227
Earp, Warren 145, 148
Earp, Wyatt 43, 145–152, 162–163, 226–227
Earp, Wyatt (Mrs.) 145
The Earp Brothers of Tombstone (1960) 150
Eastham, Richard 260
Eastman, George 141
Ebehardt, Norma 207
Eddy, Kay [Bonnie] 233
Eden, Chana 245
Edwards, Alan 153
Edwards, Blake 171
Edwards, Bruce 207
Edwards, Burt 107
Edwards, Cliff 243
Edwards, Jennifer 171
Edwards, John 107
Edwards, John Newman 61
Edwards, Penny 36, 127
Edwards, Ronnie Clair 215
Eestrate, Edwin 92
Efron, Marshall 169
Egan, Richard 87
Eggles, Amy 214
Eiland, Michael 219
Eitner, Don 240
Elam, Jack 51, 108, 160, 162, 164
Elam, Joan 243
Eldredge, George 198, 208, 210, 251, 262
Eldredge, John 207–209
"Election Day" (1958, TV) 240
Elhardt, Kaye 254
Elic, Josif 49
Elkins, Saul 83–84
Elliott, Biff 94
Elliott, Bill 154–155, 180, 188, 190, 193–201
Elliott, Cecil 209
Elliott, Dick 26, 126, 156, 191
Elliott, Edythe 200
Elliott, John 18, 20, 30, 73, 191
Elliott, Sam 172, 219

Ellis, Frank 18–19, 22, 24, 28–30, 32, 83, 91, 126, 154, 157, 184, 188, 191, 230
"Elusive Baguette" (1960, TV) 254
Elwes, Cassian 108
Emerson, Faye 78, 199
Emery, Gilbert 78
Emmett, Fern 122, 156
Emory, Richard 36, 241
"End of the Line" (1961, TV) 260
Engel, Roy 241
Engel, Samuel G. 159
Englund, George 142
Enright, Kevin 127
Enright, Ray 23, 199, 231
"Episode in Eden" (1961, TV) 260
Erickson, Leif 126, 202
Erskine, Lauri York 94
Erwin, Bill 243
Erwin, E.L. 127
Erwin, Roy 210
Erwin, Stuart 121
Esformes, Nate 53
Espey, Hortense 70
Estevez, Emilio 51–54
Ethier, Alphonz 152
Ethridge, Ella 208
Evans, Charles 234
Evans, Douglas 208
Evans, Ed 107
Evans, Gene 51, 101, 130, 202
Evans, Jack 18, 21, 24, 184, 188, 196–197
Evans, Jesse 4
Evans, Linda 171
Evans, Michael 213
Evans, Richard 49
Evans, William Michael 108
Everett, Tom 53
"The Ex-Convict Story" (TV) 207
Eyre, David 128

Fadden, Tom 78, 202
Fahey, Jeff 174
Fairbanks, Anne 47
Falcon (horse) 32
Fallman, Gill 89
Falwell, Marshal 107
Famous Sheriffs and Western Outlaws 151, 179
Farina, Dennis 108
Farley, Jane 193
Farley, Jackie 47
Farley, James 181
Farmer, Frances 193
Farmer, Richard 35
"Farmer with a Badge" (1961, TV) 263
Farnsworth, Dick 210, 216
Farnum, Franklyn 126, 138, 154, 189
Farnum, William 185

Farrell, Sharon 128
Farrell, Tommy 89
"The Fatal Garment" (1961, TV) 263
Faulkner, Edward 46, 101
Fawcett, William 36, 37, 100, 206, 208
Fay, Dorothy 196
Faylen, Frank 164
Featherstone, Eddie 189
Fees, Paul 220
Fenady, Andrew J. 46, 100
Fenton 125, 209
Ferguson, Al 15, 88, 154, 189
Ferguson, Frank 91, 96, 233, 255
Fern, Fritzi 184
Fernandez, Emilio 51
Ferrara, James 158
Ferrior, Gianni 45
Fesetti, Doris 251
Fessler, Michael 33, 91
A Few Bullets More (1969) 45
Field, Todd 108
Fielding, Edward 193
Fierro, Paul 254, 256
"The Fighter" (1958, TV) 237
Fighting Man of the Plains (1949) 85
Film Daily 80, 122, 182, 202
Filmer, Robert 208–209
Filmindia 93
Films and Career of Audie Murphy 102
Films and Filming 213–214
Fimple, Dennis 128
Fine, Bud 234
Fine, Travis 218
Finn, Mickey 97, 262
Finnegan, Joe 217
Fischer, Bruce M. 169
Fischer, Shug 167
Fisher, Steve 91, 130
Fiske, Richard 193–194, 196
Fiske, Robert 188–189
Fitzgerald, Dallas 189
Fitzpatrick, John 128
Fix, Paul 51, 85–86
Flaherty, Dennis 252
Flanery, Sean Patrick 108
Flavin, James 73, 121, 138
Fleer, Harry 241, 263
Fleming, Rhonda 97, 164, 204
Fletcher, Bill 168
Fletcher, Louis 238
Flicker, Ted 216
Flint, Sam 82, 87, 206–210
Flippen, Jay C. 233
Floeers, Jim 108
Flood, Harry, Jr. 149
Flori, Jean Jacques 48
Flowers, Jim 207
"Flume to the Mother Lode" (1960, TV)
249
Fonda, Henry 73–74, 76, 159
Fontaine, Jacqueline 125
Foote, Bradbury 16
Foran, Dick 209
Foran, Mary 139
Forbes John [John Carpenter] 210
Ford, Buck 107
Ford, Charles E. 11
Ford, Charlie 65
Ford, Constance 243, 252
Ford, Francis 154, 159, 186
Ford, Fritz 100
Ford, Harrison 101
Ford, John 159, 167, 182
Ford, Paul 36
Ford, Philip 232, 233
Ford, Robert (Bob) 64–66
Ford, Ruth 197, 200
Ford, Steven 128
Ford, Wallace 38, 91, 139, 162–163
Forest, Michael 210, 252
Forrest, Frederic 217, 220
Forrest, William 44
Fortnight 27
Fortune, Richard 234
"The Fortune Telling Story" (TV) 208
Foster, Edward 209
Foster, Jerry 153
Foster, Mike 207
Foster, Preston 84–85, 154, 161
Foster, Ron 250, 263
Foulger, Byron 84, 87, 90, 124, 206, 208,
210
Foulk, Robert 40, 253
Fowler, Gene 16
Fowley, Douglas 164, 173, 207, 216, 234
Fox, Wallace W. 200
Fox, William 182
Foy, Charley 229
Foy, Eddie, Jr. 156
Fraker, William A. 216
Frame, Milton 238
Franciosa, Anthony 215
Francis, Anne 101
Francis, Kay 121
Francis, Olin 190
Frank, Tony 53
Frank and Jesse (1995) 108
Franklin, Don 218
Franklin, Paul 194
Frankovich, Mike 81
Fraser, John 47
Fraser, Sally 207
Frayer, Hal 43
Frederic, Norman 92
Frederici, Blanche 10
Fredericks, Charles 208–209, 242, 257

Freedom to Love (1970) 47
Friedkin, Joel 200
Fristoe, Bersheba 57, 59
Fritts, Donnie 51, 107
Frome, Milton 237
Frontier Marshal (1934) 152–153
Frontier Marshal (1939) 155–156
Frontier Scout (1938) 187
Frost, Terry 34, 36, 125, 206, 208
Frutin, Sharon 169
Frye, Gil 210
Fugitive of the Plains (1943) 28
Fuller, Lance 239, 259
Fuller, Samuel 84
Fulton, Lou 22
Fung, Willie 193
Furlough, Kevin 171
Furthman, Jules 26
Fury, Barney 185
Fusco, John 51, 53

Gad's Hill, Missouri, Holdup 61
Gahan, Oscar 11, 14, 154, 184
Galindo, Nacho 91
Gallatin, Missouri, Holdup 59, 61
Gallaudet, John 239, 248
The Gambler Returns: The Luck of the Draw
  (1991) 171, 236
Gamet, Kenneth 124
Gammon, James 101, 174, 221
Gangelin, Paul 122
Ganzhorn, Jack 201
Garcia, Carlotta 53
Gardner, Jack 181
Garland, Richard 92, 126
Garner, Don 159
Garner, James 97, 168, 171
Garralaga, Martin 26, 36–37, 40, 255
Garrett, Don 209
Garrett, Pat 4, 8–9, 37, 42, 51, 54
Garrick, Richard 161
Garrison, Lloyd 234
"Garrison Finish" (1959, TV) 248
Garson, Greer 39
Garth, Otis 37
Garver, David 219
Gashade, Billy 67
Gas-s-s-s (1970) 47
Gates, Larry 168
Gates, Nancy 161, 255
"The Gattling Gun" (TV) 209
Gatzert, Nate 154
Gay, Eula 229
Gaye, Lisa 166, 241, 246, 263
Geary, Bud 230
Gebert, Gordon 208
Geddes, Jack 35
Geer, Lennie 44

Geer, Leonard 162
Geer, Will 36, 233
Gehring, Ted 101, 216
Genevieve Savings Bank Holdup 60
Geoffrey, Lewis 142
George, Christopher 46
George, Chief Dan 214
George, Sue 127
George, William 208
Geraghty, Gerald 196
Gerald, Hal 207–208
Gerard, Carl 181
Gerard, Joseph 184
Geray, Steven 100
Getty, Balthazer 53
"Ghost Town Lady" (TV) 209
"Ghost Town Story" (TV) 206
Gibson, Dale 53
Gibson, Helen 185
Gibson, Henry 43
Gibson, Margaret 107
Gibson, Tom 188
Gibson, Virginia 210
Gibson, William 185
Gierasch, Stefen 215
Gifford, Frances 78, 158
Giftos, Elaine 47
Gillette, Ruth 153
Gilpin, Mark 216
Gilson, Tom 257
Ging, Jack 255
Ginger, Johnny 43
Girard, Joseph 189
A Girl Is a Gun (1991) 48
Gish, Annabeth 174
Gittens, Wyndham 189
Gladwin, Frances 30
Glart, Joseph W. 189
Glass, Ned 190, 193, 197
Gleason, Redmond 128
Glendale, Missouri, Train Holdup 65
Glendon, Frank 184
Glenn, Scott 128
Glickman, Mort 81
Glover, Bruce 215
Glover, Richard 53
Goblenz, Walter 216
Goff, D.C. (Dash) 108
Goff, Ivan 216
Going, Joanna 174
"Gold Is Where You Steal It" (1960, TV)
  255
"The Golden Rainbow" (TV) 209
Goldsmith, Martin M. 235
Goldstone, James 217
Gombell, Minna 33
Gomez, Augie 14, 19–20, 23, 25, 83
Gomez, Nicholas Sean 53

Gomez, Thomas 122
Gonnet, Jean 48
Gonzales, Pedro Gonzales 46
"The Good and the Bad" (1961, TV) 261
"Good Indian" (TV) 210
Goodwin, Gary 36
Goodwin, Gay 210
Goodwin, Harold 36, 73
Goold, Jane 219
Goonz, Bill 203
Gordon, Bruce 247
Gordon, Gavin 198
Gordon, Glen 258
Gordon, Harris 120
Gordon, James 182
Gordon, Leo 238, 255
Gordon, Mary 121, 157
Gordon, M.R. 178
"The Gorilla of Owl Hoot Mesa" (TV)
    208
Gorman, Annette 101
Gorman, Patrick 221
Gorshin, Frank 94
Gortner, Marjoe 221
Gould, William 78, 188
Graaf, Irene De 47
Graf, Annemarie 47
Graham, Fred 81, 83, 91, 202
Graham, Ronnie 49
Graham, William A. 100, 107
Grahame, Margot 154
Granger, Dorothy 121
Grant, Esther 42
Grant, Morton 83
Granville, Joan 252
Grapes, Charlie Elledge 107
Gravage, Robert 102
"A Grave Situation" (1960, TV) 253
Graves, Jessie 188
Graves, Peter 162–163
"The Graves for Swan Valley" (1959, TV)
    244
Gray, Gary 33
Gray, Lorna [Adrian Booth] 189
Grayson, Charles 199
The Great Adventures of Wild Bill Hickok
    (1938) 188
The Great Jesse James Raid (1953)
The Great Missouri Raid (1950) 86
Great Northfield, Minnesota Raid (1972)
    102–103
Great Western Pictures II 105, 107–108, 129,
    170
Green, Duke 83, 88
Green, James 169
Greenberg, Dan 169
Greene, Harrison 195–196
Greenhalgh, Jack 26

Greenway, Tom 95, 246
Greer, Allan 185
Greer, Dabbs 246
Greer, Len 206
Gregg, Virginia 260
Gregg, Walter 168
Grenne, Joseph 209
Grever, Robert 101
Grey, Duane 210
Grey, Joel 42
Griffies, Ethel 16
Griffin, Bob 91
Griffin, Merv 38
Griffin, Robert 37
Griffith, Helen 81, 88
Griffith, James 37–38, 85–86, 92, 161–162
Griffith, Melanie 219
Gross, Jack J. 231
Gruber, Frank 85–86, 204
Guajardo, Roberto 53
Guard, Kit 77, 154, 187, 189, 231
Guihan, Frances 187
Guillon, Peter 42
Guest, Christopher 104
Guest, Nicholas 104
Guhl, George 121
Gulager, Clu 42
Gulliver, Dorothy 154, 184–185
Gun Belt (1953) 160
Gunderson, Bob 97
The Gunfight at Dodge City (1958) 235
Gunfight at the O.K. Corral (1957) 164
Gunfire (1950) 89
Gunmen of the Rio Grande (1964) 168
Gunn, Earl 16
Gunn, Eddie 16

Haade, William 136, 206, 209, 234
Hack, Human 14, 23, 29, 81, 88, 188, 197
Hackett, Karl 15, 18, 22, 25, 27-29, 31, 79,
    184, 189, 230
Hackman, Gene 174
Haden, Sara 207
Hadley, Nancy 238
Hadley, Reed 84–85, 87, 91, 188, 202, 237
Haggerty, Don 36, 247
Hagney, Frank 16, 31–32, 208, 234
Hahn, Paul 210
Halaleck, Dan 47
Hale, Alan, Jr. 37, 206–208, 240
Hale, Alan, Sr. 83, 94
Hale, Bill 206, 237
Hale, Creighton 185
Hale, Jonathan 242
Hale, Monte 206, 210, 232
Hale, Richard 80
Hall, Arch, Jr. 19, 212
Hall, Arch, Sr. 212

Hall, Ben 153, 159
Hall, Fern 91
Hall, Harry 70
Hall, Henry 122
Hall, Lola 206
Hall, Porter 78, 186, 204, 229
Halloran, John 80, 85
Halton, Charles 73, 158, 208
Hamet, Kenneth 233
Hamill, Pete 169, 170
Hamilton, Charles 189
Hamilton, Chuck 80, 188, 234
Hamilton, Don 156
Hamilton, Fran 49
Hamilton, John 33, 85, 88, 202
Hamilton, Ray 260
Hamlin Joey Joe 53
Hammer, Alvin 139
Hampden, Walter 39
Hampton, Orville 35, 38, 98, 166
Hampton, Ruth 161
"Hands Across the Border" (TV) 208
Hands Across the Rockies (1941) 195–196
Haney, Betty Jane 11
Hanley, Jim 20
Hannah, Will 53
Hannon, Chick 14, 18, 88, 136, 154
Hansen, Peter 240
Hansen, Velda J. 102
Hanson, Speed 157
Hardin, John Wesley 145
Hardin, Ty 98
Hardy, Rod 219
Harens, Dean 238, 248
Harlan, Kenneth 193, 196
Harmon, John 166
Harmon, Mark 174
Harmon, Pat 136
Harnesberger, Robert 219
Harper, Patricia 29, 32
Harper's Magazine 199
Harr, Silver 31
Harris, Bill 227
Harris, Jack 253
Harris, Lucille 107
Harris, Robert H. 102
Harris, Stacy 164, 234
Harrison, Dan 141
Harrison, James 85
Harrison, Jan 248, 260
Harrower, Elizabeth 207–209
Hart, Bill 216
Hart, John 38, 216
Hart, Neal 152
Hart, William S. 180–181, 229
Hartman, Marx 256
Hartung, Phillip T. 41
Harveth, Charles 202

Harvey, Al 260
Harvey, Don 206–207, 209–210, 248
Harvey, Harry 126, 189, 200, 208, 231
Harvey, Lew 16, 33
Harvey, Michael 33
Harvey, Paul 186, 205
Harvey, Robert 53
Haskell, Al 14, 29, 188
Hatcher-Travis, Elizabeth 108
Hatfield, Hurd 30–41
Hatton, Raymond 125, 152, 206–209, 240
Hawkins, Jimmie 91
Hawks, Howard 26
Hawks, J.G. 181
Hawley, Norman 108
Hayden, Charlie 255
Hayden, Don 206
Hayden, Harry 156
Hayden, Helene 91
Hayes, Allison 166, 240, 244, 250, 252, 254
Hayes, George [Gabby] 33, 75, 77, 80, 136, 186, 191, 231–232
Hayes, Ronald 166, 249, 252, 256, 263
Haysee, A.R. 188
Hayward, Chuck 167, 217
Haywood, Robert 225
Hayworth, Joe 160
Head, Harry 227
"Heading for Trouble" (TV) 208
Healey, Myron 96, 140, 234–235, 243, 246
Hearn, Edward 188–189
Heckler, John Jay, Jr. 107
Heisler, Stuart 78, 201
Helldorado (1928) 151
Hellman, Les 238, 250, 257
Hellman, Sam 76, 155, 159
Hell's Crossroads (1957) 95–96
Hemmings, David 217
Hemmingway, Mariel 171
Henderson, Del 156
Henderson, Douglas 127
Henderson, Marcia 244, 248
Henderson, Ray 14, 16, 18–20, 24, 188
Hendricks, Jack 20, 24
Hendrix, Wanda 258
Hendry, Len 243
Henry, Bill 208, 210, 238, 251
Henry, Buzz 208, 210
Henry, Carol 89, 206, 208, 233
Henry, Thomas Browne 38
Henry, William A. 162
Henson, Sudie 108
"Hepsibah" (TV) 207
Herbert, Charles 164
Herbert, Hugh 193
Hereford, Claud 170
Herek, Stephen 52

Hern, Pepe 209
Herrill, Mary Jane 107
Herring, Aggie 10
Herron, Bob 101
Hersh, Andrew 108
Heston, Charlton 172, 204
Hetchner, Tracy 214
Heyburn, Waldon 230
Heydt, Louis Jean 38, 86
Heyes, Douglas 161–162
Hickey, William 214
Hickman, Howard 138
Hickman, Mark 95
Hickman, William 256
Hickok, Wild Bill 43, 145, 151, 177–221,
   224
Hickox, Harry 210
Hicks, Russell 76
Hiecke, Carl 154
"High Card Loses" (1960, TV) 256
High Noon (1952) 104
Hill, Betty 231
Hill, Doris 136
Hill, Julie 128
Hill, Riley 206, 208
Hill, Robert F. 183
Hill, Walter 103, 105, 220
Hillman, Lee 166
Hillman, Les 263
Hillyer, Lambert 196–197, 199–201
Hilton, Arthur 86
Hinds, Samuel S. 193
Hinton, Ed 127
Hirschman, Herbert 217
Hitchcock, Alfred 43
Hittleman, Carl K. 43, 84, 86–87, 100
Hitzig, Rupert 128
Hoagland, Eleanor 153
Hobbs, Peter 107
Hock, John 128
Hoctor, Emmett C. 70
Hodge, Patricia 171
Hodgins, Earle 33, 87, 91, 184, 188, 209–
   210
Hogan, Jack 245
Hoey, Dennis 36
Hoffman, Craig 130
Hoffman, Dan 107
Hoffman, Dustin 214
Hoffman, Harry 70
Hoffman, Pato 221
Hogan, Jack 246, 261
Hogan, Pat 204
Hohl, Arthur 229
Holden, Willima 78
Holland, Erik 102
Holliday, James D. ["Doc"] 146–149, 162
Holliman, Earl 164

Hollywood Reporter 11, 26, 35–37, 39, 43,
   49, 51, 88, 92–93, 95, 125, 139, 142, 160–
   162, 164, 167, 169–171, 187, 196, 198, 203,
   205, 215–216
Holman, Harry 73, 80
Holman, Rex 43, 98
Holt, Jack 125, 136
Holt, Nat 33, 80, 85–86, 204, 231
Holt, Stephen 251
Holt, Tim 159
"Homer Atchison" (TV) 206
Hondo [Unbilled TV Episode, 1967) 100
Hoose, Fred 206
Hope, Bob 97–98
Hopkins, Bo 128, 173
Hopper, Dennis 42, 164
Hopper, Jerry 204
Hopton, Russell 152
Horan, James D. 179
Horizons West (1969) 102
Horne, James W. 189
Horse, Michael 216
Horton, Brian 164
Horton, Clem 190
Horton, Robert 83–84
Houck, Joy 125
Hour of the Gun (1967) 168
House, Billy 231, 233
Houseman, Arthur 16
Houston, George 187
Houston, Norman 231
Hoven, Adrian 212
"How I Killed Jesse James" (Play) 65
Howard, Alan 214
Howard, David 157, 216
Howard, Mary 16
Howat, Clark 241
Howell, Jean 96
Howes, Reed 12–13, 18–19, 128, 185, 206,
   208, 234
Howlin, Olin 75, 137, 233
Howling, Wolf 185
Hoxie, Jack 183
Hoy, Robert 216
Hoyt, Clegg 95
Hoyt, John 101
Hsueh, Nancy 167
Hubbard, John 126
Hubbard, Tom 208
Hubert, Ted 88
Hudman, Wesley 162, 208, 237
Hudson, John 126, 164
Hudson, Larry 206–207, 253
Hudson, Rock 233
Huerta, Cris 212
Huggins, Roy 215
Hughes, Howard 26, 126
Hughes, Tony 85, 208

Hughes, Whitey 203
Hugo, Mauritz 36, 235
Hulette, Gladys 182
Hull, Henry 73–74, 76, 87, 229
Hulswit, Mart 169
Human Life (Feb., 1907) 150
Humans, Robert 209
Hunandez, Jose [Joaquin Marchant] 211
Hungerford, Marguerite 70–71
Hunt, J. Roy 33
"The Hunter" (1960, TV) 256
Hunter, Jan 16
Hunter, Jeffrey 94
Hunter, Tab 160
Hurst, Brandon 78
Hurst, Paul 232
Hurt, John 221
Hussenot, Olivier 168
Huston, Anjelica 219
Huston, Virginia 125
Huston, Walter 26, 152
Hutton, Paul Andrew 150, 220
Hutton, Robert 209
Hyatt, Bobby 208–209
Hyer, Martha 207

I Killed Wild Bill Hickok (1956) 210
I Married Wyatt Earp (1983) 170
I Married Wyatt Earp: The Recollections of Josephine Sarah Marcus Earp 150
I Shot Billy the Kid (1950) 35
I Shot Jesse James (1949) 84–85
Iglesias, Eugene 202
Ihnat, Steve 168
In Early Arizona (1938) 154
Ince, John 15
Ince, Ralph 9, 152
Ince, Thomas H. 183
"Incident at Fort Bowie" (1960, TV) 252
"Incident at Leadville" (1959, TV) 242
"The Inner Circle" (1959, TV) 242
Independent Film Journal 35
"The Indian Bureau Story" (TV) 206
"Indian Pony Express" (TV) 206
"The Indians and the Delegates" (TV) 208
Induni, Luis 42, 45
Ingalls, Indian Territory 117
Ingraham, Lloyd 11, 71, 122, 157
Ingram, Jack 12, 21, 24, 28–29, 36, 75, 126, 154, 187, 189–190, 196, 203
International Photographer 153
The Intruders (1970) 100
Ireland, John 84, 87, 125, 159, 164
"The Iron Major" (TV) 209
Irving, Lori 203
Ivers, Robert 251, 261
Ivins, Perry 207
Ivo, Tommy 206, 209

Jack McCall, Desperado (1953) 202
Jacks, James 172
Jackson, Ginny 209
Jackson, Selmer 202
Jackson, Stoney 221
Jackson, Valarie 161
Jackson, Warren 33, 231
Jacobs, Harrison 77
Jacobs, William 204
Jacques, Ted 246
Jaeckel, Richard 46, 49, 51, 130
Jaffe, Allan 255, 258, 260
James, Jesse Edwards [Jesse James, Jr.] 65, 70–71
James, Jesse Woodson 43, 55–58, 61–62, 65–69, 70, 128, 131, 135, 151
James, John 34
James, Mary 65
James, Robert 55
James, Robert Franklin 65
James, Susan 55
James, Walter 185
James, Zerelda 155
"James Boys in Missouri" (Play) 67
James Brothers of Missouri (1950) 85
James Gang (Music Group) 142
Janovitz, Walter 44
Jarre, Kevin 172
Jay, Helen 242
Jayhawkers 58
Jeffreys, Anne 21, 33, 231
Jenks, Frank 208
Jennings, Al 119
Jenson, Roy 100
"Jeopardy at Jackson Hole" (1961, TV) 263
Jergens, Adele 39
Jergens, Linda 170
Jerry, Toni 208
Jesse James (1927) 71, 73
Jesse James (1939) 73–75
"Jesse James" (1957, TV) 95
"Jesse James" (Song) 67–68
Jesse James, Jr. (1942) 79–80
Jesse James and the Civil War in Missouri 61
Jesse James as the Outlaw (1921) 71
Jesse James Meets Frankenstein's Daughter (1966) 100
Jesse James Rides Again (1947) 81
Jesse James Under the Black Flag (1921) 71
Jesse James vs. The Daltons (1954) 92, 127
Jesse James' Women (1954) 93
Jewell, Isabel 80, 139
Jim Lane's Free State 177
Jiminez, Soledad 10
"Jingles Becomes a Baby Sitter" (TV) 208
"Jingles on the Railroad" (TV) 210
"Jingles Wins a Friend" (TV) 209
Joachim, Anthony 85

"Johnny Deuce" (TV) 206
Johns, Larry 139
Johnson, Arch 254
Johnson, Brad 38
Johnson, Chubby 94, 161, 205
Johnson, Ben 46, 80, 108, 167
Johnson, Don 142
Johnson, Dorothy 7
Johnson, Duke 125
Johnson, H.J. [Major] 58
Johnson, Jeffrey Paul 108
Johnson, Julia 113
Johnson, Kay 9
Johnson, Lamont 128
Johnson, LeRoy 166, 204
Johnson, Nunnally 94
Johnson, Ralph 70
Johnson, Robert Lee 199–200
Johnson, Russell 39, 161, 166
Johnson, Teffi 8–9
Johnson, Timothy 109
"A Joke on Sir Anthony" (TV) 207
Jolley, I. Stanford 27, 32, 34, 82, 87, 97,
    140, 162, 207, 210
Jones, Chris 99
Jones, Dickie 26, 188
Jones, Elvin 142
Jones, George C. 238
Jones, Gordon 91, 206
Jones, L.Q. 51, 220
Jones, Marsha Mae 206
Jones, Miranda 249
Jones, Morgan 209, 253
Jones, Podner 154
Jones, Ray 27, 30, 91, 188, 196, 201
Jordon, Paul 89
Jordan, Robert 208, 210
Jory, Victor 78, 85, 101–102, 158, 167
Joslin, Howard 204
Joyce, Marty 185
Joyce, Stephen 42
Joyce, William 239
Judels, Charles 186
July, Jim 134
Jungmeyer, Jack, Sr. 121
Jurado, Katy 49, 51
Juran, Nathan 160
Justice, William 210

Kane, Eddy 206
Kane, Joseph 11, 75, 77, 136
Kane, Michael 216
Kansas Raiders (1950) 87
Kansas State Penitentiary 114
Karen, James 108
Karlan, Richard 209–210
Karnes, Robert 251, 257
Kastner, Elliott 108

Katsulas, Andreas 171
Katzin, Lee H. 100
Katzman, Sam 37, 92, 161–162, 202
Kaufman, Philip 102
Kay, Beatrice 101
Kaylin, Samuel 155
Keach, James 103–104
Keach, Stacy 103–104, 169–170
Keane, Robert Emmett 11
Kearney Courier 70
Keel, Howard 204
Keene, Valley 203
Keene, William 210
Kehoe, Jack 53
Keith, Brian 51, 171, 211
Keith, Byron 202
Keith-Johnston, Colin 40
Keller, Sam 93
Kelley, Barry 85–86, 161, 261
Kelley, DeForest 261
Kellogg, John 87
Kellogg, Ray 237
Kelly, Bill 132
Kelly, Jack 171
Kelly, Nancy 73, 155, 158
Kelly, Walter 51
Kelsey, Fred 189, 202, 207–208
Kemper, Charles 125, 139
Kendall, Cy 16, 136, 156
Kendall, Lee 98
Kenneally, Philip 214
Kennedy, Arthur 78, 167
Kennedy, Bill 35
Kennedy, Don 246, 248
2
Kennedy, George 262
Kent, J.B. 119
Kent, Robert E. 92, 166
Kenyon, Charles 182
Kenyon, Jack 119
Kercheval, Ken 217
Kerr, Donald 209–210
Kershaw, Doug 141
Kesterber, Rachel 48
Kesterson, George [Art Mix] 77
Keyes, Evelyn 190
Keymas, George 96
Keys, Robert 140
Khilling, Rhed 108
Kibbee, Milton 15, 21–22, 29, 32, 76, 78,
    194
"The Kid from Red Butte" (TV) 208
The Kid from Texas (1950) 35–36
The Kid Rides Again (1943) 27
Kilbride, Perry 229
Kilian, Victor 73, 76, 84, 87
Killett, Pete 208
Kilmer, Val 53, 172–173

Kimball, Anne 207
King, Alan 128
King, Arlene 128
King, Bill 227
King, Brad 92
King, Brett 251, 256
King, Charles 12, 14–15, 17–20, 23–24, 27, 29–30, 32, 81, 89, 154, 189, 198, 230
King, Edith 139
King, Jack 219
King, Joe 121
King, Louis 205
King, Luther 227
King, Cpl. Melvin 226
King, Wright 235
King, Zalman 101
King of the Gun-Players, William Barclay Masterson 228
"King of the Wild West" (TV) 32
Kinney, Jack 21, 166
Kirk, Jack 11, 23–24, 33, 77, 79, 83, 184, 191, 230
Kirkwood, James 91, 125, 234
Kitses, Jim 102
Kleven, Max 44
Klimovsky, Leon 42
Knapp, Harry 101
Knell, David 107
Knepper, Robert 53
Knight, Fuzzy 186, 193, 209
Knott, Robert 221
Knowles, Carl 195
Knowles, Patric 46
Knox, Patricia 88
Knudsen, Peggy 240, 253, 258
Kohler, Frank 186
Kohler, Fred, Jr. 97, 206–207, 210
Kohler, Fred, Sr. 11, 182
Kohners, Pancho 215
Kootenay, Cecelia 214
Kortman, Robert (Bob) 79, 90, 121, 154
Koskells, Kirk 170
Kosloff, Maurice 203
Kovack, Nancy 43
Kraamwinkel, Monique 47
Kraamwinkel, Sacha 47
Kreig, Frank 202
Kresoja, Bruno 45
Kristofferson, Kris 9, 49, 51, 107
Kroeger, Barry 85
Kronhausen, Phyllis 47
Krone, Fred 166
Kroopf, Scott 52
Kruschen, Jack 245
Kulick, Seymour 205
Kulky, Henry 207–209, 235
Kunde, Al 234

Kurlander, Tom 53
Kuter, Kay E. 101

Lackteen, Frank 136, 183–184, 188, 210
Lacy, Alva 202
"Lady Luck" (1959, TV) 247
"The Lady Mayor" (TV) 206
"The Lady Plays Her Hand" (1960, TV) 258
"The Lady School Teacher" (TV) 206
Laidlaw, Ethan 26, 80, 86, 97, 121, 122, 156, 164, 188, 195, 198, 233
Laird, Effie 208
Lait, Jack, Jr. 157
Lake, Florence 210
Lake, Stewart N. 146, 150–151, 153, 155, 159
Lamb, Harold 186
Lamb, Karl 35
Lambert, Jack 126, 139, 242, 259
Lambert, Paul 242, 249, 256
Lamond, Don 43
LaMotte, Marguerite De 183
Lancaster, Burt 128–129, 164
Landa, Miguel 251
Landau, Richard 91
Landis, James 212
Landman, Hannie 44
Lando, Joe 109
Landon, Hal, Jr. 52
Landon, Michael, Jr. 108
Lane, Allan 36
Lane, Bruce 188
Lane, Diane 128, 221
Lane, Dick 35
Lane, Mike 210
Lane, Morgan, 164
Lane, Nora 72
Lang, Fritz 76–77
Lang, Jennings 102
Lang, Perry 128
Lang, Stephen 172
Langan, Glenn 46
Lange, Hope 94
Langton, Paul 255
Lansford, William 100
Lansing, Joi 246
Lapp, Richard 101
Larch, John 244
Largay, Raymond 92
Larsen, Keith 140
Larson, Christine 139, 206
Larson, David 230
Larue, Frank 14, 190
LaRue, Lash 125, 164, 234
LaRue, Walt 101
Laskey, Jesse 71
The Last Day (1984) 130

The Last Days of Frank and Jesse James
(1986) 107
The Last Frontier (1933) 183
Last of the Desperados (1955) 38–39
"Last of the Night Raiders" (1960, TV)
257
Last Stand of the Dalton Boys (1918, circa)
120
"Last Stop to Austin" (1960, TV) 257
Latham, Dwight 193
Lathrop, William Addison 120
Laughlin, Tom 217
Laughton, Eddie 195, 198, 200
Laurence, Ann 202
Lauter, Ed 216
Lauter, Harry 38, 166, 209, 232, 235, 252
Lavagnino, Angelo Francesco 212
Law and Order (1932) 151–152
Law and Order (1940) 152
Law and Order (1942) 23
Law and Order (1953) 152, 160–161
"Law of the Land" (1960, TV) 255
The Law vs. Billy the Kid (1954) 37
Lawrence, Barbara 92, 255
Lawrence, Bert 97
Lawrence, Jay 197
Lawrence, Peter Lee 45
Lawson, Eric 128
Lawson, Frank 136
Lawson, Priscilla 16
Lawson, Slick 107
Lazar, Paul 219
Learn, Charles 116
Leary, Nolan 88, 230
Lease, Rex 15, 18, 77, 126, 160, 184–185,
205, 207, 230
Leaud, Jean-Pierre 48
Leavitt, Norman 98
LeBaron, Bert 81, 88
Lebeau, Madeleine 168
LeBorg, Reginald 91
Ledbetter, Bud 119
Lederman, D. Ross 194
"Ledger of Guilt" (1961, TV) 261
Lee, Laura 93
Lee, Lanny 172
Lee, Lisa 260
Lee, Ruta 243
Lee, Virginia 120
Lee, Wendy 35
Lees, Paul 86
Leewood, Jack 98–99, 213
The Left-Handed Gun (1958) 8, 40–41
The Legend of Jesse James (1965–1966) 99
The Legend of the Lone Ranger (1981) 216
Le Gon, Jeni 84
LeGult, W.L. 215
Lehmann, Ted 210

Leigh, Nelson 92, 164, 208
Lennon, Percy 203
Leo, Melissa 218
Leonard, Terry 217
Leong, Al 52
LeRoy, Mervyn 39
LeSaint, Edward 73, 153, 156
Leslie, Bethel 246
Leslie, Joan 91
Leslie, Maxine 24, 28
Lesser, Len 254
"A Lesson in Violence" (1961, TV) 260
Lester, Jack 212
Lettiere, Louis 208, 210
Lettis, Dennis 108
Letz, George [Montgomery] 11
Levering, Joseph 154
Leverington, Shelby 104
Lewis, Alfred Henry 228
Lewis, Gene 231
Lewis, Geoffrey 107
Lewis, George J. 82, 124, 206, 207
Lewis, Mitchell 16, 183
Lewis, Nancy 101
Lewis, Vera 78
Libby, Fred 139, 159, 206, 208
"License to Cheat" (1959, TV) 240
Lieb, Robert P. 101
Life and Legend of Wyatt Earp (1955–1962,
TV) 164, 234
The Life and Times of Wyatt Earp 146, 150
*The Life and Times of Wyatt Earp, Leg-
endary Lawman* (1993) 172
Lincoln County War 4
Linden, Judith 196
Lindgren, Orley 206
Lindsey, Marilyn 91
Line, Helga 212
Linley, Chad 108
Linn, James R. 33
Linn, Jo 101
Linn, Rex 174
Lippert, Robert L. 84
Lippert, Robert L., Jr. 91
Litel, John 122, 126
Little, Little Jack 212
Little Big Man (1970) 214
Little Star, Robert 214
Littlefield, Jack V. 210
Littlefield, Lucien 209, 210
Lively, William 15, 88
Livermore, Paul 91
Livingston, Robert 206, 207
Lloyd, Christopher 216
Lloyd, George 199
Lloyd, Suzanne 251
Locke, Jon 130
Lockhart, Gene 16

Loeb, Art 234
Loft, Arthur 26, 75, 196
Loftin, Carey 81, 83
Lollier, George 154
London, Dirk 164, 234
London, Jerome 109
London, Pop 258
London, Tom 16, 31, 33, 81, 122, 154, 156, 188, 189, 195, 229–230
The Lone Star Vigilantes (1941) 198
Long, Hal 136
Long, Richard 87
Long, Walter 121
The Long Riders (1980) 103–105, 143
Longview, Texas: First National Bank Holdup 116
Loomis, Rod 52
Lorch, Ted 77, 197
Lorimer, Louise 208
Los Angeles Daily News 90
Los Angeles Herald Examiner 81, 105, 202, 205
Los Angeles Times 38, 45, 94, 127, 161
"The Lost Indian Mine" (TV) 207
"Lottery of Death" (1959, TV) 243
Loughery, Jackie 263
Love, Montagu 72, 78
Lovejoy, Frank 96–97
Lovering, Otho 26
Lowe, Rob 108
Lowell, Jack 40
Lowery, Dick 171
Lube, Henry A. 127
Lucas, Wilfred 157
Lule, Karen 221
Lull, Louis 61
"Lumber Camp Story" 207
Luna, Alvaro De 168
Lund, John 91
Lupton, John 100
Lydecker, Howard and Theodore 81–82, 88
Lyden, Pierce 33, 36, 126, 196
Lyles, A.C. 130
Lynch, Ken 242
Lynch, Theodore 207
Lynn, Emmett 81, 90, 219
Lynn, Patricia 209
Lynn, Robert 240, 258
Lyons, Cliff 154
Lyons, Richard E. 170, 213

Maaske, Dee 170
MacArthur, Charles 9
MacAteer, Alan 209
MacBurnie, John 36, 81–82
MacDonald, Etta 154
MacDonald, J. Farrell 85, 124–125, 139, 154, 159, 182, 183, 199

MacDonald, Kenneth 33, 126, 139, 195, 199
MacDuff, Tyler 38
Mace, Rita 42
Macgowan, Kenneth 76, 137
MacGregor, Casey 81
MacGregor, K.C. 127
MacGregory, Lee 90
Mack, Cactus 21, 29–30, 32, 88, 124, 157, 185
Mack, Buck 16
Mack, Wayne 43
MacKenzie, Aeneas 229
MacLane, Barton 38, 96
MacLaren, Ian 121
MacLeod, Angus 254
MacLeod, Gavin 101
Macnee, Patrick 171
MacNeil, Evan 249
Macready, George 125, 258
Madison, Guy 168, 180, 205, 206
Madsen, Chris [Marshal] 119, 151
Madsen, Michael 174
Magginetti, Kathleen 89
Mains, Marlene 229
Mainwarning, Daniel 96
Mala, Ray 188
Malden, Karl 167
Mallison, Rory 36–37, 91–92, 126, 206, 208, 232
Mallory, Chad 206, 208
Mallory, Wayne 209, 245
Malone, Dorothy 161
Maloney, John 246
Maloney, Kathy 48
"Man of Action" (1959, TV) 243
The Man Who Killed Billy the Kid (1967) 45
Mann, Anthony 233
Mann, Delbert 182
Mann, Hank 156
Manners, Marjorie 29, 32
Manning, Jack 102
Manning, Ron 170
Mansfield, John 204
Mansfield, Sally 208
Mantley, John 39
Mantoya, Patrick 216
Maples, Ted 26, 81, 91, 136, 197, 201
Mara, Adele 237
Marchant, Carlos R. 212
Marchant, Joaquin Romero 211
Marchant, Rafael Romero 212
Marco, Henry 35
Marcus, James 10–11, 182
Marcus, Josephine Sarah [Earp] 147, 149, 150, 152
Margolin, Stuart 101, 215

Marin, Edwin L. 83–85
Marion, Beth 187
"Marked Deck" (1959, TV) 241
Markham, Monte 168
Marlow, Res 212
Marlowe, Don 209
Marlowe, Frank 81
"Marriage Feud of Ponca City" (TV) 208
Marsh, Mae 138
Marshal, Adam 95
Marshal of Mesa City (1939) 157
Marshall, George 120–122
Marshall, John 233
Marston, Theodore 120
Martell, Donna 38, 240
Martell, Gregg 162, 164, 209, 233
Martin, Chris-Pin 11, 139, 156, 158
Martin, Christopher 10
Martin, Dewey 87
Martin, Douglas D. 168
Martin, Eugene 257
Martin, George 42
Martin, Irene 207
Martin, Lewis 166, 204
Martin, Marion 229
Martin, Ross 170–171, 238
Martinelli, Elsa 141
"Marriage Mixup" (TV) 206
Masak, Ron 101
"Masked Riders" (TV) 206
Maslin, Janet 54
Mason, James 22, 234
Mason, Leroy 81, 184, 194
Mason, Louis 76, 234
Mason, Tim 20, 22
"Masquerade at Moccasin Flats" (TV) 208
Massett, Patrick 53
Massey, Raymond 202
Massini, Per 47
Massot, Joe 142
Masters, Howard 15, 19
Masterson, Bat 43, 145–147, 150–151, 162, 223, 228
Masterson, Edward 223
Masterson, Thomas 223
Masterson, Tom, Jr. 228
Masterson of Kansas (1954) 161, 234
"Masterson's Arcadia Club" (1960, TV) 253
Mathers, Don 209
Matheson, Chris 52
Matheson, Tim 130
Mathews, Carl 12, 23–24, 30, 185, 187–188, 197
Mathews, Carole 207
"A Matter of Honor" (1959, TV) 243
Mature, Victor 159
Maurer, Norman 43

"The Maverick" (TV) 208
Mayer, Ken 100, 252, 262
Maxey, Paul 87
Maxwell, Charles 100, 237, 247, 262
Maxwell, John 162
Maxwell, Lucien 193
Maxwell, Pete 4
Mayall, Herschel 181
Mayer, Ken 210, 214
Maynard, Kermit 16, 24–25, 28–29, 32, 79–80, 85, 138, 162, 188
Maynnard, Richard 108
Mayo, Frank 78
Mazurki, Mike 97, 167
McCabe, J.P. 70
McCabe, Peter 207
McCall, Jack 180
The McCanles Affair 177–179
McCarroll, Frank 27, 29–30, 32, 36, 136
McCarthy, John 109
McClary, Clyde 184
McClory, Sean 167
McClure, Bud 188
McClure, Dove 171
McClure, Greg 124
McClure, Tipp 256
McConnell, Fred 183
McCormack, William 207, 234
McCormick, Merrill 24, 193
McCoy, Tim 184
McCrea, Joel 162–163, 235–236
McCroy, Kent 108
McCullough, Harrell 115–117
McCullough, Philo 156
McDaniel, Sam 78
McDaniels Tom 60
McDonald, Francis 207, 234
McDonald, Frank 140
McDonald, Miki 101
McDonnell, Ed T. 43, 236
McDonough, Tom 91
McDougal, Annie [Little Britches] 118–119
McDowell, Malcolm 171
McDowell, Nelson 10, 152
McElhanie, Bill 113
McEveety, Vincent 130
McGann, William 158
McGeehan, Pat 203
McGlyn, Frank 186
McGlynn, Frank, Jr. 185, 231
McGowan, J.P. 188
McGrail, Walter 12, 21
McGrath, Larry 33, 87, 231
McGrath, Roger 220
McGregor, Buddy 173
McGregor, Park 206–207, 209
McGuinn, Joe 12, 15, 157, 198, 200–202

McGuire, Paul 140, 208
McGuirk, Catherine 223
McIntire, John 233, 235
McIntire, Reba 171, 219
McIntyre, Richard 42
McKay, Cole 108
McKay, George 190
McKay, Wanda 23
McKee, Lafe 122, 185
McKee, Tom 209, 237
McKellen, Joan 203
McKenzie, Bob 11, 121
McKenzie, Fay 121
McKenzie, Richard 169
McKenzie, William 206
McKim, David 188
McKim, Sammy 188–189
McKinney, Bill 215
McKinney, Mira 87
McLaglen, Andrew V. 46
McLaglen, Josh 46
McLaglen, Mari 46
McLeod, Norman 97
McLerie, Allyn 205
McLowery, Frank 148–149, 227
McLowery, Tom 148–149, 227
McMinn, Frazer 34
McMullen, James 211
McMurphy, Charles 122
McMurty, Larry 219
McMyler, Pamela 46
McNally, Stephen 96, 233
McNamara, J. Patrick 52
McPeak, Sandy 107
McQueen, J.W. 116
McQuinn, Joe 200
McSween, Alexander 4, 9
McTaggart, Bud 21
McVey, Patrick 244
McVey, Tyler 237, 252
McWade, Edward 76
Meade, Bill 206
Meader, George 207
Meador, Steve 217
Means, Bobby 212
Means, Russell 219
Mecklenburg, Margit 47
"The Medicine Show" (TV) 207
Meehan, Lew 188, 198
Meek, Donald 73, 76
"Meeting at Mimbers" (1961, TV) 261
Meher, Ray 154
Mejan, Juan 168
Melford, George 138, 156
Mell, Randle 174
Melton, Sid 87, 97
Melville, Sam 168
Mendoza, Harry B. 164

Mercier, Louis 159
Meredith, Charles 234
Meredith, Iris 27
Meredith, Judi 211
Meredith, Madge 231
Merlin, Jan 96, 257
Mern, E. 168
Merrick, Lynn 79
Merrill, Tony 164
Merriwether, Nicholas 212
Merton, John 12–14, 22–25, 28, 35, 184, 207, 209
"Meteor Mesa" (TV) 210
Metz, Leon 220
"Mexican Gun Running" (TV) 207
"Mexican Rustlers" (TV) 206
Meyer, Emile 98, 241, 245, 248
Michnelis, Dario 168
Middleton, Charles 73, 75, 138, 158
Middleton, John 132
Middleton, Robert 237
Mikler, Mike 51
Mila, Miguel 45
Milan, Lita 40–41
Miles, John Peere 189
Miles, Robert J. 204
Miles, Vera 162–163
Miljan, John 186, 191
Milland, Gloria 45, 212
Milland, Victor 209
Millar, Stuart 214
Miller, Bran 115
Miller, Clell 62
Miller, David H. 16–17, 167
Miller, Kristine 206
Miller, Marvin 262
Miller, Ty 218
Miller, Walter 188
Miller, Winston 37, 159, 182
Millican, James 85–86, 124, 160, 208, 233
Mills, Mort 247
Milner, Martin 164
Milton, George 31
Milton, Gerald 245, 256
Milton, Zachary 128
Mimms, Bill 210
Mimms, Zerelda 59, 62, 65
Minaud, Michael 48
Mineo, Sal 167
Miranda, Steve 214
Mirisch, Walter 235
Misiorowski, Bob 172
Missouri State Guard 57
"Mr. Fourpaws" (1960, TV) 250
Mitchell, Cameron 39
Mitchell, Carlyle 260
Mitchell, Frank 197–198, 200–201
Mitchell, Howard 81

Mitchell, Millard 233
Mitchell, Pat 206–207
Mitchell, Steve 257
Mitchell, Thomas 26
Mitchum, Christopher 46
Mitchum, John 46, 96
Mitchum, Robert 172
Mix, Art [George Kesterson] 136, 152, 188, 190, 195, 200–201
Mix, Ruth 185
Moffat, Donald 102
Mohr, Gerald 244, 260
Monagaw Hotel 60
Moniot, Robert 108
Monk, Isabell 217
Monroe, Tommy [Tom] 35, 207, 209
"The Monster in the Lake" (TV) 208
Montague, Edward J. 9
Montague, Monte 157, 190
Montalban, Ricardo 167
Montana: The Magazine of Western History (1995) 150
Montana Belle (1952) 126–127, 131, 139–140
Montgomery, Elizabeth 106–107
Montgomery, George 139, 160, 161, 162, 166, 202
Montgomery, Jack 188
Montoya, Alex 140, 202
Montoya, Julia 209
Moody, Ralph 39, 242
Mooney, Jesse 135
Moore, Barbara 212
Moore, Charles 77
Moore, Clayton 36, 81–82, 207, 217
Moore, Dennis 18, 20, 126, 164, 246, 251
Moore, Dorothy 122
Moore, Eugenie 112
Moore, Ida 33
Moore, Joanna 247–248
Moore, Michael 204
Moore, Pauline 75
Moore, Tom 208
Moorehead, Agnes 94
Morante, Milburn 18, 184–185
Moray, Tom 200
Moreno, Antonia 202
Moreno, Felix 128
Moreno, Jorge 128
Moreno, Robert 214
Morgan, Boyd [Red] 127, 160, 208
Morgan, Dennis 78
Morgan, George 189
Morgan, Harry 130
Morgan, Lee 126
Morgan, Melissa 212
Morgan, Ray 88
Morgan, Read 212

Moriarty, Pat 186
Morin, Alberto 46
Morning Telegraph 228
Moroff, Mike 128
Morrell, George 14–15, 18–20, 22–23, 27, 30, 185, 188, 193, 195, 197
Morrice, John 132
Morris, Adrian 76
Morris, Frances 206, 229
Morris, Wayne 78, 83–84, 241
Morrison, Chuck 196
Morrison, Pete 184
Morrow, Brad 210
Morrow, H. 168
Morrow, Neyle 206–207
Morrow, Scott 209
Morse, Robin 91
Morton, Charles 81
Morton, James 121
Morton, Mickey 260
Morton, Nanomba [Moonbeam] 167
Moss, Charles 49
Motion Picture Daily 90
Motion Picture Herald 11, 41, 204
Moullet, Lue 48
Moullet, Patrice 48
Moulton, Buck 195
"The Mountain Men" (TV) 209
Mowbray, Alan 159
Mower, Jack 78
Muckleroy, Matt [Marshal] 116
Muir, Gavin 243
Mulhall, Jack 185
Mullaney, Jack 214
Mulligan, Richard 214
Mulroney, Dermot 51, 171
Mulvey, Paul 198
"Murder Can Be Dangerous" (1960, TV) 256
Murdock, Jack 217
Murphy, Audie 36, 87, 101–102, 126
Murphy, Ben 215, 220
Murphy, Charles 121
Murphy, Donald 162, 166, 252
Murphy, Geoff 53
Murphy, Horace 11
Murphy, Michael S. 52
Murphy, Richard 79
Murphy, Sam 128
Murphy, Skip 101
Murphy, Terry 101
Murphy-Dolan 4
Murray, Don 101, 213
Murray, Forbes 79
Murray, Zon 36, 202, 206
Muse, Clarence 138, 157
"The Music Teacher" (TV) 209
Mustin, Burt 101

My Darling Clementine (1946) 159–160
Myers, Alton B. 135
The Mysterious Rider (1942) 25
Myton, Fred 20, 27, 199, 201

Nagel, Conrad 241
Nash, Robert 210
Natham, Norman 214
Natteford, Jack 11, 33, 75, 80, 86
Navarro, Anna 261
Nazarro, Ray 160
Neal, Richard 184
Neal, Tom 35, 91, 125, 207
Nedar, Vladmer [Lina Wertmuller] 141
Needham, Leo 241
Neff, Mary 108
Neff, Ralph 209
Neil, James 70–71
Neill, Noel 82, 88
Neise, George 244
Nelson, Bek 260
Nelson, Bobby 185
Nelson, Ed 166, 263
Nelson, Gene 242
Nelson, Herbert 102
Nelson, Kirk 53
Nelson, Lloyd 42
Nelson, Rick 100
Nelson, Sam 188
Nelson, Sid 35
Nelson, Willie 107
Nestell, Bill 184
Neufeld, Sigmund 12, 14–15, 17–25, 27–32, 38–39
Neumann, Dorothy 210
Neumann, Kurt 35–36
Neville, Daphne 219
New York Rock Ensemble 142
New York Times 11, 52, 54, 95, 153, 171, 175, 214
Newcomb, "Bitter Creek" 115, 118–119
Newcomb, George 113
Newfield, Joel 19, 22
Newfield, Sam 12, 14–15, 17–25, 27–32, 38–39, 184, 187
Newell, William 26, 210
Newlan, Paul 200
Newman, Joseph M. 235
Newman, Paul 8, 40–41
Newman, Walter 94
Newman, William 107
Newton, Charles 182
Nicholas, Charles 60
Nicholas, Robin 219
Nichols, George Ward 172, 180
Nichols, Ray 11
Nickoll, Nick 242
Nicol, Alex 161

Nielsen, Leslie 213
Nigh, Jane 85
Nimoy, Leonard 108
Nite, "Big Asa" 115–116
Nite, Jim 115–116
Nix, E.D. 119
Nixon, Allan 208
"No Amnesty for Death" (1961, TV) 261
"No Funeral for Thorn" (1959, TV) 246
Nolan, Jeanette 261
Noonan, Tom 84, 87
"A Noose Fits Anybody" (1958, TV) 238
Norris, Edward 156
North from the Lonestar (1941) 196
Northfield Bank Holdup (Minnesota) 62
Norton, Mark 100
Novack, Shelly 101
Novak, Kim 216
Novello, Jay 136, 254
Nugent, Carol 210
Numkena, Anthony 39

Oakland, Simon 211, 213
Oakman, Wheeler 184
Oates, Warren 243, 261
Ober, Philip 259
Obon, Raymond 42
O'Brian, Hugh 87, 97, 126, 164, 165, 171, 173, 234
O'Brien, Dave 18–19, 22–24, 187
O'Brien, Edmond 101
O'Brien, Erin 251, 262
O'Brien, George 153, 156–157, 167, 182
O'Brien, Joan 240, 247, 256
O'Brien, Laurie 217
O'Brien, Rory 214
O'Byrne, Bryan 130
O'Callohan, Foxy 18
O'Connor, Frank 11, 88, 234
O'Connor, Kathleen 181
O'Dea, John 202
O'Donnell, Jacklyn 98
O'Donnell, Joseph 14–15, 18, 30–31
O'Driscoll, Martha 122–123
O'Flynn Damian 234
O'Hanlon, James 204
O'Hara, Catherine 174
O'Hara, George 73
O'Hara, Jimmy 167
O'Hearn, Eileen 200
O'Herlihy, Michael 170
Ohmart, Carol 244, 250
Ojena, Louis 101
O.K. Corral 148, 150–151, 159
O'Kelly, Don 254, 257
"Ol' Pardner Rides Again" (TV) 208
"Old Cowboys Never Die" (TV) 209
Oliver, Ted 154

Olkewicz, Walter 217
O'Loughlin, Jack 120
Olsen, Larry 233
Olson, Nancy 37–38
Olsson, Robert A. 120
O'Mahoney, Jock [Jack] 125, 233
O'Malley, Charles 182
O'Malley, Pat 156
"One Bullet from Broken Bow" (1959, TV) 240
O'Neal, Charles 33
O'Neal, William 161
O'Neill, Henry 16
O'Neill, Johnny 98
O'Neill, Shannon 207
Onyx, Narda 100
Oppenheimer, Alan 214
O'Quinn, Terry 51, 172
Orlandi, Felice 104
Ormond, Ron 34, 124–125
Ortego, Artie 18, 28–29, 184, 188
Osborne, Bud 33–34, 37, 75, 78, 80, 83, 88, 92, 125, 154, 189, 190, 200, 207, 210, 233
Osceola, Missouri, Shoot-Out 62
O'Shea, Jack 77, 154, 230
Osmond, Clif 211
Osmond, Marie 170
Ossmon, David 142
Osterloh, Bob [Robert] 86, 125
The Outlaw (1943) 8, 26
"Outlaw Flats" (TV) 206
The Outlaws Is Coming (1965) 43, 99, 141, 168, 236
"The Outlaw's Portrait" (TV) 209
"Outlaw's Son" (TV) 207
Overall, Park 171
Overton, Frank 94

Pacheco, Rafael 211
Packer, Netta 193
Padden, Sarah 23, 231
Padjan, Jack 182
Padula, Marguerita 10
Page, Bradley 190, 193, 198
Paige, Janis 83–84
Paiva, Nestor 40, 80, 100
Pakula, Joanne 172
Palance, Jack 51, 128, 219
Pallias, Dorita 36
Palmer, Bob 95
Palmer, Gregg 46
Palmer, Max 238
Palmer, Tex 14–15, 18, 20, 81, 154
The Panhandle Trail (1947) 25
"Papa Antinelli" (TV) 207
Pappas, Iris 53
Pardee, Ida 120

Parfrey, Woodrow 215
Paris, Darla 101
Parish, James Robert 105, 107–108, 129
Park, Jacquelyn 210
Park, Post 88, 91
Parker, Eddie 81, 83, 121
Parker, Fess 97
Parker, Fred 184
Parker, Holt 53
Parker, Isaac 132, 134
Parker, Jean 39
Parker, Willard 91, 98, 141
Parks, Michael 53
Parks, Post 156
Parnell, Emory 26, 80, 206–207, 209
Parnell, James 253
Parnell, Jim 207
Parrish, Leslie 254–255
Parson and the Outlaw (1957) 39–40
Parsons, Milton 78
Parsons, Patsy Lee 11
Parsons, Ray 208
Passing of the Oklahoma Outlaws (1915) 119
Pat Garrett and Billy the Kid (1973) 8, 49
Patrick, Dorothy 207
Patrick, Lee 125
Patten, Bill 157, 188
Patterson, Elizabeth 137
Patterson, Hank 87–88, 250, 258
Patterson, Pat 47
Patton, Billy Joe 53
Paul, Taffy 262
Paull, Morgan 107
Pawl, Nick 263
Pawley, William 76, 156
Pawnee, Indian Territory Farmers and Citizens Bank 115
Paxton, Bill 108, 172
Paxton, John 108
Payne, Sally 77, 121, 136, 191
Payton, Barbara 91, 202
Pearce, John 102
Pearl Younger and the FallingStarrs 132
Peckinpah, Sam 9, 49
Peil, Edward, Sr. 15, 17, 26–27, 77, 87, 182, 189
Pellow, Cliff 216
Pendleton, Steve [Gaylord] 86, 89, 91, 206–208
Penn, Arthur 40–41, 214
Penn, Leonard 89, 206–207, 209–210
Pennick, Jack 159
Pepper, Barbara 76
Perkins, Gil 81, 210
Perkins, Jack 220
Perna, David 168
Perrin, Jack 12, 35, 87, 188, 205

Perrott, William 34, 139
Perry, Frank 169–170
Perry, Jack 38
Perry, John Bennett 170, 216
Perry, Pasqual 14, 19, 21, 75, 77, 81
Perry, Roger 100
"A Personal Matter" (1959, TV) 240
Peters, House, Jr. 34, 82, 207
Peters, Kelly Jean 214
Peters, Ralph 15, 194
Peterson, Arthur 102
Peterson, Dan 70
Peterson, William 53
Petrie, Howard 249, 253, 255
Petti, Carl 91
Peyton, Claud 184
Phelan, Brian 47
Phelps, Lee 76, 188, 206
Phelps, Tex 20
Phillips, Barney 94
Phillips, Eddie 21
Phillips, Joe 83
Phillips, John 36
Phillips, Lou Diamond 51, 54, 108
Phillips, Robert 168
Phillips, William [Bill] 37, 92, 101, 139
Phipps, William 164, 206, 240
"The Photographer's Story" 207
Pica, Antonio 45
Pichel, Irving 233–234
Pickard, John 46
Pickens, Slim 38, 51, 216
"A Picture of Death" (1960, TV) 249
"The Pied Piper of Dodge City" (1960, TV) 249
Pierce, Charley 113, 118–119
Pierce, James 72, 122, 195
Pierce, Maggie 255
"Pigeon and Hawk" (1960, TV) 249
Pimon, Bernard 48
Pinkerton Detective Agency 60, 62
The Pioneer Peacemaker (1913) 181
Pitillo, Maria 108
Pittman, Tom 95
Pitti, Carl 16
Pitts, Charlie 62
Pitts, Michael R. 105, 107–108, 129
The Plainsman (1937) 180, 186
The Plainsman (1966) 213
Platt, Edward C. 242
Plowman, Melinda 43, 84
Plummer, Armanda 128
Plummer, Rose 30
Plympton, George 17, 183
Police Gazette 131, 135
Pollard, Michael J. 9, 49–50
Pony Express (1953) 204
"Pony Express vs. Telegraph" (TV) 206

Pooderall, Earl 107
Potts, Cliff 106–107, 128
Powell, Charles Arthur 188
Powell, Patricia 241
Powell, Russ 122, 196
Power, Tyrone 73–74
Powers, Bill 113–114
Powers, Richard [Tom Keene] 33
"Prairie Flats Land Swindle" (TV) 208
Prairie Gunsmoke (1942) 201
Prairie Schooners (1940) 193
Prather, Lee 197
Pratt, Judson 167
Pratt, Purnell 186
Prendes, Luis 45
Prescott, Guy 248
"The Prescott Campaign" (1961, TV) 259
Press, Marvin 208
Price, Hal 12, 17–18, 23–24, 28–30, 200
Price, Stanley 33, 84, 124–125
Price, Sterling [General] 57
"Price of Paradise" (1961, TV) 259
Priestley, Jason 172
Prince of the Plains (1949) 232
Prine, Andrew 42, 46
Procopio, Lou 47
Proctor, Phillip 142
"The Professor's Daughter" (TV) 207
"Promised Land" (1959, TV) 244
Prosser, Hugh 195
Pryor, Ainslie 40, 96
Puglia, Frank 16, 140
Pullen, Bill 209
Pullman, Bill 174
Pulver, Herman 40
Punnell, Larry 263
Purcell, Lee 49
Pyle, Denver 38, 40, 167, 208, 210, 241, 259
Pyper-Ferguson, John 108

Quade, John 128
Quaid, Dennis 103–174
Quaid, Randy 103–104, 128
Qualen, John 167
Quanah, Chief 226
Quantrill, William Clark 57–58, 132
Quartero, Nena 26
Quinn, Anthony 186
Quinn, Pat 142

Ragan, Mike 38, 206, 208, 243
"Rage of Princess Anne" (1960, TV) 256
The Raiders (1964) 211
Raiders of Red Rock (1947) 28
Raidler, "Little Bill" 118–119
Raine, William McLeod 151, 179
Raily, Mary 195

"The Rainmaker" (TV) 209
Rainwater, Gregg 218
Raison, Milton 24
Ralston, Annie 62, 65
Ramsey, Jeff 216
Ramsey, Quen 121
Randall, Anne 101
Randall, Stuart 204
Randall, Sue 256
Randels, Larry 216
Random, Bob 101
Rangno, Terry 242
Ranier, Joe 170
Ranson, Lois 31
Rapoport, J.C. 170
Rawlins, Judith 258
Rawlinson, Herbert 85, 229
Ray, Allan 256
Ray, Anthony 95
Ray, Antoria 169
Ray, Clark 53
Ray, Nicholas 94
Ray, Wade 88
Raymond, Paula 243, 250, 257
Raynor, William 140
Reach, John 210
Reade, Charles 257
Reagan, Ronald 161
Real West 132
"The Real West—The Dalton Gang"
   (1994, TV) 130
Reason, Rhodes 220
Red Crow, Floyd 219
Red Fox, Chief 70
Redd, Mary Robin 102
Reed, Diana 70–71
Reed, Edward 132, 134–135
Reed, George 138
Reed, Jim 57, 132
Reed, Marshall 88, 124, 206, 208, 251
Reed, Pamela 104, 143
Reed, Tom 152
Reed, Walter 33, 101, 167
Reel, David 212
Reeves, Bob 77, 83
Reeves, Dick 239
Reeves, Keanu 52
Reeves, Richard 40, 44
Reevies, Steve 221
Regan, Mike 140
Regehr, Duncan 53
Reid, Carl Benton 162
Reid, Pamela 104
Reid, Wallace, Jr. 26
Reisner, Dean 89
"The Reluctant Witness" (1960, TV) 166,
   252
Remar, James 221

The Remarkable Andrew (1942) 78–79
Remer, James 104
Renaldo, Duncan 78
The Renegade (1943) 31
"The Return of Chief Redhawk" (TV) 209
The Return of Frank James (1940) 74, 76
The Return of Jesse James (1950) 86–87
Return of the Bad Men (1948) 33, 83, 124
Revere, Anne 86
Rey, Pilar Del 36
Reyes, Gene 169
Reynolds, Francisco 128
Reynolds, Jack 206–207
Reynolds, Marjorie 136
Reynolds, William 126
Rhed, Joyce 93
Rheia, Al 196
Rhodes, Eugene Manlove 118
Riano, Renie 207
Ricci, Aldo 168
Rich, Christopher 171
Rich, David Lowell 213
Rich, Dick 206
Richards, Addison 193, 211
Richards, Ann 80
Richards, Jill 209
Richards, Keith 81, 88, 208–209
Richards, Paul 244, 258
Richards, Robert L. 233
Richmond, Felice 35
Richmond, Ted 126
Richmond, Warner 10–11
Rickabaugh, Lou 227
Ride Lonesome (1959) 101
Riebe, Loren 81
Riesner, Dean 100
Riggio, Jerry 34
Riggs, Lynn 186
Righini, Francesca 141
"The Right of Way" (TV) 208
Riley, Robin 255
Rinehart, Jim 88
Ringo, Johnny 43, 227
Riordan, Robert 81
Rippey, Leon 53
Riss, Dan 166
Ritchie, Will M. 183
Ritter, Tex 162, 196–198, 200–201
Rivas, Carlos 128
"River Boat" (1959, TV) 241
Riveria, Luis 45
Rivero, Julian 15, 17, 26
Rizzi, Gene 26
Roadman, Betty 11
Roaring Frontiers (1941) 197
Rob Wagner's Script 27
Robards, Jason, Jr. 51, 168, 216

Robards, Jason, Sr. 33, 231
Robbins, Gale 205
Robbins, Sam 23
Robbins, Walt 184
Roberson, Chuck 46, 81, 84, 88, 160, 169, 233, 251
Roberts, Allene 233
Roberts, Ben 216
Roberts, J.N. 101
Roberts, Lee 88–89, 124, 126
Roberts, Lynn 11–12
Roberts, Roy 126, 159, 233
Roberts, William 216
Robertson, Cliff 102–103
Robertson, Dale 40, 85, 95, 127–128, 141
Robertson, Willard 73
Robin Hood 8
"Robin Hood of the Old West" (TV) 55
Robinhood of the Pecos (1941) 136
Robinson, Ann 126
Robinson, Dewey 152
Robinson, Edward G. 167
Robinson, James G. 51
Robinson, Roger 215
Rochelle, Claire 196
Rockwell, Jack 10, 31, 35, 75, 77, 122, 158, 188, 191, 196
Rodriguez, Estelita 100
Rodriguez, Orlando 209
Rodriguez, Percy 213
Rogers, Cameron 137
Rogers, Charles [Buddy] 39
Rogers, Christopher Cody 171
Rogers, Howard Emmett 16
Rogers, John W. 160–161
Rogers, Kasey 253, 257
Rogers, Kenny 130, 171–172, 236, 240
Rogers, Marianne 171
Rogers, Roy 8, 11, 12, 75, 77, 97, 136, 191–192
Rogers, Walter 182
Rogers, Will, Jr. 37–38
Rojas, Alfonso 45, 212
Rojo, Antonio Molina 212
Roland, Gilbert 167
Rolfe, Sam H. 215
Rolph, Alice 208
Roman, Ruth 139, 202
Romanoff, Constantine 189
"The Romany Knives" (1959, TV) 245
Romero, Carlos 245, 255
Romero, Cesar 155
Rooker, Michael 172
Rooney, Mickey 171
Roosevelt, Buddy 15, 87, 161, 202, 207
Roper, Jack 196
Roquemore, Henry 121

Rosa, Joseph G. 220
Rosell, Earl 214
Rosemond, Clinton 138
Rosenberg, Aaron 155, 233
Rosenor, George 188
"Rosie Lee" (TV) 132
Ross, Earl 209
Ross, George 210
Ross, Thomas W. 78
Ross, William 80
Rossellini, Isabella 174
Rosser, Bill 130
Rossovich, Ric 171
Roth, Eugene [Gene] 126, 202, 256
Roth, Joe 51
Roundtree, Richard 108
Rousseau, Louise 232
Routh, John Jackson 107
Rowan, Dan 121
Rowland, Betty 101
Rowland, Henry 208
Royal, Charles Francis 196
Royce, Frosty 88, 196, 201
Rubenstein, John 142
Rubenstein, Zelda 171
Rubin, Benny 37, 162
Ruck, Alan 53
Rudabaugh, Dave 146
Ruhl, William 206–207
Ruller, Lance 253
"Run for Your Money" (1961, TV) 260
"The Runaway Wizard" (TV) 210
Rush, Barbara 130
Russ, William 128
Russek, Jorge 51
Russell, Bing 44, 167
Russell, Ed 91
Russell, George 128
Russell, Jane 8, 26–27, 126, 139
Russell, John 73, 127
Russell, John [scenarist] 182
Russell, Jorge 168
Russell, Kurt 172–173
Russell, William D. 90
Rutherford, Ann 193–194
Ryan, Dick 255
Ryan, Fran 104
Ryan, Robert 33, 90, 168, 231–232
Ryan, Ted 91
Ryder, Alfred 211
Ryley, Courtney 186

Sackheim, Jerry 98
Sadler, Nick 108
The Saga of Billy the Kid 6, 9, 16
Sage, Willard 49
"Sagebrush Manhunt" (TV) 209
St. Aubrey, Robert 97

St. John, Al [Fuzzy] 12–15, 17–32, 34, 79, 125, 187
St. John, Betta 37
Saint Johnson 151
Sais, Marin 18, 189
Sale, Richard 215
Sale, Virginia 80, 231
Salkow, Sidney 202
Salmi, Albert 53, 168
Salvador, Jimmy 127
Sampson, Will 216
Samuel, Rubin 57–58
Sancho, Fernando 168
Sande, Walter 36, 122, 162
Sanders, Hugh 160, 249
Sanders, Sandy 162, 208–209
Sandoz, Mari 167
Sands, Gaston 42
Sanford, Ralph 207, 234
Sanjuan, Manuel Hernandez 42
Sann, Paul 179
Santa Fe (1951) 233–234
Sanz, Francisco 212
Sanz, Paco 45
Saturday Evening Post 91
Saunders, Gloria 206
Saunders, Jerry 108
Saunders, Mary Jane 209
Savage, Ann 91
Savage, John 128
"Savvy, the Smart Little Dog" (TV) 207
Sawaya, George 259
Sawtell, Paul 33
Sawyer, Joe 26, 138, 154, 156
Saxon, Aaron 95
Saxon, John 101
Saylor, Syd 92, 210
Sayre, George W. 24, 28
Scanlon, John 169
Scannell, Frank 209–210
Schaefer, Rube 157, 210
Schallert, William 168, 250, 258
Schayer, Richard 160
Schiff, Paul 51, 53
"The School Teacher Story" (TV) 204
Schreiber, Liev 219
Schrock, Raymond 199
Schroeder, Doris 79
Schwalb, Ben 96
Schwartz, Jack 203
Schwenk, Gordon 212
Scott, Jacqueline 245, 248
Scott, Morton 82
Scott, Randolph 33, 73, 80, 85, 121, 125, 155, 231–234
Scott, Robert 204
Scott, Sherman 17–24, 26–27
Scott, Walter 217

Scullin, George 164
Scully, Peter 140
Searl, Jack 257
Sears, Fred F. 166
Seavey, Marjorie 153
Seay, James 140, 202, 252, 257
Sebell, Bert 153
"The Secret Is Death" (1959, TV) 244
Sedley, Bruce 43
Seiler, Lew 153
Seitz, George B. 136, 183
Selander, Lesley 139
Selden Lindsey 115–117
Seldes, Marian 94
Sells, Paul 77
Selzer, Milton 215
Sepulveda, Carl 12, 28, 31, 75, 81
Serato, Massimo 168
Sessions, Almira 206
Seven, Johnny 258
Seven Hours of Gunfire (1964) 211
Seven Men from Now (1956) 101
Seymour, Jane 109
Seymour, Jonathan 209
"The Shadow of Jesse James" (1960, TV) 98
Shafer, Philip 169
Shahan, Rocky 88
"Shakedown at St. Joe" (1959, TV) 247
Shane (1953) 104
Shannon, Harry 33, 96, 261
Shannon, Paul 43
Shannon, Richard 204
Sharpe, Dave 83, 88, 126, 206–207
"Sharpshooter" (1959, TV) 241
Shaw, Paula 47
Shayne, Robert 206
Sheehan, John 26, 125
Sheehan, Winfield R. 153
Sheen, Charlie 51
Sheldon, Kathryn 156
Sheldon, Lee 210
Sheldon, Norman 33
Shemayne, Steve 214
Shepard, Jan 259
Sheppard, Jim 168
Sheppard, John 137
Sheridan, Dan 96, 240
Sheridan, James 185
"The Sheriff of Buckeye" (TV) 210
Sheriff of Sage Valley (1942) 24
"The Sheriff Was a Redhead" (TV) 208
"The Sheriff's Secret" (TV) 209
Sherman, Fred 207, 210
Sherman, George 79
Sherman, Harry 229
Sherman, Teddie 229

"Sherman's March Through Dodge City"
  (1958, TV) 239
Sherwood, Choti 19
Sherwood, George 207, 234
Shibell, Charles 146
Shields, Arthur 244
Shields, Joannie 101
Shields, Randy 101
Shiff, Richard 53
Shipman, Barry 95
Shirley, Charlotte 131
Shirley, Cravens 131
Shirley, Ed 57, 131–132
Shirley, Glenn 131
Shirley, John 131
Shirley, Mansfield 131
Shockley, William 109
Sholdar, Mickey 101
Shoot-Em-Ups 77
Shoot-Em-Ups Ride Again 217
Shor, Sol 81–82, 88
Short, Dorothy 200
Short, Paul 35–36, 87
Short, Luke 147
Short, Robin 84
Shot, Dan 52
Shumate, Harold 120
Shumway, Lee 26, 79, 81, 189
Sickel, Dale Van 81–82, 88–89
Sides, Anthony 207
Siemaszko, Casey 51
Silva, Geno 107
Silva, Henry 213
Silva, Howard Da 78
Silver, Johnny 239
Silver King (Horse) 72
"The Silver Mine Protection Story" (TV)
  206
"Silver Stage Holdup" (TV) 206
Silvera, Frank 126, 245
Silverheels, Jay 97, 162, 202
Simmonds, Leslie 184
Simmons, Richard 91
Simms, Benjamin 57
Simon, Robert F. 258
Simpson, Dan 53
Simpson, Mickey 159, 243, 256
Simpson, Richard 219
Simpson, Russell 10, 78, 152–153, 159, 199,
  206, 229
Sinclair, James 107
Sirens, Bob 42
Sitka, Emil 43
"Six Feet of Gold" (1960, TV) 250
Sizemore, Tom 174
Skerritt, Tom 130
Slate, Jeremy 247
Slater, Christian 53

Slattery, Page 100, 254
Slifar, Lis 209
"The Slocum Family" 207
Smile, Ted 203
Smiley, Sam 53
Smith, Bernard 167
Smith, Charlie Martin 51
Smith, Clifford S. 181
Smith, Dean 167
Smith, Earl 170
Smith, Gerald O. 207
Smith, Hanley 217
Smith, Irby 51, 53
Smith, Jack C. 156, 187
Smith, John 162
Smith, John M. 217
Smith, Lennie 203
Smith, Lewis 174
Smith, Lois 39
Smith, Paul 40
Smith, Paul Gerard 199
Smith, Savannah 104
Smith, Steven 103
Smith, Tom 16, 20, 184, 191, 197
Smith, Tom [Marshal] 179
"The Snare" (1960, TV) 251
Snell, Earl 33, 75
Soble, Ron 46
Soderling, Walter 121
Sodja, Joe 40
Sofaer, Abraham 46
Sofronski, Bernie 217
Soisson, Joel 52
Soldani, Charles 126
Solomon, Ed 52
Sommerfeld, Elga 212
Son of Belle Starr (1953) 139–141
Son of Billy the Kid (1949) 34
Son of the Renegade (1953) 203
Sondergaard, Quentin 257
Sontag, Hedy 169
Sooter, Rudy 11
Sorenson, Paul 209
Sothern, Hugh 78
Southerland, Boots 219
Sowards, George 16
Space, Arthur 244
*Spaghetti Westerns—the Good, the Bad and
  the Violent* 46
Spahn, Paul 40
Spain, Fay 24
Spangler, Dick 101
Spence, Pete 227
Spencer, Douglas 96
Spies, Simon 47
Spillsbury, Klinton 216–217
Springsteen, R.G. 96
Sprotte, Bert 181

"Spurs for Johnny" (TV) 210
Stack, Robert 193–194
Stacy, Michelle 107
"Stage to Nowhere" (1960, TV) 252
Stagecoach (1939) 159–160
Stahl, Andy 107
Stallings, Lawrence 9
Stamp, Terence 51
"Stampede at Tent City" (1958, TV) 237
Standing, Wyndham 9
Stanhope, Ted 206
Stanley, Edwin 11
Stanley, Forest 210
Stanton, Dean 242
Stanton, Harry Dean 51, 101
Stanton, Paul 234
Starr, Belle 43, 57, 131–143
Starr, Flossie 135
Starr, Henry 119
Starr, James E. 69–70
Starr, Jennette 135
Starr, Pearl 132, 134, 135
Starr, Ruth 135
Starr, Sally 43
Starr, Sam 132, 134
Starr, Tom 135
Staunton, Ann 209
Steadman, Ted 52
"The Steam Wagon" (TV) 210
Steel, Ray 184
Steele, Bob 8, 12–18, 38, 40, 42, 173
Steele, Karen 245
Steele, Tom 81–82, 88, 206, 230
Steele, William 26
Steen, Mike 95
Steiger, Rod 128–129
Stein, Elayne 170
Stein, Sammy 193, 199
Stephens, Harvey 158, 238, 247
Stephens, Rachel 94
Steppling, John 9
Sterling, Jan 204
Sterms, Herb 27
Stevens, Angela 202
Stevens, Charles 33, 139, 156, 158–159,
    184, 198, 207
Stevens, Clarke 34
Stevens, Harry 121
Stevens, Jennie ["Cattle Annie"] 118–119
Stevens, Leslie 40–41
Stevens, Lewis [Louis] 126, 233
Stevens, Marya 262
Stevenson, Robert J. 239, 252
Stewart, Art 255
Stewart, Charles 210
Stewart, Elaine 256
Stewart, Jackie 108
Stewart, James 167, 233

Stewart, Peggy 33, 206, 230
Stewart, Peter 12, 14–15
Stillwell, Frank 227
Stiritz, John 108
Stirling, Linda 81
Stockdale, Carl 26, 157
Stockman, Boyd 160
Stock-Poyntor, Amy 52
Stockwell, Guy 213
"Stolen Church Funds" (TV) 208
Stone, George E. 153
Stone, Harold J. 243
Stone, Milburn 122, 206
Stonewall (Horse) 70
Stoney, Jack 156
Storey, Edith 9
Storm, Gale 36, 77
Strang, Harry 156
Strange, Glenn 19–21, 27, 29–30, 75, 97,
    126, 193, 201
Strange, Robert 136
Strange Lady in Town (1955) 39
Stratton, Bob 210
Stratton, Inger 102
Stratton, William 107
Strauss, Robert 257
Street, Elliot 128
Strickland, Mabel 185
Stricklyn, Ray 42, 98
Stromsoe, Fred 100
Stroud, Claude 35, 89
Strudwick, Shepperd 36
Stryker, Amy 104
Stuart, Randy 164
Stuart, Tina 101
Sturges, John 164, 168
Stutenroth, Gene [Roth] 81–82, 88
Sugarfoot (1957–1960) 42
Suhor, Yvonne 218
Sujata 207
Sullivan, Barry 42, 51, 229
Sullivan, Beth 109
Sullivan, Brad 171
Sullivan, Donald 209
Sullivan, Elliott 199
Sullivan, Liam 251, 259
Sullivan, Tim 166, 209
Sully, Frank 37–38, 76
Summers, Don 81
Summers, Jo 40
Summerville, Slim 73
The Sunday Oklahoman 220
Sunset (1988) 171
Sutherland, Boots 53
Sutherland, Kiefer 51, 53
Sutherlin, Wayne 102
Sutton, John 242, 248
Sutton, Paul 158

Swam, Robert [Bob] 210, 238, 260
Swapp, David 127
Swenson, Karl 168, 238
Swerling, Jo 215
Swit, Loretta 130
Swofford, Ken 101
Swope, Herbert B., Jr. 94
Sydes, Anthony 206
Symon, Burk 85

Tabor, Joan 263
Taeger, Ralph 100, 253
Taggert, Ben 199
Talbot, Lyle 125, 206–209
Talbot, Slim 202
Talbott, Gloria 97, 207, 238, 254
Taliaferro, Hal [Wally Wales] 77, 158, 191, 197, 200, 229
The Tall Man (1960–1962) 42
The Tall T (1957) 101
Talmadge, Richard 210–211
Talman, William 36
Tannen, Charles 73, 76
Tannen, William 37, 92, 202, 208, 234, 238, 250, 257, 262
Tansey, Sherry 12, 14–15, 17, 154
Tarter, L.L. 173
Tate, Lincoln 216
"The Tax Collecting Story" 206
Taylor, Al 11, 24, 77, 136
Taylor, Buck 128, 172, 216
Taylor, Cliff 34, 124
Taylor, Dub 51, 171, 190, 193–196
Taylor, Duke 81, 83, 88
Taylor, Ferris 156, 206
Taylor, Forrest 15, 17, 33, 38, 198, 208, 231
Taylor, Jack 42
Taylor, Joan 85
Taylor, Joyce 251
Taylor, Kent 122, 158, 251
Taylor, Madeleine 102
Taylor, Ray 34, 122
Taylor, Robert 8, 16
Taylor-Gordon, Hannah 219
Teague, Frances 182
Teague, Guy 83, 207–208, 210
Teal, Ray 16, 36, 46, 126, 193, 199, 246, 255
Television episodes, miscellaneous 220
"Tempest at Tioga Pass" (1961, TV) 258
Templeton, Bob 204
Tenney, Jon 172
Terrell, Ken 81, 83, 88, 230, 247
"Terror on the Trinity" 260
Terry, Ethel Grey 181
Terry, Tex 33, 81
Teters, Verne 203
Thayer, Carl 94

Theodore, Ralph 200
This Was the West That Was (1974) 215
Thomas, Arlette 101
Thomas, Heck [Marshal] 119, 151
Thomas, Lonnie 210
Thomas, R.J. 210
Thomas, Sharon 51
Thomason, Bryce Anthony 108
Thompson, Al 188
Thompson, Ben 145, 226–227
Thompson, Bill ["Bully"] 227
Thompson, Evan 254
Thompson, Glenn 202
Thompson, J. Lee 215
Thompson, Peter 233
Thompson, William 203
Thomson, Fred 72–73
Thornton, Cyril 121
Thorpe, Jim 154, 187
"Three Bullets for Bat" (1960, TV) 251
The Three Stooges 43, 99
Thunder Cloud, Chief 80, 185, 188, 234
Thurston, Carol 206, 234
Tibbs, Casey 101
Tichy, Gerard 168
Tierney, Gene 76, 137
Tierney, Lawrence 80, 90
Tilghman, William [Bill] 118–120, 145, 151
Tiller, Lucy 169
A Time for Dying (1969) 101–102
"A Time to Die" (1960, TV) 257
Tinker, Mark 108
Tittle, Jimmy 107
"To the Manor Born" (1959, TV) 246
Tobey, Kenneth 164, 250
Toby, Doug 217
Todd, Ann 78
Todd, James 85
Tolan, Michael 168
Tolbert, R.L. 216
Tomas-Blanco 42
Tombstone (1929) 151
Tombstone (1993) 151
Tombstone—The Town Too Tough to Die (1942) 152, 158
Tombstone Nugget 227
Tomes, Andrew 80
Toomey, Regis 140
Toones, Fred 75
Toovey, Shawn 109
Torgerson, Skippy 38
Totter, Audrey 91
Tourneur, Jacques 162
Tovay, Jose 39
"The Town in Hell's Background" (TV) 200
"Town Without Law" (TV) 210

Townes, Harry 128
Tozzi, Fausto 45
Tracy, Marlene 101
Traeser, Rick 216
Trahey, Madalyn 39
"Trail Pirate" (1958, TV) 239
Trail Street (1947) 231
"The Trapper Story" (TV) 207
Travis, Randy 108
Treadway, Wayne 258
"The Treasure of Worry Hill" (1958, TV) 238
"Treasure Trail" (TV) 209
Treen, Mary 91
The Trianas 39
Trimble, Larry 9
The Trimmed Lamp (1918) 116
Trotti, Lamar 137
Trout, Tom 36
Trowbridge, Charles 138
Truax, John 210
The True Story of Jesse James (1957) 55, 94–95
Trumbo, Dalton 78
Tuchock, Wanda 9
Tucker, Denis 107
Tucker, Forrest 46, 100, 126, 140, 200, 204
Tucker, Melville 232
Tufts, Sonny 39
Tulsa Jack 119
"The Tumbleweed Wagon" (1959, TV) 242
Tunstall, John H. 4, 37
Turich, Felipe 34, 100
Turich, Rosa 34, 36, 83, 208
Turkel, Joseph 238, 253
Turner, Don 207
Twist, John 90, 201
Twitchell, Archie 35, 125, 191
The TV Collector 236
Tyler, Beverly 126
Tyler, Harry 73, 210
Tyler, Richard 207
Tyler, Tom 33, 78, 80, 83–84, 86, 90, 156, 207
Tylor, Harry 234
Tyrrell, John 200

Ullman, Daniel B. 162, 235
Ullman, Elwood 43
Under Western Stars (1938) 11
The Untold West (1993) 54, 108
Urecal, Minerva 91
Uris, Leo 164
Urrutia, Rederico De 45
Usher, Guy 196

Vale, Virginia 157

Vallon, Mike 206–207, 210
Vallon, Rick 207
Valmont, Jean 48
Van Cleef, Lee 164
Vanderwusten, Franulka 47
Vanderwusten, Kess 47
Van Fleet, Jo 164
Van Husen, Werner 169
Van Nutter, Rick [Clyde Rogers] 212
Van Patten, Dick 49, 142
Van Sloan, Edward 154
Van Tyle, Helen 206
Varconi, Victor 186
Varela, Nina 91
Variety 12, 15–17, 19, 21–25, 28–31, 33, 36–37, 39–41, 48–49, 51–52, 75–80, 85–90, 93, 95–96, 98–99, 102–103, 105, 109, 122, 125, 127, 129, 137, 138, 140, 155–157, 160–162, 166, 169–170, 173, 175, 181, 183, 187, 188, 190–191, 193–198, 200, 203–205, 211, 216–217, 220, 229
Varno, Roland 206–207
Varsi, Gianni 141
Vaughn, Dorothy 11, 78
Vaughn, Ned 53
Vaughn, Robert 42, 96
Vaughn, William 257
Vegas, Ray 212
Veiller, Anthony 201
Veo, Carlo 45
Verbit, Helen 214
Vereen, Ben 47
Vernon, Wally 35, 89
Vetching, Bill 208
Viagran, Herbert 38
Vickers, Yvette 239
Victorian West: Class and Culture in Kansas Cattle Towns 225
Vidal, Gore 41–42
Vidor, King 9
"Vigilante Story" (TV) 207
Villa, Trinidad 46
Vincent, Billy 33, 231
Vinson, Gary 238
Vint, Alan 107
Vint, Jesse 107, 214
The Virginian (1929) 159
Vischer, Blanca 15
Vitale, Joseph A. 210
Vivyan, John 243, 256
Vogan, Emmett 193
Voight, Jon 168
Volkie, Ralph 46
Von Eltz, Theodore 208
Votrian, Peter 207
Vye, Murvyn 283

Wagenheim, Charles 101

Waggner, George 182
Wagner, Jack 238
Wagner, Robert 94
Waighman, George 118
Walcott, Gregory 39, 166, 250, 263
Waldron, Wendy 206
Wales, Ethel 75, 190
Walker, Clint 171, 216
Walker, Francis 188, 196, 198, 201
Walker, Greg 216
Walker, Nellie 81
Walker, Ray 209
Walker, Robert 184–185, 188
Walker, Terry 14
Walker, Tom 91
Wall, Jack 70
Wallace, Beryl 158, 229
Wallace, Edgar 134
Wallace, Houston 116
Wallace, Jim 115–116
Wallace, Lew [Governor] 4
Wallace, Morgan 11
Waller, Eddy 73, 188, 195–196
Walling, Will 182
Wallis, Hal B. 164
Walsh, Arthur 159
Walsh, M. Emmet 171, 214
Walter, Tracey 219
Walters, Emma 228
Walters, Luana 184, 198
Walton, Douglas 79
Waltz, Patrick 237, 250, 262
Wanger, Arthur 152
"Wanted—Alive Please" (1960, TV) 253
"Wanted—Dead" (1959, TV) 246
War Eagle, John 233
Ward, Bill 203
Ward, Blackjack 10, 188, 190
Ward, Fred 107
Ward, Luci 33, 80
Ward, Robert 128
Warden, Jack 216
Warfield, Emily 108
Warner, Franklyn 187
Warner, Hansel 30, 75
Warner, Jack L. 49
Warren, Charles Marquis 204
Warren, James 80
Warren, Jerry 42
Warren, Phil 231
Warren, Richard 237
Warren, Steve 252
Waterman, Willard 243, 250
Waters, Frank 150
Waters, L.V. 9
Watkin, Pierre 77
Watson, Mills 49, 128
Watson, Minor 78

Watters, William 212
Watts, Charles 38, 202
Watts, George 78
Wayland, Len 101
Wayne, Billy 138
Wayne, Carole 188
Wayne, John 46
Wayne, Michael 46
Wayne, Patrick 51, 167
Weaver, Dennis 161
Webb, Harry S. 189
Webb, Ira 34
Webb, James R. 77, 167
Webb, Richard 78
Webster, Chuck 262
Webster, M. Coates 36
Weisbart, David 37
Welch, James 182
"Welcome to Paradise" (1960, TV) 253
Welden, Ben 210
Welles, Rebecca 242
Wellman, Horace 178
Wells, Allan [Alan] 86, 209
Wells, Jacqueline 191
Wells, Randy 170
Wells, Tiny 53
Wells Fargo Company 146
Welsch, Howard 122
Wengraf, John 245
Wenland, Burt 208–209
Werker, Alfred L. 71
Wescoatt, Rusty 208, 210
Wescott, Helen 160, 210
Wessel, Richard 210
Wessen, Gene 162
Wesson, Dick 205
West, Adam 43, 236
West, Frank 134
West, Pat 26, 122
West, Red 53
West, Victor 89
West, Wally 14–15, 17–21, 31, 92
Westbound (1959) 101
Westerfield, James 237
Westerfield, Jim 235
Western Badmen 7
Western Cyclone (1943) 29
Western, Johnny 127
Western Movies 91
Westman, Nydia 78
Whalen, Michael 97
Wheatcroft, Stanhope 182
Wheeler, Rick 53
Wheeler-Nicholsom, Dana 108, 172
Whelan, Tim 80
When the Daltons Rode (1940) 121
When the West Was Young 151
Whipper, Leigh 136

Whitaker, Charles [Slim] 14, 16, 19–20, 22, 25, 154, 157, 187–188, 191, 195
Whitcomb, Cynthia 219
White, Dan 23–24, 31, 100, 251, 260
White, Daniel 42
White, Dean 33
White, Francis 125
White, Jacqueline 33
White, Lee [Lasses] 26
White, Ted 216
White, Wesley 16
The White Buffalo (1977) 215
White Lightnin' 142
White Spear, Chief 182
Whiteford, Blackie 234
Whiteford, Brad 53
Whiteman, Russ 33, 207
Whitman, Ernest 73, 76
Whitman, Kip 100
Whitmore, James, Jr. 104
Whitney, Claire 229
Whitney, Grace Lee 261
Whitrow, Glenn 42
"Who'll Buy My Violence?" (1959, TV) 247
Whyte, Patrick 210
Wich, Nathan 141
Wichita (1955) 162–163, 234
Widmark, Richard 130, 167
"The Widow Muldane" 206
Wiedlin, Jame 52
Wilcox, Frank 36, 96, 199, 204
Wilcox, Larry 128
Wild Bill (1995) 320
Wild Bill Hickok (1923) 180–181, 229
Wild Bill Hickok: Gentlemen of the Old West (1996) 220
Wild Bill Hickok Rides (1941) 199
"Wild Bill's Odyssey" (TV) 209
The Wild Bunch 52
Wildcat of Tucson (1941) 199
"Wild White Horse" (TV) 207
Wilke, Robert [Bob] 39, 88, 99, 122, 162, 230, 237, 247
Wilkerson, Guy 38, 88, 233–234
Wilkerson, William 208
Wilkins, June 121
Wilks, Darrell 107
Willes, Jean 237, 248
William, Warren 199
Williams, Bill 85–86
Williams, Cora 216
Williams, Charlie 107
Williams, Cindy 47
Williams, Guinn ["Big Boy"] 16, 209
Williams, Jack 39, 44, 251
Williams, JoBeth 174
Williams, John T. 37

Williams, Kate 107
Williams, Mike 179
Williams, Oscar 202
Willimas, Rhys 85, 252
Williams, Rush 210
Williams, Sumner 95
Williams, Zack 136
Willingham, Calder 214–215
Willingham, Willard 101, 204, 212
Willis, Austin 168
Willis, Bruce 171
Willis, Jean 161
Willis, Leo 181
Willis, Matt 85
Willis, Norman 138, 190
Willmering, H.E. 127
Willowbird, Chris 231
Wills, Chill 16, 51, 137
Wills, Henry 191, 216, 230
Wills, Walter 188
Wilson, Alex 47, 49
Wilson, Jack 203
Wilson, J.S. [Major] 209
Wilson, Scott 53
Wilson, Stanley 36, 88
Wilson, Terry 213
Wilstach, Frank J. 186
Winchester '73 233
Windom, William 168
Windsor, Marie 39, 237
Wingreen, Jason 95
Winkler, Robert 78
Winningham, Mare 194
Winter, Alex 52
Winters, Gloria 208
Winters, Shelley 233
Withers, Bernadette 209
Withers, Grant 16, 36, 96, 159
Witney, Mike 169
Wolfe, Bill 77, 191
Wolfe, Bud 81, 83, 88
Wolfe, Dave 87, 126
Wolfe, Ian 83
The Woman of the Town (1943) 229
The Woman They Almost Lynched (1953) 91
Wong, Kit 216
Woodard, Chalayne 219
Woodell, Barbara 35, 84, 87, 89, 91, 209
Woods, Donald 249
Woods, Harry 72, 75, 90, 152, 154, 156, 159
Woods, Harry [Editor] 227
Woods, James 178
Woods, Robert 141
Woodward, Bob 187, 207
Woodward, Morgan 130, 234, 254

Wooley, Sheb 38
Warden, Hank 46
Wormser, Richard 36
Worth, Michael 75
Wren, Claire 218
"The Wrestling Story" (TV) 207
Wright, Jenny 51, 53
Wright, Mack 188
Wright, Richard 47
Wright, Will 97, 202, 241, 252, 259
Wurlitzer, Rudolph 49
Wurtzel, Sol M. 153, 155
Wyatt, Al 127, 166
Wyatt, Bobby 208
Wyatt Earp (1994) 151, 236
Wyatt Earp—Return to Tombstone (1994) 173
Wyatt Earp: Walk with a Legend (1994) 175
Wyatt Earp, Frontier Marshal 150, 155
Wyman, Jane 78
Wynant, H.M. 128, 240

Yarbo, Lillian 199
Ybarra, Ventura 156
"The Yellow Haired Kid" (TV) 206
Yesterday's Saturdays 14
York, Duke 206
Young, Carleton 12, 14–15, 17, 20, 87, 90, 167, 193
Young, Clifton 87
Young, Evelyn 193, 199
Young, Harry 181
Young, Mary 97
Young, Waldermar 186

Young Bill Hickok (1940) 191
Young Guns (1988) 51–52
Young Guns II (1990) 53–54
Young Jesse James (1960) 98, 141
The Young Riders (1989) 218
Younger, Bruce 132
Younger, Henrietta 63
Younger, James [Jim] 57–63
Younger, John Harrison 57–61
Younger, Pearl 132, 134–145
Younger, Retta 59
Younger, Robert [Bob] 57–60, 62–63
Younger, Thomas Coleman 43, 57–64, 68–69, 128, 132
The Younger Brothers (1949) 83–84
Younger's Bend 134
Youngs, Gail 107
Yowlachie, Chief 233
Yrigoyen, Joe 83, 91
Yule, Joe 16
Yulin, Harris 169–170

Zachariah (1971) 141–142
Zachary, Ray 212
Zane, Billy 172
Zanuck, Darryl F. 75–76
Zanuck, Fifi 220
Zanuck, Richard D. 220
Zerbe, Anthony 218
Zero, Natividad 168
Zinnemann, Tim 103
Zito, Louis 95
Zogbaum, Ferdinand 169
Zukor, Adolph 71
Zurakowska, Diank [Dianne Zura] 45